MEDIA EFFECTS AND SOCIETY

LEA'S COMMUNICATION SERIES
Jennings Bryant / Dolf Zillmann, General Editors

For a complete list of titles in LEA's Communication Series, please contact Lawrence Erlbaum Associates, Publishers

MEDIA EFFECTS AND SOCIETY

Elizabeth M. Perse
University of Delaware

LAWRENCE ERLBAUM ASSOCIATES, PUBLISHERS
2001   Mahwah, New Jersey   London

Lawrence Erlbaum Associates, Inc., Publishers
10 Industrial Avenue
Mahwah, NJ 07430

Cover design by Kathryn Houghtaling Lacey

Library of Congress Cataloging-in-Publication Data

Perse, Elizabeth M.
  Media effects and society / Elizabeth M. Perse.
      p. cm.—(LEA's communication series)

    Includes bibliographical references and indexes.
  ISBN 0-8058-2505-3 (cloth : alk. paper)
    1. Mass Media—Influence. 2. Mass Media—Social aspects.
      I. Title II. Series.

  P94 .P384 2000
  302.23—dc21   00-050301
                                                          CIP

Books published by Lawrence Erlbaum Associates are printed on
acid-free paper, and their bindings are chosen for strength and
durability.

Printed in the United States of America
10   9   8   7   6   5   4   3   2   1

To Jeff

Contents

Preface

It seems that many students enter the study of mass communication with interests in producing media content. Some are intrigued with technology and equipment. Others enjoy the sense of accomplishment and recognition that comes with knowing that messages they have created are being watched, read, and heard by audiences. Still others relish the sense of power that accompanies producing messages designed to persuade. This enthusiasm for media production, however, is not usually accompanied by an appreciation for theories of message effectiveness. The study of media effects, though, is the study of media effectiveness. In the years that I have been teaching media effects, I've watched students enter my course with a sense of distrust for "theories." But, after a short while, they begin to understand how theories can be tools in understanding the power of mass communication. The study of media effects is the study of how to control, enhance, or mitigate the impact of the mass media on individuals and society.

This book is the result of my years of teaching about media effects. It is based on the assumption that the mass media *do* have effects. Most communication scholars would be reluctant to argue that mass media are the sole or most substantial change agent in society, but it is clear that mass communication is an agent or catalyst to a variety of shifts and changes in people and institutions. It is certainly true that there was violence in society long before there was mass communication, but that does not mean that new media forms and content cannot serve as stimuli to violence. Certainly children were socialized before the development of television, but that does not mean that children's educational media cannot increase children's knowledge about the world.

The most commonly studied areas of media effects are well known, but it would be impossible to identify all the potential media effects. So, the goal of this text is not to identify the domain of the study of media effects; the breadth of the existing literature of the field illustrates the range of interests of the scholars of media effects. Instead, my goal is to focus on *how* media effects occur—to focus on theoretical explanations for media effects. It is my belief that these explanations can be effective tools in understanding message effectiveness. If we understand how media effects occur, then we can increase the likelihood of positive effects and lessen the chance of negative effects. The goal of this book is to enable students to understand how to enhance mass communication's prosocial effects and mitigate its negative effects.

This book was written for those who study and conduct research in media effects. I hope that my contribution serves some integrative function for the scholars of our field, those who produce our knowledge about media effects. The theoretical discussions of media effects are also designed to stimulate the intellectual inquiry of graduate students. I have not intended the chapters in this text to be comprehensive summaries of various areas of media effects; excellent overviews are available in another text, *Media Effects: Advances in Theory and Research*, edited by Bryant and Zillmann (1994). Instead, I hope that the synthesis of different theories might increase graduate students' understanding of the process of media effects and stimulate their interest in new and creative approaches to research on media effects.

This book is also designed for undergraduate students, like those I teach at the University of Delaware—students with a background in mass communication and an interest in the products of our field. I have found that the study of media effects is a subject that is easy to make relevant to students. Almost every year some salient event illustrates the power of mass communication to affect the audience. In just the last decade of the 20th century, we've seen the Persian Gulf War, the death of Princess Diana, two U.S. presidential elections, devastation by earthquakes and hurricanes, political concerns about rap music, violent television programs, movies, and computer/video games, the growth of the World Wide Web as a source for pornography, the O. J. Simpson trial, the introduction of new entertainment and news channels, the near impeachment of a president, and so on. In all of these and others, the mass media have played a critical role. The students of today were also raised in a media-rich environment. They can easily remember the impact of television programs like *Sesame Street* on their own early lives. They can recall how they might have been influenced by product advertisements and media celebrities as they were socialized into adulthood. The study of media effects can be a personal experience. Coupled with students' interest in producing effective media messages, I have found that my students become excited about the study of media effects.

This book is organized to serve two purposes. First, after the first two introductory chapters, each chapter presents an abbreviated summary of some of the major areas of interest as well as some representative research findings. More important, each chapter presents a theoretical explanation to guide thought about that domain of study. That theoretical explanation guides the analysis of media effects and provides the explanation for understanding how those effects come about. Each chapter builds on previous chapters, so that the final chapters of the book use theoretical explanations presented in previous chapters.

The first chapter provides an overview to the study of media effects. In it, I present reasons for the importance of the area of study. I explain my presumption of media effects and spend some time discussing reasons that limit evidence for media effects. In general, there are good reasons to believe that the effects of the mass media might very well be stronger than social science concludes. The chapter ends with the first set of concepts that serve as tools to understanding media effects—ways to define and categorize media effects.

The second chapter begins with a brief history of the "received view" of the study of media effects. This commonly accepted history of the field can provide a context for the substance of the chapter—the four models of media effects. These four models, Direct Effects, Conditional Effects, Cumulative Effects, and Cognitive–Transactional Effects, are simplified explanations of the process of media effects. Each places different emphasis on different causes for media effects. These four models are the basis for the theoretical explanations in the following chapters.

Chapter 3 discusses media effects in crisis situations. Because crises are some of the most critical times in a society, different media functions become especially important. So, Wright's discussion of the functions of mass communication serves as the theoretical grounding of this chapter. The effects of dependency (Ball-Rokeach & DeFleur, 1976) help explain how media effects tend to be more direct and uniform during times of crisis.

The fourth chapter tackles a broad topic—media effects on public opinion. Effects of concern focus on politics and voting. A persuasion model, the elaboration likelihood model, serves as the theoretical grounding of this chapter. Media effects on public opinion are presented as conditional on the political expertise, interest, and involvement of the audience. This chapter includes discussions of agenda setting, news framing, the spiral of silence, effects of polling, how reporting affects voter turnout, and concerns about the impact of television on national elections.

Chapter 5 is another broad chapter. Its focus is learning from the mass media. Two general theoretical orientations to learning serve as the theoretical introduction. Learning is presented as either an active process, in which the audience invests interest and mental effort into cognitively processing media messages, or as a passive process, in which passive audiences absorb effectively created media messages. Specific issues of media effects include a discussion of when it is that children are old enough to learn from and be affected by media content, how television affects academic achievement, and knowledge gaps. This chapter provides important information for subsequent chapters that focus on the effects of learning prosocial and antisocial media content.

The sixth chapter covers one of the topics of media effects that has been of consistent concern to parents, educators, and scholars—the socialization effects of mass communication. Mass communication is certainly functional for society, but there are consistent concerns that entertainment programming instills in children and adolescents inaccurate, unhealthy, and potentially harmful beliefs, values, and behaviors. The main focus of this chapter is the acquisition of stereotypical schemas and the social learning of inappropriate and/or unhealthy behaviors.

Concerns about the effects of violent media content emerge regularly as a result of particularly salient violent events in society. The seventh chapter builds on theories and models of earlier chapters to describe how it is that media violence translates into behavioral, cognitive, and affective effects. The theories are organized into those that provide primarily cognitive explanations (e.g., social learning theory, information-processing, priming), those with physiological explanations based on audience arousal reactions, and those that hold that media violence is not the cause of aggressive behavior.

Chapter 8 uses Linz and Malamuth's (1993) discussion of moralist, feminist, and liberal perspectives on the effects of sexually explicit materials as the overview of thinking about effects of pornography. Because most of the concerns about this sort of content focus on connections to sexual violence, I apply what our field knows about effects of media violence to understanding effects of sexually explicit materials. The chapter concludes with a discussion of some of the controversies that surround this area of research, because they illuminate some of the larger issues in studying media effects.

The final chapter is an afterword. It is clear that the study of media effects will be ongoing with the development and extension of new media technologies. It is my assertion that our field already has a wealth of models and theories that allow us to hypothesize how effects can emerge from new media (e.g., the World Wide Web), new forms of media content (e.g., specialized cable networks), and new technologies (e.g., HDTV). As a summary, I show how the four models of media effects can be applied to new areas of study.

ACKNOWLEDGMENTS

Throughout my professional career I have been fortunate to interact and work with so many outstanding scholars. Their influences have not only facilitated my own work, but shaped my research and thinking. I owe special appreciation to my friends and colleagues at Kent State University, especially Alan and Becky Rubin. Their instruction and direction gave me the tools and skills that I use every day of my professional life. Their mentoring showed me how to work efficiently and productively. My closest professional friends, Carole Barbato and Beth Graham, have provided so much support in helping me navigate through academia. My colleagues in the Department of Communication at the University of Delaware have stimulated my thinking by exposing me to new perspectives and ways of looking at our field. I work with a group of vibrant scholars. What a pleasure it is to interact regularly with intellectually stimulating (and good natured) colleagues. Thanks to my colleagues and friends, John Courtright, Nancy Signorielli, Doug McLeod, Charlie Pavitt, Beth Haslett, and Wendy Samter.

This book grew out of more than a decade of teaching a senior-level class on media effects, my favorite class. My thoughts on this topic have evolved, to a large extent, as a result of my students. I no longer remember which students gave me which ideas, but I appreciate their insights into the topics and (probably too extensive) readings I've assigned over the years.

Special thanks to Jennings Bryant for encouraging me to complete this book and the staff at Lawrence Erlbaum Associates, especially Linda Bathgate, who made this book a pleasant project. Thanks to this volume's reviewers who offered specific suggestions and welcomed insights into how to present my ideas.

Finally, personal thanks to my family. My children, Rebecca and Jonathan, keep me grounded and remind me that I am not infallible and that sometimes people "just watch TV." I know that I would not be where I am today without the love and support of my husband, Jeff Bergstrom. He is my wisest and most trusted advisor, my best friend, and the love of my life.

—Elizabeth M. Perse

1

Introduction: Do Media
Have Effects?

One of the primary focuses of the study of mass communication has been the social, cultural, and psychological effects of media content and use. Despite Berelson's (1959) warning that our field was "withering away," the study of effects has remained active and robust. Much of the empirical research published in the major mass communication journals concerns the effects of the mass media. There is no longer discussion in that literature about whether the media have effects or not; nor is our field as interested in identifying the different effects that media do have. Instead, most current research attempts to improve our understanding of media effects by refining our theoretical explanations of the processes by which media effects occur.

This chapter is an initial critical analysis of the effects of the mass media. It begins by presenting the domain of the study of effects, but then notes the limitations inherent in focusing on the media as a prime mover or cause for effects. Despite these limitations, though, it is important to focus our study on how media effects occur so that we can mitigate harmful effects and enhance positive ones.

WHAT KIND OF EFFECTS DO THE MASS MEDIA HAVE?

Mass media have been hypothesized to have effects across a broad range of contexts. McGuire (1986) noted several of the most commonly mentioned intended media effects: (a) the effects of advertising on purchasing, (b) the effects of political campaigns on voting, (c) the effects of public service announcements (PSAs) on personal behavior and social improvement, (d) the effects of propaganda on ideology, and (e) the effects of media ritual on social control. He also pointed out the most commonly mentioned unintended media effects: (a) the effect of media violence on aggressive behavior, (b) the impact of media images on the social construction of reality, (c) the effects of media bias on stereotyping, (d) the effects of erotic and sexual material on attitudes and objectionable behaviors, and (e) how media forms affect cognitive activity and style. McQuail's (1994) summary of the main streams of effects research adds these other areas of media effects: (a) knowledge gain and distribution throughout society, (b) diffusion of innovations, (c) socialization to societal norms, and (d) institution and cultural adaptations and changes. Liebert and Sprafkin (1988) believed that some of the important questions facing media scholars who study television's impact on children are (a) how television instigates antisocial behavior, (b) how it leads children to be more accepting of violence, and (c) how television's images cultivate social attitudes and stereotypes.

There are other, less obvious and less studied possible media effects. During the summer of 1996, for example, some retailers blamed the slump in consumer purchases to women's interest in and viewing of the summer Olympics (Pauly, 1996). Watching the Olympics, retailers thought, kept women out of stores. Teachers and parents have been concerned that television viewing by children will take the place of reading, leading to lower reading skills and educational achievement (e.g., Corteen & Williams, 1986; Hornik, 1978). Pediatricians have been concerned that the unhealthy eating practices portrayed on television coupled with an emphasis on slim models contributes to increases in eating disorders (e.g., Dietz, 1990). Although there are few positive images of smoking on television programming now, print media that carry tobacco play down the dangers of tobacco in their editorial content (e.g., Kessler, 1989). Public health officials are concerned about how print advertising affects adolescents' attitudes toward smoking. There are reports of increased family violence associated with television sports viewing (Capuzzo, 1990). Legal scholars struggle with the industry's responsibilities in instigating criminal behavior in particularly susceptible radio listeners, television and movie viewers, and listeners to popular music who imitate antisocial media actions (Dee, 1987). Scholars are still sorting out how news coverage affects solidarity and consensus during crises (D. M. McLeod, Eveland, & Signorielli, 1994), perceptions about political protest (D. M. McLeod, 1995), and on narcotization (Lazarsfeld & Merton, 1948).

In general, media effects are usually described as cognitive, affective, or behavioral (Ball-Rokeach & DeFleur, 1976; Chaffee, 1977; Roberts & Maccoby, 1985). Cognitive effects are those that concern the acquisition of information—what people learn, how beliefs are structured (or restructured) in the mind, how needs for information are satisfied or not. These effects include concerns about what is learned as well as how much is learned. Whereas news and public affairs information is often the focus of cognitive effects, the cognitive impact of entertainment is also an important area of study. Affective effects involve the formation of attitudes, or positive or negative evaluations about something. Other areas of affective effects concern emotional reactions to media content, such as fright or amusement, or the development of feelings toward other objects as a result of media exposure, such as the generation of fear in society as a result of watching violent television programming. Behavioral effects are observable actions that are linked to media exposure. The most studied kinds of behavioral effects focus on anti- or prosocial behavior.

THE PRESUMPTION OF MEDIA EFFECTS

One of the first and most important assumptions of the study of mass communication has been the presumption that media and their content have significant and substantial effects. In 1922, Lippmann argued that mass communication could become the basis for people's view of the world. About the same time, Lasswell (1927) considered mass communication as a tool for manipulation and social control. This focus on media effects continued throughout the middle part of the 20th century with the applied (and theoretical) research of Lazarsfeld's Office of Radio Research (later the Bureau of Applied Social Research). Concern about the negative impacts on children has been the basis of a "legacy of fear" (DeFleur & Dennis, 1994) and numerous government investigations and hearings that accompanied the introduction of each mass medium—movies, radio, comic books, and television (Rowland, 1983; Wartella & Reeves, 1985). Most recently, there has been a renewed political spotlight on television as a cause of violence in society and fears that material on the World Wide Web (WWW) will not only increase terrorist activity (by reporting militia and other "fringe" political groups' philosophies and bomb-construction techniques) and corrupt children (because of indecent, sexually oriented content).

This presumption of media effects is easy to understand. It makes common sense that anything that consumes so much money ($206 billion in 1992, according to Bogart, 1995) and time (about 20% of the time we are awake, according to Robinson, 1981) must have some impact on our lives. Daily household television watching time is about 7 hours and the average person listens to the radio about 22 hours per week, according to the National Association of Broadcasters (1996). We know from personal experience that movies can frighten us or make us cry, that children learn their letters and numbers from *Sesame Street*, integrate ideas and characters from movies and television programs into their play, and that much of the world seems to revolve around U.S. football during Superbowl week. Even media conglomerates acquire a variety of media outlets to create *synergy*, or cross-media spinoffs and promotions of products and personalities. (It was not surprising when the casts of *Roseanne* and *Full House* both visited Disney World shortly after the Disney–ABC merger).

It is important to realize, though, that there is a good deal of self-interest in promoting a belief in strong media effects. Media companies derive profit by promising that they are effective vehicles for advertisements or product placements, messages designed to persuade consumers to purchase. Although consumers rarely see them, advertising-supported media regularly promote themselves in trade publications as being able to "deliver" valuable demographic groups to advertisers. This notion of potent advertising effects is reinforced by the advertising business itself, which profits from advertising production and placement. Although advertisers are often reluctant to take credit for product trial (as in the case of underage alcohol or tobacco use), they do maintain that advertising does lead to brand switching and/or reinforcement.

Some politicians, who use the media for reelection and to gain support for their political goals, seem to accept without question a view of strong media impact. During the 1980s, for example, Senator Jesse Helms was interested in taking over CBS so that he could shape its news coverage (presumably to eliminate a liberal bias as well as to promote a more conservative agenda). During the 1992 campaign, Vice President Dan Quayle attempted to bring the issue of "family values" to the media and public agenda. One of his strategies was to show how the media legitimize unwed motherhood by depicting respected professional women, like the fictional televison character, Murphy Brown, becoming pregnant outside of marriage. The 1996 Republican candidate, Robert Dole, decried the violence in films (with Arnold Swartzenegger standing at his side) and congratulated producers of films that promote wholesome values, such as *Independence Day*'s celebration of patriotism.

Although some politicians are motivated to promote public interest and media responsibility, others see media as convenient and easily understood scapegoats for social problems. Although there certainly are reasons to be concerned about the level of violence in our society, it is clearly simplistic and misleading to hold that violent themes in popular music, movies, comic books, or television might be the major cause for delinquency and the violent crime rate. But opposition to media violence is a less politically charged position than advocating dealing with other roots of crime, such as poverty, drug and alcohol use, dysfunctional home life, substandard or inadequate educational facilities, and easy access to weapons. Media companies might be especially compliant political targets right now, with corporate mergers dependent on U.S. Justice Department antitrust scrutiny and changes in Federal Communications Commission (FCC) ownership rules. The broadcast networks and the National Association of Broadcasters, for example, might have been less likely to raise a commotion about the 1996 requirements that they offer 3 hours of quality children's programming because they are lobbying for the privilege of using radiowave spectrum space without having to pay for it.

Even academic scholars have strong vested interest in holding that media have substantial effects. As McGuire (1986) wrote, "It would hardly enhance the self-esteem or status of academic researchers ... to find that mass media effects studied by many in their discipline are trivial" (p. 174). The study of media effects is based on empiricism and rewards results. We cannot "prove" the null hypothesis and nonsignificant findings are typically not publishable. Most academics enter their fields hoping "to make a difference" in the real world. The contribution of communication research to the development and success of *Sesame Street* (Ball & Bogatz, 1970) illustrates how much our field has to offer. So, for academics, the assumption of effects offers practical value (and funding opportunities) to improving media effectiveness (along with the possibility of consulting) and the opportunity to influence government policy.[1]

THE STRENGTH OF MEDIA IMPACT

The question of whether media effects are strong or substantial has certainly not been settled; some of this disagreement is definitional. There is consensus, for the most part, among scholars that media do have some impact on various dimensions of social life and structure. But, as McGuire (1986) suggested, the effects seem quite small, given the amount of time, money, and energy devoted to producing and consuming media content. Metaanalysis, a statistical technique that combines the quantitative results of a body of research to examine effects and to estimate effect sizes, attests to the modest effects of media content on some commonly examined areas of media effects.

Hearold (1986) conducted a large metaanalysis of a variety of television effects. She found that television's impact on antisocial effects (e.g., aggression, materialism, use of drugs, cultivation perceptions, stereotyping) was $d = .30$.[2] For prosocial effects (e.g., altruism, counterstereotyping, activism, imaginative play), television's effect size was somewhat stronger, $d = .63$. Paik and Comstock's (1994) update of Hearold's (1986) analysis found that television violence had an overall effect size of ($d = .65$ $r = .31, r^2 = .10$). Television's negative impact, though, was higher in experiments ($d = .80, r = .37, r^2 = .14$) than for surveys ($d = .38, r = .19, r^2 = .03$).

Wood, Wong, and Chachere (1991) sought to uncover the effect size of media violence in studies that were ecologically valid. They focused on 28 studies of experimental exposure to filmed or television violence that used as their dependent variable aggressive behavior in naturally occurring social situations (free play for child samples or unconstrained social interaction for adult samples). In 16 studies, the experimental group was more aggressive ($d = .27$ for weighted analy-

---

[1]Simpson (1994) suggested that one reason for communication scholars' involvement in study of psychological warfare during the Cold War era was they believed that it was an enlightened and peaceful way to achieve world peace.

[2]The effect size is based on standardizing different measurement scales so that they can be compared. It is computed much like a Z score—the difference between the means of the experimental and control group divided by the standard deviation (Rosenthal, 1984). It is usually interpreted to indicate the size of the difference, in terms of standard deviations, between the exposure and control groups. An effect size of .30, then, indicates that the groups differ by .30 of a standard deviation.

ses, $d = .40$ in unweighted analyses). Similarly, Hogben's (1998) metaanalysis of naturally occurring variance found that television violence and viewer aggression were related ($d = .21$).

Television's effects on sex-role perceptions have also been isolated: $r = .101, r^2 = .01$, for nonexperimental studies, and $r = .207, r^2 = .04$, for experiments (Herrett-Skjellum & Allen, 1996). Pornography's effect on rape-myth acceptance is a bit smaller: $r = .146$ ($r^2 = .021$) for laboratory experiments and $r = .018$ ($r^2 = .0003$) for surveys (Allen, Emmers, Gebhardt, & Giery, 1995).

These analyses demonstrate that, although media's impact is significant, it is not very substantial. Variance accounted for by media exposure is quite small. But are these effects trivial? Hearold (1986) gives a context for interpreting these effect sizes. Metaanalyses have found these other effect sizes: gender on height, $d = 1.20$, one year of elementary school on reading, $d = 1.00$, psychotherapy, $d = .85$, tutoring on mathematic skills, $d = .60$, drug therapy on psychotics, $d = .40$, and computer-based instruction on mathematic skills, $d = .40$.

According to Cohen's (1988) classification of effects size, most media effects would be considered small ($r = .10, d = .20$), or moderate ($r = .30, d = .50$), but rarely large ($r = .50, d = .80$). But there is another way to consider effects size. Rosenthal and Rubin (1982) developed a way to translate these effects sizes into terms that can be understood by those not trained in statistics. The binomial effect size display (BESD) suggests that r be interpreted as a measure of difference between control and experimental groups. So that, if we could find a group of people who had never been exposed to television, and show them violent television programming, they should be 37% more aggressive (using Paik & Comstock's 1994 estimate) than a comparable group that did not view the programming.[3] Using this same method, Hogben (1998) estimated that eliminating television violence would reduce viewer aggression by 10%. Herrett-Skjellumm and Allen (1996) also pointed out that media effects may be especially strong for the heaviest media users. Using their television sex-stereotyping effect size estimates for nonexperimental studies, they argue that television's

---

[3]The binomial effects size display may make some more sense when applied to medical settings. In 1981, for example, a drug study was prematurely discontinued because researchers decided that the effects were so significant and substantial it would be unethical to deny treatment to the control group. The effects size for this study was $r = .02, r^2 = .004$ (Rosenthal, 1984). Clearly, a success rate of 2% can be quite meaningful.

heaviest viewers, compared to the lightest viewers, are almost twice as likely to hold sexist attitudes.

SOME PROBLEMS IN INTERPRETING EVIDENCE OF MEDIA EFFECTS

Despite the bias of the presumption of effects and the evidence drawn from metaanalyses, not all scholars agree that media have effects in all areas. There has, for example, been little consistent evidence that television affects academic achievement (Morgan & Gross, 1982) or children's cognitive development (Anderson & Collins, 1988). After examining their evidence, the 1970 report of the Commission on Obscenity and Pornography concluded that pornography had little negative impact. Analysis of the results of "naturalistic" studies of television violence observed that in 7 of the 23 studies in which direction of effect (30.4%) could be determined, the control group was more aggressive (Wood et al., 1991). Studies of the introduction of television found that children in a town without television were not significantly less aggressive than children in towns with television (Joy, Kimball, & Zabrack, 1986). The connection between availability of pornography and sex crimes is not well supported (Brannigan & Kapardis, 1986). And, despite the stereotypical and segregated portrayals of African Americans on television, television exposure is linked to more positive attitudes and higher self-concepts among African American children (Graves, 1993; Stroman, 1986).

Moreover, media's impact does not seem to be consistent across cultures. There is a good deal of open and available sexual content in Japanese media, for example, but a much lower incidence of sexual crime (Abramson & Hayashi, 1984). Similarly, Japanese television in 1977 was about as violent as U.S. television, but Japan is a less violent society (Iwao, Pool, de Sola, & Hagiwara, 1981). Cultivation effects, commonly identified in the United States (Gerbner, Gross, Morgan, & Signorielli, 1994), have not been observed with heavy British television viewers (Wober, 1978).

Some scholars argue that there is a "publication bias," in which effects are more likely to be inferred because studies that do not find effects are less likely to be published. Paik and Comstock (1994) found no evidence, though, that stronger effects were found in published studies. However, they drew these conclusions based on examining unpublished studies that were readily available as dissertations, the-ses, conference papers, and ERIC documents. There may be many other studies with null findings, though, that never become even that available (cf. Rosenthal, 1979).

It is clear that the most substantial media effects are located in laboratory settings. There is a good deal of value in conducting research in the tightly controlled setting of the laboratory (Kerlinger, 1973). Laboratory experiments allow a high level of control over conditions, subjects, and extraneous variables, so specific effects can be isolated and error variance minimized. Because treatments can be manipulated and time order can be controlled, causation can be determined. But there should be some caution interpreting effects from laboratory experiments. The control that is a strength of laboratory setting is also one of its greatest weaknesses. Laboratories are artificial; they do not account for the possibility of selective exposure available to people in the real world. For example, some subjects greatly affected by pornography in a laboratory might never choose to expose themselves to it voluntarily. Dependent measures (such as hitting a Bobo doll or pushing a button) limit the possible range of realistic responses to the stimulus (Brannigan & Goldenberg, 1987) and may not be valid or realistic measures of the study's construct (Freedman, 1984). The laboratory also lacks the normal social constraints on behavior. Studies have found, for example, that children are more likely to act aggressively when the experimenter leaves them alone than when an adult is present (Stein & Friedrich, 1975).

Experimenter effects may also account for some of the effects found in laboratory research. When a researcher presents media content to subjects, the subjects may presume that the experimenter approves of it, even if it is violent or pornographic. And when subjects are given the opportunity to act in what might be otherwise considered inappropriate or undesirable ways, they may be more likely to do so in the laboratory setting. Subjects may believe that they have the permission of the experimenter to act. Rosenthal (1979) estimated that these "experimenter effects," or the influence of the experimenter and the hypotheses on the results, range from $d = .23$ to $d = 1.78$. So, experimenter effects alone might account for the media effects located in experimental settings.

The major concern with evidence of media effects is inferring a causal relationship between media exposure and various effects. Metaanalyses demonstrate that there is some relationship between media exposure and some media effects. The relationship, though, does not necessarily reflect that media content leads to effects. There are two other possible explanations for that relationship. It is possible that certain predispositions may lead people to seek out certain types of media content. For example, people who hold more traditional sex-role beliefs may choose to watch television programs that reinforce those views. Or, cultivation effects might reflect that people who are more fearful may prefer to spend time safely in their own homes, watching television. A correlation between two variables may be spurious, or due to similar influence of a third variable on both. So, the strong correlation between the number of churches and bars in a community certainly does not indicate that as people drink and carouse more, they find the need to pray more. The relationship might be more easily explained by population size. As the number of people in a town increases, so does the number of churches, bars, stores, sidewalks, automobiles, schools, and so on.

WHY AREN'T MEDIA EFFECTS STRONGER

If the mass media do have effects on individuals and society, why doesn't research find evidence of strong and substantial media effects? Of course, it is possible that the media do have effects, but they are slight, compared to the influences in the environment. But, there are several reasons to believe that the strength of media effects may be underestimated by research.

For ethical reasons, many studies limit dependent variables to those that do not harm subjects. For example, researchers studying the effects of pornography are more likely to measure attitudinal effects, rather than behavioral effects that might lead subjects to commit crimes or act in ways that would lessen their self-esteem. So, Malamuth, Haber, and Feshbach (1980) asked male subjects if they would act like the rapists in a rape scenario rather than providing the subjects an opportunity to act sexually aggressive. Josephson (1987) gave boys the chance to play a game of floor hockey after exposure to media content and used the number of fouls committed as a measure of aggression, rather than let the boys have a chance to act in a less socially sanctioned aggressive way. These "diluted" measures may not be very accurate ways of assessing effects of media exposure.

Measures of media exposure in natural setting are often imprecise and subject to a good deal of random error (e.g., Webster & Wakshlag,

1985). Use of the broadcast media is typically inattentive (Bechtel, Achelpohl, & Akers, 1972) and fragmented now with widespread use of remote control devices (e.g., Walker & Bellamy, 1991). Newspaper exposure is usually operationalized as time spent reading or attention to different parts of the newspaper (e.g., D. M. McLeod & Perse, 1994), although people's reading speeds and interests vary. This error in measuring exposure can increase the amount of error variance in the study and reduce the relationship among the variables (Kerlinger, 1973), so media effects may seem less substantial.

For the most part, research designs tend to assume that media effects develop linearly. That is, as more media content is consumed, the greater the likelihood of effects. Our field depends on statistical techniques that are based on linear relationships, such as correlation, regression, and analysis of variance. If the media effects process is not a direct, linear process, our techniques may underestimate effects (e.g., Eveland, 1997). Persuasion research, for example, has found that the relationship between repetition and message impact is *curvilinear*. That is, as messages are repeated, not only does impact diminish, but, after a point, repetition may lead to less persuasion (e.g., Cacioppo & Petty, 1979). McGuire (1986) pointed out that there are models of advertising effects that are based on a threshold model (e.g., Bemmaor, 1984). That is, media content may have no impact until a certain level, or threshold, of exposure is reached. On the other hand, some media effects may have "ceilings," or points of diminishing returns.

Greenberg (1988) suggested that media content may have "drench" effects. According to the *drench hypothesis*, the media effects process is not a linear and cumulative "drip, drip" one. Instead, some media personalities, programs, and portrayals may be so potent that, although most images are ignored, these command attention and account for a good deal of media impact. An epidemiological approach to analyzing media effects would suggest that the media effects process may be very subtle and effects not noticed until media cause an imbalance in the social system. Then, media impact increases dramatically (e.g., Centerwall, 1989a, 1989b). If scholars are searching for linear media effects, then nonlinear ones will be less likely to be identified.

Media effects may appear to be less substantial because of conflicting processes. Television's heaviest viewers, young children and older women, are less likely to be aggressive, so television's effects may not be noticed. The cultivation hypothesis holds that heavy television viewers are more likely to believe that the real world is a violent as television's fictional programming (Gerbner et al., 1994). So, these heavy viewers are more fearful and less likely to venture outside at night. Other theories maintain that high levels of media violence lead people to act more aggressively (e.g., Bandura, 1994; Huesmann, 1982). These two processes, though, may serve to cancel each other out. If heavier viewers are more likely to stay indoors out of fear, they may be less likely to encounter situations where they may act aggressively.

Some writers argue that the thin performers and models in the media contribute to the prevalence of eating disorders among young women (Dietz, 1990). Adolescent girls are unable to attain the hyper-thin look of these media portrayals, so they become anorexic or bulimic. Yet, most research shows that reading and viewing media are inactive pastimes, associated with obesity and lack of exercise (Dietz & Gortmaker; 1985; Tucker, 1986). So media's influence on thinness may be offset by media's displacement effects. Other theoretical processes may hide the effects of media violence. If movie and television viewers become desensitized to violence because of heavy exposure to it, they may be less likely to be subject to arousal or priming effects (Jo & Berkowitz, 1994; Zillmann, 1982).

Some media may be so pervasive and so consistent in their effects that their impact is not noticeable. After all, it is almost impossible to find someone who doesn't watch television in industrialized societies. And those light viewers associate regularly with others who do watch television. Morgan (1986) suggested that "the longer we live with television, the smaller television's observable impact may become" (p. 135). Similarly, media's pervasiveness means that people are often exposed to conflicting messages. In the case of political advertising, for example, effects of ads for one candidate may be canceled out by ads for the opposition. The net media effect, then, may not be noticeable in situations where there are many contradictory media messages (Zaller, 1996).

The main reason that media's impact is not more substantial is that other aspects of life have stronger influence on people. As early as the Payne Fund studies (Jowett, Jarvie, & Fuller, 1996) of the 1920s and 1930s researchers were aware that the movies' impacts on children were dependent on age and cognitive abilities (Wartella & Reeves, 1985). Lazarsfeld, Berelson, and Gaudet (1968) observed that people's voting decisions were influenced more by the social groups (family, friends, and coworkers) than by media information and political advertising. When people are deciding whether to adopt an innovation (new idea, product, or way of doing something), mass media's impact is usually secondary to personal trial and social influence (Rogers, 1995). Public affairs knowledge gain associated with news use declines dramatically when the influence of demographics (gender, age, education, income, and religion) is removed (Robinson & Levy, 1996). Knowledge gap research demonstrates that learning information from the media is highly dependent on socioeconomic status (education and income; Tichenor, Donohue, & Olien, 1970). Declining credibility of the news media may cause some people to discount their information (Pew Research Center, 1996). Adolescents' decisions to drink beer and wine are more strongly linked to peer group influence than to exposure to alcohol advertising (Atkin, Hocking, & Block, 1984). Cultivation effects have been explained better by a variety of other demographic and life-situation variables, such as the neighborhood in which people live or their personal experience with crime (e.g., Doob & Macdonald, 1979; Hughes, 1980; Weaver & Wakshlag, 1986). Pornography is viewed as only one aspect of a range of individual conditions and social forces that influence the development of antisocial attitudes and behaviors toward women (Malamuth & Briere, 1986). The family communication climate may block some the harmful effects of sexual media content on adolescents' moral development (Bryant & Rockwell, 1994).

It is clear that media impact is often diminished because many messages are avoided by those who might be the most affected by them. Selective exposure research has noted that many people seek messages that confirm their beliefs and feelings and avoid those that are discrepant (e.g., Cotton, 1985). So smokers may be more likely to avoid public service announcements (PSAs) that urge them to give up tobacco and pay attention to those messages that deny harmful effects of tobacco (e.g., Brock & Balloun, 1967). One of the primary uses of remote control devices is to avoid objectional television content, such as commercials and political messages (Walker & Bellamy, 1991). Even when people do encounter messages that might affect them, they tend to reinterpret the messages to reinforce their preexisting beliefs and attitudes. Selective perception has been noted by communication scholars for decades. Football fans of different teams see different numbers of fouls (Hastorf & Cantril, 1954) and political candidate supporters are more likely to believe that their candidate was the "winner" in presidential debates (Kraus, 1962). When Norman Lear created *All In The Family* in the early 1970s, he hoped to make people aware of their prejudices and reduce bigotry. Vidmar and Rokeach (1974) found, however, that both high- and low-prejudiced viewers used the arguments between Archie and his son-in-law, Michael, to bolster their own beliefs. So selective perception leads people to interpret media content in accordance with their own beliefs. Finally, many people tend to select media content to maintain or achieve equilibrium. That is, people chose media content that brings them to emotional and arousal states that make them feel comfortable (e.g., Kubey & Csikszentmihalyi, 1990). Bored people seek media content that is exciting whereas anxious people seek relaxing content (Bryant & Zillmann, 1984; Zillmann, Hezel, & Medoff, 1980). The search for equilibrium may make media effects harder to notice.

These explanations suggest that media effects might be obscured by methodological imprecision, theoretical forces, and many personal, social, and situational constraints. Clearly, the probe for media effects demands continued efforts, refined theories and methods, and the integration of a wide range of intervening variables into research designs.

CRITICISM OF MEDIA EFFECTS APPROACHES

Scholars who hold critical and cultural studies perspectives argue that the study of media effects is limited and the results of those studies obscured because of faulty assumptions. Gitlin (1978) explained that the dominant paradigm in the study of media effects is a behaviorist approach that directs scholars to be concerned with a very narrow definition of "effects." Because behaviorism focuses on outcomes that can be observed, much research has been limited to short-term manifestations of "effects" that can be easily measured in laboratories or in surveys. Effects have been defined in most studies as attitude change or in specific, discrete behaviors. This means that, for the most part, research has not considered the effects of long-term, cumulative media exposure.

Gitlin (1978) also pointed out that most media effects research is grounded in "administrative" modes of research, which yield data to marketing or policy decision makers so that they can predict the impact of media campaigns. Administrative research, then, also places value on short-term media impact that can be identified in pretests designed to help prepare campaigns or in postcampaign evaluations. Moreover, administrative media effects research is typically interested in variables in the campaign that can be manipulated or controlled, such as media production variables or frequency of exposure. Systemic variables, such as media ownership and organization, are not relevant because they are the part of the assumptions and administrative structure driving the research. So, structural variables, that may shape media production and content, are rarely studied in connection with media effects, so their impact rarely considered.

Because media effects research has its roots in the United States (Rogers, 1994), it has been grounded in the assumptions of capitalism and democracy. Central to both is the value in "freedom of choice." There are two problems with the notion of choice. First, reinforcement, or rejection of media attempts to change one's choice, is viewed as evidence of limitations on media power (Klapper, 1960). But, the maintenance of the status quo is often a powerful, though less noticed, effect. Second, believing in freedom of choice assumes that various alternatives are indeed real choices. Different people might select different network news programs for different reasons (e.g., Palmgreen, Wenner, & Rayburn, 1980), for example, but are the programs sufficiently different to lead to different effects? Gerbner (1990) argued that because television content, even that seen with videocassette recorders (VCRs) and cable, is created, for the most part, by the same producers with the same end goals, so it will all share common themes and patterns of images. So, freedom of choice may be an illusion that leads scholars to hold beliefs about limited media power.

For these reasons, then, critical and cultural scholars are not surprised that only "limited," or modest media effects have been identified. Because of the assumptions and methods of the "dominant paradigm" (Gitlin, 1978), more powerful, yet subtle effects, such as social control, manufacturing of consent, and reluctance to challenge the status quo, are unable to be studied; so they are ignored.

WHY IS IT IMPORTANT TO STUDY MEDIA EFFECTS

With all these questions about the existence and substance of media effects, why is it important to continue to study them? Students in introductory mass communication courses are often reminded that mass communication is functional in society (Wright, 1986) and an important field of study because of its role as a major societal institution.

Mass communication is an important economic force in the United States. In 1993, the entertainment industry alone (movies, music, cable television, and home video) brought an estimated $50 billion into the U.S. economy. Network television advertising added an additional $30 billion (Warner, 1993).

Mass communication is also an important political force, acting as a watchdog over official actions and as the platform for political information and activity. The Watergate scandal, for example, was brought to light by the *Washington Post* and the Pentagon papers were first published by the *New York Times*. Political campaigns are now built around television. In 1992, the Republicans spent two-thirds of their budget on television advertisements for George Bush. Talk shows and news program coverage are crucial to campaigns. Our political leaders contact the public primarily through the mass media—press conferences, political talks. Ronald Reagan noticed that there was little political news that was made during the weekends, so he (an old radio announcer, himself) began to make radio addresses about various issues on Saturday mornings. These addresses got so much news coverage (Martin, 1984), in part because there was so little else happening, that Saturday morning radio talks are a current presidential practice.

At the same time, mass media are a major source of entertainment and the main source for news for most people. In 1995, a majority of people in the United States turned to media for news: 70.3% were regular viewers of local television news, 67.3% were regular viewers of network television news, and 59.3% read a daily newspaper. In addition, 48.6% listened regularly to radio news and 31.4% read a news magazine regularly (Stempel & Hargrove, 1996).

Beyond the importance of mass communication in society, there are two main reasons for continuing to study media effects. The first reason is theoretical. Although most scholars acknowledge that mass media effects can occur, we still don't know the magnitude and inevitability of the effects. That is, we don't know how powerful the media are among the range of other forces in society. And, we don't know all the conditions that enhance or mitigate various effects. Most importantly, we don't understand all the processes by which mass communication can lead to various effects. Research in media effects must continue to add to our knowledge.

A second reason for studying media effects is practical and policy oriented. If we can elaborate the conditions and understand the various processes of media effects—how media effects occur—we can use that knowledge. At a practical level, understanding the processes of media effects will allow media practitioners to create effective messages to achieve political, advertising, and public relations-oriented goals. Additionally, agencies will be able to formulate media campaigns to promote prosocial aims and benefit society as a whole. That is, understanding the processes of media effects will allow media practitioners to increase the likelihood of prosocial media effects. Most importantly, understanding how media effects occur will give parents, educators, and public officials other tools to fight negative media effects. If we understand the processes of media effects, we will also understand how to mitigate negative effects. No longer will changing or restricting media content be the only methods to stop media effects. We will be able to mitigate negative media effects by also targeting aspects of the process of impact.

WAYS TO CONCEPTUALIZE MEDIA EFFECTS: DIMENSIONS OF MEDIA EFFECTS

Over the years, scholars have suggested that it is useful to analyze media effects along specific dimensions (Anderson & Meyer, 1988; Chaffee, 1977; McGuire, 1986; J. M. McLeod, Kosicki, & Pan, 1991; J. M. McLeod & Reeves, 1980; Roberts & Maccoby, 1985). Some of the dimensions delineate the type of effect; other dimensions elaborate the conditions of media impact.

Cognitive–Affective–Behavioral Dimension

Media effects are commonly described along a cognitive–affective–behavioral dimension, which marks a distinction between acquisition of knowledge about an action and performance of the action. Mass communication scholars have been greatly influenced by persuasion models that see human action as logical and driven by cognition (e.g., McGuire, 1985). This dimension is important in keeping scholars from assuming that knowledge and attitudes translate directly into action. Persuasion research during World War II, for example, found that although media content may be quite effective at teaching information, it had less influence on attitude formation and motivation to act

(Hovland, Lumsdaine, & Sheffield, 1949). The Theory of Reasoned Action (Fishbein & Ajzen, 1975) posits that, although knowledge and attitudes have some impact on behavior, their influence is mediated (or eliminated) by social constraints.

Micro- Versus Macrolevel

Another dimension that describes the type of effect is one that focuses on the level of media influence: micro- versus macrolevel. Most concern about media effects focuses on impressionable audiences and has been grounded in psychological approaches. So, there is a wealth of research on media effects at the individual, or microlevel. It is a fallacy, however, to assume that all media effects are accumulations of individual-level effects. Scholars recognize that a focus solely on individual-level media effects can obscure more subtle societal-level effects. Research on the effects of *Sesame Street*, for example, showed that children of all socioecomic status (SES) classes learned from the program. But, that learning led to another, unintended effect: a widening gap in knowledge between higher and lower SES groups. Although all children learned from the program, children from higher SES families learned at a faster rate (Cook et al., 1975). So, individual knowledge gain may lead to greater inequities in society.

Another area in which an accumulation of individual-level effects might conceal more macrolevel effects is news learning. Although many researchers have uncovered various media-related influences on public-affairs knowledge (e.g., J. P. Robinson & Levy, 1986, 1996), these studies cannot assess the completeness, accuracy, or objectivity of media's presentations about public affairs. Several scholars argue that larger influences on news gathering and reporting may make individual-level knowledge effects inconsequential because news sources and practices present only limited public affairs information to the public (e.g., Gitlin, 1980; Herman & Chomsky, 1988; Tuchman, 1978). So, knowledge gain by individuals may not necessarily be functional for society.

Several important effects of mass media may be at the societal, institutional, or cultural level. Over the years, for example, the expanding telecommunications revolution has changed, and no doubt will continue to affect how political campaigns and the workings of government are conducted. Clearly, scholars need to consider various levels of media impact.

Intentional Versus Unintentional

Another dimension of media effects directs scholars to consider whether the effects are intended versus unintended—planned for or accidental. Although this dimension is a descriptive one, it also offers some insights in the processes of media impact. For example, the development of knowledge gaps between high and lower SES children who watched *Sesame Street* is generally considered an unintended effect of the flow of media information. So, scholars and media policymakers study ways to close accidental knowledge gaps by increasing access to a variety of sources of information, by making information more relevant to lower SES groups, or by increasing the motivation of lower SES audience members to seek additional information. The identification of these knowledge-gap effects as accidental, then, has led scholars to focus on how knowledge is carried by the mass media, how audiences access that knowledge, and how people use media-delivered information.

Another example of the relevance of the intended versus unintended dimension is one effect of television violence. The cultivation hypothesis suggests that one, often overlooked, effect of television violence is that it affects social perceptions of heavy viewers and leads those groups who are victimized in television drama to feel fearful, alienated from society, and distrusting of others (Gerbner & Gross, 1976; Gerbner et al., 1994). If scholars believe that these effects are unintentional due to the conventions of television drama production, they might advocate certain remedies to help mitigate these effects, such as television program ratings to help fearful people avoid certain programs or to help parents screen what their children watch. If, on the other hand, scholars believe that cultivation is an intentional effect designed to reinforce the existing power structure in society by structuring reality for women and minorities so that they avoid involvement in political affairs, possible solutions would be quite different. Those scholars (at the very least) would be less trusting of television program ratings affixed by television producers and probably not advocate that sort of solution to cultivation effects.

Studying unintended effects can be a way of increasing media effectiveness. Dramatic story lines in soap operas and telenovelas have been found to not only captivate their audiences but bring about knowledge gain and some prosocial attitudinal effects (e.g., Singhal & Rogers, 1989). So this dimension of media effects directs scholars to search for a range of effects, beyond those planned for the media producers.

Content-Dependent Versus Content-Irrelevant

The content-dependent versus a content- irrelevant distinction reflects the impact of specific classes of media content as opposed to the impact of media use itself. The most visible media effects research has focused on the effects of specific media content, such as stereotypes, violence, and pornography. This research assumes that specific content is linked to specific effects. As J. M. McLeod and Reeves (1980) paraphrase the nutritional analogy, "We are what we eat": We are what we watch. So, one way to reduce aggressive behavior in children would be to reduce the amount of violent media content that they read or watch. Or, one way to reduce sexual aggression against women would be to reduce access to media content that depicts violence against women. Although there is a good deal of evidence of the effects of specific media content, scholars should also be aware that some effects are due less to specific media content, and more to the form of the content or the act of media use.

Displacement effects are a commonly identified content-irrelevant effect. Lazarsfeld and Merton (1948) suggested that political involvement could suffer if people become politically "narcotized." That is, public affairs media use might replace real political action and some people might be informed, but politically apathetic. Watching television has been attributed with lower academic achievement because children are replacing homework and study with television watching (Armstrong & Greenberg, 1990; Hornik, 1978).

Other content-irrelevant effects may be due to the form of the media presentation. Tavris (1988) is one writer who has suggested that television's regular commercial interruptions has led to shorter attention spans. Scholars (Shannon & Weaver, 1949) investigating how information theory is relevant to media effects have found that the randomness of television's formal features are connected to aggressive responses (Watt & Krull, 1977). Kozma (1991) speculated how the form and use of different media lead to different learning styles and outcomes. And there is a good deal of evidence that arousing media content, whether it is violent, pornographic, or suspenseful, can lead to similar excitation effects (Zillmann, 1980, 1982). In order to understand how media effects occur, we need to uncover, first, if they are content-relevant or content-irrelevant.

Short Term Versus Long Term

Media effects can be long or short term. This dimension is not only a descriptive one, but also helps describe the process of media effects. When we examine media effects, we need to question how long the effect is theoretically expected to last. Some effects, such as increased arousal (or relaxation) are relatively short term, and disappear quickly. Others, such as agenda setting, may last somewhat longer, but may disappear as the media agenda changes. Still other effects, such as the social learning of aggressive behavior, are expected to be fairly enduring, especially if the aggressive behavior, once performed, is rewarded.

Some theories do not specify the persistence of their effects. Do the stereotypes that children learn from television persist even as children watch less and less television as they get older? How long do the effects of televised political ads (and their associated voting intentions) last? What are the possibilities that new ads (and new information) will change voting intentions?

And what are the implications of differing periods of influence? Clearly, short-term effects can have a profound impact. If, for example, a short-term arousal effect of a violent film leads someone to get involved in a fight, permanent injury could result. But, if agenda-setting effects last only as long as an issue stays near the top of the media agenda, what long-lasting impacts can result? Media effects scholars should be clear in specifying the duration of the effects that they study.

Reinforcement Versus Change

A final dimension of media effects is that of reinforcement versus change. Does media exposure alter or stabilize? The most visible media effects studies focus on how media content or exposure changes the audience (or society or culture). For example, we are concerned how placid children might be changed into aggressive ones by watching violent cartoons. Or that respectful men will change into uncaring desensitized oafs through exposure to pornography. Or that voters might have their political values adjusted through exposure to political ads. Or that ignorant citizens will become knowledgeable through exposure to public affairs news. And so on.

There is evidence, though, that communication's strongest effect, overall, is reinforcement and stabilization. Selective exposure leads people to prefer media messages that reinforce their preexisting views. Selective perception points out that people interpret media content to reinforce their attitudes. Because it is often easier to observe change than reinforcement, we often neglect media's power to stabilize. Advertisements that keep supporters active in a political campaign and keep them from wavering in support yield important effects. Media content that reinforces the already existing aggressive tendencies of a young boy may be an even more important influence than prosocial messages that have little impact. We must be careful not to equate reinforcement effects with null effects.

CONCLUSION

The study of media effects is grounded in the belief that mass communication has noticeable effects on individuals, society, and culture. Evidence for these effects, though, is problematic. On one hand, despite consistence findings of effects, the variance accounted for is typically small. Moreover, the strongest effects are usually relegated to laboratory settings, which are highly artificial settings. There are, however, several reasons to expect that research underestimates media effects. Our models, theories, and methods are still imprecise; we still cannot offer complete explanations for media effects. The study of media effects remains important so that we can increase understanding of the role mass communication plays in shaping our lives. Awareness of the process of media effects will allow us to use mass communication effectively—to maximize desirable outcomes and minimize negative effects.

2

Models of Media Effects

This chapter begins with an overview of the chronicle of the study of media effects. Although there is some disagreement about the progression of theory about and study of media effects, throughout the history of our field there have been bodies of research that emphasize different forces as the impetus for media effects. Those beliefs can be summarized by four basic models of media impact. This chapter presents these four models that will be the structure for the following chapters. Because this book focuses on understanding *how* media effects occur, these four models serve to highlight aspects of media content and the audience that serve as the basis for influence so that we can understand the process of media effects.

THE "RECEIVED VIEW" OF THE STUDY OF MEDIA EFFECTS

Many of the textbooks of our field (e.g., Baran & Davis, 1995; DeFleur & Ball-Rokeach, 1989; McQuail, 1994) described the study of media effects as a series of "phases" marked by paradigm shifts—shifts in theoretical assumptions, the ways the scholars look at problems, and the ways that they interpret empirical results. According to this *received view* (i.e., generally accepted history of the field), there are three basic phases to the study of media effects.

The first phase covered the early 20th century through the 1930s. Its focus on media effects was based on the stimulus–response model drawn from psychology and grounded in mass society theory drawn from sociology. The "magic bullet"[1] or "hypodermic needle" model held that the media were so powerful that the audience was powerless to resist their influence. This model was based on observations that the technological improvements in public communication and mass production of popular culture had created a mass audience attending to the same messages (Curran, Gurevitch, & Woollacott, 1982). The emphasis on instinct and stimulus–response learning drawn from psychology reinforced the notion that powerful stimuli, such as effective media messages, could induce people to respond mechanically, immediately, and relatively uniformly, consistent with the intentions of the creators of the messages.

At the same time, sociologists believed that the industrial revolution had led to a fragmentation of the social bonds in society, so that people no longer felt part of social communities but felt isolated and disconnected from others. A society based on the personal bonds of kinship and friendship, *Gemeinschaft*, was replaced by a society marked by personal distance and contractual obligations, *Gesellschaft* (see DeFleur & Ball-Rokeach, 1989, pp. 153–154, for a discussion of Tönnies, 1957). The social and psychological isolation brought on by the industrial revolution created a mass society in which people were aimless and disconnected from others. These masses, then, were especially susceptible to the influence of powerful, persuasive forces in society, such as mass communication.

This phase reflected the views of scholars of the era and found some support in some of the published research. Lasswell's (1927) analysis of propaganda, for example, was based on the assumption that the effective messages of World War I could teach scholars how to create messages to manipulate the masses. Studies of war bond drives of World War II (Merton, 1946) focused on the appeal of Kate Smith, a down-to-earth singer whose sincerity impressed radio listeners so much that they pledged millions of dollars to the war effort. Her appeal, according to Merton, grew out of listeners' desire for *Gemeinschaft* in the mass society. And, although the Princeton study of the audience response to the "War of the Worlds" radio broadcast (Cantril, Gaudet, & Herzog, 1940) showed that the impact of the program was limited by a

---

[1]Chaffeee and Hochheimer (1982) pointed out that the term "magic bullet" may actually be a misnomer. In the medical literature, a magic bullet is a "specific medication, which hits only those few in the population who are diseased; it is 'magic' because it passes through all the others without any effect" (p. 286). In the context of media effects, a magic bullet would have specific effects on only a limited portion of the audience.

variety of audience factors, news coverage and anecdotal accounts reinforced beliefs that mass communication could instill extreme emotions and reactions in the audience.

The second phase of media effects research is often called the era of *limited effects*. This phase is marked by regarding media as having only minimal influence on the audience. Klapper (1960) expressed the limits on media effects: "Mass communication *ordinarily* does not serve as a necessary and sufficient cause of audience effects, but rather functions among and through a nexus of mediating factors and influences" (p. 8). Klapper elaborated two conditions under which mass communication could influence the audience: if normal barriers to effects are not operating or if mediating factors are congruent with media's influence. But his statements about the minimal effects of mass communication were supported by pages of evidence that filled most of his book. His generalization about the conditions of media influence received a good deal less attention in his work and the subsequent research of the era.

The reason for media's limited effects was the power of the audience to selectively choose and use media content. In other words, people controlled media and their content through various selectivity processes: (a) selective exposure, or control over what they watched, listened to, or read in the media; (b) selective attention, or control over which elements of media messages people would pay attention to; (c) selective perception, or control over how messages were interpreted; and (d) selective recall, or control over how and what was learned from the media.

This view of the power of the audience grew out of persuasion and election research that found that media's impact was limited by the social connections among people, the influence of people in the flow of information from mass media (Katz & Lazarsfeld, 1955; Lazarsfeld, Berelson, & Gaudet, 1968), and by a host of personal experiences and attributes (e.g., Hovland, Lumsdaine, & Sheffield, 1949). Social connections drew people together and led to shared interpretations of media messages. People's personal characteristics led them to seek out media content that reinforced their beliefs and preexisting attitudes. So, media's impact was seen as quite limited in this era. Social and personal characteristics of people influenced their selective approach to mass communication so much that media's main and most common impact was believed to be *reinforcement*.

This phase lasted until the 1960s and led several scholars to question the value of continuing to study media effects (e.g., Berelson, 1959). There seemed to be little justification to studying media effects, if media's influence was so minimal. The introduction and widespread adoption of television, though, brought scholars to a new phase of effects research.

Television was quickly embraced by the public. In 1950, only 9% of U.S. homes owned a television. By 1955, 64.5% of U.S. homes owned a television; by 1965, the percentage had increased to 92.6% (Television Information Office, 1985). Television became the dominant medium as people replaced radio listening and movie going with television viewing. By 1963, the typical household was watching television more than 5½ hours a day (Comstock, Chaffee, Katzman, McCombs, & Roberts, 1978). And by 1961, television replaced newspapers as the most believable medium (Roper, Starch Worldwide, 1995). Scholars began to question whether selective exposure was feasible in such a television-saturated media environment. During this period, several studies began to show that it was possible for the mass media to overcome the tendencies of the audience toward a selective approach to using mass communication. In fact, this era is often referred to as "the return to the concept of powerful mass media" (Noelle-Neumann, 1973, p. 68).

McClure and Patterson (1974) noted that television had the possibility to overcome some selectivity processes. During elections, political advertisements on television were so prevalent during prime time that people could not avoid them. Although people might selectively avoid news programs, it was much more difficult to avoid political ads interspersed during entertainment programming. McClure and Patterson found that people learned about the candidates from the many political ads on television, even if they weren't particularly interested in the election.

Other studies found *strong media effects*; that is, consistent reiteration of important news items led people to adopt the media's agenda as their own (McCombs & Shaw, 1972). *Agenda setting* marked the ability of the mass media to tell people "what to think about." Gerbner and Gross (1976) found that the heaviest viewers of television were the most likely to be "cultivated" by its patterns of images and accept the television world view as their vision of reality. These heavy viewers, of course, were relatively unselective in what they watched on television.

Notice that these studies did not focus on obvious, behavioral media effects. McClure and Patterson (1974) did not argue that exposure to political ads led people to change their voting behavior, but that these ads had "dramatic and direct" (p. 3) impact on people's beliefs about candidates. McCombs and Shaw (1972) did not argue that media were powerful in telling people what to think, but what to think *about*. And Gerbner and Gross (1976) did not argue that the violence on television made people act aggressively, only that watching large amounts of television violence made people feel afraid. So, this era of media effects focused on media's power to bring about subtle, yet direct media effects.

An Appraisal of the Received View

Although the received view sees a progression of ways of looking at media effects, it is probably a simplistic report of the development of the study of media effects. Moreover, several scholars have argued that it is not a realistic account of the full range of media effects study. Wartella and Reeves (1985) suggested that the received view reflects an emphasis on the study of public opinion, voting, and marketing decisions, and ignores other areas of interest. The received view particularly does not describe the progress of research on the child audience. The Payne Fund Studies, some of the earliest studies of the impact of movies on children, were conducted from 1929 to 1932, during the era of "direct effects." Yet, the various studies focused on a broad range of influences that mediated harmful effects of the movies, including age, gender, parental influence, family and social environment, predispositions, and experiences—the same kinds of influences considered in studies of the effects of television decades later. The effects of the movies were hardly considered direct by the Payne Fund researchers.

Others have argued that the "limited effects" phase of study is a misrepresentation of the research findings of the era. Chaffee and Hochheimer (1982) pointed out that effects identified during that period only seemed limited because of the marketing orientation of Lazarsfeld's research bureau. In the Erie County voting study (Lazarsfeld, Berelson, & Gaudet, 1968), voting was conceptualized as a marketing decision—a one-time choice at the polls. So the researchers were concerned only with voting intention and ignored other possible political effects (see also Gitlin, 1978). Other effects, such as knowledge gain, or participation in political parties and other political activities were ignored, even though these might have greater impact on the political process as a whole.

Moreover, Lazarsfeld and his colleagues may have understated the impact of the media and overstated the role of personal influence. The data do not support a heavy reliance on interpersonal communication over mass media as a source of influence. When the Erie County panelists were asked to name the sources of information that influenced their voting decision, 56% of the men and 52% of the women made no mention of a personal contact as "influential." Three-quarters of the panelists made no mention of a personal contact as "most influential" (Lazarsfeld et al., 1968, p. 171). On the other hand, 68% found radio "helpful" in their voting decision; 66% reported that newspapers were "helpful." Of all the information sources, 38% found radio to be the "most important" source and 23% named newspapers (Lazarsfeld et al., 1948, p. 127). The media's role in voting was clearly strong and one that was important to the panelists.

The assertion of limited media effects also needs to be placed in the context of media industry connections to academic research. During that era, much research was funded by media industries[2] and academia provided the training for several notable names in the business.[3] Because the era of limited effects held that media served mainly to reinforce, rather than bring about change, the research of this era served as evidence that fears about media effects were groundless. Klapper's (1960) book, one of the most influential works of this era, was used politically by the television networks to argue against regulation. Klapper not only worked as a graduate student with Lazarsfeld's research bureaus, but was Director of Social Research at CBS when his book was published (Rowland, 1983).

FOUR MODELS OF MEDIA EFFECTS

Although the received view is not a completely accurate depiction of the full range of the study of media effects, it illustrates that different emphases were placed on different contexts and different explana-

---

[2]*The People's Choice* (Lazarsfeld et al., 1998) received some funding from *Life* magazine for rights to the story. Merton's (1949) study of opinion leadership in "Rovere" was funded by *Time*. MacFadden Publishing provided $30,000 to underwrite *Personal Influence* (Katz & Lazarsfeld, 1955; see Rogers, 1994, p. 296).

[3]Frank Stanton, president of CBS, for example, had worked with Lazarsfeld at the bureau. He was the first PhD in the broadcast industry (Rogers, 1994).

tions for media effects. This section of the chapter presents four different models of media effects. These models depict four different processes of media effects, drawn from the various bodies of research of our field. These models differ because each places emphasis on different aspects of media content or the audience as the primary force driving media effects. It is important to remember that these four models are designed to focus explanations. So, they are simplified. Because each model focuses on only one part of the cause of media impact, no single model can be a complete explanation for media effects. But these models are valuable because they can direct study of the processes of media effects.

DIRECT EFFECTS

The direct effects model focuses on *media content* as the most important explanation for media influence. Effects are seen as immediate (occurring fairly shortly after exposure), relatively uniform (similar across all audience members), and consistent with the goals of the media producer. Moreover, effects within this model are observable ones. The emphasis of this model is on effects that represent change, not reinforcement. Effects are either behavioral, cognitive, or affective effects that lead directly to noticeable actions. For example, the direct effects model is applicable in understanding how political ads might lead to voting for a specific candidate (a behavioral effect), or knowledge gain that would lead to a voting decision (a cognitive effect), or attitude acquisition that influences voting choice (an affective effect). The direct effects model, however, would not be useful in explaining how political campaigns would lead to feelings of political disenfranchisement.

The direct effects model ignores the role of the audience in the media effects process. People are assumed to be incapable of countering media's impact. They may lack the mental capacity to analyze media messages. So young children may be the targets of direct effects. Or people may have little background knowledge or context about certain events and issues and be reliant solely on media content. In these situations, effects may be direct. Most commonly, however, people are seen as reacting involuntarily and automatically to certain aspects of media content. Although people may have the mental abilities to evaluate content, the direct effects model holds that they are unable to resist the attentional "pull" of some of the features of presentation. Within this model, then, skilled media producers can create media content that is likely to invoke fairly predictable and uniform reactions from large parts of the audience.

IMPORTANT VARIABLES IN THE MODEL

Variables associated with media content are the most important to understanding direct effects. Most central are aspects of media content that (a) are perceived more automatically by people—such as those that attract orienting responses (involuntary attention) or unconscious responses; (b) are associated with increases in arousal; and (c) are depicted realistically.

Structural and Content features.   Structural and content media features, such as commercial breaks, cuts and edits, and camera and lens movement, are associated with the orienting response. The *orienting response* is involuntary and automatic attention that is unrelated to the meaning of the media stimulus (e.g., Lang, 1990). These structural features' demand on attention is usually explained by the natural need to detect movement so one can control and understand one's immediate environment (Reeves, Thorson, & Schleuder, 1986). Welch and Watt (1982), for example, hypothesized that children's attention to educational programs was a necessary antecedent to learning effects. The researchers found that shifts in scenes in television programs were associated with children's visual attention to the screen. Negative media images may attract the orienting response out of a survival instinct (Reeves, Newhagen, Mailbach, Basil, & Kurz, 1991). So people may remember negative news stories better because of that attention.

Some features of media content (such as certain musical themes or the presence of certain types of characters) may attract less conscious attention because people have learned to associate pleasure with those features. Levin and Anderson (1976), for example, speculated that children focused visual attention on the television screen when female adults, other children, and familiar animals were on because these were familiar sources of enjoyment. In contrast, media depictions of dangerous people, animals, and situations may evoke fear reactions because of stimulus generalization (Cantor, 1994). That is, some stimuli invoke conditioned or unconditioned fear responses. Realistic media representations may elicit those same automatic reactions. Features such as camera angles and distance influence how people perceive images. Low camera angles, for example, make objects seem bigger. Camera angles have been found to influence perceptions of the credibility of political candidates (McCain, Chilberg, & Wakshlag, 1977) and impressions and recall of characters in pictures (Kraft, 1987). Shots that mimic interpersonal distance are hypothesized to lead to more personal reactions to media personalities (e.g., Meyrowitz, 1982). All of us realize how "spooky" below-key lighting is (such as shining a flashlight up at our face from below our chin). Zettl (1973) suggested that "we affix this outer distortion to an inner disorientation. The face appears unusual, ghostly, brutal" (p. 30).

Arousal.   Media content variables may be important to media effects because they increase arousal. *Arousal* is an automatic, nonspecific physiological response that is conceptualized as an activator or energizer. Arousal is usually not under the control of an individual; it is stimulated by the environment. But, interpretation or labeling of what the arousal is due to *is* controlled by the individual (Zillmann, 1991). Arousal is important to understanding media effects because it is associated with greater attention (Eysenck, 1993), so arousal can be associated with cognitive effects. As an activator, arousal has also been linked to increased affective and behavioral responses (e.g., Zillmann & Bryant, 1974). Arousal is increased by some structural features of media presentations, such as larger television screens. Detenber and Reeves (1996) speculated that larger images are "compelling and significant stimuli" (p. 77) and humans have adapted to be "wary of big things." Arousal is also a common result of exciting media content, such as violence and erotica (Zillmann, 1991). Comstock et al. (1978) considered the salience of a television act as an important antecedent to explaining media effects (see Fig. 2.1). *Salience* involves the arousal inherent in the depiction as well as its vividness of the image.

Realism.   When media content more closely resembles real-world counterparts, various theories hold that it is more likely to have an effect. Cultivation, for example, is based in part on the realism of television content, so that heavy viewers are more likely to accept television's distorted depictions as reality (Gerbner & Gross, 1976). So-

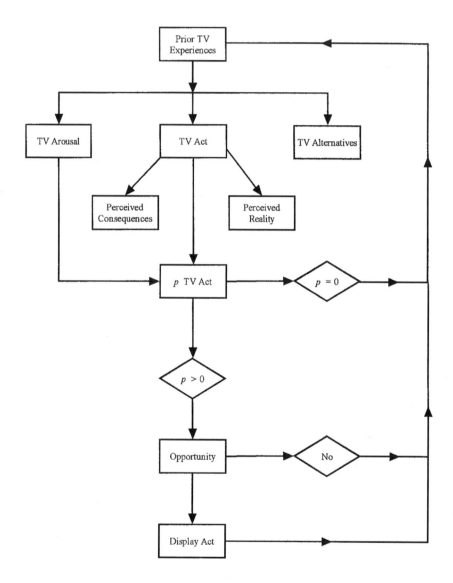

FIG. 2.1.   Comstock's psychological model. Adapted from Comstock's Psychologi-
cal Model of Television's Behavioral Effects. From: Comstock, G., Chaffee, S.,
Katzman, N., Mccombs, M., & Roberts, D. (1978). *Television and human behavior.*
New York: Columbia University Press, p. 400.

cial learning theory holds that people are more likely to learn behaviors that are presented more realistically (Bandura, 1994). And more realistic media content is more likely to activate mental images (e.g., Jo & Berkowitz, 1994).

Summary

The direct effects model holds that media content invokes fairly predictable and uniform reactions from large parts of the audience. This model may appear to bear some resemblance to the outdated, early conceptions of the "propaganda," "magic bullet," and "hypodermic needle" models. Certainly, few mass communication scholars still accept the viability of these models, although the notion of a passive audience helplessly manipulated by enticing media images still invades the writings of popular authors. But the value of the direct effects model should not be dismissed. There are certain conditions when this model may be useful in understanding how media effects occur: (a) when the audience is incapable or unable to analyze and/or evaluate media messages or (b) when media content stimulates people to react unconsciously or automatically. Central to this model is the impact of media content variables to arouse and command attention. For this reason, most direct effects are relatively short term. This model and media content features may be an especially fruitful area of media effects research as new technology brings media content closer to reality (e.g., filmic special effects, high definition television—HDTV, and virtual reality).

CONDITIONAL EFFECTS

This model is drawn from the limited effects model described by the received view. Like the limited effects model, the *conditional model* places emphasis on the audience and is based on notions of selectivity (selective exposure, attention, perception, and recall) and social influence. The limited effects model downplays the possibility of most media effects beyond reinforcement, whereas the conditional model recognizes that media effects can occur and offers explanations for those effects. This model is called the conditional model, because media effects are conditional on the audience member. This model recognizes that all media exposure is not bound to result in media effects. The audience has the power to avoid exposure and reject influence. And, when media effects occur, they are certainly not uniform. Different people may be affected quite differently by the same media content.

To give a simple example: Certainly not everyone is going to cry at the end of a sad movie (such as *Terms of Endearment*). Some may never watch the movie because they dislike the actors or the story device. Even some of those who watch the movie will dislike it, and some may go to a movie they don't expect to like, just to accompany someone. And even those who like the movie may not cry. Different people have different feelings about expressing emotions in public places. Still others may be profoundly affected by the movie and find themselves sobbing at certain scenes. So, the conditional model holds that the explanation of the effects of the movie rests with the individual audience member.

Effects, according to the conditional model, can be cognitive, affective, or behavioral. The effects can occur immediately after exposure or require repeated exposure to similar messages. And the effects may be short term or long term. The conditional model, because it focuses mainly on the individual audience member, can be used to explain almost any media effect at an individual level.

The individual is the focus of media effects because of the individual's power to be selective. The audience member is central to the conditional model (and media content is ignored, for the most part) because of selectivity processes that act as barriers to intended media effects. People selectively expose themselves to media content. Mainly, they choose media content that is consistent with their interests, personal experiences, and their own needs and desires. Even when they are using media content, people pay attention quite selectively. For example, people often listen to what's happening on television while they do something else. They turn their complete attention to the set only when something interesting is happening. Finally, when they watch, read, or hear media messages, people selectively perceive those messages and interpret them within the framework of those interests, experiences, and needs. Selective exposure, attention, and perception, then, are barriers to effects that lead people to reject messages unless they fit into preexisting knowledge or interests.

But media effects often go beyond reinforcement. Change as a result of media exposure is likely. When change effects happen, they are conditional on some attribute of the audience. Although selectivity is generally seen as a barrier to effects, audience characteristics may act as lenses, and focus media's influence. Audience characteristics are conditions of influence.

This model is called conditional because when effects do occur, they are conditional on some attribute of the audience. For example, learning from the news might be conditional on the reasons the viewer is watching. Or cultivation effects from watching prime-time television might be conditional on whether the viewer has had personal experience with crime. Or, the effects of political messages about changes in Medicare funding might be conditional on the age of the audience member.

So, this model focuses discussion and explanation on the audience member. And audience variables are important—especially variables that deal with the social connections of people and those variables that concern how the audience interprets messages.

Important Variables in the Model

There are three classes of audience variables that can intervene in the process of media effects according to the conditional model: social categories, social relationships, and individual differences. These three classes of variables can act either as a barrier to media effects or as a lens to enhance the likelihood of media effects.

Social Categories.   Social categories variables are aspects of people that are fairly easy to observe or uncover. They may be demographic characteristics of people, such as gender, age, SES, ethnicity, educational level, and geographic location of their home. Social categories may also reflect common self-designations such as religion, political party membership, and occupation. Social categories variables are often the variables measured by the U.S. census. Social categories are ways to separate people into broad groups. These variables are meaningful because we assume that, for the most part, everyone in one category is alike, and that people in one category are different from those in another category. For example, television programmers know that they can target certain types of television programs at women, because, for the most part, most women will prefer certain program genres. But, as a whole, women will prefer different types of television programs than men. So, gender is a meaningful social category for explaining television program preference. Another social category is age. Young children (ages 3 to 5) may be more likely to be frightened by television programs that do not frighten older children. So, a child's age is a meaningful way to explain some of the fright effects of the mass media.

Social categories variables provide explanations for media effects because the categories represent the common frames of reference of different groups of people. These frames of reference are reflected in shared interests, experiences, and abilities that affect selective exposure, attention, perception, and recall. So, social categories are really shorthand explanations for media effects.

The reason that young children are more likely to be frightened by some televison programs is not solely because they are young. Age is really a shorthand for levels of cognitive development. Young children's minds process environmental information quite simply (Flavell, 1963). They rely on superficial, physical features of a stimulus. Because of that reliance, they cannot understand the psychological motivation underlying action. So, Sparks and Cantor (1986) showed that younger children were more frightened by David Banner's transformation into the Incredible Hulk than older children, because younger children were not cognitively able to understand that the Hulk was really a good character. They saw the Hulk acting aggressively, and saw no connection between the Hulk and Banner.

Malamuth (1996) argued that gender is an important social category in understanding the effects of pornography for two reasons. First, evolution has favored males who have many, fertile sexual partners (echoing the content of much pornography). Second, males and females are socialized about sex differently in most societies and receive different messages about the rewards and dangers inherent in sexual activity.

Knowledge gap research hypothesizes that SES is an important social category in understanding knowledge gain from the mass media. Higher SES groups (reflecting higher education and/or income) typically learn more and gain knowledge more quickly than low-SES groups. Socioeconomic status is such a powerful explanation because it represents many other individual factors, including greater access to more sophisticated information sources, better communication skills, greater social utility for public affairs knowledge, and political interest (D. M. McLeod & Perse, 1994; Tichenor et al., 1970). So higher SES groups are more likely to selectively expose themselves to news and selectively remember information that is useful to them.

Social Relationships.   Social relationships variables represent the social connections and interpersonal interactions among people that mediate media effects. This set of variables gained importance in communication research with the Erie County voting study (Lazarsfeld et al., 1968). Subsequent studies noted that people play a role in the flow of mass communication. The two-step flow holds that interested people pay attention to specialized media and pass along that information to others to whom they are socially connected. Researchers found that media messages flowed from opinion leaders to family members, friends, and even more casual coworkers. The two-step flow has several implications for media effects. First, people might become aware of and be influenced by media messages that they have not directly encountered. Second, the information passed along by opinion leaders is not necessarily isomorphic with that delivered by the media. As individuals, opinion leaders are affected by selectivity processes of selective exposure, attention, perception, and recall. Third, the personal influence represented by the two-step flow can be an especially powerful barrier to or the enhancement of media effects (Rogers, 1995).

Social relationships variables are also represented in the mediating impact of the social context of media exposure. Whether it is going to the movies, watching videotapes, or just sharing time in front of the television, group exposure to mass communication is quite common. The *social facilitation hypothesis* suggests that people should enjoy media content more in group settings than when alone. Often comedians seem funnier when we're watching their routines with friends than watching a cable special alone. Televison producers have recognized the impact of an audience on enjoyment and routinely add studio audience applause and laugh tracks to programs (see Neuendorf & Fennel, 1988). These elements may increase enjoyment because they help reduce uncertainty about whether something is supposed to be funny, or they may increase the arousal inherent in the viewing or listening experience. The arousal inherent in group viewing of sporting contests can also increase the pleasure of sports viewing (Zillmann, Bryant, & Sapolsky, 1989).

Who is in the audience with us can also influence our responses to media content. College men who watched a horror film with women enjoyed the experience more than men who did not watch the film with women (Zillmann, Weaver, Mundorf, & Aust, 1986). There are some possible explanations for this sort of effect. First, comforting a frightened companion might provide an excuse for bodily contact. Or the increased arousal offered by the frightened partner might be "transferred" into pleasurable feelings by the young man.

Children frequently watch television with their parents or other children (e.g., Alexander, Ryan, & Munoz, 1984; Rubin, 1986). Group viewing is a powerful mediator of television's effects on children. Even when children are watching with other children, they discuss the programs (Alexander et al., 1984). These discussions can increase awareness, attention, understanding, and knowledge. Parents have many opportunities to influence how their children are affected by television. Messaris (1986) pointed out that parents can mold their children's interpretation of television through discussion while viewing. Parents can help children learn about the conventions of the medium and distinguish fact from fantasy. They can highlight characters' motivations, provide background for unfamiliar content, and add explanations for confusing action. Most important, parents can emphasize positive aspects of programs and evaluate and criticize antisocial actions and characters.

Chaffee, J. M. McLeod, and Atkin (1971) initiated research on family communication patterns (FCP). These patterns represent the general orientation of parent–child interaction. According to their measures, family communication can be oriented toward maintaining harmony (sociooriented) or oriented toward exploring issues and ideas (concept oriented). These orientations are important to understanding children's media use and effects. Concept-orientated families encourage more news and public affairs media use; socio-oriented families are likely to comment more about imitating television characters (Chaffee, J. M. McLeod, & Wackman, 1973; Messaris & Kerr, 1983).

Individual Differences. *Individual differences variables* are those aspects that differentiate one person from another. These are characteristics that are unique to an individual. Unlike social categories variables, which are characteristics of groups of people that make them similar to others, individual differences variables are characteristics of people that make them different from other people—even from others in the same social category. So, although, as a whole, boys are more likely to act more aggressively than girls after watching a violent television program, boys are not equally aggressive. Several individual differences can explain why some boys are more or less aggressive than others (e.g., Cantor & Orwant, 1980). Individual difference variables not only explain how people differ from one another, but also can explain how each individual's response to mass communication can be different at different times. For example, someone might typically be calm and not riled up by radio talk shows. But after a rough day at work (with many pressures from a demanding boss), that same person might get angry and aroused by the same talk show host. So individual difference variables are those characteristics that make people unique.

There are as many individual difference variables as there are differences among people. Some of the most commonly researched individual differences are: personality, prior experiences, preexisting attitudes, physical and mental states, attitudes toward the media, and gratifications sought from the media.

Personality is usually conceptualized as the set of beliefs, values, and preferences that predispose people to act, think, feel, and behave in consistent ways. Personality is a trait; it is a fairly stable part of a person. Each individual's personality makes him or her unique and different from others. Research has shown that personality traits can be intervening variables in the media effects process, primarily because they affect selective exposure and attention. Neurotics (people who tend to be more anxious and socially isolated) avoid television comedy but prefer news programs (Weaver, 1991b). People who score higher on a psychoticism scale (those who have a lack of constraint and tend to reject rules and regulations) seem to prefer horror and/or slasher films (Weaver, Brosius, & Mundorf, 1993). Need for cognition, or a personality trait to mark preference for complex mental activity, is linked to attention to public affairs information in local news reports (Perse, 1990e). Sensation seeking, a personality trait that predisposes people to engage in highly arousing activities (see Zuckerman, 1994), is related to selective exposure to more stimulating media content, such as horror films (Edwards, 1991) and pornography (Hirschman, 1987). People low in sensation seeking avoid sexual and violent media content (Zuckerman & Litle, 1986) and prefer more "bland" music (Litle & Zuckerman, 1986).

People's own unique experiences are important in the conditional model. Several scholars hold that exposure to media content can shape perceptions of reality through cultivation (e.g., Gerbner & Gross, 1976). So, heavy media users are more likely to perceive a world that is like that depicted in the media. But media content is merely a source of vicarious experience. The real experiences that people have in their day-to-day lives are likely to have a mediating impact on the effects of media content. The kind of neighborhood in which someone lives, for example, has a greater impact on people's perceptions of about how susceptible they are to crime than how much television they view (Doob & Macdonald, 1979). Weaver and Wakshlag (1986) found that cultivation effects were mediated by people's direct, personal experience with crime.

The attitudes that people hold are potent individual difference variables that influence selectivity processes as well as media effects. Some interesting research conducted about *All in the Family* illustrates how racial prejudice affected perceptions about the television program. Critics of the program raised concerns that the show provided a platform for the bigoted views of the main character, Archie Bunker, a middle-age blue-collar worker who lived with his wife, daughter, and liberal son-in-law, Mike. Norman Lear, the show's creator, argued that the program's humor would be an effective weapon against prejudice because Archie's outrageous and inaccurate attitudes would be rebutted in arguments with Mike. Lear, however, did not anticipate the impact of selectivity. Brigham and Giesbrecht (1976) found that southern White viewers who expressed racial prejudices were more likely to like and agree with Archie Bunker and see his racial views as valid. Vidmar and Rokeach (1974) found similar connections between racial prejudice and perceptions about the program; those with more prejudicial attitudes were more likely to identify with Archie and believe that he made more sense in arguments with his more liberal son-in-law, Mike.

Mental and physical states are variables that are important in the conditional model because of their impact on selective exposure and perception. We all know how our moods can affect our choice of media content. We all know what kind of music people prefer when they have just broken off a relationship—sad songs. It is clear that we use the mass media to help us manage our moods (e.g., Zillmann & Bryant, 1985). If we are bored, we might seek out exciting movies or television programs; if we are stressed, we might listen to calming music. We select media content that helps us feel better. We might also select media content that helps us forget about or escape from aversive, or bad moods. McIlwraith and Schallow (1983), for example, suggested that some people selected highly arousing media content to "block" hostile and negative mental preoccupations. Similarly, physical states can influence selective exposure to media content. Some interesting research has suggested that hormonal changes can affect women's television program preferences throughout pregnancy (Helregel & Weaver, 1989) and the menstrual cycle (Meadowcroft & Zillmann, 1987).

The attitudes that people hold toward media and their content can be a barrier to effects or a condition that enhances effects. Media credibility, for example, or how trustworthy one believes the media to be, may influence whether audience members accept what they hear, see, or read, or whether they reject or ignore the messages (Gaziano & McGrath, 1986; Kim & Rubin, 1997). Perceived realism, or how realistic one believes media content to be, is another attitude that intervenes in media effects (Potter, 1988). Perceptions of television realism are linked to greater television influence on perceptions of social reality, or cultivation effects (Perse, 1986), parasocial interaction, or pseudo-friendships with television characters (Rubin, Perse, & Powell, 1985), and social learning from television (e.g., Bandura, 1994). And, perceptions about how difficult it is to learn from different media amount of invested mental effect (AIME), affect how children mentally process media information and the effects of that information processing (Salomon & Leigh, 1984).

Another set of individual differences variables that intervenes in media effects is drawn from the uses and gratifications perspective. This perspective holds that the reasons that people use mass communication (or the gratifications that they seek from media use) influences the effects from that use (Rubin, 1994). Different media use motives lead to selective exposure to specific media and content, as well as to selective attention to different aspects of the message. In addition, different reasons for using mass media influence how involved (or uninvolved) people are with the content. So, media use motives are conditions of media impact. Media-use reasons that lead to greater attention to and involvement with the content generally facilitate effects (Kim & Rubin, 1997). Media use reasons that lead to less attention to content may inhibit effects.

Research has shown, for example, that watching television to gain information for use in one's daily life leads to watching news and magazine programs on television (e.g., Rubin, 1981a). In contrast, watching television just to pass time leads to inattentive channel surfing (Perse, 1990a). The reasons that people have for watching television enhance certain media effects. Watching news for information is linked to greater knowledge gain (Gantz, 1978; Perse, 1990d). Watching news and soap operas for entertainment explains cultivation effects of local news and soap operas (Carveth & Alexander, 1985; Perse, 1990b). Perse (1994) uncovered four main reasons that college students have for using erotica: sexual enhancement (for information and foreplay), diversion (entertainment and relaxation), sexual release (solitary fantasy), and substitution (to replace a partner). Of these reasons, three were directly or indirectly related to greater acceptance of rape myths, or lack of sympathy toward rape victims. The other, sexual release, was a barrier to accepting rape myths. Clearly, it is important to understand why people use media in order to understand the effects of that use.

Summary

The conditional model, then, is an audience-centered model of media effects. It holds that media effects are conditional on the audience because people have the power to selectively expose themselves to messages, pay attention only to those aspects of the content that interest them, selectively interpret the content along with needs, interests, and experiences, and recall messages within their own individualized mental frameworks. Like the limited effects model of the received view, the conditional model recognizes the power of the audience to reject media influence. But, unlike the limited effects model, the conditional model holds that reinforcement effects are not the only effects. Change effects are also quite likely, but conditional on the audience. Audience variables provide important explanations for media effects, especially social categories, social relationship, and individual differences. This model is especially valuable when the focus is on individual-level effects and when individuals are able to select from among a range of media content, assumed to be mentally active and aware, and mentally process and interpret media content.

CUMULATIVE EFFECTS

The *cumulative effects model* is drawn from the "return to powerful effects" era of the received view of media effects history. The main emphasis of this model is the ubiquitous nature of certain media content that overrides any potential of the audience to limit exposure to certain messages. This model focuses on the consonance and repetition of themes and messages across media content. The explanation for media effects, then, rests in media content—its consistent make-up and depiction. The audience is not relevant to this model because it is not within their power to avoid certain media messages. Some media content is so pervasive that selective exposure is impossible, so everyone is affected in ways that are consistent with media messages. So, amount of media exposure (as a measure of audience immersion in media content) and content analyses (as a measure of media's messages) are essential components to explaining media effects.

Unlike the direct effects model, this model explains that media effects are a result of cumulative exposure, not due to a single event. Through repeated exposure to similar content across channels, people are moved. The effects of this model are generally reality-construction effects. That is, through cumulative exposure, people begin to adopt the media's framing as their own representation of reality. Effects, according to the cumulative model, are limited to cognitions (belief and attitude acquisition) and affect (emotional reactions). This model, then, focuses on more subtle effects. Although behaviors may be linked to how people think and feel, behaviors are not seen as a direct results of media exposure. Effects are assumed to be fairly enduring because media content tends to be fairly consistent across time. If content changes, then effects might diminish.

Agenda setting can be viewed as a cumulative effect (e.g., McCombs, 1994; McCombs & Shaw, 1972). *Agenda setting* is conceptualized as the power of the news media to direct our concerns toward certain issues. The effect is a fairly limited cognitive one: the news media don't tell us what to think, but what to think about (Cohen, 1963). Agenda setting is based on observations that news content tends to be fairly consonant across news channels. Broadcasting, cable, and print news media highlight the same types of stories, issues, events, and people. Moreover, the processes of newsgathering and production enhance the similarity of news across channels. In the past, news wires have been prime sources for national and international news. Now, concentration of ownership and economy of scale have lead to proliferations of different news channels drawing from the same resources (e.g., CNN and CNN Headline News; NBC, CNBC, and MSNBC). Observations have noted that news organizations tend to be influenced by the same prestige news sources (e.g., Stempel & Windhauser, 1989).

In our society, almost everyone sees some type of news. News is presented regularly on the radio, television, and on various cable networks. Newsbreaks pepper network television. Even newspaper headlines are displayed for sale in newsstands and boxes on street corners. Even if people don't seek news out, it is almost impossible not to become aware of the top stories. Selective exposure is not a realistic option. Over time, people accept those issues on the media agenda as important issues.

Traditional cultivation research is another example of a limited effect (Gerbner & Gross, 1976; Gerbner et al., 1994). Through repeated, heavy exposure to television, viewers begin to believe that the real world is similar to the television world. The most researched area of cultivation effects is that of fear of crime. Heavy television viewers become more fearful. The cultivation effect, is both cognitive (developing a world view based on television content) and affects (fear). Behavioral effects are not the domain of this approach.

Cultivation is based on the results of content analyses that reveal that violence of some kind and patterns of group victimization cut across all prime-time television content (e.g., Signorielli, 1990b). Because most people watch television during those hours, they see those patterns of violence and images; selective exposure is not relevant. Because patterns of television viewing are fairly stable, cultivation researchers imply that effects are fairly enduring.

Important Variables in the Model

Media content is central to the cumulative effects model. The nature of the images and issues in the news media are important because they define what the effects are. The specific issues of the media agenda translate to audience agenda. The patterns of victimization in prime-time dramatic programs (who aggresses against whom) translates into fear for those groups who are represented as victims.

More important, though, is the consonance of media content, or its consistency across channels. Because this model holds that selective exposure is not possible, media messages need to be fairly consistent across a range of readily accessible media outlets. The cumulative effects model is less applicable for specialized, or one-shot media messages, presented on a limited range of channels. The changes in the media environment may threaten the validity of the cumulative effects model. If the Internet becomes an important and widely used news source, personalized news services and menu-based news selection could undermine agenda setting effects. Some scholars have argued that the specialized nature of some cable channels may reduce cultivation's effects because viewers can avoid traditional television programming (e.g., Perse, Ferguson, & D. M. McLeod, 1994). Other scholars, though, point out that most television content is still programming created by the same producers (e.g., Gerbner, 1990).

Summary

The cumulative effects model focuses on media content as the prime explanation for media effects. This model finds that the audience is not important to understanding media effects because some media content is so pervasive that it is impossible for people to ignore it. So, this model is appropriate when the focus is the effects of media content that are readily accessible and fairly consistent across media channels and context. According to this model, people are affected in fairly predictable ways by cumulative exposure to similar kinds of content. So, this model is not useful for considering one-shot media exposure. This model assumes that because media exposure patterns are fairly stable, effects are fairly enduring.

COGNITIVE–TRANSACTIONAL MODEL

This model is drawn from cognitive psychology. It applies the notion of schematic processing to the media context. Several theorists have explained that how humans mentally process environmental stimuli affects how we interpret and learn new information (e.g., Fiske & Taylor, 1991). The key to this model is the *schema*. Knowledge, according to this approach, does not exist as isolated chunks in our brains. Instead, all knowledge is organized into schemas. A schema is a mental structure that represents knowledge about a concept. Schemas contain the attributes of the concept and the connections among those attributes. Schemas have a hierarchical structure, so that some elements are more central than others. Schemas may exist independently or they may be interrelated through commonly shared elements. When we think of Pat Sajack, for example, we might also think about Vanna White, because of the common element *Wheel of Fortune*.

There is a good deal of scholarly as well as common-sense evidence to support the existence of schemas. Word association tests support the notion that some concepts are linked more closely than others. Which is easier to remember: blue *bird* or blue *frame*? We all have experienced how some environmental stimuli bring to mind a whole host of other concepts. The scent of a certain perfume may bring to mind thoughts of a relative or a past relationship. The smell of turkey roasting certainly arouses memories of past Thanksgivings.

Some of the earliest scholarly evidence for the existence of schemas comes from Bartlett (1932). He observed that when people retold stories that took place in other cultures, they altered the details so that they were consistent with their own culture. Bartlett suggested that people had mental patterns that described the stories of their cultures.

Schemas exist for all domains: (a) role schemas (e.g., what a college professor is like), (b) person schemas (our understanding of others we know), (c) self-schemas (how we think about ourselves), (d) group schemas (e.g., males vs. females), and (e) event schemas (e.g., scripts). All these are mental representations of our knowledge about various people, events, and issues. It is clear that schemas are also relevant in the mass communication context. We not only apply our schemas to interpreting mass media content (e.g., group schema and how women on television ought to act or person schema to help us anticipate how a favorite talk show host will deal with guests), but we also have schemas that help us understand mass media content specifically. We know, for example, that when we see a teen-age girl begin to undress in an empty house in a horror film, mayhem is almost sure to follow.

Schemas not only organize knowledge, but they serve several other functions that influence media effects. First, they direct selective exposure, perception, attention, and recall. The schema that is in use directs attention to certain aspects of the environment that are relevant to that schema. Second, because they organize knowledge, schemas control how new information is integrated with prior knowledge. How a news story is framed (with headlines, graphics, or introduction) influences which schema is used to interpret the information and which schema any new knowledge is associated with. Third, schemas allow people to make inferences about new situations and help reduce uncertainty about what to think or how to act. When we attend the first class in a semester, for example, we have a fairly good idea of what will happen during that meeting, even if we've never been in one of that professor's classes. Fourth, schemas allow us to go beyond the stimuli and make inferences about things that are not shown. Most soap opera viewers, for example, know what is happening in the "fade to black" that ends a romantic sex scene.

There are two ways that schemas operate: through controlled or through automatic processing (Bargh, 1988). *Controlled processing* is individual-controlled mental activity. It usually involves goal-directed, thoughtful mental action. When students are studying for a test, for example, they very consciously look for links among the course concepts and try to connect class readings with lecture materials. Or, when well-educated, politically involved people read the newspaper, they may concentrate and try to integrate the new material with prior beliefs about political issues. In controlled processing, the individual chooses and self-activates the schema that they believe is relevant to the task. In a sense, controlled processing involves a good deal of selectivity. When one is goal-directed, he or she may focus only on those media messages that have relevance for the task.

Much media use, however, is not controlled. People are often more automatic in their approach to mass media consumption. Much television viewing grows out of entertainment or relaxation motives, for example, that leads viewers to be more automatic in their viewing. When people are relaxed or distracted, they may react more automatically to the environment. *Automatic processing* is an effortless, low-involved mental processing of environmental stimuli. In this case, environmental stimuli (media content) may *prime* or activate schemas. When a schema is primed, it is, in a sense, energized and moves to the top of the mind. As long as it is top of mind, that schema will be used to interpret stimuli; that schema will influence selective exposure, attention, perception, and recall. Priming is an unconscious, relatively short-term effect; a schema rarely is top of mind for more than a few hours. But, once a schema has been primed, it retains some of its energy, and is more easy to bring to top of mind again. One way to think about priming is to think about a filing system. When a schema is primed, it is pulled from the mental files. As other schemas subsequently primed, that first schema gets "buried." But, it is easy to find and reactivate if few other schemas have been used.

The cognitive–transactional model has a number of implications for media effects. In the case of controlled processing, media effects are influenced, to a large degree, by the goals of the individual and the schemas that he or she uses to interpret media content. With highly controlled processing, effects are likely to be cognitive, conscious, and fairly long term. But the kind of effects depend on the schema that is self-activated. For example, when people seek out political information, they may use one of several schemas to evaluate candidates (e.g., Lau, 1986): (a) party identification (looking for consistencies or inconsistencies on political party stands), (b) issues (stands on relevant political issues), or (c) a personality scheme (the kind of person the politician is). What people get from their media use, then, is influenced by their goals and the schema that they use.

In the case of automatic processing, media content can be an especially potent prime. Effective media messages can activate certain schemas that direct attention and influence the interpretation of and reaction to the stimuli. Advertisers know, for example, that putting a kitten or a baby in a commercial for toilet paper can associate a schema that includes the attribute "soft," which then might be associated with the product (see also, Baran & Blasko, 1984). Beliefs in the acceptability of rape and interpersonal violence can be primed through observations of violent sexual films (Malamuth & Check, 1981) and evaluations of people's hostility can be primed by observations of hostile behaviors on videotape (Carver, Ganellen, Froming, & Chambers, 1983). Media content can also prime sex-stereotyped schemas. Women who viewed gender stereotyped television commercials are more likely to deemphasize achievement and emphasize homemaking in their personal goals (Geis, Brown, Walstedt, & Porter, 1984) than women who viewed commercials with women in nontraditional roles. And adolescent girls who view cosmetic commercials are more likely to rate physical appearance more important than girls who view neutral commercials (Tan, 1979).

And, once primed, schemas are more readily accessible, so a primed schema can also influence the interpretation of and reaction to subsequent stimuli. Researchers have observed that overhearing pro- versus antisocial news stories on a radio affected research participants' reactions in games, as well as judgments about the decency of the average person (Holloway, Tucker, & Hornstein, 1977; Hornstein, LaKind, Frankel, & Manne, 1975). Hansen (1989) observed that participants who watched sex-stereotyped music videos followed by a supposedly unconnected video of a male–female interaction, evaluated the woman in the interaction more favorably when she acted more compliantly. Watching some media content, then, can prime schemas that affect how we evaluate other stimuli that we encounter shortly after exposure.

Important Variables in the Model

The cognitive–transactional model is called *transactional* because both media content and audience factors are important to understanding media effects. Media content is important is its ability to prime. The audience members are important because schemas can be quite individualized.

Media Content. The salience of visual cues is important to understanding what can prime. When objects in the environment stand out, people pay attention to them (Kahneman, 1973). We notice quite easily, for example, the flashing lights and sirens of police and emergency vehicles. So, aspects of content that attract involuntary attention are more likely to prime. Sexual and violence content may be especially potent primes. Other characteristics of media content may increase salience. Berlyne (1970), for example, observed that people pay more attention to bright, complex, and colored stimuli. Studies have found that subjects paid more visual attention to people on television with more brightly colored clothing and hair (McArthur & Post, 1977; McArthur & Solomon, 1978).

Other content attributes are likely to facilitate priming. Berkowitz and Rogers (1986) pointed out that aggressive ideas are more likely to be activated when content is realistic. Subjects who believed they had watched violent documentaries were more likely to display aggressive behaviors than subjects who believed they had watched fiction (Berkowitz & Alioto, 1973; Feshbach, 1972).

Character identification may also increase priming effects because people might imagine themselves imitating the actions of characters with whom they identify (Dorr, 1986). Turner and Berkowitz (1972), for example, found that subjects who were instructed to imagine themselves as a boxer acted more aggressively after viewing a prize fight. Identification may increase the salience of the actor and stimulate more thoughts related to the observed action.

Audience Variables. The audience is also important to the cognitive model because the schemas that direct selectivity can be individualized. So media content that has the ability to prime may prime different kinds of schemas in different types of people. For example, a photo of a Saint Bernard might prime an image of good dog (e.g., Beethoven) for some people or an image of a violent killer (e.g., Cujo) for others, depending on the elements of each's schema about that breed of dog. Research suggests that political sophistication is reflected in the kinds of schemas that people use to evaluate political candidates (Lau & Sears, 1986). People who know relatively little about politics may make voting decisions based on more general, person schemas (is the candidate a good person?). Those who are politically knowledgeable may make decisions based on a candidate's public records on certain important issues. Social categories, social relationships, and individual difference variables are relevant to explaining the content of audience schemas.

The individual goals that people have when they approach media exposure influences controlled processing. More goal-directed media use is more selective (Rubin, 1984), so people may reject media messages that do not help them achieve their goals. To use an earlier example, if a politically sophisticated person is seeking information about political candidates, he or she may reject talk shows that focus on candidates' personal lives and habits.

People's moods can also affect the schemas that are more easily brought to mind. As Fiske and Taylor (1991) summarized: "All else being equal, people in a good mood are more likely to see the good sides of other people, and sometimes people in bad moods see others' bad sides" (p. 146).

Summary

The cognitive–transactional model is one that has a dual focus. It holds that media impact grows from cognitive reactions to media content. So, the model focuses on the mental organization of knowledge—the schema. Schematic processing is seen as the basis for selective attention, perception, and recall as well as subsequent media effects due to that processing. Schematic processing, though, can be automatic or controlled. When processing is automatic, the audience is considered to be less active and the focus turns to media content. Some aspects of media content are salient, and prime schemas. When schemas are primed, they direct attention, perception, recall, and other reactions to environmental cues. Variables that affect the salience of media content are important to understanding automatic processing.

TABLE 2.1
Comparing and Contrasting the Four Models of Media Effects

| | *Models of Media Effects* | | |
	Nature of Effects	*Media Content Variables*	*Audience Variables*
Direct	Immediate, uniform, observable Short-term Emphasis on change	Salience, arousal, and realism	Not relevant
Conditional	Individualized Reinforcement as well as change Cognitive, affective, and behavioral Long- or short-term	Not relevant	Social categories Social relationships Individual differences
Cumulative	Based on cumulative exposure Cognitive or affect Rarely behavioral Enduring effects	Consonant across channels Repetition	Not relevant
Cognitive–transactional	Immediate and short-term Based on one-shot exposure Cognitive and affective; behavioral effects possible	Salience of visual cues	Schema make-up Mood Goals

When processing is controlled, schemas are self-activated. People are goal-directed and channel their thoughts toward their goals. They select the schemas that they believe will help them achieve their goals. Media content is interpreted, then, according to the individual audience member's goals and schemas.

This model sees effects as a result of cognitive reactions to media content, in the case of automatic processing, or as a result of conscious mental effort, in the case of controlled processing. Effects are cognitive and affective, though reactions to the environment can also have behavioral aspects. The cognitive model accounts for short-term effects as a result of priming. But long-term effects can emerge as a result of controlled processing.

Some Notes of Caution About the Four Models

These four models are simplified depictions of explanations for media effects. They are designed to focus attention on specific explanations for media effects. No single model is complete. It is, of course, unrealistic to ignore entirely the nature of media content as contributing to media effects as the conditional model does. It is just as unrealistic to ignore the possibility that different individuals will react differently to media content, as the direct effects model does. The most complete explanations for media effects are those that combine explanations from each model. For example, the most complete explanations for cultivation effects are those that combine aspects of the conditional and cumulative models. That is, when cumulative exposure to prime-time television drama is combined with certain aspects of the audience (e.g., educational level, gender, neighborhood of residence), more variance in fear of crime is accounted for. The value of each model, though, is in its ability to focus on the most important explanation for media effects.

3

Media Effects and Crisis

Graber (1989) defined crises as "natural or manmade events that pose an immediate and serious threat to the lives and property or to the peace of mind of many" (p. 305).[1] Crises emerge suddenly and arise from attacks on political leaders, such as the assassination of John F. Kennedy (1963) and the attempted assassination of Ronald Reagan (1981); from attacks by and threats from external forces, such as the Yom Kippur War (1973), the hostage situation in Iran (1979 to 1981), and the Persian Gulf War (1991); from natural disasters such as the eruption of Mount St. Helens (1980), the San Francisco earthquake (1989), and hurricane Andrew (1992); from technical disasters such as the nuclear accidents at Three Mile Island (1979) and Chernobyl (1986), the Challenger space shuttle explosion (1986), and airline accidents, such as the crash of TWA flight 800 in 1996; from internal conflicts such as the National Guard shooting of nine students at Kent State (1970) and the Los Angeles riots following the first Rodney King verdict (1992); and from terrorist activity, such as the bombings at the World Trade Center (1993) and the Oklahoma Federal Building (1995). Crises affect large numbers of people and are marked by sudden onset, un-

---

[1]Graber (1993) distinguished crises from "pseudo-crises." There are events that get "crisis-like" attention from the news media, but offer no real immediate threats to society. These events, such as the Clarence Thomas hearings, the attack on ice skater Nancy Kerrigan, and the criminal trials of William Kennedy Smith, Lorena Bobbitt, O. J. Simpson, and Marv Albert consume media and audience attention. Although some of these may focus on important issues, such as sexual harassment and spousal abuse, their coverage is due more to the appeal of celebrity or interest in salacious details.

certainty, and lack of control, emotional reactions, and threats to lives and property.

No matter what the cause, times of crisis are extraordinary periods that are marked by instability, uncertainty, stress, and emotional significance because of fear of undesirable outcomes. Normal activities cease. When President Reagan was shot in 1981, for example, Congress recessed in the midst of debate, the New York and American stock exchanges halted trading, and the Oscar presentations, scheduled for that evening, were postponed. Times of crisis heighten the importance of the role of the mass media in providing information and explanation. Because of their resources and unique access to government agencies and officials, society relies on the media to collect information and guide public response.

THEORETICAL FOCUS: THE FUNCTIONS OF MASS COMMUNICATION

One approach to analyzing the relationship of mass media to society is structural functionalism. Functionalism is based on a biological analogy. *Society* is viewed as a complex system of interrelated parts—all of which perform specific activities that are designed to maintain society's even and steady functioning. These activities are termed *functions*. Functions are repetitive activities that are designed to ensure harmony and stability in society. If there is a disruption in society, various aspects of society act to ensure a return to a state of equilibrium (Merton, 1968).

C. R. Wright (1986) summarized much of the writing about the functions of mass communication and notes that mass media serve both latent (hidden) and manifest (obvious) functions for society, individual, societal subgroups, and culture. Based on Lasswell (1948), Wright points out that mass communication serves four major functions for society: surveillance, correlation, socialization, and entertainment. He also notes that these activities of the media may not only be functional, or positive, but they may also be dysfunctional and have negative consequences.

Surveillance is the information function of mass communication. As a society grows and becomes more complex, it becomes important to have a sentry or watch dog monitor the environment so that other groups in society can devote themselves to other functional activities. Complex societies rely on mass communication for surveillance most typically through news reports. The mass media collect, summarize, and report the information that various groups need to conduct their own work (e.g., stock market reports, weather, or summaries of legislative activity). We also rely on mass communication as an advance warning system to alert society in times of danger and crisis.

As a result of its surveillance activity, mass communication performs other functions for society. Surveillance can increase perceptions of equality in society. Because many forms of mass communication are publically accessible, information can be available to all members of society and everyone has a chance to benefit from that information. Through ethicizing, surveillance allows society to maintain social control by pointing out deviant behavior and holding it up to ridicule. And coverage by the mass media raises awareness of as well as the social standing of those issues, events, and people that they cover through the status conferral function (Lazarsfeld & Merton, 1948).

Surveillance, though, can also be dysfunctional. "War nerves" is a phenomenon that emerges during crises in which people become stressed and anxious because of information overload. Some alerts may also lead to overreaction and panics or paralysis through fear. One latent dysfunction is narcotization. Lazarsfeld and Merton (1948) feared that media surveillance could begin to replace political activity in society. That is, as people try to keep up with news and public affairs information, they actually become more apathetic toward society issues. The sheer amount of time spent with the media may displace political action. Or, the intellectual analysis of political information misleads people into thinking they are actually involved in the political process, when they are not. Media use for surveillance, in this case, replaces political activity. As Lazarsfeld and Merton (1948) said, people may "mistake *knowing* about problems of the day for *doing* something about them" (p. 106).

Correlation is the editorial and explanation function of mass communication. Information is often complex. Through correlation, mass media clarify and explain the relevance of information. If through surveillance the mass media tell us what is happening, through correlation the mass media relay what it means to us. Correlation is a correction of some of the dysfunctions of surveillance. Information overload, for example, can be reduced through synthesizing and digesting information to highlight the most important bits of news. Correlation is common in the mass media. Editorial pages in newspapers present opinion and suggestions about public affairs. One simple example of correlation is the typical weather forecast. Through surveillance, the weathercaster displays maps that mark cold and warm fronts, jet stream movement, and isobars. Unless we're familiar with climatology, these markings often make no sense. But, the weather forecaster explains these to the viewers and relays what we can expect the weather to be, based on those data.

Correlation can be dysfunctional for society. If people rely too heavily on mass media's interpretation of news, they may lose their own critical abilities to evaluate information on their own. Or, media organizations may be hesitant to criticize and editorialize against powerful institutions and people in society out of fear of retaliation. Media organizations rely heavily on government sources, for example, and might be reluctant to lose access to those sources (e.g., Herman & Chomsky, 1988).

Socialization is the function of mass communication that deals with the transmission of social values and cultural heritage. A society is marked by commonly shared cultural norms, values, and experiences. Mass communication serves to display and reinforce those values and experiences. Mass communication can also integrate new members of a society, children and immigrants, by teaching and relaying those norms, values, and experiences. Through socialization, mass communication promotes societal integration and cohesion.

An emphasis on cohesion, however, can be dysfunctional. If mass communication ignores subgroups in society, regional and ethnic differences may be diminished, reducing cultural and intellectual diversity in society. Mass media content often is not a multifaceted presentation of societal norms and values. Unfortunately, because of demands of the marketplace, media content is often simplified, stereotyped, and representative of the values of the dominant social class. Those images may lead to improper socialization and learning inaccurate, slanted representations of societal values.

The *entertainment* function serves as a source of rest, respite, and diversion. The strong work ethic in our society led to mass media entertainment being considered dysfunction for many years. Some writers were concerned that popular culture would debase people and might even displace more intellectual pursuits (see Mendelsohn, 1966). But, it is clear that amusement and relaxation are functional. Individually, people need to rest and regroup. For society, entertainment provides shared experiences, like media events such as the Olympics (e.g., Rothenbuhler, 1988) and a source for social cohesion. But, entertainment can also be dysfunctional. Mass media entertainment can displace other more worthwhile activities. And, much of the concern about antisocial effects focuses on violent or sensational media content.

Functionalist approaches to understanding mass communication have been criticized (e.g., Elliott, 1974). Some argue that the approach is *tautological*; that is, it is based on the assumption that something exists, it must serve some purpose, so it is functional. Existence, then, is equated with function. Moreover, functionalism's emphasis on stability means that it is unable to provide an explanation for change in society. Despite these limitations, understanding society's and individuals' expectations about mass communication may help in understanding the role that it plays and the effects that can emerge in times of societal upheaval.

Functions of Mass Communication During Crises

Graber (1993) explains that crises have several stages. The first stage is the discovery of the crisis or threat of disaster. At this phase, uncertainty is the highest and the threat least understood. Mass media organizations react by sending resources to the scene and contacting officials, agencies, and experts who can explain what is happening. The broadcast media react rapidly and interrupt or suspend regular programming to cover the crisis. It is radio and television that become primary sources for information—even for those involved in the crisis. During the initial hours of the Persian Gulf War, for example, world leaders followed CNN's news coverage of the bombing of Baghdad. Even the Federal Emergency Management Agency monitors ABC, CBS, NBC, and CNN during natural disasters (Goldman & Reilly, 1992). News anchors typically become conduits for disconnected reports from those on the scene—professionals, experts, eyewitnesses, and onlookers. The news is viewed as a "command post" that coordinates and disseminates pertinent news information (Quarantelli, 1981). These bulletins are often unedited and unverified. Crises almost eliminate gatekeeping (Waxman, 1973). Rumor and disinformation are passed along side accurate reports (Dynes, 1970).

Coverage of a crisis can consume media. As the most immediate and most relied upon medium, television devotes extraordinary resources to crisis coverage. For 4 days in November, 1963, television reported without interruption on the assassination and funeral of President John F. Kennedy. The launch of the Challenger space shuttle was initially minor news, covered live only by CNN. But immediately after the explosion that killed the seven astronauts, including teacher Christa McAuliffe, all three networks turned to live, continuous coverage. Media focus continued throughout the evening, especially when President Reagan canceled his State of the Union address. Dramatic aerial shots were key to coverage of the San Francisco earthquake that occurred during the 1989 World Series. Television's images continued until there was no more natural light. ABC's *Nightline* was born as *America Held Hostage* during the Iranian hostage crisis. ABC was the only network to have a reporter in Teheran during the first week of the crisis and was the clear champion in media coverage. Expanded news reports filled late evening, after the local news. These reports proved to be so popular that the program was continued as *Nightline*, even after the crisis passed. The Persian Gulf War is a good case study of increased news coverage. The National Media Index, which tracks the news in the three major networks, five major newspapers, and the three major news magazines, reports that during January 21, 1991, through February 3, 1991 (the weeks following the air strike on Baghdad), news increased to 130% of its normal volume; almost 93% of all news was Gulf War related (Dennis et al., 1991).

During times of crises, the mass media's functional importance dramatically increases. Schramm (1965) noted that crises heighten society's needs for information, interpretation, and consolation. Intense uncertainty coupled with fear of danger lead people to rely on the only central source that has access to news sources and information. During the 1973 Yom Kippur war, "the media had become central to people's lives" (Peled & Katz, 1974, p. 52) for information about family members at the front. Because the blackout required everyone to stay indoors, 53% of the Israeli respondents wanted television to devote most of its time to surveillance and correlation. Another one-third expected tension release and solidarity building from television. During the Persian Gulf War, respondents believed that television's most important function was providing information ($M = 6.09$, on a 7-point scale), followed by explanation ($M = 5.76$), building solidarity ($M = 5.52$), and reducing tension ($M = 4.95$).

The functional importance of the media to provide surveillance and correlation is reflected in increased news use during crises. On hearing startling news, people often turn to the media, usually television, for confirmation and details (e.g., Greenberg, 1965; Riffe & Stovall, 1989). News ratings can be extraordinarily high during times of crisis. On hearing of President Kennedy's assassination, five out of six people who could abandoned their daily routine and turned to television for further information (Sheatsley & Feldman, 1965). President Kennedy's funeral a few days later attracted 81% of the television audience. George Bush's address the evening of the January, 1991, air strike on Baghdad was seen by 79% of all U.S. households (Record-Breaking TV Audience, 1991). During the first week of the 1973 Yom Kippur War, almost all Israelis were listening to radio and television; 68% listened to the radio all day long and 55% even reported that they listened to the radio while they were watching television (Peled & Katz, 1974). Thirst for news was so great that people stayed up late listening to the radio and wanted the daily television news expanded. After hearing of the attempt on President Reagan's life, 90% of Gantz's (1983) respondents watched television or listened to the radio; 28% continued to follow the news after 11:00 p.m.

News use increased during the 1991 Persian Gulf war. National polls reported that 70% of the U.S. public followed war news "very closely" almost 80% stayed up late to watch more news (Gallup Organization, 1991). New Castle County (Delaware) residents reported watching television news for almost 3 hours a day and listening to radio news for nearly 1½ hours a day (compared to watching the news for about 1 hour and listening to radio news for just over ¾ hour a year later; D. M. McLeod et al., 1994). Reuters reported that video rentals dramatically decreased during the first week of the Gulf War (Gaunt, 1991). Video store managers speculated that news use replaced movie viewing at home.

Greenberg, Cohen, and Li (1993) reinforced the importance of television in the initial stages of a crisis. Their study of the diffusion of the start of the Persian Gulf air war found that over one-third of their respondents (36%) turned immediately to television for news. CNN was the preferred news source for between 49 to 54% of all the respondents. The authors note that *"recognizing that CNN is available in only about 61% of the homes in the country, its domination of viewers is even more remarkable. In virtually every home with access to CNN, it became first choice"* (italics in original; p. 150). People clearly relied on specialized news with resources in the Persian Gulf region.

Natural disasters are also marked by heightened need for information and increased news use. On the day of the eruption of Mount St. Helens in 1981, 85.4% of respondents living in eastern Washington turned to television for information; 81.8% used the radio. Information-seeking remained high the following day; 89.1% turned to television for news and 86.6% also listened to the radio (Hirschburg et al., 1986). The researchers concluded that uncertainty increased the importance of the media and people's reliance on them for news.

Surveys of Galveston, Texas, residents who had experienced the 1983 devastation of Hurricane Alicia further point to the importance of the media. Researchers interviewed these residents about their reactions to the 1985 warning for Hurricane Danny (it bypassed Galveston and struck the Louisiana coast (Ledingham & Walters, 1989). About half of the residents reported that media sources were the most important information about what to do during Danny's warnings but only 15.8% spent more time watching television. Over three-quarters of the residents (77.7%), however, watched television specifically to monitor the storm's progress or to watch the weather forecasts. Although time with the media did not increase for many, storm-related news may have displaced entertainment viewing.

Wenger (1980) found that residents of communities that have experienced various disasters (hurricanes, floods, and tornadoes) relied on the media for disaster information during the emergency. He noted that for many, "the media were not only an important source of information, they were the only source" (p. 243). Respondents relied especially on the electronic media because of their immediacy; from 58.3% to 74.5% named radio and television as their first choice for disaster information.

Surveillance and correlation are the most apparent functions of the mass media during crises, but the mass media also serve solidarity-building and tension-reduction functions. During the days following the assassination of President Kennedy, television coverage provided emotional support to help viewers deal with their shock and grief (Mindak & Hursh, 1965; Schramm, 1965). Although surveillance and correlation were most important, about one-third of Israelis expected television to reduce tension and build solidarity during the Yom Kippur War (Peled & Katz, 1974). Dramatic programming, such as action adventure and movies, were linked to tension reduction. Peled and Katz (1974) suggested that these programs distracted viewers from their war fears. Even news reports helped to reduce tension and build solidarity. The authors note that these effects might have been due to morale-bolstering approaches to news reporting. During natural disasters, emergency relief workers encourage media coverage for two reasons: to expedite the flow of emergency information to victims (surveillance and correlation) and to build public sympathy to encourage donations and aid (Sood et al., 1987).

More recent crises have also illustrated the tension reduction and solidarity functions of mass communication. The Challenger explosion was associated with wide reports of sadness and grief. The intense news coverage seemed to comfort many television viewers (e.g., Kaye, 1989). Indeed, people who were upset by the explosion were more likely to spend time watching the news (Kubey & Peluso, 1990; Riffe & Stovall, 1989). Media coverage is often geared to tension reduction and solidarity building. During the Persian Gulf War, news stories built on the "yellow ribbon" theme. Kaid, Harville, Ballotti, and Wawrzyniak's (1993) content analysis of newspaper coverage of the Gulf War, for example, concluded that the U.S. involvement in the war was portrayed negatively in only 3% of the stories. Newhagen (1994) found that network television news was also mainly more supportive and less critical of U.S. involvement in the war. Dennis and his colleagues (1991) reported that 3 weeks prior to the air strike, stories focusing on the controversy about entering the war outnumbered stories about supporting the war stories by 45 to 8. In the following weeks during the air and ground wars, "yellow ribbon" stories outnumbered "controversy" stories 36 to 19.

Crisis Coverage as a Media Event

Even as society becomes complex, it is still important for social rituals and events to reinforce shared values and traditions. Symbols represented in social rituals, such as parades celebrating patriotic holidays, bond individuals to each other and to society (Durkheim, 1893/1964).

More recently, though, a society's social rituals are displayed and experienced through television. Katz (1980) conceptualized these *media events* as the coronations (parades, weddings, and funerals), contests (in which super-powers compete), and conquests (the stories of heros) that reinforce the shared traditions and values of a society (Dayan & Katz, 1992). According to Katz (1980), media events (a) are broadcast live so that the coverage allows viewers to feel as though they are experiencing the event as it happens; (b) are planned to ease access to and coverage by television; (c) are dramatic and contain emotional and symbolic content; (d) compel viewing as participation in history; (e) are suspenseful (although the event may be planned, the ultimate outcome is unknown); (f) are framed to capture and hold the audience's attention; and (g) focus on the people involved as symbols.

Many crises are covered by the media as media events. As soon as news is released of a crisis, intense television coverage transports the audience to the locale—Baghdad, Oklahoma City, Cape Canaveral. Although the crises themselves are rarely planned, the media have policies and plans and devote resources immediately to coverage of the crisis. The coverage focuses on the dramatic and is framed as a contest (will the United States be able to secure the release of the hostages in the embassy?), as a conquest (Schwarzkopf's "How we won the war" speech after the Persian Gulf ground war), or as a coronation (Johnson's swearing-in after Kennedy's assassination). Personalities become central to the coverage: the bravery of Jacqueline Kennedy; the firefighter carrying the rescued youngster from the bombed-out Oklahoma federal building; Christa McAuliffe. And symbols represent the crises: the yellow ribbons of the Gulf War; the single rose standing in the surf after the memorial service for those who died on TWA flight 800.

The framing of crises as media events can fulfill surveillance and correlation functions by providing coverage of the incidents, but mainly they serve to socialize and entertain. A prime function of media events is to facilitate and reinforce societal cohesion. The live coverage by television, accessible to all, gives viewers a sense of connection to others who are sharing a common experience. The symbols that dominate the coverage give rise to common emotional reactions. The media coverage of crises endows a shared memory. Most baby boomers will always remember the Kennedy assassination. Their children will remember the Challenger explosion. Media events also serve an entertainment function; the coverage of the Persian Gulf war especially illustrates its framing, in part, as entertainment. CNN gave its war coverage a title ("A Line in the Sand") and a theme song (rhythmic drum roll). The glorification of the success of U.S. military equipment was reminiscent of video games (e.g., smart bombs) and sporting events (the Patriots vs. the Scuds).

DO THE MEDIA FULFILL THEIR FUNCTIONS?

The functions of mass communication become particularly apparent during times of emergency. The press devotes resources to fulfilling the public's needs for information, explanation, socialization, solidarity, and tension release. The effects of mass communication during times of crises can be understood within this framework. Through their surveillance and correlation roles, media may increase awareness of threats through news diffusion and contribute to other cognitive and/or learning effects. Through solidarity and tension-reduction roles, media may contribute to rally effects and the formation of other attitudes.

Diffusion of News

One of the most researched effects of mass communication during crisis situations is news diffusion. This area of study focuses on the information role of mass communication. News diffusion research examines the means through which people learn about news events and how rapidly news of an event is spread throughout a system. The study of the diffusion of news events not only has theoretical importance for understanding the role of mass communication in the spread of information, but it also has real practical value. Officials need to know the most rapid and effective way to alert the public about impending disasters and subsequent relief efforts. DeFleur (1987) reported that first quantitative news diffusion study considered how people found out about the death of President Franklin D. Roosevelt in 1945. Since the 1940s, many other studies suggest the following conclusions about diffusion of news.

The more important an event, the higher the rate and amount of diffusion. The prime determinant of how quickly and completely news of an event spreads is the importance of the event. News of life-threatening hazards can diffuse quite rapidly; in 1982, 80% of a Chicago sample had been alerted about the cyanide-contaminated Tylenol capsules within 24 hours (Carrocci, 1985). The assassination of a leader is perhaps one of the greatest crises a society can experience. The news of the assassination of President Kennedy spread rapidly; 42% of people heard of the shooting within 15 minutes (Greenberg, 1965); by 60 minutes, 90% of the country had heard; within 3 hours of the shooting, almost everyone had been informed. The spread of the news of the attempted assassination of President Reagan was not quite so rapid (Weaver-Lariscy, Sweeney, & Steinfatt, 1984); within 1 hour, 64% knew; this percentage increased to 81% within another 30 minutes. News of the attempted assassination of Pope John Paul II was still less rapid; 60% knew within the first hour and 71% within the first 90 minutes (Weaver-Lariscy et al., 1984). Schwartz (1973-1974) found that news of the attempt on presidential candidate Governor George Wallace's life spread to 60% of his sample in 2 hours.

The 1986 assassination of Sweden's Prime minister, Olof Palme, provided the context for a large-scale international comparative study of news diffusion. Researchers from 11 different countries conducted studies of the spread of news of the event (Rosengren, McQuail, & Blumler, 1987). The results of these studies confirm the role of news importance in amount of news diffusion. In the five Nordic countries (Sweden, Iceland, Norway, Denmark, and Finland), almost 100% of the population was aware of Palme's death within 12 hours (see Fig. 3.1; Rosengren, 1987). In the United States, however, after 48 hours, only 72% of the public was aware (Gantz & Tokinoya, 1987). These differences reflect the distance and importance of Swedish influence in Europe and the United States.

Comparisons of the diffusion of different news events reinforces that the impact of the event determines the rate and level of awareness. In 1960, researchers (Budd, MacLean, & Barnes, 1966) compared news diffusion of two events that occurred within a day of each other: the ouster of the Soviet Premier Nikita Khrushchev (a major event during the cold war era) and the arrest of a presidential assistant, Walter Jenkins, on a morals charge (a more minor event). The researchers concluded that "in less than one and a half hours, a higher percentage of persons were aware of the Khrushchev incident than knew of Jenkins after 15½ hours" (p. 225). The first hour after the announcement of each event, 30% were aware of Khrushchev but only 13% were aware of Jenkins. After 8 hours, almost everyone (93%) was aware of Khrushchev; only 50% were aware of Jenkins. Clearly, diffusion is determined by impact of the news.

The time of day that the news is released determines both the communication channel that is the first source of news as well as the rapidity of diffusion. Life's daily rhythms determine the primary initial source of news. As Mayer, Gudykunst, Perrill, and Merrill (1990) concluded af-

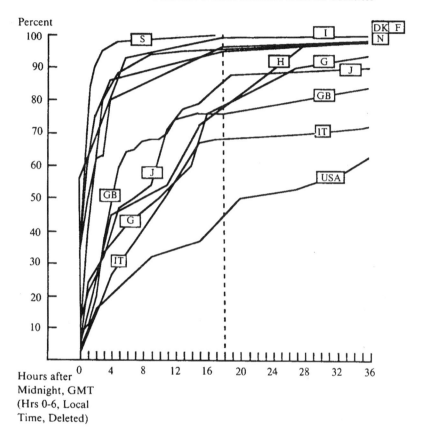

FIG. 3.1.   Diffusion of news of Palme's assassination in 11 countries. From: Rosengren, K.E. (1987). Conclusion: The comparative study of news diffusion. *European Journal of Communication, 2,* 227–255, p. 247. Reprinted by permission of Sage Publications Ltd..

ter their analysis of awareness of the Challenger explosion: "*where* one is affects *how* one discovers the occurrence of a major news event ... *how* one discovers the event then affects *how quickly* one hears of the event" (p. 121).

Greenberg (1965) reported that interpersonal contact was quite important to the spread of the news of the Kennedy assassination for his sample of San Jose, California, residents. Of those who first heard of the shooting in the first 15 minutes after it happened, about 38% learned from someone else. Of those who learned within the next 15 minutes, 55% learned from interpersonal contact; 57% of those who learned in the next 15 minutes cited interpersonal channels as their source. Kennedy was shot at 10:30 a.m. Pacific time, a time when many people are at work or busy with errands. At a time with fewer televisions and fewer television stations, television would be less important as an initial source. Mendelsohn (1964), however, in his sample of teens and adults in Colorado, found that radio was an important first source for news of Kennedy's shooting; 39% cited radio as their source. Media habits of the teens, who had radio as a typical accompaniment to daily activities, may explain its importance in that study.

A study of diffusion of the news of the air strike on Baghdad illustrates how time of day influences the channel of first information. Greenberg and his colleagues (1993) collected data across all four time zones of the United States. The bombing first occurred at 6:30 p.m. EST, when many were watching the evening news to see the U.S. reaction to Iraq's failure to withdraw troops from Kuwait by the January 15 deadline. In the eastern time zone, television was the first source of information for 68% of the respondents. Television's role grew smaller for respondents in earlier time zones; 53% and 50% first heard via television in the mountain and Pacific time zones respectively. Interpersonal sources were more likely sources earlier in the day: 16% of respondents learned from interpersonal channels, 21% and 29% relied on those sources in the mountain and Pacific time zones. The researchers concluded that earlier in the day people are more likely to be outside the home, working or running errands, and more likely to hear news from interpersonal sources. Those at home were more likely to hear the news from television, a home-centered medium. These findings confirm Gantz's (1983) conclusions about channel use and news diffusion. How people find out about an event is due mainly to where people are when the news is released—at work or at home. For those at home, radio or television are usually the first source of news; for those at work, where media are less likely to be readily available, interpersonal communication is usually the first source.

The timing of a fraternity house fire on the Indiana University campus that resulted in one death and several injuries illustrates the impact of people's routines on awareness (Gantz, Krendl, & Robertson, 1986).

The fire occurred early on a Sunday morning. Because there were no classes scheduled that day, most students were off campus. Although this was important to the student community and news of the fire diffused fairly rapidly throughout the day (by 6:00 p.m., 78% of students were aware of the fire), fewer than one in five of the respondents named any mass media channel as their source of awareness. Instead, over 80% heard the news from interpersonal sources. This finding may be due to the lack of media coverage or availability to students living on and off campus.

The time of day also influences news diffusion because of journalists' routines. Diffusion of news about Palme's assassination was slower to take off in some Nordic countries than in Japan or Iceland. Part of the explanation is due to time zone differences. Palme's death (which occurred around midnight Swedish time) was announced about 8:00 a.m. Saturday morning in Japan and at 12:30 a.m. in Iceland. But the slow initial rate of diffusion in Sweden was also due to journalist and government routines. At that hour, Swedish news desks were closed for the evening. Moreover, the intense importance of the assassination required confirmation before it could be publicly announced. Swedish broadcasting was handicapped by the late hour because of personnel shortages and because it was difficult to reach government officials to confirm the event. So, the first announcement of the tragedy wasn't until 1:10 a.m. (Rosengren, 1987).

The more important the event, the smaller the role of audience characteristics in its diffusion. A Swedish diffusion study of the assassination of Olof Palme found one minor difference in time of awareness among people: Men got the news a bit earlier than women (Weibull, Lindahl, & Rosengren, 1987). All other differences could be explained by people's daily routines. Younger people tended to stay out later on Fridays, so they were more likely to learn about the event earlier; older people learned the next morning. Similarly, Hill and Bonjean (1964) concluded that any differences between males and females in awareness of news events in diffusion studies of that era were due to daily routine. If an event occurs on a workday, there are differences in routines for males and females. In those days, because more males worked outside the home than females, gender influenced the source of knowledge through its link to where the individual was.

Other studies have supported the limited role of demographics in the diffusion process. Awareness of the death of ex-President Eisenhower in 1969 was not related to age or education (O'Keefe & Kissle, 1971). Although older Americans might find the news of his death more relevant because of his importance as a leader of World War II military forces and as president during the 1950s, personal relevance did not influence how quickly someone became aware of the death; nearly everyone was informed of Eisenhower's death.

There has been some conflicting evidence about the role of emotional response to news and diffusion. There are theoretical reasons to expect that those who are more upset when they hear of a major news event would seek out others for comfort. College students who were upset about the Challenger explosion were more likely to inform others of the tragedy (Kubey & Peluso, 1990). But, although adults who were more upset by the space shuttle explosion ultimately were more likely to talk to others about it, they were not more likely to pass along the news immediately (Riffe & Stovall, 1989).

Characteristics of the critical news event, then, appear to influence the rate and amount of diffusion. Certain audience variables, especially certain social categories, have an impact on rate of diffusion and communication source of first knowledge through their impact on daily routines.

Effects of Surveillance and Correlation Media Content

Do the Mass Media Provide Surveillance and Correlation? Nature of Media Content.   By their very nature, crises erupt suddenly. The threat of natural, technological, or political disturbances stress the public, but strain the resources of news-reporting agencies. Organizations have general plans and policies for covering crises and disasters (e.g., Kueneman & Wright, 1975), but in the midst of the situation, journalists' normal routines are upset (Tuchman, 1978). News organizations have many goals in mobilizing their coverage of crises. The need for profit and ratings demands speedy coverage and the "scoop," but coverage also is driven by public service. News agencies try to alert the public, calm fears, provide an official channel for information, and create public sympathy to increase humanitarian aid efforts (Kueneman & Wright, 1975; A. F. Simon, 1997; Sood et al., 1987). Although their goals are noble, news organizations often fail to fulfill the public's need for information.

Crises can disrupt normal newsgathering and reporting. All too often, natural disasters create havoc; electricity is lost, travel is dangerous or impossible, and communication links are cut. When Hurricane Andrew hit south Florida early Monday morning on August 24, 1992, the nation's news media were focused on the Louisiana coast. It wasn't until almost 24 hours later that we had any notion of the devastation the winds and rain had wreaked on the area. Hurricane Andrew devastated local media (Goldman & Reilly, 1992). The CBS-owned station, WCIX, was off the air for most of Monday. Andrew's winds toppled the microwave tower linking ABC with its affiliate. CNN could not contact its two affiliates and its Miami satellite truck had been damaged in the storm; reporters could not transmit video of the damage. The only video out of South Florida early on Monday was shots of Miami's mayor in largely undamaged downtown Miami. Obstacles to media reporting led initial reports of the damage to be greatly underestimated and relief efforts delayed.[2]

Crises impede communication to the outside world. Initial reports of the damage to the Caribbean island of Dominica by Hurricane David initially contained several inaccuracies because of poor telephone connections to and within the area. The need to travel off-island to file reports meant that much of the coverage was dated by the time it was broadcast.

During disasters and crises, those who are in positions to answer questions and provide explanations are often those who are too busy to talk to the news media. Firefighters and police officials are in the midst of rescue efforts; medical personnel are treating patients; government and military leaders are planning strategy. The public was largely uninformed about President Reagan's true medical condition for quite a while after the assassination attempt. But, we should be grateful that the medical personnel spent their time with the President rather than with reporters.

During the first stage of crisis coverage, news organizations struggle with demands for immediate information and the need for accuracy in reporting. The public's demand for information is so great at these times that radio and television usually interrupt normal programming and devote all their resources to coverage of the crisis. But because of strains on newsgathering, there is often a shortage of news, and the

---

[2]Not only was the American public generally unaware of the extent of the damage left by Hurricane Andrew, but the Federal Emergency Management Agency (FEMA) also was uninformed. FEMA monitors and relies on the four major news networks (ABC, CBS, NBC, and CNN) for information from disaster fronts (Goldman & Reilly, 1992). So, federal relief efforts depend on news coverage.

need for news outstrips the information available. Experts and commentators rush to the television studios. And televison stations play every bit of video that they have; but there may be long minutes when there is nothing new to release. Reports and speculation are repeated. As a television station manager said when interviewed after the Kennedy assassination, "Every bit of wire news was aired, re-aired, broadcast again and again" (Nestvold, 1964). What little video is available is played over and over. Most Americans surely have two news images burned in their memories forever: that of President Reagan waving, crumbling, and being pushed into the limousine to be rushed to the hospital and the image of the space shuttle Challenger replaced by the Y-shaped trail of smoke.

Normal gatekeeping is abandoned and almost all information passes through the gates—whether it has been verified or not (Waxman, 1973). Home video is aired (often with the caption "unedited video"). News anchors take telephone calls on the air from bystanders.[3] Reports may be incomplete, inaccurate, and conflicting. Early reports after the attempted assassination on President Reagan's life, for example, announced that James Brady had been killed. Immediately after the 1989 San Francisco earthquake, all four news networks initially underestimated the strength of the earthquake. Although all eventually reported the accurate Richter reading (7.1), first estimates hovered between 6.2 and 6.5 (McKenzie, 1993). In the confusion following the Oklahoma federal building bombing, news organizations reported speculations about a Middle Eastern connection that was later found to be false.

Given the incomplete and misinformation given during the first stage of crisis coverage, it is clear that media do not fulfill their surveillance and correlation functions well. Peled and Katz (1974) concluded that Israeli media did not satisfy the public's need to know and understand during the Yom Kippur War. News coverage was delayed and incomplete; there were few reports about losses, and interviews with soldiers at the front painted an optimistic picture of the army's progress. There is evidence that media coverage may not only fail to inform, but it may misinform. Emergency planners recognize the existence of various, inaccurate "disaster myths." The most common el-

---

[3]There have been several instances where fraudulent calls by Howard Stern fans have been aired. The news anchor (and viewers) may not be aware that the calls are a "joke."

ement of these myths is the belief that humans act and engage in irrational and exploitive behavior in times of crisis. Disaster myths suggest that (a) panic is a common reaction, (b) most victims are in shock and unable to care for themselves, (c) those who are not disabled loot, and (d) most people leave their homes for relief shelters (Goltz, 1984; Wenger, 1980). These myths may be perpetuated by media coverage of disasters that exaggerates evacuation efforts, interviews the most easily available "victims" (those in relief shelters), and reports "nonevents" (e.g., "there were few reports of looting"). Graber (1993) suggested that surveillance and correlation may not be fulfilled until the second stage of crisis coverage, well after the initial emergency. By this time, facts have emerged and been verified and the full impact of the crisis has been assessed. At this stage, though, print media can do a more complete job of integrating and synthesizing the material and are able to provide more complete explanations.

Other Effects of Surveillance and Correlation.   There are several other potential media effects due to media coverage of crises. Some crises may become part of the media agenda long enough that agenda setting occurs. That is, the audience may accept the issue as an important one facing society. The intense coverage of the Persian Gulf War, for example, led it to the top of the audience agenda during the early months of 1991 (Iyengar & Simon, 1993). Larson (1980) suggested that media coverage of some disasters, such as plane crashes and droughts, have been followed and associated with limited agenda-setting effects. There have been few studies, though, that focused specifically on the agenda-setting effects of crisis coverage; this may be due to the short duration of stage-one crisis coverage.

More research has focused on the effects of media coverage of terrorism. Scholars suggest that this coverage can result in knowledge gain, status conferral, and contagion effects. Due to the pressures of crisis coverage (need for speed and access to information), media coverage of terrorist acts is often incomplete. That is, terrorist acts and goals are often reported and interpreted by authorities who are opposed to the terrorists (Picard, 1993); therefore, terrorists' objectives are rarely discussed. Coverage mainly focuses on the tactics the terrorists employ and the resulting harm to victims; still, some limited learning may result. Weimann (1987) pointed out that terrorist acts have led to awareness of the plight of Palestinian refuges, Lebanese prisoners, and other politically disenfranchised groups. And the intense coverage of terrorist crises can provide a window for citizens to observe how well their government officials perform under pressure.

Other scholars are concerned that media coverage might confer status on terrorist groups. Status conferral is one outcome of surveillance (Lazarsfeld & Merton, 1948). Because media coverage signals importance, coverage of terrorist acts might serve to legitimize the instigators' cause and further, to gain sympathy for their cause (Weimann & Winn, 1994). It seems reprehensible to many that terrorists might benefit from their actions; an empirical test supports the notion that media coverage leads to status conferral (Weimann, 1983). Experimental groups of college students either read or watched television news reports of two specific terrorist acts. Control groups read or watched the news without reports of those acts. Pre- and posttest responses indicated that exposure to media coverage led to a significant increase in beliefs that the problem driving the terrorist act was important, should be covered by the media, and should be solved by international organizations. Comparisons between experimental and control groups reinforced this effect.

Another concern about media coverage of terrorism is fear of contagion, or fear that the publicity given to the terrorist acts will be imitated by others.[4] Although media coverage is certainly not the direct cause of terrorist acts, several aspects of its coverage may spawn imitation (Dobkin, 1992). There are concerns that media coverage may present information about terrorist methods, strategies, and techniques. As Dobkin (1992) summarized, reports of terrorist acts may serve as triggers to other groups, may increase the morale of other terrorist groups, or encourage common criminals to adopt terrorist techniques. There is evidence to support the contagion effect. Media coverage of the Irish Republican Army acts has been linked to subsequent terrorism (Tan, 1988). Weimann and Winn's (1994) comprehensive analysis of contagion effects of terrorist acts reported or not reported on television found that terrorist acts reported on U.S. network televisions are more frequently and more rapidly replicated than those acts not reported. They found that reported acts are likely to be replicated in 16.7 days

---

[4]Concerns about the imitation of violent and other antisocial acts portrayed in the media is common. In the case of air terrorism, for example, D. B. Cooper, the first hijacker who disappeared without a trace after parachuting with a bag of money, is believed to have spawned a rash of copycat hijackings.

(compared to 25.4 days for unreported acts). And, within 60 days, a reported act is likely to be imitated 25.7 times (compared to 12.0 times for unreported acts).

Concerns about the effects of media coverage of terrorism lead to policy concerns. Media coverage of terrorist acts can be functional; coverage can stop rumors from developing and help inform the public about dangers in the area. Because media coverage is a tool to gain publicity and sympathy for terrorist causes, some advocate that terrorists be denied media coverage. Press coverage has several dysfunctional outcomes beyond status conferral for terrorist groups and their causes (Bassiouni, 1982). Media coverage can also inform the terrorists about law enforcement location and activity. Media activity in the area can impede negotiations and tie up phone lines. And, the need for information may lead the press to distract officials and negotiators with requests for interviews.

The role of the media during terrorism gives rise to some grave conflicts between media organizations and law enforcement agencies. It would clearly be dysfunctional to keep the public ignorant of terrorist acts, especially while they are ongoing. But, some fear that media feed terrorism. Solutions to the problem of what, how, and when to cover terrorism range from complete government restriction of coverage to limits on media access to the area (Bassiouni, 1982). It is difficult, though, for mass communication scholars to accept press censorship. Suggestions that press use voluntary self-restraint during coverage of terrorism is, perhaps, unrealistic, in this era of concern for ratings and profits. The positive and negative effects of surveillance and correlation functions need to be carefully researched and weighed in order to understand how the media can best serve society.

Effects of Solidarity-Building Media Content

In times of crisis, the media react to society's need for surveillance and information by devoting massive time and energy to coverage of the crisis. All too often, though, it is difficult to gather information. Yet, it would be dysfunctional for media coverage to cease until information can be collected and verified. In order to reduce tension in society, media devote a good deal of coverage to media content intended to comfort their audience. Solidarity building is functional for society in times of crisis. Media highlight the wisdom of leaders and the bravery of res-

cue workers or soldiers to reassure society that "we are all in this together" and that everything possible is being done for survival. So,
although the media may be unable to fulfill surveillance and correlation needs, they are able to offer assurance and tension reduction.
Some of the effects of this content are rally effects and willingness to
accept censorship.

Rally Effects.   Rally effects are relatively rapid increases in presidential approval ratings during and just after times of crisis. These solidarity effects are termed rally effects because they signal a patriotic
solidarity—a sort of "rallying around the flag." Coser (1956) wrote that
conflict with forces external to a society (such as wars) leads society to
ignore within-group disagreements and to mobilize against the source
of the external threat. The more dramatic and sudden the threat, the
more likely rally effects are (Mueller, 1970). Because most intense
conflicts involve the president taking some visible and decisive action,
the president benefits from expressions of patriotism and solidarity.

Rally effects result from presidential action against intimidations
from other governments, such as Kennedy's war stance during the
1962 Cuban missile crisis and Reagan's 1983 invasion of Grenada. Bush
enjoyed incredible approval ratings during the 1991 Persian Gulf War,
reaching up to 93% of the country approving of his handling of the
country.[5] Clinton's order to attack the Iraqi intelligence headquarters in
1993 was also followed by about an 11% surge in his popularity. Rally effects emerge during or after presidential reactions to terrorist threats,
such as Reagan's responses to the hijacking of the cruise ship, Achille
Lauro, in 1985. Jimmy Carter even enjoyed a brief surge in popularity in
1980 after the aborted attempt to rescue the Iranian hostages. Rally effects have followed direct violent attacks on the president. Ronald Reagan's initial popularity following his 1980 landslide election over
incumbent Jimmy Carter was beginning to fade. Two months after he
took his oath of office, Reagan's approval rating stood at only 59% and
there was a good deal of opposition to his legislative agenda. John
Hinckley's bullet, however, changed that.

Rally effects are relatively short term and fade relatively rapidly after
the crisis has been resolved (Bowen, 1989). Bush's popularity as the
leader during the Persian Gulf War did not last long enough to ensure re-

---

[5]Bush's approval ratings were so high that some political commentators were taking his
reelection as a certainty. A few even suggested that the Democrats would be wasting time
even nominating an opponent.

election in 1992. But, these short-term effects have some long-term implications such as heightened support for the president in areas unrelated to the crisis (Bowen, 1989). President Johnson, for example, enjoyed a relatively long "honeymoon" period following the assassination of his predecessor due to the support given to him by a grieving public. This support translated into legislative action; Johnson was able to guide civil rights legislation through Congress where Kennedy had failed. Before the attempt on his life, Reagan was facing a good deal of opposition to his proposals to cut taxes and the budget; after he regained his health, his proposals were adopted by Congress. As Nacos (1990) wrote, "In a sense, the crisis triggered by the shots on T Street resulted in a renewed honeymoon for the President and his policy" (p. 156).

Rally effects reflect the solidarity that emerges when society is threatened (Coser, 1956). Need for information and explanation are certainly strong during crises (D. M. McLeod, Perse, Signorielli, & Courtright, 1993; Peled & Katz, 1974). But the need for solidarity building is heightened. A panel of Delaware residents was asked during the Persian Gulf War and 1 year later about the importance of the four media roles: providing information, explanation, solidarity building, and tension reduction. Endorsement of the solidarity-building media role was significantly higher during the war; endorsement of the surveillance role was stronger 1 year later than during the war (McLeod et al., 1994). In fact, McLeod and his colleagues found that respondents were less likely to endorse restrictive attitudes toward the media a year after the conflict than during the war. During crises, the public may be looking to media to act more as a cheerleader than a watchdog.

The mass media contribute to rally effects in two ways. First, because of their resources and direct access to those in authority, media are the primary conduit of information for the public. Second, during crises, when solidarity building is important, the media take a less critical stance toward government policies; they rarely challenge presidential action. Coupled with increased media use during crises, media content is likely to contribute to rally effects.

Prior to the 1962 Cuban missile crisis, there was a good deal of national concern about the build up of Soviet offensive weapons 90 miles off the coast of Florida, but there was certainly not widespread support for Kennedy's Cuban policies. In the month preceding the blockade, Republicans, some conservative Democrats, and anti-Castro Cuban exiles demanded government action against Castro. The Kennedy administration, however, advocated caution and rejected a military intervention. At that time, press coverage of Kennedy's position was divided in support; around 40% of coverage in the *New York Times*, *Washington Post*, and *Chicago Tribune* was favorable to Kennedy's stand (from 37.3% of the stories in the *Tribune* to 43.8% of the stories in the *Times*) while between 25.2% and 46.4% was unfavorable (Nacos, 1990). Of the sources cited in news stories in those three papers, almost half were in favor of the administration's position (from 42.6% in the *Tribune* to 49.3% in the *Post*); from 14.3% to 43.7% were against the position (Nacos, 1990). When Kennedy announced the Cuban blockade (which is, technically, an act of war) on October 22, 1962, news coverage became more supportive. Of the stories in the three newspapers about the Cuban crisis, from 56.8% to 67.8% were supportive and only 13.4% to 16.1% were against Kennedy's actions. Moreover, the sources cited in the articles were more supportive (from 62.5% to 82%) and far fewer against the administration's actions (from 1.8% to 6.0%; Nacos, 1990).

During the Persian Gulf War, media content was also marked by a lack of critical discussion of the administration's actions (Kellner, 1993). Dennis et al. (1991) noted that Bush used a strategy that attempted to "unite the country under the umbrella of support for the troups rather than seeking to win over skeptics to his approach" (p. 48). The media embraced the yellow ribbon theme. According to content analyses, during the first 3 weeks of the war, newspapers devoted less than 3% of their space to antiwar activities; television news granted peace protests less than 1% of news air time.

Willingness to Accept Censorship.   Democratic nations are marked by few overt restrictions on press freedom. Yet, during crisis situations there are often more reasons for "press management." Local broadcast stations are concerned that coverage of civil disorder might lead to panic, draw crowds, and incite rioting (e.g., Graber, 1993; Kueneman & Wright, 1975). So news reports may be edited to eliminate potentially damaging information. Surveillance may be sacrificed because of possible negative effects. During war, or military threats from external forces, these fears become especially important. The history of press coverage of military activity is marked by attempts to manage the information reported by the press (Woodward, 1993). There are often essential reasons to limit front-line news reports. As early as the Civil War, news media were scrutinized for information about weapons location and troop movement (Griffith, 1986). Information is often restricted to prevent news that might reveal military strategy and tactics that could be used by the enemy. Press restrictions during war are justified to protect the lives and the security of the nation. The instantaneous delivery of news worldwide by international news sources (e.g., CNN) has fueled the military's resolve to manage news coverage of conflicts (e.g., Sharkey, 1991).

During wars, the public seems to accept these press restrictions. Typically, most people in the United States advocate press freedom. Immerwahr and Doble (1982) found that almost three-quarters of their respondents believed newspapers could print material, even if it was embarrassing to the president or the government. Fewer than 30% were willing to restrict communists from public access to television audiences. In times of military crisis, though, press censorship is more likely to be endorsed. Gaziano (1988) found that 69% of her respondents felt that the government should censor television news stories if there were threats to national security. During the Persian Gulf War, acceptance of news censorship was expressed by a majority of Delaware respondents (D. M. McLeod, Perse, Signorielli, & Courtright, 1999). Respondents seemed to prefer supportive information and sanitized coverage (e.g., no information provided by the Iraqi government, no coverage of antiwar protests, and no images of wounded or dead soldiers).

Ironically, restrictive attitudes toward the press may grow out of media coverage and people's expectations about the roles of the mass media. D. M. McLeod and his colleagues (1999) observed that television news viewing was associated with greater acceptance of government control over military coverage. The "yellow ribbon" coverage of television news (Dennis et al., 1991) as well as the human interest stories about soldiers at the front and the families they left at home may have fanned patriotic feelings and reduced scrutiny of government actions. The importance of the different functions of mass communication had significant impact on respondents' willingness to censor war coverage. Those who believed that it was less important for media to provide information were more likely to believe that the media were a threat to the war effort and want the media curtailed from showing enemy and POW videos. Those who believed that it was less important for the media to provide explanation wanted the media prohibited from showing pictures of battle and wounded soldiers and felt that the government should be trusted to know what kind of news the public should receive. Those who believed that it was important for the media to build solidarity were more likely to believe that the government should select the reporters who cover war news and also allow the media to show only supportive information. This antidemocratic turnaround by the public in times of military crisis is a dramatic, though short-term effect of media coverage and expectations about the functions of mass communication.

How Functional is Solidarity Building During Times of Crisis?
There are few doubts that solidarity building during times of crises is functional. Television coverage following the Kennedy assassination helped people overcome fears about the stability of the country as well as their own personal grief (Mindak & Hursh, 1965; Schramm, 1965). Knowing that shock and grief are widespread provide comfort in times of upheaval. Disaster workers count on human interest stories to increase humanitarian aid in areas hit by natural calamities (Simon, 1997; Sood et al., 1987).

Some have raised concerns, though, about the mass media's abdication of their watchdog role during times of crisis. No responsible media organizations would want to endanger U.S. troops through irresponsible coverage. But it is difficult to justify some military restrictions. For example, Edward R. Murrow, during World War II, was initially denied permission to broadcast live during war raids by Britain's Ministry of Information (Woodward, 1993). The damage done by the German bombers was certainly visible to the pilots; few military secrets could be exposed by the broadcasts. Other details of World War II were kept out of the press by U.S. military censors. The public was not fully informed about the extent of the damage at Pearl Harbor; nor were they told about the kamikaze boat and plane attacks near the end of the war. Press restrictions have become even broader in recent conflicts. There was a total news blackout of our invasion of the small Caribbean island of Grenada and press restrictions during the Persian Gulf War have been called "unprecedented" (Sharkey, 1991). The Center for Public Integrity concluded that

> increasingly, information about Defense Department activities is being restricted or manipulated not for national security purposes, but for political purposes—to protect the image and priorities of the Defense Department and its civilian leaders, including the President. (Sharkey, 1991, p. 1)

Some writers have suggested long-term outcomes of acceptance of censorship. First, it is clear that military restrictions yield a sanitized and distorted image of warfare. A public that does not understand the horror of war might be more likely to endorse future military engagements and less likely to demand diplomatic solutions to international problems. There could even be a residual agenda-setting effect that leads the public to accept military issues as important along with increased support for military spending (perhaps at the expense of other spending).

Perhaps more important, though, is how the media's performance during military crises may affect the public's perceptions about the media's roles in society. Scholars have argued that media have important responsibilities in democratic societies (Gurevitch & Blumler, 1990). The press should provide news to allow citizens to make informed decisions. They should encourage discussion of public affairs and be a platform for a wide variety of different viewpoints. The media should act as a watchdog, and approach official statements skeptically and critically. Finally, the media should fend off attempts to curtail their democratic role. During international crises, governments make decisions and take actions that can have serious long-ranging consequences. If media abdicate their responsibilities during those critical times, it may be difficult to regain their position in society—relative to those they are supposed to be watching and those to whom they owe a responsibility.

Explaining Media Effects in Times of Crisis

Which models of media effects can explain these effects during crises? There is striking evidence that many of the initial and most noticeable effects are almost universal and uniform. During crises, people overwhelmingly turn to the medium that is the most immediate source of news: television (e.g., Gallup Organization, 1991; Gantz, 1983; Hirschburg et al., 1986; Peled & Katz, 1974; Sheatsley & Feldman, 1965). Diffusion of news is rapid and complete (e.g., Greenberg, 1965; Rosengren, 1987; Weaver-Lariscy et al., 1984). Rally effects reflect dramatic increases in presidential popularity (e.g., D. M. McLeod et al., 1994; Nacos, 1990). Most people prefer solidarity building than information from the media (e.g., D. M. McLeod et al., 1999).

Audience variables seem to play little role in explaining these effects. Social category variables offer only limited variation in effects (e.g., Hirschburg et al., 1986). The time an event happens interacts with people's daily routines to explain when and where news is heard (e.g., Gantz, 1983; Hill & Bonjean, 1964; Weibull et al., 1987). Preference for television as a news source may also be linked to lower educational levels (e.g., Peled & Katz, 1974). But, overall, the role of audience variables seems to be quite small (e.g., McLeod et al., 1993, 1999). Instead, the driving force for many of the effects of crisis media coverage seem to derived from the nature and content of the media coverage.

The direct effects model may provide a good explanation for these media effects. People respond almost immediately and uniformly to media messages about crises. When people overwhelmingly turn to the media, selective exposure is irrelevant. Moreover, their responses are determined, to a large degree, by the content of the media, rather than people's interpretations of that content. Many of the effects, though, seem to be relatively short term. After crises, people return to the concerns of their normal lives; typical media use patterns resume; rally effects dissipate. Of course, there may be other long-term implications and outcomes of crisis situations. But, the most commonly mentioned media effects may be best explained by the direct effects model. Why is the role of the audience in the media effects process reduced during times of crisis?

Dependency Model of Media Effects

Ball-Rokeach and DeFleur (1976) and DeFleur and Ball-Rokeach (1989) articulated a theoretical statement that explains the varying power of the role of mass media in the media effects process. According to their dependency model of media effects, how dependent the audience is on mass media to fill needs is a key variable in understanding media effects. *Dependency* is defined as "a relationship in which the satisfaction of needs or the attainment of goals by one party is contingent upon the resources of another party" (Ball-Rokeach & DeFleur, 1976, p. 16). Dependency on the mass media is likely to be higher under two conditions. In the first condition, as societies become more complex, mass media perform specialized and unique functions—especially gathering and disseminating news. A second condition that heightens audience dependence on the mass media is crisis, conflict and change, which creates uncertainty in society and, in turn, increases the audience's needs for information, tension reduction, and solidarity. These needs can be supplied typically only by the mass media, because of their role in society and their superior resources. As Ball-Rokeach and DeFleur (1976) wrote,

> The potential for mass media messages to achieve a broad range of cognitive, affective, and behavioral effects will be increased when media systems serve many unique, and central information functions. That potential will be further increased when there is a high degree of structural instability in the society due to conflict and change. (p. 7)

Crises are times of great conflict, potential change, or upheaval. Because of their resources and access, media have the unique abilities to gather information and make it available to the audience. Crises are times when the audience is highly dependent on the mass media. Mass media have the ability to control what news is reported and how it is framed. Mass media also take the responsibility to explain the significance of various bits of information. In crises, because there are few, if any, other sources of information, the media, to a large degree, are able to limit how information is interpreted. So, with standardized information comes fairly uniform interpretations. Times of heightened dependency, then, are marked by fairly uniform and universal media effects (Hirschburg et al., 1986).

Ball-Rokeach and DeFleur (1976) noted that media dependency can intervene in several cognitive, affective, and behavioral effects, such as ambiguity reduction, attitude formation, agenda setting, belief acquisition, value clarification, emotional reactions, feelings of alienation or solidarity, and behavioral activation or deactivation. In times of crisis, increased dependency makes it more likely that media effects will be direct. But dependency may also be conceptualized as a variable—a condition of influence—that can intervene in the process of media effects even when society is not threatened. We consider later in this volume how other media effects can be heightened when people, for various reasons, might be more dependent on the mass media than on other sources of information.

Summary

Functional approaches to understanding the role of mass media in society point out that mass media serve society by providing surveillance, correlation, socialization, and entertainment. Although these functional activities are constant, during times of crisis, the functional nature of mass communication is especially apparent. Because of heightened uncertainty and fear, people rely on mass media for information, explanation, and solidarity. Mass communication is an important source for news diffusion, or alerting people to events and threats. But, because of constraints on news gathering, the information function of the mass media is often quite limited during the acute phase of a crisis. Media's solidarity-building function, though, is valued by society and the audience. For short periods of time, media solidarity building can have effects on how the public perceives its leaders. Ironically, solidarity building may also be seen in public acceptance of limits on press freedom.

Many of the media effects during crises seem to be fairly uniform and universal; audience variables offer little explanation for these effects. Effects during crises can be explained by the direct effects model because of increased dependency on the mass media. Heightened needs brought on by conflict and uncertainty lead to greater reliance on the major source for information and explanation. This state of dependency reduces differences among people. The media's tight control of information limits selective exposure and perception, so effects are directed by the nature of media content. Many of these effects, however, although they are dramatic, are often short term. Research, though, needs to explore if and how these short-term effects might have long-term ramifications for people, the media system, and society.

4

Shaping Public Opinion

Public opinion is a concept that is difficult to define because it has roots in the concerns of a number of different of disciplines (Price, 1992). What, for example, is a public? What counts as an opinion? Can a group of people hold a single opinion? Fields of sociology, psychology, political science, political philosophy, polling, and communication all consider different aspects of the phenomenon referred to as public opinion. Graber (1982), though, provided a definition that is serviceable for communication scholars: Public opinion is "group consensus about matters of political concern which has developed in the wake of informed discussion" (p. 556).

This definition illustrates that public opinion is something that is marked by being endorsed by a number of people (a group). Public opinion is not the expression of narrow views of political isolates. Public opinion focuses on matters of political concern. Sentiments that large groups of people share are not necessarily public opinion. Beliefs in the innocence or guilt of O. J. Simpson may have been the basis for the questions of many polls, but his guilt or innocence is not a political matter. Expressions about bias in our judicial system, though, might be the content of public opinion. Graber (1982) also stated that her definition of public opinion assumes that people are mentally active and involved in forming and supporting their opinions.

Scholars suggest that public opinion has several different roots. Ideally, active and knowledgeable public opinion should emerge from political ideology. *Political ideology* is a set of general principles about how society ought to function, usually described in terms such as "liberal" or "conservative." Ideology, though, explains only part of the public's opinion. Other sources for public opinion are self-interest, social group identification, opinion leadership, the expression of personal values, and interpretations of history and events (Kinder & Sears, 1985). In most societies it is also clear that mass communication plays a role in the formation of public opinion. The political matters that are the substrate for public opinion are rarely unobtrusive, that is, directly experienced (McCombs, Einsiedel, & Weaver, 1991). In complex societal systems, politics often take place in centralized locations, managed by political specialists. For most, politics is unobtrusive, experienced vicariously through the reports of the mass media. Through its surveillance function, mass communication watches, monitors, and reports on political matters. It is through the mass media that most people learn about political issues, assess which issues are important, and gauge which positions are endorsed by the majority. Mass communication, then, is the platform on which political matters are discussed and political events are played out.

The opinions that people express about matters of political concern, though, are not always thoughtfully derived. People may express views about issues that they know little about. Surveys of news awareness consistently demonstrate that many people are both uninformed and misinformed about current events (e.g., D. M. McLeod & Perse, 1994; Robinson & Levy, 1996). Even when the United States has been engaged in high-profile international events, such as the building of the Berlin Wall (Converse, 1975) and United States' involvement in the Persian Gulf War (Jhally, Lewis, & Morgan, 1991), many people are mistaken about the facts underlying those events. People may even express opinions without any basis. Schuman and Presser (1980) asked respondents about the Agricultural Trade Act of 1978, a piece of legislation so little known that even their well-informed academic colleagues did not recognize it. Given its obscurity, the "don't know" option should have been the overwhelming option chosen by their survey's respondents. Instead, nearly one-third (31%) offered an opinion about the act (see also G. F. Bishop, Oldendick, Tuchfaber, & Bennet, 1980, for opinions about bogus legislation).

It is clear, then, that public opinion has different meanings. For some, public opinion is well formed, grounded in solid knowledge, fairly stable, and predictive of political action. Others, though, hold "pseudo" public opinion, which is a more short-term reaction to political issues or politicians and candidates and not based on depth of prior knowledge. This chapter focuses on the role of mass communication in the formation and expression of public opinion. The effects of mass communication, though, are not uniform. The existence of real and pseudo public opinion suggest that media effects are conditional, based on the political involvement and abilities of people.

THEORETICAL FOCUS: ELABORATION LIKELIHOOD MODEL

The elaboration likelihood model (ELM) was formulated by Cacioppo and Petty as a general theory of persuasion or attitude change. While much persuasion research has been conducted outside the field of mass communication, it is clear that persuasion is at the heart of understanding many media effects. Now, more than ever, media channels are used to persuade people to support candidates or issues, to try products, to adopt healthy practices, and to support charitable causes (Petty & Priester, 1994). Petty and Cacioppo (1986) noted, however, that even though the study of persuasion had compiled a substantial set of theories and data, "there was surprisingly little agreement concerning if, when, and how the traditional source, message, recipient and channel variables … affected attitude change" (p. 2). The ELM is a theoretical approach that attempts to explain the disparate findings of persuasion research.

The ELM is based on several assumptions (Petty & Cacioppo, 1986). The first is that people want to hold *correct attitudes*. Correct attitudes are those that have some underlying rationale. Correct attitudes are also ones that people believe will help them function in their daily lives. So, attitudes have some sort of basis that makes sense to those who hold them. Moreover, there is no single way or process in which these correct attitudes can be formed.

The second assumption is that, although people want to hold correct attitudes, people's capacity to process persuasive messages is limited. The ideal view of attitude formation is a mindful one, in which people pay attention to a message, learn its content, and yield to its suggestion (McGuire, 1985). There are times, when issues are important to us and outcomes may affect us directly, that we put a great of effort and energy into forming our attitudes. We may do our own extended research, acquire a good deal of knowledge about the topic, and evaluate messages about the issue carefully against that knowledge. It is impossible for us, however, to carefully scrutinize and evaluate every persuasive message that we encounter. If we did, we would get very little else done because we would be spending so much time thinking about the many messages we encounter daily. And, intense analysis of persuasive messages would distract us from other more interesting and valuable aspects of our lives. So, we pay only fleeting attention to messages that aren't very relevant to us. Even if messages may be relevant, we may be forced to make snap decisions because we haven't the time to analyze and evaluate the arguments of the messages. Or, we may form attitudes based on the authority or expertise of the message source simply because we haven't the background knowledge to understand completely the complexities of the message's arguments.

Based on these two assumptions, Petty and Cacioppo (1986) proposed that there are two general routes that mark people's mental strategies when they encounter persuasive messages: central and peripheral routes. Attitude change is the result of either of two major influences: the content of the message or the characteristics of the situation (Stiff, 1986). Figure 4.1 illustrates the process of persuasion according to the ELM.

The central route is motivated by consideration of the issues and arguments in the message—the central information in the message. This route reflects the ideal way that public opinion is formed. The recipient considers the information in a message, compares it to prior knowledge, and either integrates the new information or rejects it. Attitudes formed via the central route are more long term and fairly predictive of behavior.

The peripheral route is the route followed by recipients who are either not motivated to devote mental energy to considering the message, or are not able to totally understand the information (due to mental abilities or environmental context, such as distractions). Persuasive effects are still possible in the peripheral route, but they are based on peripheral cues, such as source attractiveness or credibility, or the number or arguments, and so on. Attitudes formed by the peripheral route are generally shorter term and not necessarily predictive of behavior.

Different variables are relevant to the ELM because of their impact on the likelihood of elaborating on messages. These variables are typically receiver variables, or variables that relate to the audience, and affect the

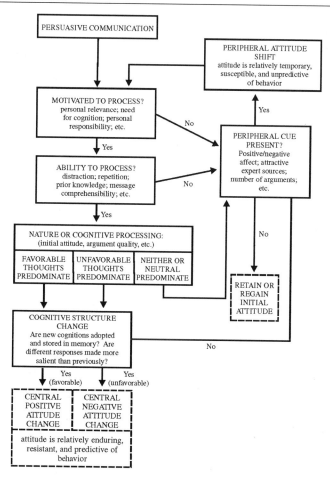

FIG. 4.1.   The elaboration likelihood model of persuasion. From: Petty, R. E., &
Priester, J. R. (1994). Mass media attitudes change: Implications of the Elaboration
Likelihood Model of Persuasion. In J. Bryant & D. Zillmann (Eds.), Media effects:
Advances in theory and research (pp. 91-122). Hillsdale, NJ: Lawrence Erlbaum
Associates, p. 99. Reprinted by permission.

motivation or ability to engage in central message processing. Message
variables, or those that deal with message construction, are relevant because they describe peripheral cues related to attitude change.

RECIPIENT VARIABLES

In general, *recipient variables* can be classified as influencing either motivation or ability to engage in central message processing. Motivation to
process messages has been linked to personal relevance and personal

characteristics (Petty & Cacioppo, 1986). One truism of persuasion research is that people react differently to messages that are personally
relevant (Johnson & Eagly, 1990). Various approaches to persuasion
have noted the importance of personal relevance or involvement: social
judgment theory (C. W. Sherif, M. Sherif, & Nebergall, 1965), attributional
approaches (Taylor, 1975), cognitive response approaches (Petty,
Ostrom, & Brock, 1981), cognitive dissonance (Festinger, 1957), and
functional approaches (Katz, 1960). When people hear messages that
affect them in important ways, they pay more attention to the messages
and put more mental energy into considering their content. So, for example, Rothschild and Ray (1974) found that people's recall of political
ads depended, in part, on the importance of the election. They reasoned
that the outcome of the presidential elections was more personally relevant to people than the outcomes of local elections. P. L. Wright (1974)
found that people thought more about advertisements for products
when they were going to be given one of the products than when there
was no vested interest in the ads. So, greater personal relevance is
linked to the central route to persuasion. When people are not involved
with the message topic, they put less mental effort into message reception and follow the peripheral route.

There is evidence that some people are intrinsically motivated to follow the central route. Some people share a personality trait, need for
cognition (NFC), that leads them to enjoy thinking and relish putting effort into cognitive activity. Those who score high on NFC measures prefer complex mental tasks as opposed to simple, repetitive activities.
They enjoy puzzles. They are also more likely to be employed in jobs
that require a lot of thinking (Cacioppo & Petty, 1982). When they encounter arguments, those higher in NFC think about the messages
more and more likely to follow the central route—even with political
messages (Cacioppo, Petty, Kao, & Rodriquez, 1986).

Other recipient variables affect the ability to engage in message elaboration. Intelligence or educational level, for example, might be related
to being able to understand messages better, which enables greater
elaboration and thought about the implications of the arguments. For
those with lower intelligence or less education, some arguments may
be too complex, so the listener pays attention, instead, to easy-to-com-
prehend peripheral cues. Petty and Cacioppo (1986) pointed out that
prior knowledge affects thinking about messages. Because prior knowledge is often reflected in schemas, prior knowledge may result in cen-

tral, but biased, elaboration. So, schematic-based central processing may be colored by the nature of the prior knowledge.

An individual's social context may also affect the route of thinking. Distractions reduce the ability to think about a message. So, distractions reduce the likelihood of elaboration and disrupt central processing. Studies confirm the effects of distractions on processing and persuasion (Petty & Cacioppo, 1986). When messages are heard in distracting contexts, recipients are less able to generate positive thoughts about the message, so distraction reduces persuasion. But, distractions also keep recipients from generating negative thoughts, or counterarguments, resulting in lower likelihood of rejecting the message.

MESSAGE VARIABLES

Message variables typically have their greatest impact on persuasion by acting as peripheral cues. Source credibility is perhaps one of the most-researched persuasive techniques. Sources who are credible are ones with superior knowledge (expertise) and can be trusted to present material objectively (Hovland, Janis, & Kelley, 1953). Messages that are attributed to more credible sources will be associated with heightened attention and persuasion (McGuire, 1985). The ELM, however, points out that source credibility is more important to persuasion through the peripheral route, when arguments are not scrutinized (Petty, Cacioppo, & Goldman, 1981).

Source attraction is another message factor that is not directly related to central argument quality. This peripheral cue, though, has predictable impacts on persuasion. In general, more attractive sources are more persuasive (Chaiken, 1979).[1] There are several explanations offered for this effect: (a) Attractive sources may also be perceived as credible; (b) they may serve as distractions from weak arguments; or

---

[1]One of the most notable examples of the effect of source attraction is the outcome of the 1960 presidential candidate debate between John F. Kennedy and Richard M. Nixon. One of the myths surrounding that first debate was that television viewers were captivated by Kennedy's youthful attraction and put off by Nixon's discomfort and "sickly" appearance. So, television viewers believed that Kennedy won the debate. Radio listeners, though, were impressed with Nixon's command of the facts and believed he won (e.g., Diamond & Bates, 1992; Jamieson & Birsdell, 1988). Others, though, questioned the factual basis of these reports (Vancil & Pendell, 1987). Kraus (1996) concluded, however, that there was evidence to support the popular "myth." It is interesting to note, thought, that even in 1960, the total television audience for the first debate was estimated to be 4 ½ times larger than the radio audience (Kraus, 1996).

(c) the positive feeling associated with attraction may enhance favorable thoughts toward the message.

Other message variables that serve as peripheral cues are the number of arguments in a message and the number of people endorsing a message. In general, the number of arguments used in a message increases persuasion because the position appears to be more strongly supported. But, this factor works only in the peripheral route, when recipients do not scrutinize whether the arguments are strong or valid (Petty & Cacioppo 1984). Similarly, when a message contains endorsements, a greater number of endorsements acts as a peripheral cue ("If so many use this product, it must be good"; Axsom, Yates, & Chaiken, 1987). This cue is very much the "bandwagon" effect of propaganda analysis (Lee & Lee, 1939).

There are, however, some indications that some message techniques can increase the likelihood of central processing by motivating people to become more involved with the message. Unexpected or unusual newspaper headlines may "surprise" readers and lead them to scrutinize an article that they would normally only skim (Baker & Petty, 1994). Research has also shown that questions (compared to statements) and implied (rather than explicit) conclusions can draw people into thinking about messages more (e.g., Hovland & Mandell, 1952; Petty, Cacioppo, & Heesacker, 1981).

The channel of origin on which a message is carried can also affect the ability to process the message. In general, media with reception pacing controlled by the audience (e.g., print or Web) enable central processing (P. L. Wright, 1981). Newspaper readers, for example, can stop and think about ideas and issues whenever they like. But other media's presentations are often out of the audience's control. Television and radio, for example, continue on, whether the audience wants to stop and think or not; so, these media lower the likelihood of elaboration. P. L. Wright (1981) also pointed out that the typical reception context of audio-visual media is a busy and distracted one. So, audio-visual media reception is likely to follow the peripheral route. Different media may also interact with peripheral cues. Visual media, for example, are more effective to deliver messages that use source attraction appeals.

MULTIPLE ROLES FOR MESSAGE VARIABLES

Petty and Priester (1994) pointed out that it is impossible to classify any message variable as absolutely central or peripheral. Different variables can serve multiple roles; they can, at different times, serve as central or peripheral cues, depending on personal relevance. When a topic is particularly personally important, it is possible for source credibility to backfire. A message about the importance of hiring more police officers may include several strong arguments, including the need to reduce drug crime. But, if the source is the public safety official who stands to benefit from increased personnel, financial resources, and political power, highly involved and knowledgeable audience members might detect the bias in the advocacy of hiring more officers. And, source attraction might serve as a very central cue in messages that advocate diet, fitness, and beauty products. A trim, attractive model, for example, can illustrate the effectiveness of exercise equipment (e.g., Petty & Cacioppo, 1980).

VALUE OF THE ELM FOR THE STUDY OF MEDIA EFFECTS

The *elaboration likelihood model* offers some utility to understanding the process of media effects. It provides an explanation for a distinction between long-term and short-term effects of persuasive messages. It specifies the aspects of messages that might be more important in understanding media effects. It specifies the characteristics of people that influence their reactions to media messages.

The elaboration likelihood model offers several connections to models of media effects. First, the ELM has some similarities to the cognitive model. Both suggest that individuals can engage in different types of thought. The central route may be similar to controlled processing; the peripheral route may be like automatic processing. Both central and controlled processing are intentional, individual controlled, and goal directed. Both peripheral and automatic processing are more passive and affected more by characteristics of the message stimulus. Like the conditional model, selective exposure is important to the ELM. Both suggest that people process information that is relevant to their own situation.

The ELM has wide utility and broad scope, however, scholars have criticized it for lack of specificity and because it is difficult to disprove (Stiff & Boster, 1987). Because different variables have been described as having different effects depending on personal relevance, the ELM may be more descriptive than predictive. That is, it may be easier to describe what has happened, after the fact, rather than predict the specific effects of different variables. For that reason, any number of different effects of persuasive messages can be explained by the model.

Stiff (1986) advocated an alternate explanation for the processes delineated by the ELM. Based on his metaanalysis, Stiff found that highly involved individuals evaluate both central and peripheral cues, contrary to his characterization of the ELM's assertion that people process only central or peripheral cues. Stiff suggested that Kahneman's (1973) elastic capacity model presents a more ecological explanation of message processing. According to Kahneman, people can manage several cognitive tasks at the same time, depending on the amount of mental capacity the tasks require. Stiff's metaanalysis found that when message involvement is low, people process few central or peripheral cues; as involvement increases, processing of both central and peripheral cues both increase—up to a point. When involvement is high, processing focuses on central cues. According to Stiff, the capacity model explains that at high involvement, cognitive capacity is focused on central information, so little capacity is left to consider peripheral cues.

There may be some validity to persuasion scholars' concerns about the multiple, unspecified roles of different variables in the process. The *conditional model*, though, operates at the individual level and recognizes that effects are conditional on aspects of people. Clearly, different message aspects can affect different people in different ways. Petty, Wegener, Fabrigar, Priester, and Cacioppo (1993) also pointed out that, although most research on the ELM has used experimental analysis of variance (ANOVA) designs, the true process cannot be described as a dichotomy. In reality, people do not follow either a central or peripheral route. The likelihood of elaborating on messages is most likely a continuum. The ELM is relevant when considering the effects of the mass media in the political realm because of the distinction between "pseudo" and "true" public opinion (Graber, 1982).

THE DISTINCTIONS BETWEEN INFORMED AND PSEUDO PUBLIC OPINION

Noelle-Neumann's (1993) discussion of the evolution of the concept of public opinion highlights that a belief in rationality undergirds many definitions. As early as 1923, Young defined public opinion as " the social judgment of a self-conscious community on a question of general import after rational, public discussion" (pp. 577–578). Blumer (1946) saw public opinion as an aspect of social relations: People confront an issue of concern and explore different solutions to the issue through public discussion. This notion of a rational public engaging in public discourse about political matters is grounded in Libertarian philosophy—discussion eventually leads to knowledge of the truth (e.g., Siebert et al., 1963). But scholars quickly realized that not all political opinions are based on rationality and public discussion. People may not be able to develop thoughtful opinions because they don't have the education, background knowledge, or mental resources to understand political matters or they may not have access to the information they need to make informed opinions (Price, 1992).

Graber (1982) built on these limits to the development of public opinion and suggested that there are two general sorts of public opinion. *Informed public opinion* is the thoughtful, rationally based opinion formed after consideration and discussion with interested and informed others. Informed public opinion is held by political elites in society who are especially attentive to political matters. *Public pseudo-opinions*, on the other hand, are "opinions expressed by various publics which lack a sound information base and the honing that comes from dialogue and debate" (Graber, 1982, p. 556). Graber likens pseudo-opinion to snap judgments or top-of-mind reactions. These opinions may be based on impressions, moods, recollections of past opinions, or the plagiarism of opinion leaders' opinions. Pseudo-opinion is held by political nonelites, who pay only superficial attention to political matters, if they pay attention at all. Graber (1982) characterized such opinion as "ill-considered, fleeting, and unstable" (p. 556).

Role of the Mass Media in the Formation of Informed and Pseudo Opinion

Because political events and issues in modern societies typically take place in specialized locations, most citizens experience politics vicariously. So they rely on the surveillance function of the mass media to monitor and report on important events and issues. For most, then, media content is the symbolic input for public opinion—informed or pseudo. Graber (1982) argued that the role of the media in the development of public opinion differs for elites and nonelites. For elites, information from the media becomes just one of many sources of data. Because of their political involvement and interest and their vast base of prior knowledge, elites treat media coverage as foreground, or sources of new and/or specific information. Elites analyze new information from the media and compare it to prior background knowledge they have. As a result, new information may be integrated with prior knowledge to reinforce existing opinion, or it may lead to some changes in opinion, or it may be rejected entirely. Nonelites, on the other hand, are not so interested in politics, and they have relatively little prior knowledge about political issues. For nonelites, media coverage is not only a source of new data, but their only source of information. For nonelites, media content is both foreground and background.

Media Use by Elites and Nonelites.   Elites and nonelites differ dramatically on their choices for learning about politics. Although television is an almost universal leisure activity, television news use is generally unrelated to political activity (e.g., D. M. McLeod & Perse, 1994). Televison news use, as well as television viewing in general, though, is linked to lower levels of education (e.g., Shoemaker, 1989). Viewers with less education tend to seek entertainment rather than news and information from television (e.g., Rubin, 1984). Rhee and Cappella (1997) found that political sophistication was negatively correlated with television news exposure.

Research on newspaper reading (Bogart, 1989) supported the conclusion that the newspaper is a preferred news source by politically active people. D. M. McLeod and Perse (1994) found significant links between newspaper use and both political interest and political involvement. Frequent newspaper readers are more likely to talk about politics and current events in daily conversations than infrequent readers. They are more likely to vote (75% compared to 55% of infrequent readers). More frequent newspaper readers (43%) consider newspapers important to them as citizens and voters, compared to only 19% of infrequent readers. The infrequent newspaper reader tends to rely on television for political news and may be politically uninvolved. Bogart (1989) reported that infrequent newspaper readers under the age of 35 "appear to include the most transient, unsettled, alienated element of their age group" (p. 88) who are turned off by news almost totally, including that of their own community.

The audience for specialized news media is also more likely to be politically active (e.g., Lamb & Associates, 1988). While the C-SPAN audience is still rather small, its viewers are more likely to be registered to vote (86% compared to 76% of nonviewers), more likely to have voted in the 1984 presidential election (93% compared to 53% of nonviewers) and in the 1986 congressional election (69% compared to 37% of nonviewers). They are more likely to discuss politics with family or friends three or more times a week (44% compared to 21% of nonviewers), more likely to read a daily newspaper (76% vs. 44%), and watch television news (80% vs. 50%). Robinson and Levy (1996) observed that news awareness was predicted by watching specialized television news programs such as the *MacNeil/Lehrer NewsHour, 60 Minutes, 20/20,* and *C-SPAN.*

The ELM, coupled with differential use of television, newspapers, and specialized media for news, can explain the development of pseudo- and informed public opinion. First of all, newspapers and television differ dramatically in the amount and kind of information they present. Newspapers, the preferred medium of those who are more likely to be public opinion elites, provides more in-depth central information; television presents more peripheral information. Limited learning via television news has been explained by television news' information constraints because of space and time. Most television news compresses the stories to fit a limited time—22 minutes for network national news, for example, after subtracting time spent on commercials. So, television covers far fewer stories than newspapers. Moreover, television news stories are far shorter and present fewer details than comparable newspaper stories (Graber, 1990; Neuman, Just, & Crigler, 1992). Although some argue that television's visuals adds information that newspaper cannot furnish (e.g., Graber, 1990; Katz, Adoni, & Parness, 1977), most research confirms television's limited effectiveness in transmitting information (Robinson & Levy, 1986).

Television's mode of presentation is also less suited to imparting central information. Whether is it because of reliance on attention-grabbing visuals, or limited time and space, or a general orientation to "infotainment," television frames news stories in ways that limits development of viewers' understanding. *Framing* is defined by Entman (1993) as the highlighting of certain aspects of a news story to make them more noticeable. Framing works to encourage a particular interpretation of the news story. Most television news is framed episodically rather than thematically (Iyengar, 1991; Postman, 1985). *Episodic framing* depicts "public issues in terms of concrete instances or specific events" (Iyengar & Simon, 1993, p. 369), such as covering crime by covering criminal acts and their victims. *Thematic framing* "places public issues in some general or abstract context" (Iyengar & Simon, 1993, p. 369), such as discussing the causes of crime or the changes in crime rates and occurrences. Framing can limit in-depth understanding of public issues by simplifying complex problems.

Second, differences in newspaper and television's typical exposure situations suggest that television news viewing is more likely to follow the peripheral route. Because of the way that television news is presented, the audience is less likely to be able to follow the "central route." Because television's presentation and pacing are real time, audiences are not able to review or reflect on what they have seen or heard or ponder something that they do not understand (Wright, 1981). Newspaper reading, on the other hand, is reader controlled. Readers can stop and think about stories at their own pace. Television news viewing is a more distracted activity, accompanied by daily routines (Levy & Windahl, 1984; Rubin & Perse, 1987). So levels of attention to news stories fluctuate, and viewers may miss entirely some aspects of stories. Some scholars have observed that television encourages "heuristic" modes of information processing (Chaiken & Eagly, 1983; Spencer, Seydlitz, Laska, & Triche, 1992). Heuristic processing is very much like the peripheral route; heuristic responses are more automatic and respond to salient messages cues.

Finally, television news viewing and newspaper reading are associated with different motives for use. Although information seeking motivates the use of both news media (Perse & Courtright, 1993; Rubin, 1981b), television news viewing typically includes a strong entertainment component (e.g., Palmgreen et al., 1981; Rayburn, Palmgreen, & Acker, 1984; Rubin et al., 1985). Frequent newspaper readers, however, are more oriented toward seeking information from print media. They read newspapers more for information than for entertainment and are also more likely to use other print media for information, such as news magazines (Bogart, 1989).

Political Schemata of Elites and Nonelites

One axiom of news research is that education is a significant and substantial predictor of learning from the news (Berry, 1983; Gunter, 1987; Price & Czilli, 1996; Robinson & Levy, 1986; Tichenor et al., 1970). Education may have an impact because it signals sharper cognitive skills and abilities to process information. But, education's greatest impact may be due to its association with prior knowledge (Berry, 1983; Price & Czilli, 1996; Robinson & Levy, 1986). Greater prior knowledge may grow out of the use of superior information sources, higher cognitive ability, and greater interest in the news. Many scholars also explain that "people who possess large stores of information need well organized schemata to organize it, and these schemata aid in the acquisition of new information" (Price & Zaller, 1993, p. 138).

Public opinion elites may be seen as political sophisticates (Rhee & Cappella, 1997). *Political sophistication* is expertise in the political arena. It is marked by greater prior knowledge about political matters (Price & Zaller, 1993), more ideological stances on issues (Rhee & Cappella, 1997), and more analytic processing of political messages (Hsu & Price, 1993). Political experts have more complex and developed schemas about political matters than novices (Fiske & Kinder, 1991). Rhee and Cappella (1997), for example, found that political sophistication was related to higher argument quality and greater construct differentiation (i.e., number of distinct concepts) about the healthcare debate. Elites, then, not only have greater political knowledge as background, but have more complex political schemas.

Most of the research on political novices, or nonelites, focuses on their lack of elaborate political schemas. Nonelites, then, learn less from news and are not as analytical when encountering political messages. The ELM might suggest that nonelites follow a more peripheral route when encountering political information. There has been little speculation about what sorts of schemas nonelites use, however. An interesting finding drawn from news research suggests that nonelites might simply transfer accessible schemas from daily life to the political context. Price and Czilli (1996) found that human interest and personalized news stories are associated with greater learning, regardless of prior knowledge. Their least knowledgeable respondents (2 standard deviations below the mean) recalled 82% of news stories focusing on people in the news, but only 33% of nonpersonality stories. Graber (1988) suggested that human interest stories are remembered because they easily tap schemas that refer to people's own personal experiences.

Together, these findings illustrate that there are two general kinds of schema that may be reflected in pseudo and public opinion. When forming political opinions, elites may use schemas that have been developed specifically for political information processing and decision making. These schemas are ideologically based, and concern party or political stands or beliefs about political issues (Lau, 1986). Nonelites, on the other hand, may simply transfer schemas that they use every day to the political arena. These schemas most likely deal with political leaders and candidates as persons and as personalities.

MEDIA EFFECTS OF POLITICAL COMMUNICATION AND THE ELM

The elaboration likelihood model and Graber's concepts of public opinion elites and nonelites focus on the importance of two models to explain the effects of political communication. The conditional model suggests that effects will depend on whether audience members are elites or nonelites and whether they follow central or peripheral political information processing. The cognitive model suggests that the schemas that people use affect the effects of political messages. These two models will be applied to help understand a variety of traditional political media effects.

Agenda Setting

Agenda setting is theory about the news media's power to structure the importance of political issues in the public's mind. Quite simply, agenda setting holds that, through gatekeeping, the news media select and highlight certain events, people, and issues. Through repetition and because of consistency across media, the public begins to adopt the news media's agenda and believes that these same events, people, and issues are salient and important.

Even before the seminal Chapel Hill study of the role of the news media in establishing issue salience in undecided voters in the 1968 election (McCombs & Shaw, 1972), the notion of news media as the constructors of social reality was recognized by scholars. Lippmann (1922) speculated that people respond to the pictures of the world that they have in their heads, not to events in the real world. Lazarsfeld and Merton (1948) held that media performed a status-conferral function for society by focusing attention on important people, events, and issues.

Researchers have found a good deal of support for agenda setting. The original 1972 study (McCombs & Shaw, 1972) found a substantial .98 rank-order correlation between amount of news coverage of issues and the rank ordering of those same issues by undecided voters. Since then, support for agenda setting mounted. Dearing and Rogers (1996) listed over a 100 studies confirming the agenda-setting hypothesis. There is strong evidence of a causal connection between news prominence and public salience. Funkhouser (1973a, 1973b) and MacKuen and Coombs (1981) looked at agenda setting over long periods of time. These studies make it clear that media coverage of issues such as urban unrest, the Vietnam war, and drug use, does not always follow real-world indicators. In fact, at times, the news media highlight issues as they become less serious. And, most interesting, the public's beliefs in the importance of issues corresponds more closely to news coverage than to real-world indicators. Experimental manipulations of the evening news (Iyengar & Kinder, 1987; Iyengar, Peters, & Kinder, 1982) reinforced the connection between news coverage and issue salience. When participants watched news reports over the course of a week that highlighted stories about U.S. defense preparedness and pollution, they rated those issues more important than participants who had seen news reports providing only minimal coverage of those issues.

This conceptualization of agenda setting is an effect that can be described by the cumulative model of media effects.[2] Agenda setting is not an effect that occurs after a single exposure to the news. Instead, salience emerges in the public's mind because of consistent coverage of certain issues over a period of time.[3] And, selective exposure to specific newscasts is not relevant to agenda-setting research. There is remarkable consistency in the top stories across most news outlets (e.g., Dearing & Rogers, 1996). Moreover, the agenda-setting effect is limited to certain cognitions. Agenda setting does not claim that the news media shape our opinions or direct our actions about an issue, only that they establish the issue's importance in the minds of the public.

Agenda Setting as a Peripheral Effect.   Considering how central agenda-setting research has been in the study of mass communication effects, it may be interesting to note that it can be characterized as a peripheral effect. That is, issue salience does not depend on careful consideration of the content of news stories. Instead, it is signaled by peripheral cues inherent in news coverage. How is it that we know which stories are the

---

[2]There is a fair amount of research on agenda setting based on the conditional model. Hill (1985), for example, examined the impact of audience demographics (social categories) on agenda setting. McCombs and Weaver (1985) argued that agenda setting was based on an active audience and that people who were higher in "need for orientation" (an individual difference) were more likely to adopt the media agenda. This body of research has found that there are certain conditions that increase the likelihood of agenda setting (see Wanta, 1997). Including these conditions in research designs generally leads to greater variance explained (beyond the impact of news exposure) in agenda-setting effects.

[3]There is no established length of time that it takes for agenda setting to occur. Researchers have found agenda setting effects after time lags as short as 1 week to as long as 9 months (Wanta, 1997). W. Williams (1985) found that the correlations between media and audience agendas remain fairly stable for 3-, 6-, and 9-week time lags. W. Williams (1985) suggested that 3 weeks is the optimal time lag for establishment of the audience agenda; Wanta (1997) accepted 4 weeks.

most important in the news? Quite simply, journalists give simple signs to signal importance. The most important stories are those that are reported at the beginning of a newscast, are placed on the front page, take up the most space in the newspaper or the most time in a newscast. Frequently, journalists alert us to a story's importance by interrupting television programming or by even summarizing "today's top stories." These cues are noticeable and peripheral; they do not affect the information content of the news stories.

Agenda-setting scholars also based their analysis of the media agenda through an analysis of peripheral cues. Most studies determine the most important stories in the news through frequency; researchers simply count the number of stories about an issue as a measure of the media agenda (e.g., Brosius & Kepplinger, 1990; Funkhouser, 1973a, 1973b, Iyengar et al., 1982; McCombs & Shaw, 1972). Others may weigh a news story by its proportion of the total news (e.g., Wanta, 1997). W. Williams (1985) summarized other content analytic measures of news prominence: story placement, headlines, photos, column inches for print media, and videotape and static visuals for television news (see also Watt, Mazza, & Snyder, 1993). All of these are peripheral signals, not central news content.

Additional evidence for agenda setting being a peripheral effect emerges from the study of the kinds of issues that are most easily transferred from the media agenda to the audience agenda. In general, issues can be characterized as *obtrusive*, that is, directly experienced, or unobtrusive, distant from one's daily experiences. Agenda setting seems to be stronger with unobtrusive issues than with obtrusive ones (e.g, Deemers, Craff, Choi, & Pessin, 1989; Iyengar et al., 1982; Watt et al., 1993; Weaver, Graber, M. E. McCombs, & Eyal, 1981; Zucker, 1978). This is easily explained. When issues are obtrusive, or directly experienced, such as inflation, the public does not need the news media to alert them to its importance. But, the less direct experience that they have with an issue, the more they depend on the news media for awareness. So, agenda setting appears to be stronger for less personally involving issues. There is also some limited indication that the politically involved may be less likely to adopt the audience agenda (Iyengar et al., 1982; J. M. McLeod, Becker, & Byrnes, 1974; Weaver et al., 1981; but see McCombs & Weaver, 1985; Wanta, 1997). Just as Graber (1982) described public opinion elites, politically involved elites do not need to rely on the news media for information. Their involvement and interest leads them to use the mass media only as one source of foreground information. They have many other, more direct sources of information. Moreover, their political involvement leads them to establish issue priorities based on their own interests and knowledge. Wanta (1997) explained that the politically involved probably are more active and critical when using the news. The low-involved are those who passively accept the media agenda.

One final bit of evidence suggests that agenda setting arises from the peripheral route: Agenda-setting effects are relatively short term. Without reinforcement from the news, the public's memory about issues decays (Wanta, 1997; Watt et al., 1993). Agenda setting's endurance varies by medium (newspaper's impact seems to last longer, Wanta, 1997) and by issue. This, of course, makes common sense; issues drop from both the media and audience as news coverage brings new issues to prominence.

If agenda setting is a peripheral effect, relatively short term, with its greatest impact on nonelites and strongest for uninvolving issues, what makes it an important media effect? Is the power to structure political reality important for those who are least interested in politics? There are many answers to that question. First, the study of agenda setting alerts us to the power of the news media to highlight certain issues at the expense of coverage of other issues. During the Persian Gulf War, for example, war coverage effectively drowned out the chance for any other issues to reach the public agenda, including the massive increase in cost needed to bail out failed savings and loans. Such an issue might have attracted more media and public attention if we were not focused on the war. As Dearing and Rogers (1996) suggested, the newsworthiness of issues (especially in terms of their conflict) affects media interest in those issues.

Rogers and Dearing (1988) and Dearing and Rogers (1996) also pointed out that although the focus of most agenda-setting research is the causal connection between the media and audience agenda, there is evidence that the media and audience agenda can also have an impact on the policy agenda. That is, agenda setting may have an impact on the actions of legislators and government officials.

Most important to the development of public opinion, agenda setting may ignite political interest and involvement—even in nonelites. The 1984 media coverage of the Ethiopian famine provides a good example of the impact of the media agenda on the development of public opinion and political action. A famine in a distant country on the African continent is usually a story relegated to the back pages of the international news section. But, a dramatic BBC story about the Ethiopian famine (a famine of "biblical" proportions) rebroadcast on the *NBC Nightly News* on October 23, 1984, started a massive relief effort across the Western world. The report was long for network news, about 3½ minutes. It featured the plaintive wails of starving children and grieving parents. It showed the death of a 3-year-old child, the last of her mother's children, from starvation and noted that "it was a good evening, by Korem standards, 37 dead last night."

After this story's broadcast, pictures of starving children were on the covers of news magazines as one part of the dramatic increase in media coverage of Ethiopian famine (Dearing & Rogers, 1996). It seems that everyone wanted to do something to assuage the suffering. The Save the Children foundation was blessed with phone calls and contributions. Rock musicians joined to promote the relief effort, culminating in concerts across the country and a recording, "We Are the World," whose profits were contributed to famine relief. The Ethiopian famine stayed on the media agenda for 10 months (Dearing & Rogers, 1996), but many not normally involved in political matters became, at least for that time, interested and involved.

Petty and Priester (1994) pointed out that what is a peripheral cue for one might be a central cue for another. The BBC news story, although it lasted 3½ minutes, gave relatively little verbal information about the cause of the famine or the organizations behind the relief effort. But, the video and soundtrack offered heart-wrenching visuals and vivid descriptions of the agony and despair of the starving families. For nonelites, these visuals might have been powerful central cues that commanded their attention and stimulated intense affective reactions. Through agenda setting, then, the media may bring issues to public attention and activate elites and nonelites alike. Agenda setting might be a stimulus to bring nonelites to political activity.

Agenda Setting as a Cognitive-Transactional Effect.   Since the 1980s, agenda setting has grown into a theoretical approach to media effects much broader than originally proposed. Scholars have expanded agenda setting to the cognitive–transactional model. According to this model of agenda setting, the media agenda does not merely establish a set of issue priorities in the public; it may also set the criteria that the public use to judge the effectiveness of political leaders. The work of Iyengar and his colleagues (Iyengar & Kinder, 1987; Iyengar et al., 1982; Iyengar & Simon, 1993) has demonstrated that when the news media focus on certain political issues, the public uses the president's performance on those issues as the gauge to how well he is doing his job. For example, in 1988, the economy was an important issue on the media agenda. In 1991, however, the economy was overshadowed by intense coverage of the Persian Gulf crisis. President Reagan's public approval rating in 1998 was more strongly explained by his performance on economic issues than his performance in the arena of international affairs. In 1991, however, the reverse was true for President Bush. His approval rating was more strongly linked to his performance on foreign policy than on the economy (Iyengar & Simon, 1993).[4] President Carter's approval rating was also affected by the media agenda. Iyengar et al. (1982) found that experimental manipulations that inserted stories about defense preparedness into network news coverage led to greater weight being attached to Carter's performance on defense.[5]

A cognitive–transactional model explanation of these effects suggests that when the news media highlight certain issues or events as important, these become salient issues and events to the public. The salience of these issues primes them in the minds of the public. Repeated news coverage repeatedly primes these issues. Moreover, when thoughts have been primed, they are more easily accessed. So, when people are asked to evaluate the president's performance, greater weight is given to his performance on those recently primed issues and events. In a sense, the media agenda sets the criteria for judging the president.

The evidence of agenda setting as priming offers some interesting implications, both theoretical and practical. First, this notion of agenda setting as priming might provide an explanation for rally effects, such as presidential support during times of international crisis (chap. 3). Crises are characterized by intense media coverage. During crises, the media agenda may be consumed by stories about critical events. As

---

[4]Iyengar and Simon's (1993) research may also offer an explanation for Bush's quick decline in approval. Their graph of the public response Gallup poll's question about the most important problem facing the country showed that the Persian Gulf War quickly dropped in importance after the cease fire. Concerns about the economy, which had maintained steady mentions over the year, steeply rose in the public mind. Although Bush could be evaluated very positively with the U.S. success in the Persian Gulf War, his performance on the ailing economy could hardly have been seen by the public as effective. His approval ratings quickly declined. The virtually "unbeatable" president during the Persian Gulf War lost the 1992 election.

[5]These findings might also provide an explanation for Carter's defeat in the 1980 election. The hostage situation in the Iranian embassy was an important issue on the media's agenda at the end of Carter's term. His failure to achieve either a diplomatic or military end to the crisis probably led to his being evaluated quite unfavorably by the public.

that event is placed on the media agenda, it may become the primary criteria for judging how well the president is performing his job. Because much media coverage during times of crisis serves a solidarity-building function, it is most likely favorable to our government. Because the public is dependent on the news media for information about the crises, their sole source of information is favorable. Hence, an increase in the public's approval of the president—a rally effect.

Second, is agenda setting as priming a central or peripheral effect? It too might be characterized as a peripheral effect. Priming is a result of more automatic information processing that responds to environmental stimuli (or salient media content). Nonelites, or those who are less politically interested and knowledgeable, might be more likely to rely on salient media coverage as the basis for evaluating political leaders. The elites, who are more politically involved and aware, might be more likely to rely on more stable criteria, based on their wealth of background knowledge.

Does that mean that agenda setting as priming is not important because it is a peripheral effect? As a conditional effect, the media's agenda setting impact affects people only under certain conditions. The ELM suggests that one of those conditions is political interest and involvement. Although we cannot know the exact proportions, it is clear that the majority of U.S. citizens are not public opinion elites.[6] For nonelites, almost all political issues might be nonobtrusive, so their perceptions about political issues might be easily affected by the media agenda. Moreover, with less interest in politics, nonelites might be easily primed by salient coverage of certain political issues. Also, for nonelites, impressions of political candidates might be based on evaluations drawn from criteria on the media agenda. In the 1992 election, for example, Dan Quayle, Bush's vice president, gave a speech in which he tried to bring "family values" to the media (and public agenda). His strategy boomeranged, but it was not ill advised. Bush's approval ratings had declined since the end of Gulf War. The economy was the issue that was at the top of the public mind, and the economy was not improving. Quayle might have been attempting to replace con-

---

[6]Lau (1986) reported that about 20% to 30% of respondents in 1972 and 1976 representative samples held no political schemas. Another 10% to 21% held schemas that focused, not on issues or ideology, but on personality. The rest of the respondents held schemas that dealt with political issues, political ideology (Republican vs. Democrat), or issues based on the political activities of various groups. It is probably from these groups that elites are drawn. The concerns about growing political apathy since the 1970s certainly suggests that the numbers of politically knowledgeable people are decreasing.

cern for the economy with a concern about family values. This issue was one against which Bush would be evaluated more favorably than his opponent, Bill Clinton. Political messages during elections might be looked at as ways to manipulate and control the media agenda, and so, control the criteria that the large number of nonelites use to judge the effectiveness of candidates. In an election, nonelites' votes count the same as the votes of the elites. If the media can sway a large number of nonelites, this is certainly no meaningless effect.

News Framing

The news media are not limited to merely establishing the salience of certain topics. *News framing* research holds that how the news is presented also affects what people think about issues, people, and events. News framing concerns the structural aspects of news stories—the symbols that are used in constructing the news story. Framing involves selection and emphasis: "To frame is to *select some aspects of a perceived reality and make them more salient in a communicating text, in such a way as to promote a particular problem definition, causal interpretation, moral evaluation, and/or treatment recommendation*" (Entman, 1993, p. 52).[7] So, news stories about the alleged relationship between President Clinton and a former White House intern can be framed many ways: as a story about government corruption, as a story about moral corruption, or as a sex scandal. These different frames can be constructed by journalists through their selection of different story introductions, different details, different video clips, and different story wrap-ups. As Entman (1993) summarized, frames define problems, diagnose causes, make moral judgments, and suggest remedies. Ghanem (1997) further explained that frames embody what is included in the story, the size and placement of details, and affective tone of the presentation. News frames, then, are media content attributes that can be identified through content analysis (e.g., Iyengar & Simon, 1993; Neuman et al., 1992). News frames are characterized by salient media content.

---

[7]Another, colloquial term for a news frame might be a "spin." Political advocates frequently put their own party's "spin" on a fact, story, or event. That means that they are interpreting the fact in a way that is favorable to their own political view. During the Clinton sex scandal, for example, the public was usually treated to two different interpretations (or spins) of the various revelations.

News framing effects go beyond setting an agenda and establishing issue salience. Framing effects involve how people interpret the news and the judgments they form after viewing or reading the news. News framing activates "some ideas, feelings, and values rather than others," and "can encourage particular trains of thought about political phenomena and lead audiences to arrive at more or less predictable conclusions" (Price, Tewksbury, & Powers, 1997, p. 483). News frames can affect political opinions.

News framing effects can be explained by the cognitive model: Salient media content attributes lead to relatively automatic and predictable responses (see Scheufele, 1999). Price and Tewksbury (1997) explained that news frames have effects because of two separate, psychological processes. First, during message reception, salient message elements activate certain thoughts and ideas. Then, because these thoughts and ideas have been recently brought to mind, they are more accessible when people have to make subsequent judgments. Iyengar (1991) termed this framing effect on subsequent judgments "accessibility bias." Ghanem (1997) pointed out that framing effects are related to other theoretical concepts: priming, or the activation of certain schemas, and indexing, or the highlighting of certain arguments over others.

There are some news frames that are used quite commonly (e.g., Iyengar, 1991; Iyengar & Simon, 1993; D. M. McLeod & Hertog, 1992; Neuman et al., 1992). *Episodic framing* involves a focus on the presentation of concrete examples. Episodic framing relies on visuals and individual examples of a larger problem. Episodic framing of poverty, for example, might highlight the plights of individuals in poverty, what brought them there, how they live day to day, or how they use government aid. *Thematic framing* presents an issue in context. It does not focus on individual examples, but on collective experiences and conclusions. Thematic framing is not visually oriented and involves a more abstract presentation. Thematic framing of poverty might present statistics about the prevalence of poverty currently and over time; it might also explain causes of poverty. Other frames identified by researchers are the protest paradigm (D. M. McLeod & Hertog, 1992). The *protest paradigm* is more episodic than thematic. It frames protest stories as battles between police and protestors, and focuses on violence, conflict, and deviance, rather than an explanation of the issues driving the protest.

Framing effects have been identified. There is support for the psychological nature of framing effects. Researchers using thought-listing techniques found that different news stories using different frames about education, crime, and economic issues resulted in different kinds of thoughts about the issue (Price et al., 1997; Valkenburg, Semetko, & de Vresse, 1999). Different news frames activate different cognitive reactions. Episodic and thematic framing of news stories result in different attributions of the causes of social problems and the solutions to their problems (Iyengar, 1991). Episodic framing of poverty in America, for example, led viewers of news stories to hold the poor themselves responsible for their plight and see the cause for poverty as the individual's own kind of (or lack of) education and character.[8] Framing has also been found to be related to the kinds of solutions to political problems that people endorse. Iyengar and Simon (1993) found that episodic framing dominated television news coverage of the Gulf War. During the early months of 1991, television news focused on summaries of the military actions during the air and ground wars at the expense of discussing diplomatic movements. This, of course, is not surprising, because television is a visual medium and episodic framing is visually oriented. The researchers hypothesized that exposure to this episodic framing would be related to endorsing a military, rather than a diplomatic, solution to the conflict. Their hypothesis was supported; exposure to television news was significantly, though modestly, related to endorsing a military solution to the Gulf crisis.

Differently framed news reports of the same political protest had different effects on viewers (D. M. McLeod & Detenber, 1999). Experimental participants viewed one of three news stories that differed in the tone and substance of their coverage of an anarchist protest that resulted in protester–police confrontation. Viewers of the "high status quo bias" story (a frame that presented protesters as a threat to police and to society as a whole) were less likely to support the protesters, less critical of the police, and less likely to attribute widespread support for the protesters' cause. Although research has not been able to link viewing of a single news story to changes in public opinion, there is

---

[8]This finding directly contradicts the folk wisdom of American journalism (Chaffee, 1992). Journalist have traditionally used the examples of specific individuals to dramatize abstract stories, in the belief that individuals' plights would arouse public opinion. Iyengar's (1991) research pointed out that episodic framing leads people to absolve the government from blame for individuals' problems.

concern that negative coverage of political protest might lead to accessible opinions that protest might be deviant, that protest should be contained, and that protest is not an effective method of changing society. This, of course, is troubling to those who see political protest as an expression of free speech, as one basis of our form of government, and as a way to introduce social change (e.g., Gitlin, 1980).

News framing research, then, posits that the structure and content of news stories have short-term effects that may have long-term implications. Directly after watching the news, framing effects are seen in the thoughts and impressions of the audience. These thoughts and impressions may become more accessible and affect more long-term impressions and political opinion. News framing research also suggests that framing effects are rather predictable for two reasons. First, the frames that news organizations employ are rather limited. News values and demands of the medium direct use of a rather limited number of frames (e.g., Iyengar, 1991; Iyengar & Simon, 1993; McLeod & Hertog, 1992; Neuman et al., 1992). Second, because framing effects are explained within the cognitive model, audience response is more automatic and depends on media content.

Are Framing Effects Central or Peripheral?

Within the ELM, framing effects might be described as more peripheral effects. Price and his colleagues (1997) were able to stimulate different effects with the same news substance, framed simply by different introductory and closing paragraphs. Framing elements might be characterized by peripheral cues. Discussions of the protest paradigm suggest that news stories frequently marginalize protest because journalists do not allow the protesters to speak for themselves and do not explain the reasons or ideology driving the protest; so, protests stories may lack central information.

Studies also suggest that political ideology may lead people to resist framing effects. That is, framing seems to have its largest impact on those who are not political partisans (e.g., Iyengar, 1991) or politically involved (e.g., Kinder & Sanders, 1990). Democrats, for example, are more likely to attribute societal causes for poverty, even in the face of episodic news story framing (Iyengar, 1991). News story framing effects are conditional, then, on the political ideology of the viewers; strong partisans are less affected by framing. Another interesting finding was that news viewers with high political interest (e.g., elites) were more affected by thematic framing than by episodic framing (Iyengar, 1991). This suggests that elites might find episodic news stories less relevant because these stories are less likely to offer central information. News framing effects might be characterized as peripheral effects, then, because they are more pronounced among the less partisan, less politically involved—the nonelites.

Spiral of Silence

The *spiral of silence* (Noelle-Neumann, 1991, 1993) is an approach that contends that the mass media are a powerful force, not only in establishing public opinion, but in reducing the number of divergent opinions in a society.[9] The spiral of silence is a theory about the expression of public opinion. This theory has two central elements that contribute to the public expression of political opinion: individuals' fear of isolation and the mass media. According to Noelle-Neumann (1991, 1993), people are essentially passive; one of their main goals is to avoid social isolation. One way to avoid social isolation is to avoid expressing opinions that might be rejected by the dominant groups in society.[10] So, before expressing any political opinion, people monitor the political views expressed in society. There are two main arenas in which people monitor political views. In the interpersonal arena, people are aware of the political views of those with whom they interact. If people see interpersonal support for their political views, they will express them. The second arena is the mass media. Noelle-Neumann (1991, 1993) saw the mass media as a powerful creator of social reality through their coverage of public opinion. The mass media project their construction of the political views in society (which may not be an accurate representation of the majority public opinion). Without interpersonal support for their views, people will not express opinions that diverge from the mainstream—as presented by the media. So, according to the *spi-*

---

[9]Questions about the influence of a scholar's own political beliefs on theory development and testing have been raised about Noelle-Neumann's (1984) spiral of silence (Kepplinger, 1997; Simpson, 1996, 1997).

[10] Noelle-Neumann (1993) based her assertion that fear of isolation was a potent motivating force on research by Asch (1956) and Milgrim (1974). In Asch's study, 76% of research participants yielded to group pressure to agree that lines were the same length when they obviously were not. Milgrim's research focused on the willingness of research participants to inflict pain on someone at the urging of the experimenter. About two-thirds of the participants yielded to the experimenter even in the presence of evidence that the other participant was in pain.

ral of silence, the mass media serve as the representation of the dominant views in society. And, without interpersonal support, people will not express political views that do not conform to media coverage. So, a spiral of silence grows; divergent opinions become less likely to be expressed. The mass media, then, can be quite powerful in establishing public opinion and maintaining social control. Noelle-Neumann's (1993) definition of public opinion reflects the power of social control: "Public opinions are attitudes or behaviors one *must* express in public if one is not to isolate oneself; in areas of controversy or change, public opinions are those attitudes *one* can express without running the danger of isolating oneself" (p. 178).

The spiral of silence is an effect that is best explained by the cumulative effects model. In fact, the spiral of silence is one the theories that alerted media scholars to "the return to the concept of powerful mass media" (Noelle-Neumann, 1973, p. 68). As a cumulative effect, the spiral of silence focuses on the importance of consonant media content. Media coverage of the dominant opinion is consistent across a range of media outlets. Because the approach assumes a passive audience, people's selective actions are not particularly important because people are not likely to seek out divergent media messages in alternative media. And, Noelle-Neumann (1993) assumed that a fear of isolation is fairly constant across people. So, the effects of the spiral of silence arise after cumulative exposure to consistent media depictions of the dominant public opinion.

Noelle-Neumann (1984) reported various polling results that suggest that the spiral of silence can lead to changes in public opinion. In the 1965 German election, for example, reports about voting intentions for one of the two parties were fairly similar over the course of the campaign. But, as the campaign progressed, polls found that an increasing proportion of the German public believed that the Christian Democratic Union (CDU) party would be the victor. The final days of the election saw a swing in voting intentions, as more people moved toward support of the CDU. Despite the neck-and-neck race, the CDU won the election. Polling about support for the death penalty (Noelle-Neumann, 1993) also suggested how perceptions about public opinion can lead to changes in public opinion. As perceived support for the death penalty (perceptions about what *most* people felt about the death penalty) declined in Germany, public opinion supporting the death penalty also declined.

The spiral of silence, however, deals more centrally with political discussion. The notion of public opinion growing out of reasoned search for truth is grounded in valuing free and open discussion. Without discussion, the truth cannot be identified (Siebert, Peterson, & Schramm, 1963). Informed public opinion depends on discussion to crystalize ideas and identify faulty assumptions, data, and logic. Graber (1982) pointed out that informed public opinion can develop only in the "wake of informed discussion" (p. 556). The importance of political discussion is reinforced by news acquisition research that finds that interpersonal discussion about issues in the news is a potent predictor of knowledge about the news (Robinson & Levy, 1986). Knowledge gaps between groups develop, in part, because higher socioeconomic groups tend to have more social contacts for whom knowledge is relevant (Tichenore, Donohue, & Olien, 1970). The stifling of public expression of opinion is an important effect in democratic societies.

There is only limited research support for the spiral of silence. Most of the research has focused on Noelle-Neumann's concept of fear of isolation and found that it is not substantially related to fear of expression opinion. Glynn and J. M. McLeod (1985) tested Noelle-Neumann's assertion that public opinion "hard cores" (those most strongly involved in political issues) would be less affected by fear of isolation and be willing to express minority opinions. The researchers found no support for Noelle-Neumann's hypothesis. Strength of opinion was not related to willingness to engage in political discussions with those who hold other opinions. Salmon and Neuwirth (1990) found that perceptions of public opinion were unrelated to willingness to speak to television reporters about the abortion issue (a highly public type of conversation). Moreover, perceptions of the local opinion climate (with presumably more immediate sanctions for deviance) had no stronger impact on willingness to speak out than perceptions of the national opinion climate. After a metaanalysis of over 100 studies that examined the relationship between fear of isolation and willingness to speak out, Glynn, Hayes, and Shanahan (1997) found no overall support for this aspect of the spiral of silence. Moreover, Kennamer (1990) reminded us of the wealth of theory and research about selectivity processes (i.e., selective exposure, attention, perception, and retention) that argue against Noelle-Neumann's proposal. Through such processes as cognitive dissonance, egocentrism, and psychological projection, people tend to attribute their own opinions to others. That is, people avoid information that conflicts with their own attitudes. When confronted with contrary information, however, they tend to interpret that information in a way so that it does not contradict their own attitudes. So people should not be so swayed by media depictions of public opinion.

There has been relatively little research on the impact of the mass media on peoples' willingness to express minority opinions. United States scholars conclude that U.S. media do not present a consonant and consistent view of the dominant public opinion (e.g., Glynn & J. M. McLeod, 1985). United States media typically may be more even-handed than German media in presenting political issues (Prince & Allen, 1990). But, there may be times when U.S. media do not necessarily represent public opinion accurately. Eveland, D. M. McLeod, and Signorielli (1995) found that people tended to over-estimate support for the Persian Gulf War. In their survey of Delaware respondents during the second and third weeks of the air war, only 46.9% of respondents supported the war. But, 81.4% believed that "most people in the United States support the war." The researchers suggest that the overwhelming supportive war coverage of the U.S. news media (see Dennis et al., 1991; Kaid, Harville, Ballotti, & Wawrzyniak, 1993; Newhagen, 1994) contributed to this "pluralistic ignorance."

It may be that the spiral of silence is a uniquely German theory that does not transfer well to other societies with different media systems (Glynn & J. M. McLeod, 1985; Salmon & Kline, 1985). The United States values free speech and dissent. Fear of isolation might be less important in the United States than freedom of expression. González (1988) noted that the spiral of silence offers no explanation for the 1986 Philippine revolution that ousted the Marcos regime. The Philippine media under the Marcos regime were tightly controlled by allies of the government and presented a highly consonant and consistent view of government support. But, their ubiquity and power were not able to squelch rebellious factions of society. Moreover, there is evidence that people sought out the limited number of alternative newspapers that published alternate views. Different cultural values may limit the scope of the spiral of silence.

Are Effects Central or Peripheral?   The spiral of silence might be characterized as a more peripheral effect. The effect seems to be explained less by the arguments that the media present to support a political view. Instead, the spiral grows out of a kind of "bandwagon" effect. Media coverage implies that a certain view is dominant in society, supported by the majority. So, it is the amount of support that is important to this effect more than the quality of the idea. This may be characterized as a peripheral cue.

There are other indications that the spiral of silence is a peripheral effect; it may have its greatest impact on those who hold pseudo public opinion. Although Noelle-Neumann (1993) argued that, for most part, the effects of the spiral of silence are fairly uniform, she does recognize that there are some groups that fall outside its influence: the hard core and the avant garde. The hard core are the "minority that remains at the end of the spiral of silence process in defiance of the threats of isolation (p. 171). The avant garde are those who do not fear isolation or are willing to pay the price of being isolated. These groups are the knowledgeable and politically involved who introduce new ideas to society or keep nondominant views alive. The spiral of silence, then, might have some aspects of the conditional model. Effects might be conditional on one's political involvement. The politically involved—the public opinion elites—might have a good deal of interpersonal resources, based on their political activity, that provide interpersonal support for their views, even if the media characterize those views as minority views. So, the social relationships of the elite might insulate them from effects of the spiral of silence. Graber (1982) might recognize the hard core and avant garde as public opinion elites. Even without the support of interpersonal networks, these groups might have the inner strength to resist the pull of societal conformity. They too would be less affected by the spiral of silence.

Nonelites, on the other hand, hold only pseudo opinions that are not well grounded in political discussion, social contact, or political activity. Because they use the mass media as both background and foreground information, they may be more likely to be affected by media reports of public opinion. Because their own political opinions are not particularly strong, they may be more likely to be pulled by the "bandwagon" of what the media depict as the dominant political view.

The Effects of Public Opinion Polls

Public opinion polls are ubiquitous and the news media have become the frontrunners in collecting and reporting public opinion poll data (Frankovic, 1998).[11] Polls are the way that the electorate can communi-

---

[11]When President Clinton spoke to the American people at 10:00 p.m. on August 17, 1998, about his extramarital affair, for example, news organizations were reporting poll reactions to his statements by the early morning news.

cate their opinions to politicians and legislators. But, it is clear that polls do more than communicate opinion; they may also shape it.

Several effects of polls have been proposed and researched. K. Lang and G. E. Lang (1984) summarized evidence that polls can have a energizing effect on voters. When people are asked their opinions by pollsters, they become more aware of and interested in an issue. Most research though, has focused on three specific effects: bandwagon effects, underdog effects, and effects on voter turnout.

Both *bandwagon* and *underdog effects* hold that public opinion polls lead to changes in public opinion. Bandwagon effects are shifts in public opinion toward the dominant opinion. That is, when people hear results of public opinion polls that show that the majority hold opinions contrary to their own, people tend to shift their opinion toward the majority. Underdog effects are the opposite of bandwagon effects. Underdog effects are shifts in public opinion toward the minority candidate or opinion. A necessary condition to both bandwagon and underdog effects is awareness of public opinion. With issues or elections that receive a good deal of media coverage, poll reports are widely reported in the media, so awareness of polls is typically quite high (e.g., Lavrakas et al., 1991). Bandwagon effects are found more commonly (see Marsh, 1984, for a summary of that research). In fact, they were found by Lazarsfeld, Berelson, and Gaudet (1968) in their Erie County (Ohio) voting study. Some undecided voters made their voting decision based on Franklin D. Roosevelt's dominance in the polls. But, there has been some evidence of underdog effects as well (e.g., Ceci & Kain, 1982). In fact, John Anderson's surprising third-party showing in the landslide 1980 election was attributed to underdog effects; people voted for him simply because they expected him *not* to win (Tannenbaum, 1986).

There are several theoretical explanations for both bandwagon and underdog effects. The spiral of silence offers one explanation. It holds that bandwagon effects result because people want to avoid social isolation, so they adopt the majority opinion. A cognitive dissonance approach (e.g., Morwitz & Pluzinski, 1996) argued that bandwagon effects are the result of dissonance reduction by voters who support a candidate who is not supported by the majority. So, when people become aware of polls that report that their position is contrary to the majority, they are likely to change their opinion. But, there is an important distinction that differentiates this cognitive dissonance approach from the spiral of silence. There are two conditions that are necessary to produce dissonance. The first is exposure to and awareness of contrary poll information. The second is belief that the poll information is correct. Morwitz and Pluzinski (1996) found that people will not change minds if they believe that their candidate will win, even in the face of contrary polling information. This approach differs from the spiral of silence because it recognizes the impact of selective perception of polls. Henshel and Johnston (1987) quite simply proposed that public opinion polls lead to bandwagon effects indirectly through their impact on campaign contributions, volunteerism, and endorsement. Large contributors, for example, might want to back a winner. Political activists may also monitor the polls to decide the candidate to which they will attach their own careers (also see Traugott, 1992).

Underdog effects have been explained by sympathy, where people vote for the loser because they feel sorry for the candidate. There is also a more rational explanation for underdog effects. Marsh (1984) suggested that underdog effects may be due to a desire to reduce the margin of victory for the winner. So voters may vote for the underdog to limit the confidence and political power of the victor because they fear of what he or she might try to do once elected.

Although there has been little research on how media report polling information on changes in public opinion, students of mass communication effects might want to consider how framing is linked to effects of public opinion polls. Over the past 10 years, tracking polls have become quite popular near the end of presidential elections. *Tracking polls* are daily public opinion measurements, either using a panel of respondents, or a cross section. Tracking polls contribute to "horse race" media coverage of elections because journalists analyze slight shifts in these daily polls reports (Frankovic, 1998). Hickman (1991), for example, reported that some of the smallest gains in polls get the largest media coverage. It is important to remember that even though all reputable media report sampling error in polls, most analysts fail to take sampling error into account in their interpretations of the polls. So statistically nonsignificant shifts in opinion are frequently characterized as "real" shifts. How the news media frame polls reports might have an impact on the effects of those reports. Framing shifts in opinion or voter preference as the result of a candidate's "momentum" (Hickman, 1991), for example, might have a larger bandwagon effect than framing the results as due to other adjustments.

But, bandwagon and underdog effects are not found universally in research. Hickman (1991) pointed out that the effects of public opinion polls on the audience are highly conditional on an individual's orientation, poll awareness, decision-making urgency, trust in polls, and political commitment. Individuals who have a higher orientation toward wanting to support the winner, who are aware of polls and find the information useful, who feel a need to make a decision quickly, place a good deal of credibility in the polls, and are not particularly committed to a candidate or a party are more likely to be affected by polling information. Conversely, those people who are less oriented toward wanting to support the winner (who may base their candidate selection on other criteria), who are not aware of or do not attach too much importance to polls, who make their decisions early in the election or at a more leisurely pace, attribute lower credibility to polls and media coverage of polls, and are politically committed, should be less affected by poll reports.

There is an indication that polls might have their strongest effects on the nonelites. Ceci and Kain (1982) observed that the greatest shifts in candidate preference (both bandwagon and underdog effects) among their experimental participants were among those participants who were not particularly committed to their candidate. Among those who felt strongly about a candidate, there was little shift after exposure to polls. Lavrakas, Holley, and Miller (1991) found both bandwagon and underdog effects in their analysis of the 1988 presidential election. But, these effects occurred almost exclusively in the less educated population. As we have seen, educational level is often a signal for political interest, knowledge, and relevant social contacts. It also signals being more able to follow the central route when considering political messages. The more educated might be more likely to be public opinion elites. Lavrakas et al. (1991) also observed that late deciders (those who made their voting decisions late in the election) were more likely to experience bandwagon and underdog effects. This finding might suggest that these effects are more common among the less knowledgeable and less politically involved—the nonelites. The effects of public opinion polls on public opinion, then, might be characterized as a peripheral effect, and one that is conditional on the political abilities and interest of the individual.

Once again, we should not assume that peripheral effects are not important effects. If less politically sophisticated people are more attentive to mainstream media's presentation of polls, they may be likely to be affected by these reports. Media coverage of the final days of an election campaign especially is filled with reports of tracking polls and election projections. If those less politically sophisticated people vote, they might have a real impact on the election outcome, simply because of their numbers.

Effects of Media Reports of Polling on Voter Turnout

Since the advent of television and more sophisticated polling and projection methods, there have been concerns that reports of election returns on presidential election days might have an impact on election-day voting. This concern exists because the United States covers three time zones (not to mention Alaska and Hawaii). So, television might begin to report election returns and projections while polls in the western part of the country are still open. Those western voters who wait until after work or dinner to vote have probably seen some reports of election returns or exit polls. Although some are concerned about the bandwagon and underdog effects, most scholars and policy researchers are concerned about the impact of election returns on voter turnout. (In fact, Gartner, 1976, believed that bandwagon effects mainly affect turnout, rather than voting; the losing candidate's supporters are less likely to vote.) These writers are concerned that reporting early returns may disenfranchise voters on the west coast and lead them to stay away from the polling booths. Few believe that the number of voters who chose not to vote could affect the outcome of an election (e.g., Lavrakas et al., 1991), but, voter turnoff is a concern in a democracy. Because our system of government is based on participation, citizen participation is valued. Voting is one of the most central and easiest ways to have a say in governance.

This problem was particularly notable in 1980. The election had appeared to be a close one up until the final day of the campaign. Early election returns, however, quickly revealed that Reagan would likely win in a landslide. The first television network named Reagan the winner by 8:15 p.m. EST, while voters in the western states were still voting. There is an indication that many western voters believed that their votes did not count and chose not to vote (Jackson, 1983). Although these votes may not have changed the outcome of the presidential election, there were many other candidates for statewide and local offices, as well as local issues on the ballot. If voters did not vote, they did not participate in elections that touched them even more closely than national offices.

Sudman (1986) explained that people vote when the perceived benefits of voting outweigh the perceived costs. Benefits derive from (a) the
importance of the election (important elections provide more benefits
for voting); (b) the closeness of the election (elections whose outcomes
are more uncertain provides more benefit); and (c) belief in the importance of voting in general. Costs associated with voting include the time
required (including travel time), interference with other activities, and
inconvenience (e.g., having to stand in line). Television reports of early
election returns, the results of exit polls, or election projections influence only the perceptions about the closeness of the election. So, media
reports that suggest that an election is not close should decrease the
benefits of voting and lead to lower turnout. On the other hand, if reports
suggest that an election is closer than earlier thought, these reports can
increase voter turnout. So, in only a few elections should there be a concern about election night reporting affecting voter turnout. Sudman
(1986) believed that only two elections in this half of the century witnessed this effect: the 1960 election between Kennedy and Nixon that
was much closer than expected, and the landslide 1980 between Reagan and Carter that was expected to be a close election (see Table 4.1 for
a summary of presidential voting data.)

This emphasis on close elections might explain the null findings of
much of the research of media effects on voter turnout. In the 1964
Johnson–Goldwater election, both Mendelsohn (1966) and Fuchs
(1966) saw no impact of election reporting on turnout in California,
even though most voters had watched some election returns. Fuchs
also found that there seemed to be few effects in that same election on
turnout for the Nevada senatorial race. Tuchman and Coffin (1971)
studied the 1968 race, but that race between Nixon and Humphrey was
so close that there were no election night projections. The winner
(Nixon) was not declared until the next morning, after western polling
booths had closed. Not surprisingly, the authors found that exposure to
election returns had no effect on either voter turnout or voting choice.

Jackson (1983) identified effects, however, in the 1980 Reagan–Carter
election. This election was expected to be a close one, but early election
returns and results of exit polls quickly revealed that Reagan would be
the overwhelming victor. NBC was the first of the television networks to
declare Reagan the victor and report that Carter was preparing a con-
cession speech at 8:15 p.m. EST, while west coast polls were still open.
Jackson found a decrease in voter turnout among voters who had still
not voted, but had seen election reporting. Based on his data, Jackson

TABLE 4.1
Voter Turnout and Election Results in Presidential Elections: 1960–1996

	Percentage of Votes Cast (Electoral Votes)	Percentage of Registered Votes	Percentage of Voting-Age People
1960		62.8	58.2
Kennedy	49.7 (303)		
Nixon	49.5 (219)		
Byrd	(15)		
1964		64.6	61.9
Johnson	61.1 (486)		
Goldwater	38.5 (52)		
1968		67.9	60.8
Nixon	43.4 (301)		
Humphrey	42.7 (191)		
Wallace	13.5 (46)		
McGovern	37.5 (17)		
1976		69.0	53.6
Carter	50.0 (297)		
Ford	48.0 (240)		
1980		68.7	52.6
Reagan	50.7 (489)		
Carter	41.5 (49)		
Anderson	6.6 (0)		
1984		71.2	53.1
Reagan	58.8 (525)		
Mondale	40.6 (13)		
1988		69.2	50.11
Bush	53.4 (426)		
Dukakis	45.6 (111)		
1992		70.8	55.2
Clinton	43.0 (370)		
Bush	38.0 (168)		
Perot	(0)		
1996		74.4	49.1
Clinton	49.2 (379)		
Dole	40.7 (159)		

(1983) estimated that "total turnout would be expected to drop from 93 percent to 81 percent if everyone who had not voted by 6 p.m. EST heard the projections [Carter's concession] speech, or both" (p. 627).

Several suggestions have been offered over the years to reduce the effect of early election returns, reports of exit polls, and election projections (e.g., Tannenbaum, 1986). Some of the suggestions are based on changing the voting day or the times that polls are open. For example, a uniform poll closing time, which would mean that east coast election polls would stay open until west coast polls close, would lead to later reports of early election returns. Other proposals include establishing longer voting periods, from 24 to 48 hours, to diffuse the impact of election result reporting. Some have suggested that election results not be released to the media and the public until all polls are closed across the country. Still others advocate public boycotts of exit polls or voluntary restraint by the news media. All of these proposals have associated problems, and none has been adopted.

It is important to remember that these effects are quite difficult to identify and, when found, are quite small. These effects, too might be limited to less politically involved voters—the nonelites. Lang and Lang's (1968) suggested that this is a reason for the small effects of election reporting and projections on voter behavior. Only a small number of voters are susceptible to influence. These effects are limited, not only limited to the portion of voters who wait to vote and watch television returns, but who are volatile voters. Those whose votes change easily are typically less politically knowledgeable and involved. And, interestingly, less involved citizens are less likely to watch election returns, so they are less likely to be aware of election night reporting. Lang and Lang (1968) further explained that election night reporting is likely to affect only those who vote based on the utility of their vote in that election. But, voters who decide based on political ideology, dedication to a candidate's cause, or beliefs in the importance of the democratic system are less likely to be affected by television reports of election returns and projections. This effect, then, is a conditional effect; elites are less likely to be influenced by media coverage of election results.

Third Person Effects

There is evidence that there is a good deal of *pluralistic ignorance*, or general unawareness of what others really think and feel (Toch &

Klofas, 1984). One implication of pluralistic ignorance is the spiral of silence; another is *third-person effects* (Davison, 1983). Third-person effects are based on perceptions that others will be more affected by negative media content than oneself.[12] So, people have a tendency to believe that media messages are persuasive and effects are common. But, they also believe that they are immune to this influence themselves. So, people overestimate media's influence on others and underestimate their influence on themselves.

There are two components to third-person effects: perceptual and behavioral. The perceptual component deals with beliefs that others are affected by negative media content. Support for the perceptual component of third-person effects is a robust research finding (Perloff, 1993). For example, people believe that others will be more affected by pornography (Gunther, 1995), political ads (Cohen & Davis, 1991; Rucinski & Salmon, 1990), violent and misogynous rap music (D. M. McLeod, Eveland, & Nathanson, 1997), news coverage about O.J. Simpson's trial (Salwen & Driscoll, 1997), neutral product advertising (Gunther & Thorson, 1992), news coverage of the Israeli–Palestinian conflict (Perloff, 1993), Holocaust-denial advertisements (Price, Tewksbury, & Huang, 1998), media images of slimness (David & Johnson, 1998), and the ABC television miniseries *Amerika* that aired in 1987 (Lasorsa, 1989).

The behavioral component of third-person effects is based on the actions that people endorse, based on their biased perceptions of others. Davison (1983) gave one of the first examples of third-person behavioral effects. During World War II, one part of Japanese propaganda was directed toward African-American soldiers, advocating that they desert. The U.S. military decided to withdraw African-American troops, but not because the soldiers were persuaded by the propaganda. It was their White commanders' fears that the soldiers would be persuaded to do so by the propaganda that led to the troop withdrawal.

This behavioral component of third-person effects makes a good deal of conceptual sense and may account for some of the calls for laws and policy change (such as in the case of election night reporting and exit polls) when so few effects have been identified. The behav-

---

[12]The emphasis on harmful effects due to negative media content is an important one. There has been little research on third-person effects of prosocial media content. Gunther and Thorson (1992), however, were unable to find any third-person effects with public service announcements (PSAs).

ioral component, however, has been less widely supported in recent research. But, third-person effects have been linked to advocating censorship of rap music (D. M. McLeod, Eveland, & Nathanson, 1997), of media violence and pornography (Rojas, Shah, & Faber, 1996), pornography (Gunther, 1995), and restrictions on press coverage of the O. J. Simpson murder trial (Salwen & Driscoll, 1997).

Third-person effects may be linked to a sense of paternalism, or a desire to protect others from harm. Or, they may be due to some desire for self-protection, If, for example, others are more affected by media violence, reducing the amount of violence in the media might lessen the likelihood of becoming a crime victim.[13] Some individual difference and social relationship variables have been offered as explanations for third-person effects. Expertise in a topic has been linked to larger third-person effects (Lasorsa, 1989). Experts may believe that their superior knowledge protects them from influence. Ego involvement, or believing that a topic is personally important, has also been associated with increased third-person effects (Perloff, 1993). As ego involvement increases, one's latitude of acceptance decreases (C. W. Sherif, M. Sherif, & Nebergall, 1965). So, ego-involved people are more likely to perceive media coverage as biased. Their own knowledge and involvement, however, protects them from influence. But, they expect others to be affected by biased media content. From a social relationships perspective, social distance appears to magnify the third-person effect. That is, people who are more similar to the respondent were perceived to be less affected by media content than those who were less similar.

The third-person effect is an interesting way of looking at the effects of public opinion and media content. Third-person effects' impact on perceptions of political opinion and endorsement of political action suggest that it may be an important process in the development of political opinion. It is not clear, however, if third-person effects are best explained by the cumulative effects model or the conditional effects model. The cumulative effect model is supported by the assumption that there is a general tendency for people to believe themselves immune from harmful effects (e.g., Weinstein, 1980; Zuckerman, 1979). But, the introduction of individual difference and social relationship variables suggest that a

---

[13]Research might want to explore third-person explanations for the cultivation effect (Gerbner & Gross, 1976).

more individual-level approach to exploring third-person effects might provide enhanced explanation for the effects.

Effects of Television on the Political Process

There is no doubt that television has had a large impact on our political process, especially on how political leaders are elected. Because political advertisements are so salient during elections, and the history of political campaigns records such notable ads as Tony Schwartz's "Daisy" for the 1964 Johnson presidential campaign,[14] we might be tempted to assume that television's biggest impact might be the effect of political ads on voting. Diamond and Bates (1992), however, believed that political ads rarely have the impact on voting that the campaigns hope for (see also Ansolabehere & Iyengar, 1996). In fact, they restate Berelson's (1948) comment about pretelevision media effects to summarize the effects of political advertisements: "some kinds of communication on some kinds of issues, brought to the attention of some kinds of people under some kinds of conditions, have some kinds of effects" (p. 347). There is a good deal of research that focuses on the effects of televised political advertisements drawn from a range of different theoretical perspectives (e.g., Biocca, 1991). This research focuses, though, on much more than merely voting intention. Other dependent variables include candidate awareness, campaign knowledge, cognitive processing of political ads, and affective reaction to ads and candidates. In all, most of the research suggests that many effects can be explained by the conditional model. Selective exposure, attention, perception, and recall limit or enhance effects of political ads. No political ad campaign can guarantee a candidate's election.

Beyond the effect of television advertising, though, television has been accused of several negative effects on the U.S. election process. These include the decline in political parties, the increased cost of political campaigning, a focus on candidate image over campaign issues, and an increase in citizen apathy.

---

[14]This classic campaign ad was shown on television only once, but has been remembered as a classic example of a negative ad. The black-and-white ad shows a little girl plucking the petals from a daisy, counting as she plucks. Her voice is taken over by a count-down. The image of the girl freezes and is replaced by that of a mushroom cloud explosion of a nuclear bomb. The ad implied that Goldwater might lead the U.S. into nuclear war.

Decline of Political Parties.   Before the age of television, the most substantial predictor of voting was political party. Political parties stood for political ideology and delivered the votes of their members to candidates. Candidates were nominated who adhered to the party platform and were judged electable by the party leaders. Between 1945 and 1974, the percentage of voters who identified themselves as members of political parties remained fairly constant. Since then, though, there has been an increase in the number who call themselves *independents* (Kinder & Sears, 1985; McCubbins, 1992). This is a concern because it may signal that more voters are naive about political issues and philosophy. Although the image exists of the knowledgeable independent carefully weighing campaign information, independents are not necessarily more politically aware. There seem to be two major types of independents: those who are aware of the political stands of the major parties (those, who in surveys are able to identify which political party they are "closer" to) and those who are not. It is this second type of independent who is more likely to be politically ignorant and uninvolved (Kinder & Sears, 1985).

Of course, television certainly allows more voters to observe the candidate and hear his or her stands on the issues. Television now takes the place of the local parties' campaign footwork. Political campaigns are now candidate-centered instead of party-oriented (McCubbins, 1992). By 1984, almost all political party identification signals disappeared from television ads (Kern, 1989). Media consultants have replaced party leaders. As a result, the political information available to the public now focuses less on party platforms and more on the candidate's personal qualifications and character. It is not surprising that since the advent of television, there has been decline in importance of party identification in explaining voting behavior (Campbell, Converse, Miller, & Stokes, 1960). Now, the candidate's personality is the most important influence on voting decisions (Graber, 1993).

Increased Costs.   The introduction of television into political campaigns has increased the cost of getting elected. From 1912 through 1952, the Democratic and Republican parties spent a fairly constant amount per vote in national elections. By 1968, campaign spending per vote had increased threefold, most of that going to pay for television ads (Diamond & Bates, 1992). By 1988, media expenses made up more than 60% of the major parties' campaign budgets (Graber,

1993); in 1972, the Bush campaign spent fully two-thirds of its budget on television. There are two major explanations for this increase. First, television is seen as the only way that candidates can reach a large audience. Most people rely on television for information about campaigns, and television delivers that information better than any other vehicle. Second, the cost of advertising on television continues to increase, despite laws to keep costs down for political candidates.

There are several implications of this increased cost. Only well-funded candidates have a real chance of election to national offices. It is not surprising that a billionaire like Ross Perot was able to mount late, third-party campaigns in 1992 and 1996. Other third-party candidates without large war chests have no real chance for national visibility. In 1996, for example, Ralph Nader was the Green party's candidate for president. Because of limited budgets, his campaigning took place on the WWW. The lack of campaign resources has recursive effects. If candidates do not have the resources to attain a real, national presence, they are excluded from news reports and political debates. So, the general public remains unaware of their platforms and goals.

A second implication of increased campaigning costs because of television is a growing interest in using "free" media to campaign (e.g., R. Davis & Owen, 1998). One goal of political campaigns has been to get as much free news coverage as possible. But, the proliferation of television channels has increased the number of nontraditional media outlets used by politicians to reach the voters. Perot, for example, declared his candidacy on CNN's *Larry King Live*. Bill Clinton visited the *Arsenio Hall Show*. And, MTV hosted candidates during the last election. Although these outlets increase the public's chances to learn about and evaluate candidates, nonnews outlets do not provide journalistic objectivity or scrutiny; candidates are treated more as celebrities. Little explication of political issues emerges from these appearances. Coverage of political issues by nontraditional, or "new" media, may also have some unintended negative effects on the political process. There are some indications that watching television talk shows is linked to greater political cynicism, lower political efficacy, and less likelihood of voting (Hollander, 1994).

Finally, the costs associated with television have led to its careful use. Like product ads, political ads have become shorter and shorter; 30-second ads are now the norm. And, a 30-second ad is not a good forum for political discussion. Issues cannot be discussed. Ads need to rely on inference drawn from short statements associated with ad visuals. Because television is not well suited to providing information in short segments, campaigns rely on television for the impact of its visuals. So, television has been accused of contributing to a focus on candidates' images over campaign issues.

Image Over Issue. Even before television, political insiders were aware that candidates are more than the political party and policy that they represent. Candidates also have personal traits and evoke feelings from the electorate. The importance of the candidate as a person, however, has been magnified by television. Televison has been accused of focusing on the candidate's image rather than the election issues. Image involves the candidate's physical appearance and the public's perceptions about the candidate's character.

It is hard to imagine some of the presidents of the past being elected today. Abraham Lincoln, for example, had a somber appearance. It is said that he grew his beard because it improved his appearance. And, William Taft, who was so overweight that he needed a special, larger bathtub installed in the White House, might have turned off voters in this era of health and fitness. Television makes the physical appearance of a candidate matter to voters. The first televised presidential campaign debate between Kennedy and Nixon in 1960 hammered this home. Nixon, who had been hospitalized before the debate, appeared tired and pale. Kennedy spent the time before the debate preparing at his family's beachfront Florida home. He appeared tanned and rested. Although the debate focused on hard, foreign policy issues, appearance seemed to have a greater impact on the viewers. Kennedy, despite his youth and relative inexperience (compared to Nixon's 8 years as Eisenhower's vice president) left the television studio a viable candidate who looked presidential.

Sabato (1993) argued that television has also instigated a journalistic focus on a candidate's character, especially if there is a character weakness. Sabato sees three eras of journalism since the advent of television. Before 1966, the news media could be characterized as "lapdog" journalism—the news media were often partisan and made few challenges to authority. Private lives of politicians were off limits. Between 1966 and 1974 was an era of "watchdog" journalism, marked by intense investigative reporting and scrutiny of the political process. This era was stimulated by the Vietnam War and the Watergate scandal. The private lives of politicians began to be a concern, but only as they related to the performance of their public duties. But since then, Sabato believes that the U.S. news media can be characterized as "junkyard dog" journalism—using aggressive, intrusive, and often sleazy journalistic practices. This change emerged because of two forces: the desire for increased profits and a loosening of the libel laws. Most news organizations now are owned by media conglomerates, so news divisions are expected to contribute to total profits. The coverage of the Watergate investigation revealed that scandal increased audience size; so, there is an interest in scandal and sensationalism to increase audience size. The fear of being sued for libel was reduced in 1964 by the Supreme Court ruling in *New York Times v. Sullivan*.[15] In this case, the Supreme Court ruled that there was a higher standard for libeling public officials. Libel required "actual malice." In 1967, this criterion was extended to all public figures including sports personalities and entertainers.

Sabato characterizes this era of journalism as a "feeding frenzy," where news organizations relish scandal and look for tears in the fabric of candidates' private lives. Some of the most notable examples are the aborted candidacy of Gary Hart in May, 1987, after it was revealed that he had been violating his marriage vows aboard the boat Monkey Business. The first half of 1998 will be remembered, along with the names Monica Lewinsky and Linda Tripp, and Clinton's presidential speech admitting an "inappropriate" relationship with Lewinsky.

Political Apathy.   Television has been accused of causing increased political apathy in the public. Some of the evidence is circumstantial; the voter turnout has decreased, for the most part, since the involvement of television in political campaigning (see data in Table 4.1) and as the amount spent on televised political ads increases (Diamond & Bates, 1992). Other reasons to link television to political apathy are

---

[15]*Times v. Sullivan* is a landmark case in libel law. A group of anti-segregationists placed a large ad in the March 19, 1960 edition of the *New York Times*. The ad criticized some government officials, including the Montgomery, Alabama Police Commissioner, L. B. Sullivan. Because there were factual errors in the ad, Sullivan sued the *New York Times* for libel. Sullivan won his case and was awarded a half-million dollars by the jury, but the verdict was reversed by the Supreme Court. The Supreme Court ruled that the press enjoyed broad First Amendment protection in criticizing public officials. Because public officials generally enjoy greater access to the media to correct errors, the Supreme Court ruled that public officials can be libeled only when they can demonstrate that the press printed errors out of "actual malice," or with the knowledge that the information is false or with reckless disregard for whether the material is false or not (*Times v. Sullivan*, 1964).

framing effects. Because television simplifies political problems and presents examples, rather than explanation, the audience is more likely to "blame" politicians personally, rather than understand how problems can be remedied (Iyengar, 1991). Increased reliance on public opinion polls in news reports may lead to political apathy because polls reduce complex political issues to simple questions (Frankovic, 1998). The personalization of the news may also contribute to increased political passivity (Price & Czilli, 1996; Rucinski, 1992). As news and campaign coverage becomes more human interest oriented and person centered rather than issue centered, people may develop uninformed and egocentric views of the political world, and, therefore, avoid political participation.

Negative campaigning is not new to the television era,[16] but concern about it has increased, especially after the particularly negative 1988 presidential campaign. There is evidence that ads that attack candidates can be effective, especially for less sophisticated voters. Negative ads might work because they command attention in an ad-cluttered environment and negative emotions tend to be remembered longer (e.g., Newhagen & Reeves, 1991; Pfau & Parrott, 1993). Evidence for concluding that negative ads contribute to political apathy is mixed. Garramone, Atkin, Pinkleton, and Cole (1990) found no connection between watching negative ads and likelihood of voting. Other studies, however, have found that negative ads are linked to lower voter turnout, less political efficacy, and more cynicism (Ansolabehere & Iyengar, 1996).

Television and Peripheral Effects.   Once again, the ELM offers a way to categorize these broad categories of television effects. First, television is not typically the medium of first choice for political elites (Graber, 1982), so its effects might be less pronounced within that group. Nonelites, though, might be more susceptible to the effects of certain peripheral cues, such as a candidate's physical appearance. Because of their lack of political background, political campaigns may be an important source of political information for nonelites. If they want to form attitudes about candidates, they may respond more positively to emotional political ads and be swayed by compelling visuals.

---

[16]Pfau and Parrott (1993) summarized that the history of negative campaigns dates back to the earliest years of the United States—to the campaigns of Jefferson and Adams in 1800.

Candidate character is likely to more relevant to nonelites. Because of their lack of prior knowledge, they probably lack complex and sophisticated political schemas. When confronted with political information, then, nonelites use schemas that are more readily accessible, such as ones they use to judge people they meet everyday (Fiske & Kinder, 1991). So, character and personality become the criteria that they use in the political arena.

For the elites, though, prior knowledge and political involvement may act as powerful selectivity filters, even when they encounter political material on television. Elites may selectively ignore political information, including negative political ads, that attack their preferred candidates.

Once again, we should be careful not to reject these effects of televison simply because they have their greatest impact on the nonelites. Voting in presidential elections is a political activity that is still done by over half of the voting age population. The nonelites among them are no doubt a sizable number. Even if nonelites are not politically involved, they might want to form attitudes about candidates so they can feel comfortable with their vote. So, they may acquire information via the peripheral route that leads them to form attitudes and voting intentions. Even if attitudes formed via the peripheral route are not particularly enduring, they might last just long enough to influence a nonelites vote (e.g, Bowen, 1994). So, within the context of political campaign, short-term peripheral effects could conceivably have an impact on the outcome of an election.

Summary

The arena of political effects of the mass media is the one that first stimulated belief that media effects were limited (Lazarsfeld et al., 1968). But, the range of political effects extends far beyond voting. Public opinion is an important concept that ties together research on news, media coverage of political affairs, political cognitions, and political activity.

The ELM, coupled with Graber's (1982) conception of public opinion elites and nonelites, provide a framework that signals the importance of the conditional model in understanding media effects on public opinion. If we consider only the elites, who use the central route when confronted with political media, media effects might be limited only to knowledge gain and attitude reinforcement. But, change ef-

5

Learning from the Media

Learning is the acquisition of knowledge about a domain. Learning increases understanding about that domain and may enhance the ability to perform a behavior related to that domain. Learning results in (a) cognitions, or increased knowledge; (b) affect, or feelings about a domain; and (c) behaviors, through the acquisition of skills or motivation to act. Learning from the mass media is at the heart of many media effects. Chapter 3 mentioned several political effects that involved learning: information acquisition that influences political attitudes and voting decisions. The next chapters (chaps. 6 & 7) will focus on how children are socialized, including how they learn values and behaviors. Most considerations of media effects imply that, somehow, media content is learned and becomes the basis for knowledge, attitudes, and action.

Mass communication research has been rather slow to develop specific theories that explain how people learn. For those theories, we need to turn to cognitive psychology, because it is the field that most directly focuses on the mental operations that lead to learning. Mass communication research, though, has not ignored explanations for learning. Because of our field's emphasis on different issues, mass communication has taken a different approach to understanding learning from the media. The focus on the functions and responsibilities of the media in democratic societies (e.g., Gurevitch & Blumler, 1990) has directed research on how much people learn from news and which medium is better for learning (e.g., Robinson & Levy, 1986). Concerns about the educational impact of television on children has directed research on children's attention to television (e.g., Levin & Anderson, 1976). Working parallel to cognitive psychology, mass communication researchers made important contributions to understanding how it is that the audience learns media content.

This chapter begins with a discussion of various learning theories drawn from cognitive psychology and mass communication. There are two basic approaches to explaining learning: *active* and *passive* approaches. The active approach is drawn from cognitive psychology. These theories assume that the audience is active and engages in mental activities that result in learning. Active learning theories fall within two models of media effects: the conditional model or the cognitive-transactional model. The active approach holds that learning occurs because people are motivated to learn and mentally engaged in the acquisition of information. The passive approach finds evidence in mass communication research. This approach assumes that people are either unmotivated or unable to learn, so effective messages must be created to attract attention and instill information, without people realizing it. Because the audience is passive, media producers must take the initiative to create media content that attracts attention and can be easily remembered. So, the main focus of the passive approach is media content variables and they fall under the direct and cumulative effects models.

Of course, the reality of learning is a combination of these two approaches. We know that learning is an interaction of both the audience's mental activity and media content. In the college classroom, for example, passive students who are asleep, distracted, or inattentive will not learn the material, no matter how gifted the instructor or how comprehensive the instructional materials. And the most active, talented, interested, and motivated students will find it difficult to learn from an instructor who is disorganized, inarticulate, and vague. It is useful, however, to consider both active and passive approaches separately, because the two approaches place different emphases on different aspects of the learning process.

THEORY: TWO APPROACHES TO LEARNING

Active Models of Learning

Active models consider learning to be "an active, constructive process whereby the learner strategically manages the available cognitive resources to create new knowledge by extracting information from the environment and integrating it with information already stored in memory" (Kozma, 1991, pp. 179-180). There are three different, but related active learning approaches. The *structures* approach sees learning as the movement of information through mental "structures." The *process* approach describes learning as an active process. The *schematic* approach is based on the cognitive model and sees learning as a result of schematic processing.

The Structures Approach

The structures approach sees learning as the result of the movement of information through mental "structures" such as the sensory register, short-term memory, working memory, to long-term memory. These structures are sequential; information must move through them in the order specified in the model. The most complete learning is the result of the movement of information through all the structures to long-term memory. But, all information is not automatically learned; not all information moves through the complete set of structures. Information that does not complete its trip through all the structures is not learned. This is an active approach because movement of information through the structures to long-term memory is due to motivation and ability (similar to the central route of the ELM). Figure 5.1 summarizes the structures approach to learning.

Sensory Register.   Information enters this system through the sensory register (Klatzky, 1980; also called the sensory store, Wyer & Srull, 1986). Information enters as sensory data from each of the five senses (sight, hearing, smell, taste, and touch). These data are held in the same form as they are received by the senses: Sounds are held in the sensory register as auditory patterns; sights are held as visual images. The sensory register is the entryway to the system; learning does not occur in this structure. In fact, humans are not necessarily consciously aware of data in the sensory register because it stores basic impressions of the environment. Data are held in the sensory structure typi-

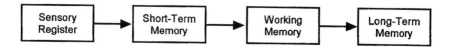

FIG. 5.1.   Structures model of learning.

cally for a very short time. The sensory data decay rapidly unless they move on to the next structure. Incoming data push out older data; in a sense, the sensory register has a self-erasing function. Note that, contrary to popular beliefs, humans do not retain an impression of everything that they encounter. Hypnosis cannot resurrect data lost from the sensory register. Meaningful data in the sensory register is not left to decay; it is converted from its raw form as sense data and moved into the next structure, short-term memory (STM).

Short-Term Memory.   Short-term memory is the state of current consciousness and awareness. Information in STM is what we are currently considering or thinking about. Short-term memory is fleeting; it decays in about 20 to 30 seconds (Brown, 1958). Short-term memory also has a very limited capacity. Humans can retain about 7 (plus or minus 2) bits, or discreet items, in STM (Simon, 1974).[1] As in the sensory register, new information crowds out the old. Humans have learned to compensate for the limits of STM. For example, students know that it is impossible to retain all the instructor's points in a class, so they take notes. In a sense, the notes are records of the information bits in STM. The information needs to be translated to a more permanent record before it decays or is replaced by a new point. If information is meaningful, and if the opportunity is there, the information moves to the next structure, working memory (WM).

Working Memory.   Working memory was originally conceived of as a component of short-term memory, but now cognitive scholars believe that there is a structure, as work space, with two specific functions. First, WM is the structure where information is prepared for long-term memory (Wyer & Srull, 1986). The structures model does not specify the processes that occur, although "rehearsal" is most commonly mentioned as the mental action in WM (J. R. Anderson, 1995; Klatzky, 1980). Another function of WM is to use information retrieved from long-term memory (LTM) in dealing with current stimuli. Working memory holds material from LTM so that we can apply that material to our current situation. The mental activity in WM, then, is conscious,

---

[1]It is possible to manipulate the length of the bits of information to increase the capacity of STM. Kozma (1991, p. 193) uses this example: The seven words "Lincoln, calculus, criminal, address, differential, lawyer, and Gettysburg" can be rearranged to three chunks: Lincoln Gettysburg address, differential calculus, and criminal lawyer.

not automatic. And, while WM is also limited in capacity, the allocation of WM resources and space may be controlled by "the total information load and, in part, by the relevance of the information to immediate processing (Wyer & Srull, 1986, p. 326). So, the displacement of information may be controlled by the individual, by deciding which information to consider. Or, displacement may be automatic, much like the "crowding out" of old information by new in the sensory register and STM. So, WM balances preparation of new information with the use of already learned information. Information can stay in WM indefinitely, as long as it is relevant to current goals. Information, though, can be displaced in working memory; if it has not been adequately prepared and transferred to LTM, it is not completely learned.

Long-Term Memory.   Long-term memory is the structure that stores what is learned. Long-term memory is often conceptualized as an orderly storage space, with no known limit, filled with various bins that hold specific types of information (Wyer & Srull, 1986). Various bins might hold episodic material about specific events, objects, or people. Some bins may hold only *semantic* material, which is the more general material that we have learned that includes the rules about how language operates, or how concepts are interrelated. Information in LTM is learned, but it is not immutable. If it is recalled to WM, it might be changed or adjusted by new information. Episodic information, because it is about specific instances, is more likely to be changed than that in semantic memory, because it is more general.

Long-term memory is usually conceived of as permanent; once something is placed in LTM it is considered to be learned. Forgetting is usually attributed to not being able to locate the correct "storage bin." Forgetting is similar to "losing" a computer file, when we have simply forgotten what "folder" we put it in. So, we might recognize the face of someone that we meet on the street, but not be able to place them, until they remind us that we met at a conference in Chicago. That data cue us to the correct storage bin. So, our memory returns. Other scholars suggest that information can decay in LTM. Evidence that younger people have better episodic memories than older people suggests that these memories in older people have decayed over time (Squire & Slater, 1975). Decay, though, could be mistaken for forgetting due to interference effects (Klatzky, 1980). Multiple associations to the same stimuli are often confused. Psychologists have found that memory for a list of paired words can interfere with prior word-list memories, if the word lists share common elements (J. R. Anderson, 1995). For example, memory for the association "book–blue" could interfere with the prior memory of the association "book–black." Forgetting attributed to age might simply reflect the greater number of associated experiences that people have stored as they live longer. Note that forgetting affects episodic memory, not semantic memory.

The Process Approach

The process approach describes learning as an active process that involves (a) attention (devoting mental energy and effort to information tasks); (b) recognition or categorizing (identifying what the information relates to); and (c) elaboration (rehearsing information, relating it to prior knowledge). Once again, learning is a complicated process done by an active audience. This conceptualization of learning as a process is derived from Craik and Lockhart's (1972) proposal that greater learning is the result of greater "depth" of mental processing. Depth "implies a greater degree of semantic or cognitive analysis" (Craik & Lockhart, 1972, p. 675). Depth is characterized by progression through different "levels" of mental processing. Craik and Lockhart (1972) defined the levels of mental activity generally as sensory analysis, pattern recognition, and stimulus elaboration. Mental structures are not important to this model; mental activities, or processes, are.

Greenwald and Leavitt (1984) built on Craik and Lockhart's ideas to propose that audience's cognitive responses to media content could be conceptualized as mental engagement with the content. Different levels of mental engagement are reflected as sequential cognitive processes that become progressively become more complex. These processes are voluntary attention, recognition, and elaboration (Greenwald & Leavitt, 1984; Perse, 1990c). This approach sees mental processing as an orderly sequence of different processes. Processing is sequentially ordered; the output from one process is the input of the next (Treisman, 1979). For information to be processed at a deeper stage, it must have been processed at all lower stages. The most complete learning occurs after information has been completely processed, after information has been attended to, recognized, and elaborated on.

Voluntary Attention.   Voluntary attention is a mental and perceptual focus on a stimulus in the environment. It is the allocation of mental, conscious effort and cognitive capacity (Kahneman, 1973). It is a readiness to process information. Cognitive capacity is limited, so when we pay attention to something, we have to reduce or eliminate attention to other stimuli. Voluntary attention is the necessary first mental process that precedes learning. Voluntary attention is contrasted with involuntary, or reflexive attention (also called the orienting response). Reflexive attention is involuntary or automatic attention. There are stimuli in our environment that attract attention because they are loud, intense, complex, novel, or threatening (Berlyne, 1960; Watt, 1979). Reflexive attention may lead to voluntary attention. For example, the siren and flashing blue lights of a police vehicle behind us on the freeway attract our attention involuntarily. If the vehicle seems to follow ours, we pay a lot of attention to it, and start to analyze why the police officer is following us. In this case, reflexive attention leads to voluntary attention. Reflexive attention, however, is not a necessary precursor to voluntary attention. Voluntary attention is controlled by the individual and originates with the individual's goals. *Voluntary attention* is a willingness to direct attention to something that we are doing, not something that is happening to us. Once cognitive effort and capacity has been voluntarily applied in voluntary attention, the information is ready for the next cognitive processes, recognition.

Recognition.   After people have paid attention to something and set aside cognitive effort for mental processing, this stage begins information processing. As Greenwald and Leavitt (1984) suggested, recognition is the process that defines the identity of the information. Recognition answers the "what is this?" question. Recognition is a three-part process of analysis, comparison, and decision. Recognition involves separating the stimulus from its context and categorizing it, first, as familiar or unfamiliar. If it is familiar, it is compared to information drawn from long-term memory, to see what it resembles (Klatzky, 1980). It is identified, coded, or labeled, based on that comparison. If, after identification, the information is still relevant, the next stage of mental processing begins.

Elaboration.   Elaboration is the most complex mental process. Elaboration is the integration of the new information into long-term memory; it is necessary for long-term learning. Elaboration involves several mental activities; it relates the new information to existing knowledge and images. The information can be mnemonically linked to similar information, placed in an organizational structure of information, or be associated with mental, affective, and behavioral responses. As elaboration continues, there are several possible outcomes. First, the information can be rejected if it contradicts prior knowledge or values. Second, the new information may be so consistent with prior beliefs and attitudes that it is absorbed without much change to what we already know and believe (a reinforcement effect). Novel information can also involve changes to existing knowledge.

Implications of Different Levels of Processing.   This model, then, sees learning as a result of progressively deeper and more complex cognitive processes. Each process is preceded by a less complex process. And information must move through the less complex processes before it can be processed more deeply. Recognition must be preceded by voluntary attention; elaboration must be preceded by recognition. But more complex processes do not necessarily follow. All information is not learned; all information is not subjected to complex mental processing. Recognition does not necessarily follow voluntary attention and elaboration does not necessarily follow recognition. Once we have paid attention to something, we may be distracted by something else, and never get to recognize the information. Or, once we recognize something as familiar, we may see that it does not interest us, or help us achieve our goal, so we stop processing it.

The Schematic Approach

The schematic approach is drawn from schema theory and firmly based on the cognitive model of media effects. A schema is "a cognitive structure that represents knowledge about a concept or type of stimulus, including its attributes and the relations among those attributes (Fiske & Taylor, 1991, p. 98). This approach to learning holds that schemas are at the heart of understanding information processing and learning. Two processes link schemas and learning: First, preexisting schemas influence what is learned; second, learning also involves the development of new schemas.

The schemas that people already hold affect learning because they affect categorization, perception, and retention (Taylor & Crocker, 1981). Humans try to make sense of their world. When they encounter a stimulus in their environment, they search their minds for what they believe is the appropriate schema to characterize or match the stimulus. The schema that is selected, then, structures how the stimulus is interpreted. Imagine the differences in what we would notice in a friend's apartment, for example, if we visited it with the intent of subletting it instead of simply attending a party there. Schemas direct attention to schema-relevant aspects of the stimulus. Schema-irrelevant aspects tend to be ignored (Hastie, 1981). Schemas affect memory; it is fairly easy to remember schema-consistent information (Taylor & Crocker, 1981). New instances that relate to preexisting schema are easily integrated into that schema and learned. *Learning*, then, is the linkage of new information to pre-existing schemas. Learning new information may alter a schema. As people gain more experience and learn more, their schemas about that domain become more elaborate. It is possible to learn schema-inconsistent information. Fiske and Taylor (1991) explained that memory for schema-inconsistent information can be the result of very thoughtful process, where people attempt to make sense of the inconsistencies. So, they try to think of explanations for the inconsistencies and link those explanations to preexisting schemas. Dealing effectively with inconsistent information, then, might be a sign of expertise in a domain of knowledge, along with larger, more complex schemas that are interlinked to other, related schemas.

This explanation of schematic learning assumes controlled mental processing. That is, the schemas that are activated are selected by the individual. Schematic processing may also be automatic; that is, the schema that is used to evaluate and learn new information may be cued or primed by the stimulus itself. The characterization of the stimulus can be cued by aspects of the stimulus itself. For example, imagine a student who has a research paper due at the end of the semester about the effects of alcohol advertising on underage drinking. When reading *Sport Illustrated* purely for recreation, the student comes across an article about the connections between alcohol advertising and sports promotion. The story most likely will cue the student to use a "research-paper" schema to read that story because it seems relevant to an important task. Once a schema is cued, it operates similarly to those schemas that are selected consciously. Schematic mental processing and learning are based on the schema that is at top of mind.

An important implication of schematic learning is that it is almost impossible to learn information unless there is a schema with which to link it (Graber, 1988). Schemas develop through experience. The more experience that we have with a domain, the more developed the schema about that domain becomes. So, learning something new involves creating a new schema. Students who are taking a class in an entirely new subject recognize how difficult it can be to develop new schemas. Typically, it involves learning a new vocabulary and definitions for a new set of terms. Learning in a new domain often involves searching one's mind to find analogies, or similar examples—a search for a schematic link. A student learning about the properties of radio waves, for example, might look for their similarities to ocean waves. Schemas develop with experience, so as we pay attention, categorize new information, and attach it to developing schemas; we can say that we are learning more about that domain.

Learning, then, is application of schematic processing (see Fig. 5.2). According to this model, what people learn is related to the schema that is activated (either self-activated or primed by the stimulus itself) during exposure. This model explains why learning might be incorrect (if an inappropriate schema is used to understand the information). This model also explains why learning is easier when there is prior

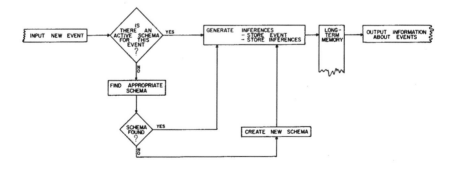

FIG. 5.2.   Schematic information processing. From: Hastie, R. (1981). Schematic principles in human memory. In E. T. Higgins, C. P. Herman, & M. P. Zanna (Eds.), Social cognition: The Ontario Symposium (Vol. 1, pp. 39–88). Hillsdale, NJ: Lawrence Erlbaum Associates, p. 45. Reprinted with permission.

knowledge—because it is easier to attach new information to existing schemas than to create a new schema.

Comparison of the Three Active Approaches

These three approaches describe three different ways to conceptualize learning, but there are several connections among them. All three models recognize that learning is a result of a top–down, or conceptually driven mental activity. Controlled schematic processing, for example, is quite clearly a top–down mental process. People pay attention to and notice aspects of the environment that are consistent with the schemas that they have selected. The structures approach holds that in WM, prior knowledge is selected from LTM for comparison and to aid pattern recognition. The process approach recognizes that the individual's goals direct mental activity (Wyer & Srull, 1986). There are, however, some distinctions between the three models. The structures and automatic schematic models, and the process model, to some extent, all describe learning as initially a bottom-up, or stimulus-driven mental process. That is, the mental activity is stimulated by what we perceive and how we mentally react to stimuli in our environment. So, the structures approach holds that information moves from the sensory register, to STM, to WM, to LTM. In automatic schematic processing, a salient stimuli in the environment cues a schema. In the process model, involuntary attention may lead to deeper mental processes if the stimuli is relevant to the individual.

Together, the three models give a fuller description of how learning occurs. Working memory may be the structure that represents the location for processes in the other approaches. Because WM involves retrieving information from LTM for comparison, it may be the location of schematic priming as well as recognition. Working memory may also be the location of elaboration and schematic learning. Readying information for LTM may involve *elaboration*, or linking the material to prior knowledge. That linkage may involve selecting the appropriate storage bin or schema.

Relevant Variables.   Several audience variables can impact learning via the structures and process approaches. As an active and audience-centered process, learning depends on the amount of effort that the individual is willing and able to put forth to learn. Motivation is a key component of learning. Cognitive scientists have proposed that there is an additional structure that contains the goals that direct the mental processing (the goal specification box, Wyer & Srull, 1986; the executive planner, Kellerman, 1985). An individual's goals direct the flow of information through the structures and control the mental actions in the various structures (Wyer & Srull, 1986). So, greater motivation is associated with greater mental activity that leads to greater learning (Kellerman, 1985).

Another variable associated with motivation is the amount of invested mental effort (AIME; Salomon & Leigh, 1984). Salomon explains that AIME represents beliefs about how easy or difficult it is to learn from a particular medium. When people believe a medium is difficult, they invest more effort and tend to learn more (Salomon, 1983; Salomon & Leigh, 1984). Because AIME is conceptually defined as "the number of nonautomatic mental elaborations applied to a unit of materiel" (Salomon, 1983, p. 42), when people believe that greater AIME is required to learn, they will invest more mental effort.

Variables associated with opportunity to process messages are also relevant to the structures approach. The pace of the presentation of the material can affect processing. If information is presented at a rapid pace, it may exceed the limited space available in STM and information may be lost. The context of information reception may also affect the opportunity to process. If one is in a distracting environment, or trying to pay attention to more than one information source at a time, effort may be divided and information learned incompletely. Television news, for example, is not learned very well by a large part of the audience (Robinson & Levy, 1986); one explanation may be the context of watching news in the household, surrounded by a variety of distracting activities (Rubin & Perse, 1987).

Motivation is also key to the schematic approach to learning. As with the structures and process approaches, strength of motivation is also important. Controlled processing takes mental effort, so greater motivation is associated with that mental effort and learning. The schematic approach also recognizes the importance of the kind of goals or motives that direct mental processing. Garramone (1983), for example, found that different goals for watching televised political advertisements (to form an impression of the candidate or to learn about the candidate's stand on the issues) were related to attention to different aspects of the ads and recall of different information. Perse (1990c) observed that different reasons for watching local news were associated with attention to and elaboration on different types of stories. Researchers conclude that different goals or motives for processing information result in the use of different schemas during message reception; so what is learned is due to the schema that is used.

Because what is learned is dependent on the schema that is used, the schematic approach also recognizes the importance of aspects of the message as priming automatic processing. Certain message elements have priming potential, or salience. Salient message aspects include: (a) prominence, larger objects or objects that are more readily seen, are more likely to prime (e.g., a graphic key in a television newscast); (b) dominance, or dominating the visual field (e.g., an image that is on camera more than any other); (c) significance, or standing out from the field because of bright colors, complexity, novelty, or movement; (d) violation of expectations (e.g., a baby break-dancing when he eats ice cream); and (e) goal-relevance, or perceived utility (Fiske & Taylor, 1991). Salient message elements not only prime related schemas, but also may attract involuntary attention. The discussion of message elements as a source of involuntary attention is presented in depth in the next section that considers passive models of learning.

Implications of Active Approaches for Media Effects.   Together, these three active approaches to learning point out that learning is not necessarily easy. Learning depends on the movement of information, elaborating on information, relating new information to prior knowledge, modifying existing schemas, and creating new schemas. Learning might also be related to following the central route of the elaboration likelihood model (ELM; Petty & Cacioppo, 1986). Learning requires motivation, effort, and opportunity. If any of those are absent, people might fail to learn, or they may learn new material incompletely or incorrectly.

The different approaches have other implications for media effects. First, focused attention is a necessary, but not sufficient condition for learning (Chaffee & Schleuder, 1986; Welch & Watt, 1982). Attention involves a visual (in the case of visual media), audio (in the case of audio and audio-visual media), and mental orientation to the information. Because attention is the entry point for the structures and process models, without attention, there is no possibility of learning. But, the active models all point out that attention is not sufficient for learning. It is merely an important first step that precedes more complex mental processes that result in the transference of information to LTM.

Second, selective attention can be conceptualized as a mental activity within the process model. The recognition stage involves categorizing information, answering the "What is this?" question. Once something has captured our attention, we compare it to previously encountered material, decide if it is relevant to our goals, and continue to process the information if it is relevant, or reject the information and stop processing it if it is not pertinent to our goals. *Attention* can be conceptualized as an intentional scanning for potentially relevant material (Katz, 1968). But recognition acts as the internal gatekeeper that admits or restricts content to further elaboration.

Third, motivation or processing goals are indirectly related to learning (Kellerman, 1985). Researchers who have explored how different motives for using media content are related to learning from the news typically have had only limited success (e.g., Gantz, 1978). These modest findings are due no doubt to ignoring that motivation has its more direct effect on mental processing. Studies have found that seeking surveillance is linked to attention to the news (J. M. McLeod & McDonald, 1985; Perse, 1990c, 1990d). Moreover, surveillance gratifications are also linked to elaborate mental processing of the news (e.g., Perse, 1990b; Rubin & Perse, 1987). Although the effects of increased and differential motivation might be reflected in greater learning, motivation's greatest effect is directly on effort, attention, and depth of elaboration.

The schematic model of learning explains why prior knowledge is associated with greater learning (e.g., Robinson & Levy, 1986). When people already have schemas about a particular news topic, they are more likely to pay attention to stories about that topic and remember information. Graber (1988) suggested that lack of appropriate schemas is an explanation for low levels of news awareness about people and politics in third-world nations. Either people do not remember stories about these topics or their memory is inaccurate and based on simplistic, stereotypical schemas (e.g., African politics are primitive). Schemas facilitate learning from the mass media.

News teasers, or promotional previews for news features, increase memory for stories (Chang, 1998; Schleuder, White, & Cameron, 1993) because they act to prime appropriate schemas so they are ready to use. When news viewers have the appropriate schema already at the top of mind, they are ready to process the news story information. Schleuder and her colleagues (1993) suggested the news directors could act in the public interest by "teasing" stories that have particular importance to insure that viewers will learn vital information.

The kinds of mistakes that people make trying to remember news stories illustrate the impact of errors in schematic processing. Findahl and Höijer (1985) reported on three types of errors in Swedish news watchers' memory for news. News viewers confused the details of two news stories about demonstrations, a peaceful one in a Swedish town and another, more contentious confrontation between protestors and police in Paris. Confusions may grow out of using the same schema to interpret two different news stories, so the details from the stories are intermingled and confused. Swedish news viewers also confused the location of an oil tanker accident. There are two large islands off the Swedish coast, Gotland and Öland. Swedish school children usually learn about these islands as a unit. So, in trying to remember news stories, some viewers overgeneralized, and remembered (incorrectly) that the tanker accident had run aground on Öland, instead of Gotland. Still other news viewers incorrectly remembered that a government organization had granted loans to industry, when they had been granted by a private bank. The researchers suggest that these mistakes were due to prior knowledge about the involvement of government institutions in granting loans.

PASSIVE MODEL OF LEARNING

The *passive model* is based on the assumption that audiences may be unable or unmotivated to acquire new information. So, learning is based on media content that will attract the attention of these inactive audience members. Children, for example, are often considered to be cognitively immature and not able to be self-motivated. So, the development of programs like *Sesame Street* built on research that identified media content elements that attracted the "passive" child audience (e.g., Levin & Anderson, 1976). Television viewing is often considered a passive pastime (e.g., Gerbner & Gross, 1976; Krugman, 1965) or opportunity for relaxation (e.g., Rubin, 1983). So learning from television news might be due more to effective presentation of the news rather than audience self-motivation. This model, then, focuses on passive learning, or learning as result of attention that occurs relatively automatically, "without regard to the *meaning* of the content to the viewer" (Anderson &

Burns, 1991, p. 19). The focus is on media content variables that attract the involuntary attention of the audience.

Formal Features of Television and Children's Attention to Television

Formal features of a medium are the production techniques and elements that are used to convey meaning. In newspapers, for example, formal features involve headline size and placement, photographs or other graphic elements, the use of quotations, and so on. In television, formal features involve visual elements, for the most part, especially the characters that are on screen, the pace of action and shots, the complexity of the screen images, camera angles, and transitions. But, the auditory aspects of television are also relevant because much television "viewing" involves listening to the television while focusing visually on other activity (Anderson & Burns, 1991). Research on the impact of formal features of television and children's learning from educational television programs focuses on identifying the program elements that are associated with children's visual attention—what they look at while they are in a room with the television on. This research is motivated by the assumption that attention is the necessary and crucial prerequisite to learning (Levin & Anderson, 1976; Welch & Watt, 1982). Although learning from television involves more than simply looking at the screen, without attention, learning cannot occur. Studies that have been conducted that vary formal features without varying the nature of the educational material find that program elements that stimulate children's attention lead to greater memory for the material (Bryant, Zillmann, & Brown, 1983; Welch & Watt, 1982).

Studies of the effects of various formal features on children's visual attention to television are based on observations of children while in a room with the television turned on. Children are usually provided toys with which to play, so that the television is not the only object of interest in the room. Then, researchers observe the children, note when their eyes are on the television, and connect visual attention to program elements to identify the formal features associated with visual attention (e.g., Anderson, Alwitt, Lorch, & Levin, 1979; Anderson & Levin, 1976; Levin & Anderson, 1976; Lorch, Anderson, & Levin, 1979; Huston & Wright, 1983; Huston et al., 1981). Children's visual attention to television is usually stimulated by the presence of females, other children, puppets, familiar animals, animation, "funny" voices, dancing, singing, rhyming, repetition, alliteration, sound effects, and the "fade to black."

Various explanations have been offered for the impact of several of these particular formal features on increased attention. Welch and Watt (1982) used information theory (Shannon & Weaver, 1949) as the basis for their study. They explained that simple, more predictable images on the screen are more interesting to children because the children were cognitively immature and unable to mentally process complex inputs. Condry (1989) offered several rationales for the impact of formal features on children's attention to television: (a) Formal features may highlight significant aspects of the content; (b) formal features may convey information about setting and context; (c) they can cue the level of mental effort needed to process the material (e.g., AIME; Salomon & Leigh, 1984); or (d) they can signal the intended audience (e.g., boys vs. girls).

Program Attributes and Learning from the News

People turn overwhelmingly to television for news. Since the early 1960s, people have named television as not only their primary source for news, but also the news medium with the highest credibility (Roper Starch Worldwide, 1995). News awareness is especially important in a representative democracy. Citizens are expected to base their votes for elected officials on knowledge about political issues and candidates views on those issues. And, people are expected to be aware of issues and to inform their elected representatives of their own views. Through its surveillance function and extensive news-gathering resources, the mass media are the conduit through which most people get their news. Research, however, paints a dismal picture of news awareness. Memory for news is usually quite low. Gunter (1985) found that Britains scored less than 50% on a test of news awareness. A U.S. sample understood the main point of only 4.6 out of 14 news stories (Robinson & Levy, 1986). More recently, Robinson and Levy (1996) determined that people remember barely half of the news. Other studies find even more disturbing levels of news ignorance. Stauffer, Frost, and Rybolt (1983) found that people remembered only 1.9 stories of the 13 presented. Neuman (1976) observed that people remembered only one or two news stories from the night before. These findings about news memory have stimulated research designed to ascertain the news production elements that will lead to greater memory for news.

This research offers several generalizations: Visuals can be used effectively to increase news recall. Compared to a "talking head" (visuals that focus on the news reader), including "interesting" video increases memory for the news (Davis & Robinson, 1986; Edwardson, Grooms & Proudlove, 1981) because it is linked to excitement, interest, and curiosity. When pictures are used to illustrate the news, there is greater recall of the story (Brosius et al., 1996). Even graphics seem to increase memory (Edwardson, Kent, & McConnell, 1985). Graber (1990) noted that people remember the visual themes of the news and close-ups of people in the news. But, not all visuals are effective. Redundancy between visuals and verbals in news increases news retention (Reese, 1984). But using nonredundant, or general file footage, does not aid recall (Brosius et al., 1996; Graber, 1990). It also matters what kind of visuals are used. For example, a negative news story is more likely to be remembered (Newhagen & Reeves, 1992), but people tend to forget the stories that precede it (Lang, Newhagen, & Reeves, 1996).

Another generalization drawn from this body of research is that people tend to remember stories about more familiar topics. Domestic news is remembered better than international news (D. K. Davis & Robinson, 1986; Katz et al., 1977). People tend to remember stories about people (Graber, 1990), human interest stories (Davis & Robinson, 1986), and stories that are personalized (Price & Czilli, 1996).

Still other generalizations about news format effectiveness are drawn from classic persuasion research (e.g., Hovland et al., 1957). Story placement in the news affects recall; stories that are either first or last are more likely to be learned than those stories in the middle (Davis & Robinson, 1986). Longer stories are more likely to be remembered than shorter ones (Davis & Robinson, 1986). Repetition (Perloff, Wartella, & Becker, 1982) and recapping increases recall (Bernard & Coldevin, 1985).

Other studies of memory for nonnews content adds knowledge about other message elements associated with learning. When a moving video camera is used, as opposed to using zooms, people recall more of the details of the image. Kipper (1986) commented that the moving camera provides viewers with more information about the image and a greater sense of the environment of the shot. Memory for information on call-in radio programs is greater than memory for the same information in a structured interview format. Andreason (1985) explained that this effect is due to an orienting response to the novelty of hearing a variety of different voices. Most recently, there has been interest in the visual elements of Web-based information that are associated with greater memory. This research found that memory for online stories is greater when both site maps and hyperlinks were present than when they were absent (May, Sundar, & Williams, 1997).

Theoretical Explanations for Passive Learning. Theoretical explanations for the effects of news content variables on learning are based on the impacts of the orienting response and arousal. The *orienting response* is an automatic response to stimuli in the environment that is associated with alertness, attention, and arousal. Orienting responses are involuntary, but they are associated with learning because of their association with attention and arousal. Certain media content features have the ability to stimulate this reaction. Changing visual images, flashing lights, visual complexity, cuts between scenes, camera movement, and object movement on the screen toward the viewer have all been associated with orienting responses in television viewing (Lang, 1990; Reeves et al., 1986). *Arousal* is a physiological response that "intensifies motivated behavior" (Zillmann, 1991, p. 54). Arousal influences learning because it increases attentional capacity (Kahneman, 1973). So, media content associated with arousal (e.g., emotional content, negative video) should be learned better because of increased attention. But, if certain media content demands a lot of attentional capacity (negative news stories or difficult concepts), attention to surrounding content will be impeded and that content will be less likely to be learned (e.g., Newhagen & Reeves, 1992; Thorson & Lang, 1992). The limited capacity of attention explains why nonredundant words and video are associated with lower learning; the need to pay attention to two separate inputs can exceed viewers' ability to pay attention (Lang, 1995). Kozma (1991) built on the limited attentional capacity concept to explain why it may be easier to learn from different media. Certain media facilitate the mental operations that are necessary to learning. Print media, for example, allow greater learning because readers control the pace that the material is presented (see also Wright, 1974). Television's fast pace crowds STM beyond its capacity.

Another explanation for the effectiveness of media content variables is that attention is a learned response to certain features. The orienting response is a "primitive" response that occurs because of novelty, surprise, and threat (Shoemaker, 1996). But, the certain media features may attract attention because people have learned to associate certain features with certain types of content (Anderson & Burns, 1991). Although the orienting response affects even the youngest children, attention due to learned response is not consistent until children have some higher cognitive processes, when they are about 2 ½ years old (Levin & Anderson, 1976). So, Levin and Anderson (1976) speculated that children pay attention to women, as opposed to men, other children, and familiar animals because they have learned that they are socially rewarding. Others explain that children pay attention to certain formal features because they have learned which ones are associated with pleasure (Anderson & Collins, 1988).

Other Passive Approaches to Learning

Krugman (1965) proposed that learning from television is a passive process that involves overlearning repeated content (such as advertisements). Repetition moves familiar content from STM to LTM, which leads to subtle shifts in the relative importance of certain attributes of objects. This learning occurs without much awareness on the part of the audience and it is unique to television. Passive learning occurs during television viewing, according to Krugman, because it is an uninvolving activity in which people make few inferences or personal connections. This sort of learning cannot be readily assessed, but Krugman (1965) argued that it was still important, because it might lead to product purchase based on the salience of product attributes, not on attitudes about the product per se. Krugman's approach might derive a theoretical explanation from schema theory. Through automatic processing of television content, certain schemas might be primed that then influence perceptions about consumer products.

Another approach to learning that marks a more passive approach to media exposure is incidental learning. *Incidental learning* is learning that occurs incidental to another task. That is, incidental learning from television could occur when viewers are watching primarily for entertainment, not to pick up information (e.g., Hawkins & Pingree, 1982). Most scholars believe, however, that incidental learning is not entirely a passive process (e.g., J. R. Anderson, 1995; Eysenck & Keane, 1992). Research that explored incidental learning of word lists revealed that the depth of intensity of mental processing predicted learning, regardless of whether research participants were trying to learn the words or not (Hyde & Jenkins, 1973). Researchers found that participants who were told to rate the words on their "pleasantness" remembered the same number of words as those who were told that their memory for the words would be tested. Participants who were supposed to count the number of "e"s and "g"s in the words, however, learned fewer words than the group who expected to be quizzed. Rating words for pleasantness required participants to consider the words' meaning and associations—a form of elaboration. Other research supports the more active nature of incidental learning. Older adults were more likely to incidentally learn details of a television program that were central to the story (Stokes & Pankowski, 1988). And, incidental learning is higher when the material is meaningful to the learner (McLaughlin, 1965).

CHILDREN'S LEARNING FROM TELEVISION

When are Children Old Enough to Learn from Television?

Chapter 6 of this book will focus on socialization effects of mass communication. Socialization, of course, is based on learning. Concerns about socialization via the mass media usually center on television, because it is a medium that appeals to and can be used by even the youngest children. Observers note that children as young as 6 months old "watch" television (Hollenbeck & Slaby, 1979; Lemish, 1987) and children from 2 to 11 years old watch about 28 hours of television a week (Comstock, 1989). Childhood is a formative time; this is when children acquire knowledge about the social and physical world. Television can be both a negative and positive source for that knowledge. But when are children old enough to learn from television? Research indicates that young children understand very little of what they see on television. Young children's learning from television is limited by their lack of attention to television, their ability to select relevant aspects of the program and to encode them properly, and their lack of understanding of the formal features of the medium and program and plot genres (Collins, 1982; Dorr, 1986). Because learning from television involves selective attention to central program events, orderly mental organization of these events, and inference of information about the implicit relations among the scenes (Collins, 1982), very young children learn very little from television.

Although young children may look at the television screen, the youngest really do not "watch television." Levin and Anderson (1976), for example, observed that 1 year olds spent only about 12% of the time looking at the television while it was turned on. The formal features that are associated with children's attention to the screen have little impact on children's attention until they are about 2.5 years old (Alwit et al., 1980). Children under the age of 6 do not pay attention to and remember much of the central plot information in programs. As a matter of fact, preschool children ignore the plots and notice and remember isolated events in the program (Collins, 1982; Dorr, 1986). It may be that the formal features attract children's attention to incidental program information. Children remember very little of television content—even when the programs are children's programs, like *Sesame Street* (Collins, 1982). Grade school children remember little about television, even though they have watched television for a number of years and learned the "grammar" of the medium (Dorr, 1986). It is not until about grade 8 that children can remember about 90% of what an adult remembers from a television program. Children can have some memory for short segments of television programs, but, as a whole they are not very good with longer programs. Even by age 4, children cannot reorder the central scenes from a 20-minute film (Anderson & Collins, 1988).

There are a few explanations for these limits on young children's memory and learning. First, young children have so little experience with the real world that almost everything that they encounter on television may be novel. All this new information may be too difficult for children to assimilate (Anderson & Collins, 1988). Collins (1982) also explained that younger children tend to "chunk" television programs into small, discrete units based on scene. Older children, on the other hand, chunk by longer segments, unified by a plot element. The smaller in size, yet large number of chunks may tax the capacity of children's STM, so they remember less. Children can also fail to understand television content if they don't have the required real-world background knowledge. For example, a young child would have a difficult time remembering aspects of a story about a "peeping tom" if he or she did not recognize binoculars or understand how they operated.

Morever, this may be why scholars have found few effects of indecent media content on children under the age of 12. Donnerstein, Wilson, and Linz (1992) suggested that because "children do not comprehend basic sexual concepts" they are not likely to understand references to those activities. "Without such an understanding, it is difficult to conceive of any negative effects" (p. 112). Jaglom and Gardner (1981) pointed out other age-related differences in children's understanding of television. Based on a 3-year observation of three children who were initially 2-years old, they noted that young children are quite limited in what they get out of television viewing. Children cannot categorize types of programs until they are about 3 to 4 years old. Even then, programs are grouped mainly by their characters. Two and three-year olds can name individual characters, but character recognition is based mainly on physical appearance. Young children often confuse characters who look alike. By the ages of 3 to 4, children describe characters by what they do, based on their traits and actions. They also notice relationships between characters (e.g., *Sesame Street*'s Bert and Ernie). By the time children are 4 to 5, they can generalize from individual characters to types of characters (e.g., monsters), and offer explanations for characters' actions. Three-year old children do not understand that television is something that is separate from their own lives. They don't recognize that programs are on only at certain times of the day. At age 2, they ignore the screen barrier between the program and themselves and believe that they can interact with and influence the characters in the programs.

These developmental (age) differences in learning from television are made clearer by Piaget's cognitive development theory (Flavell, 1963). Until about age 2, children are seen as in the *sensorimotor stage*. This stage is marked by a lack of reflexive thought—there are no symbolic representations. The child explores objects to learn to distinguish self from the rest of the world. Children may imitate actions that they see, but there is no memory of the action. The next stage (about ages 2 to 7), *preoperational*, involves mental duplication of real-world objects. This stage is marked by "perceptual boundedness," or a rather strict adherence to the physical appearance of a person or object. Most of the limited learning found in prior research occurs in children from this age group. Salience attracts attention and drives learning, because children are not able to think abstractly or think beyond what they see.[2] From

---

[2]Sparks and Cantor (1986) reported an interesting study of one of the effects of this stage of cognitive development. Children in the concrete operational stage were more likely to be frightened of the television program *The Incredible Hulk* (starring Bill Bixby as David Banner and Lou Ferrigno as the Hulk). Because children at the stage are closely tied to physical appearance, they did not understand that, as Dr. Banner changed to the Hulk, his good character remained. When David Banner got upset about some injustice, he was transformed into the Hulk, a green, muscular, angry character. Young children were frightened by the Hulk, even though he was a "good guy," because of his monster-like appearance.

ages 7 to 12, children are in the *concrete operations* stage. In this stage, children can separate appearance from reality. They are also able to perform more elaborate cognitive activities, such as relating what is seen to prior knowledge and drawing inferences. It is around this age that researchers begin to identify children's learning from television. After age 12, children enter the adultlike stage of *formal operations*.

Research on the development of children's memory reinforces the conclusion that young children may learn very little from televison (e.g., Schneider & Pressley, 1997). In general, children have few accessible autobiographical memories until they are about 3 ½ years old. *Infantile amnesia* is a widely accepted phenomenon, even with evidence that children can talk about and verbalize their experiences. This infantile amnesia may have a few explanations. Young children may be more susceptible to task interference when they are encountering the environment. Because it is more difficult for young children to selectively focus their attention, they can be easily distracted by other salient cues. So, children may be distracted from remembering what a television character says by the actions of another character in the same scene. The disruption of short-term memory can lead to less memory. Younger children are more literal and bound to physical appearance, so task interference may be an even greater problem. Young children also do not have the schemas to allow them to categorize events in their lives. So, memory is fragmented and disorganized in long-term memory. So, it is "forgotten" because it is not stored in a meaningful way. There are suggestions that discussions about events with adults aid children's memory development. This dialogue may help children verbalize their experiences as well as help them learn various story schemas. This is consistent with findings about memory for television programs; children's memory for shows/scenes improves when they talk about them with adults (Collins, 1982). But, other conversations about television content may also enhance learning from television. Alexander, Ryan, and Munoz (1984) observed that children discuss television programs while watching with their siblings. The authors suggest that children are quite an active audience and "employ a variety of verbal strategies to create a context for learning in the presence of television" (p. 360).

Although much research has focused on children's episodic memory, schemas appear to be a necessary prerequisite for memory. Schemas are the organizing framework for long-term memory. Schneider and Pressley (1997) summarized some of the research that suggests that even the youngest children have some simple schemas (e.g., they can recognize which household objects belong in the kitchen or the bathroom). But, young children's schemas generally concern events that are common to children's personal experiences, such as eating at a fast food restaurant or going to a birthday party. Because schemas aid memory, it is not surprising that Jaglom and Gardner (1981) observed that children were able to categorize and recognize advertisements earlier than any other media content. Commercials are usually quite simple and those in children's programs deal with events and products with which children have common experiences. Collins (1982) reinforced the importance of schemas in memory for television. Without story schemas, or schemas about television program genres, children answer questions about the order of scenes in programs randomly. Nor can they draw inferences about events that they haven't directly observed.

Meadowcroft and Reeves (1989) supported the importance of story schemas in children's learning from television. Rather than rely solely on age as a surrogate for schema development, the researchers assessed 5- and 8-year old children's story schema skills. Not surprisingly, children with well-developed story schemas tended to be older. The authors concluded that story schemas do not fully develop until age 7. Consistent with expectations, story schemas aided memory for television programs. Moreover, children with well-developed story schemas were able to pay less attention to television, while still learning more. Story schemas not only reduced the processing demands placed on children while watching television, but also directed attention to central (compared to incidental) story information. Story schemas not only give children a "hook" on which to hang information from televison, but also allow them to process the information more efficiently and easily. Collins (1982) concluded that schemas are essential for learning from television. Children need schemas that give them knowledge about the formats of television programs, knowledge about the kinds of stories told, and knowledge about the way that the real world works.

TELEVISION AND ACADEMIC ACHIEVEMENT

Concerns about television's impact on academic achievement have been around as long as television (e.g., Ball, Palmer, & Millward, 1986; Maccoby, 1954; Schramm, Lyle, & Parker, 1961). There is no clear evidence, though, that television viewing negatively affects reading ability or academic success. Studies have found generally only modest connections, if any, between amount of television viewed and various measures of academic achievement (e.g., Anderson & Collins, 1988; Neuman, 1991). Corteen and Williams (1986), for example, observed that, after controlling for intelligence quotient (IQ), younger children in a Canadian town without television scored better on word recognition tests than children in two towns that had television, providing some evidence that television may hinder reading achievement. Fetler (1984) reported that analyses with a large number of school children by the California reading assessment program found an overall negative relationship between amount of television viewing and reading, writing, and math test scores. This negative relationship was stronger for older students and remained significant, even when controlling for the amount of time spent doing homework and reading for pleasure. The greatest decline in academic achievement was with the group of students who watched more than 6 hours of television a day.

Hornik (1978), however, noted that, for the most part, controlling for IQ or socioeconomic status (SES) reduces or eliminates the relationship between television viewing and reading skills. Ritchie, Price, and Roberts (1987) supported this conclusion. The negative relationship between television and reading almost disappeared when other variables were controlled. Still other scholars conclude that the relationship between television viewing and academic achievement is probably curvilinear (Neuman, 1991; Williams, E. H. Haertel, G. D. Haertel, & Walberg, 1982). Watching television 10 hours or less a week is positively related to achievement; watching television for more than 10 hours a week is negatively related to achievement (Potter, 1987).

There are a variety of theoretical explanations for television's negative impact on academic achievement:

1. The passivity hypothesis (Harris, 1994a). This explanation assumes that, because television viewing is a more mentally passive activity than reading, children become mentally lazy and are less willing to invest mental effort on reading and other academic tasks. This hypothesis is supported indirectly by evidence that children believe that television is "easier" than books (Salomon & Leigh, 1984).

2. Some suggest that television weakens children's ability to concentrate, so they cannot do as well at school work. The fast pacing of most children's programming causes children to have shortened attention spans (e.g., Singer, 1980). There is some modest evidence that television viewing is associated with lower levels of task perseverance and higher levels of impulsiveness (Anderson & Collins, 1988), perhaps due to television's impact on arousal (e.g., Zillmann, 1982).

3. Kozma (1991) suggested that ability to extract meaning from a medium affects media use and preference: "The effort required for poor readers to decode the text draws on cognitive resources that would otherwise be used for comprehension, thus increasing the risk of comprehension, or leaning, failure" (p. 183). So, poor readers may spend most of their time reading trying to recognize words and their meanings. This effort detracts from their ability to comprehend the meaning of the text.[3] So, they may avoid reading and, instead turn to television, which they can more easily comprehend.

The most commonly used explanation for a negative relationship between television viewing and academic achievement is the *displacement hypothesis*. This hypothesis assumes that television viewing displaces other activities that are more cognitively beneficial to children. So, Corteen and Williams (1986) expected that television viewing would reduce that amount of time that children spent practicing their reading. So, if children had reading difficulties, television viewing would lead to less fluid and automatic reading.

The displacement hypothesis is not as simple as it sounds, however. Neuman (1991) argued that television viewing will not replace any and all activities, only certain types of activities. First, television displaces functionally similar activities. That is, children will replace television

---

[3]Active learning approaches explain this lack of comprehension. When cognitive resources are being used consciously to recognize the words and compare the words themselves to patterns drawn from LTM, there is little mental capacity left to extract meaning and attach that meaning to knowledge stored in LTM.

for other activities that fill the same needs, but do not do it as well or as conveniently. So, television viewing has been found to displace radio listening and movie going (Mutz, Roberts, & van Vuuren, 1993) as well as comic book reading. Or television may displace marginal activities that are not very important or salient. It may be that children fill more empty parts of the day, while they are "killing time," with television viewing. Neither of these examples should lead directly to reduced academic achievement.

There are several conceptual problems with the displacement hypothesis. First, it assumes that time is spent only on a single activity at a time (Mutz et al., 1993). Most observational studies document that television is often a secondary activity to other tasks (e.g., Bechtel et al., 1972). Television may not displace activities as much as accompany them. The displacement hypothesis also typically assumes that television viewing displaces only enriching activities. Television viewing is not necessarily "worse" than radio listening or movie going, the activities it is most likely to displace (Mutz et al., 1993). And, television viewing may be more mentally enriching than other time fillers, such as solitaire or "hanging out." The California assessment program suggested that the impact of displacement effects depended on what activities television viewing displaced (Fetler, 1984). For high SES groups, there was a negative relationship between television viewing and academic achievement; for low SES groups, there was a positive relationship. As Ritchie and his colleagues (1987) speculated, displacement might be negative when "viewing substitutes for more educationally pertinent conditions or activities (time spent reading, interaction with parents, supportive interpersonal climate, etc.)." Displacement effects might be positive when television "delivers something educationally valuable that would otherwise be missing from the environment (information about the distant world, vocabulary, parasocial interaction)" (p. 312).

Armstrong and his colleagues (Armstrong, 1993; Armstrong et al., 1991; Armstrong & Greenberg, 1990) propose that television's impact on academic achievement occurs through a distraction process. Based on evidence that television often serves as background to homework and reading (e.g, Lyle & Hoffman, 1972; Patton, Stinard, & Routh, 1983), Armstrong argues that television distracts children from their homework and interferes with their learning. Television can easily distract people from other activities while they are viewing by stimulating an orienting response, by competing for attentional capacity, and by interfering with or taking over the mental activities operations needed to learn new information. These distraction effects should be strongest for the viewers of a lot of television, because it is likely that television viewing should more regularly accompany homework. Research has provided some support for the distraction. Background television viewing occupies attentional capacity and reduces achievement on more difficult tasks, such as reading comprehension (Armstrong et al., 1991) and the complex analysis required to complete the Tower of Hanoi puzzle[4] (Armstrong & Greenberg, 1990). There is also evidence that background television may interfere with learning by demanding the same types of mental engagement as some mental tasks, such as visual analysis of geometric figures (Armstrong, 1993).

Armstrong and Greenberg (1990) noted that even these findings might underestimate the effects of background television because they used college undergraduates as their research participants. College students, of course, are typically better students and have already achieved a higher level of academic achievement. Television's distraction effects might be stronger with younger children who have not become habituated to watching television and have less prior knowledge and educational experience.

All of this research suggests that television can be a potentially potent distraction for children who do their homework in front of the television. Armstrong and his colleagues (1991) found that even when their research participants were instructed to ignore the television in the background, almost 70% reported that they found it difficult to do so.

KNOWLEDGE GAPS

The mass media are a source of information for society as a whole. Public communication campaigns use combinations of different media to spread messages to large groups of people. Information disseminated via the mass media is not learned equally by all societal groups, however. One unintended effect of using the mass media to spread information is the development of knowledge gaps. Knowledge gaps are inequities in information, typically based on SES.

Tichenor and his colleagues (1970) do not assert that lower SES groups do not learn, only that low SES groups learn at a slower rate than

---

[4]The Tower of Hanoi is a puzzle made up of a base with three pegs. On one peg is a series of disks, arranged from bottom-up from largest to smallest. The task is to move the "tower" of disks from that peg to another, one disk at a time, without ever placing a larger disk on a smaller one.

high SES groups, so that gaps between the groups grow larger, as more information is spread via the mass media.

> As the infusion of mass media information into a social system increases, segments of the population with higher socioeconomic status tend to acquire this information at a faster rate than the lower status segments, so that the gap in knowledge between these segments tends to increase rather than decrease. (pp. 159–169)

Knowledge gaps are problems for several reasons. Knowledge is power; so gaps in knowledge translate into gaps in power. Public communication campaigns often use the media to publicize information about health and safety, important to almost everyone in society. Knowledge gaps in these areas means that health risks will remain unequally distributed across SES groups.

The case of the television program, *Sesame Street*, illustrates how the mass media can perpetuate gaps, rather than close them. The program was initiated, in part, because children from lower SES groups were unprepared for school, compared to children from higher SES groups. *Sesame Street*'s first goal was to increase children's intellectual and cultural growth (Cook et al., 1975). Its important second goal, however, was to stimulate the intellectual growth of disadvantaged preschoolers. Researchers studying the effectiveness of the program were initially pleased with the results of the program: Children learned letters, numbers, and basic concepts that would prepare them for school. Further inquiry, though, found that children of more educated parents tended to watch the program more regularly and tended to learn more from the program (Cook et al., 1975; Katzman, 1974). So, although there was an overall increase in school preparedness, *Sesame Street* perpetuated the gaps between the advantaged and disadvantaged children.

Tichenor and his colleagues (1970) proposed several explanations for the connection between SES and knowledge gaps. First, SES is associated with education. Higher SES groups tend to be more educated than lower SES groups. With education comes communication skills. The more educated are able to read and comprehend more complex information. Education is associated with background knowledge. When people already have knowledge about a topic, it is easier to understand and assimilate new information. Higher SES groups have more relevant social contacts. So, information has social utility; information is the basis for interpersonal discussion and social rewards. Education and SES both lead to more selective seeking of information from the media.

The media system also contributes to knowledge gaps. Because of the reliance on advertising, news media tend to report stories that appeal to higher, rather than lower SES groups. This tendency is particularly notable with those media that carry the most information, the print media. The media system also favors access to those with more economic resources. The best sources of information are not free. Cable television requires monthly payment, newspapers and magazines are paid for by the issue, and online resources require access to an Internet-connected computer.

Scholars have identified some conditions that may attenuate knowledge gaps (Viswanath & Finnegan, 1996). *Ceiling effects* diminish knowledge gaps (Ettema & Kline, 1977). Ceiling effects occur when knowledge is less complex and limited. So, because knowing the numbers from 1 to 20 is a fairly defined bit of knowledge, eventually all children will learn, and gaps will disappear. Conflict reduces knowledge gaps. When there is conflict about an issue, not only is there increased media publicity about that issue—across a full range of media—but the issue becomes more salient to the public. The associated interest and interpersonal discussion can lead to fewer knowledge gaps (Donohue, Tichenor, & Olien, 1975). News diffusion of vitally important events rarely find awareness gaps (Gaziano, 1985).

Scholars have also found that knowledge gaps can disappear with motivation. That is, individuals from low SES groups can gain knowledge if they see utility in the information and are motivated to acquire it (Ettema & Kline, 1977; Genova & Greenberg, 1979). Individual motivation does appear to close some gaps. Interest in the news has been found to be a stronger predictor of news awareness than education (Genova & Greenberg, 1979). Chew and Palmer (1994) found that people more concerned about food and fitness learned more nutritional information from the television program, *Eat Smart*. Interest was more strongly linked to knowledge than education. Research on *Sesame Street* also suggests that motivation can reduce gaps. Even though Katzman (1974) found overall evidence of knowledge gaps, he observed that knowledge gaps closed for the heaviest viewers of *Sesame Street*. Although interest in the program was not directly assessed, it might be that children who had parents most interested in the program watched it more and learned from it.

The evidence for the influence of motivation is not universal, however. A study of 3,700 people who volunteered to complete a home-based learning project designed to teach diet-related cancer risk reduction strategies (e.g., food shopping and preparation skills), found that this group was a highly motivated group who felt at risk for cancer (Viswanath, Kahn, Finnegan, Hertog, & Potter, 1993). This group did learn more than a control group of unmotivated people in the general population. Knowledge gaps between education and less education, however, persisted. D. M. McLeod and Perse (1994) also noted that SES is still a potent predictor of public affairs knowledge gaps because it is linked to several motivation variables. That is, SES is linked to political interest and a desire to acquire information from both television and newspaper news reports.

Concerns about knowledge gaps continue with changes to the media environment. Children, especially, might be the victims of knowledge gaps with the increase of outlets offering children's programming. An initial study found that children with access to only broadcast television had the least diversity and variety of programming available (Wartella, Heintz, Aidman, & Mazzarella, 1990). Cable and videocassette recorders increased diversity and variety. Because cable and VCRs require extra cost, access to children's programming may be limited by SES. The growth of the World Wide Web (WWW) as a source for news and information drives other concerns about knowledge gaps. Access to online newspapers, discussion forums, and general and specific information may be limited to those who can afford the hardware and who have knowledge to operate the software and navigate the Web. Education and SES affect access to and ability to use the WWW.

Closing knowledge gaps is certainly not an easy task. Research offers some suggestions to developers of public communication campaigns. Perhaps knowledge gaps could be reduced by planning a series of campaigns, each designed to teach fairly discrete and specific bits of knowledge. Ceiling effects could limit knowledge gaps. Campaign designers should also consider ways to increase motivation and interest in the target audience before disseminating information. Increased interest and motivation may also close gaps. But, problems of access and ability offer special problems that need to be addressed by public policy. The costs and benefits to society in creating equal access to information need to be assessed.

Summary

Learning from the mass media occurs the same way that we learn from other sources. Learning involves both active and passive processes. People learn more completely when they are mentally engaged in learning, by devoting attention to the information, relating it to prior knowledge, and integrating it into mental frameworks. Learning can be stimulated by aspects of the message. Certain message elements can lead to involuntary attention, which might lead to mental engagement if the material is interesting or important.

Active approaches to learning from the media include both conditional and cognitive models. Learning from different media may be conditional on aspects of the audience, such as prior knowledge, age, and cognitive abilities. Learning involves creating new schemas or linking newly encountered information to existing schemas. Passive approaches are more media content centered. The focus is on using media content to attract the involuntary attention of the audience. Weather alerts, for example, use an annoying sound that attracts the inattentive television viewer. Passive approaches also suggest media content that will focus on things that people are interested in—such as sex appeal, celebrities, and so on. This media content centered approach assumes that people need to be pushed to pay attention to media content. Of course, attention is not the only aspect of learning, but it is a prerequisite; once attention is attracted, perhaps more active processes might come into place.

Concerns about the negative impacts of the mass media on learning can be explained by various learning approaches. Children may be hampered in their ability to learn from television, for example, because they have not developed the necessary cognitive skills to learn or the mental organization to store the knowledge. Academic achievement might be limited by television viewing, if heavy viewers try to do homework while watching television. Television can distract children from homework and reduce mental capacity needed to complete certain kinds of mental tasks.

It is clear that prior knowledge and motivation to learn increase learning throughout all groups in society. Knowledge gaps, though, also involve variables that are not under the control of the individual. Societal structure affects the cost of and access to information. For that reason, communication policy needs to address ways to close knowledge gaps.

6

Socialization Effects

Through their socialization function, the mass media teach and reinforce societal values. Because *socialization* involves learning the values and norms of society, for the most part, socialization occurs mainly at certain times of people's lives. Children, because they have had few life experiences, are the main target for socializing messages. But, socialization occurs whenever people enter a new life stage or try a new life style. Adolescence is a period of socialization as children grow to adulthood and experience new freedoms, new relationships, and new responsibilities. Even adults undergo socialization. Newly arrived immigrants, for example, need to be socialized to a new culture and society. When people begin new jobs, they often need to be socialized to the corporate culture of their workplace. This chapter builds on chapter 5, because socialization involves learning the ways, rules, and norms of society.

It is important to remember that the mass media are only one of several sources of socialization. Other societal institutions, such as the family, peer groups, school, and church can offer more immediate and personal socialization. The mass media, though, are easily accessible and attended to by large groups of people. For the youngest children, most concerns about negative effects focus on television because it is the medium that most children use and because it is viewed in the home and requires only limited skills to watch and understand. Young children (from 2 to 11) watch a good deal of television (just over 22 hours per week), compared to older children and adults (Nielsen Media Research, 1998). And although children's programming fills Saturday morning, almost 90% of their viewing takes place at some other time. A little over 20% of children's viewing occurs during weeknight prime time (8:00 to 11:00 p.m.). Children adopt the role models of the media. They imitate the way television characters dress and do their hair; they want lunch boxes and Halloween costumes emblazoned with their favorite television characters. Coupled with the realization that some children have limited social contact with other societal institutions, there is a good deal of concern about television's potential negative effects on children's knowledge about society.

ACQUISITION OF STEREOTYPES

Stereotypes are beliefs that hold that all members of a group share "the same set of characteristics, attitudes, or life conditions" (Liebert & Sprafkin, 1988, p. 189). Stereotypes are simplistic representations of social groups that deny any diversity among members of the same group. In most cases, stereotypes are negative and limiting. Children may be at risk of being exposed to stereotypes as they watch television because television is replete with stereotyped representations of social groups. Television programs rely on stereotypes because, as a business, they need to attract a large audience, so they must present content that is easily understood by a wide range of people, young and old, educated and uneducated. Much television viewing grows out of a need for relaxation (e.g., Rubin, 1981a), so content is generally not intellectually challenging. Time limitations of television programs also dictate that character development and identification be rather straightforward. There is not time for subtlety or nuances in characters in programs whose plots must be completed in 30 or 60 minutes (less time for commercials). So, producers rely on stereotypes to present easily understood and identified character types. Even television news relies on stereotypes, because producers need to illustrate news stories with representative examples (Linn, 1996).

Over the years, content analyses have found that television is filled with stereotyped images of women, minorities, and the elderly. Although these studies illustrate that stereotypical content of television has been remarkably stable over the past years (e.g., Signorielli, 1990b), there are signs that television is beginning to include more examples of nonstereotypic characters (e.g., Gray, 1989; Reep & Dambrot, 1987). But, current changes in television content do not erase concerns about stereotypes in programs that children watch because television programming has a long life in syndication. Programs created in the 1950s, 1960s, 1970s, and 1980s are still aired regularly. Many of these programs are considered "wholesome" because they contain little sex, but they are often filled with outdated stereotypes.

Stereotypes of Women

It is clear that there are strong, nontraditional female characters on television (e.g., Reep & Dambrot, 1987), but the overwhelming pattern is one of underrepresentation and traditional female images. Females are outnumbered by males by about 2 to 1 on prime-time television programs. On children's programs, there are even fewer female characters; males outnumber females 4 to 1 (Signorielli, 1993; Thompson & Zerbinos, 1995).[1] News programs also underrepresent women. A 1993 *Working Woman* analysis found that only 25% of television interviews involved females and 14% of the news was reported by females ("News Flash," 1993). Only on daytime soap operas do female characters reach parity with male characters.

When women characters appear, they are usually younger than males and are more often shown in home, family, and romantic contexts. Family and career do not mix on television; fewer than 30% of married female characters on television are employed compared to about one-half of real world married women (Signorielli, 1993). When women characters have careers and family, the programs usually focus on their home lives (e.g., Clair Huxtable of *Cosby* and Elise Keaton of *Family Ties*). Even on family oriented television programs, mothers are rarely dominant characters (Wartella, 1980). Fathers or even children are usually the most important characters. The family context also seems to restrict the mother characters' range of behaviors. Mothers, in family oriented programs, tend to show concern, and generally act as caretaker and as a source of emotional support. Female cartoon characters are usually more helpless than male characters; they ask for advice more, serve others, and show less cleverness and

---

[1]Some of the most popular and enduring children's programs over the years have underrepresented women. How many female muppets are main characters on *Sesame Street*? How many female characters were on *The Smurfs*?

ingenuity (Thompson & Zerbinos, 1995). On all programs but daytime serials, women tend to be employed in more traditional female occupations, such as nurses and secretaries (Signorielli, 1993). Because males so outnumber women, gender occupational roles on television do not reflect real-world distributions; for example, teachers on television tend to be males.

Even commercials reinforce these patterns of images. Although women are not underrepresented in commercials, they are typically subservient to men. Males are the announcers, spokespersons, and "voices of authority," even in commercials for products that women buy and use. Commercials on Saturday morning children's programming reveal gender stereotyping. Boys in commercials are seen more often, they have more dominant roles in commercials, and are more active. Girls, on the other hand, are shyer, "giggly," and less central to the ads (Browne, 1998).

The stereotype of women presented on television, then, is that women should be in the background, even in the family context. Women are valued for youth, attractiveness, and filling traditional roles. There is a good deal of research that connects television viewing to children's learning these gender-role stereotypes. With samples of children as young as 3 years old, several researchers have found that heavier viewers of television are more likely to endorse traditional, stereotypic gender role statements (e.g., Beuf, 1974; Durkin, 1985; McGhee & Frueh, 1980; Morgan, 1987). Metaanalysis of this body of literature concludes that television has an overall effect of $r = .101$ on holding gender-role stereotypes across all age groups (Herrett- Skjellum & Allen, 1996). Among children under 3, the average correlation between amount of television and holding gender-role stereotypes is $r = .33$; for children from age 6 to 10, the average correlation is $r = .16$.

Stereotypes of the Elderly

Although the cohort of adults over the age of 55 is growing steadily, they are a group that has been consistently underrepresented on television. Analyses of 1990 prime-time television programs reveal that there have been few improvements in images of the older adult population (J. D. Robinson & Skill, 1995). Even though about 12.5% of the U.S. population is over the age of 64 (U.S. Bureau of the Census, 1990), only 2.8% of 1,228 characters were over 64. And, contrary to census figures, older men outnumber older women on television. The authors conclude that there have been no real changes in representation of the older adult population since studies of the 1970s. When older characters are presented on television, they are more likely to be comic and treated disrespectfully (Bishop & Krause, 1984; Gerbner, Gross, Signorielli, & Morgan, 1980) and rarely are seen in a romantic context (Harris & Feinberg, 1977).

There is very little research on how television viewing affects children's views of older adults. There is modest evidence that television may imprint stereotypes on heavy viewing children. Gerbner and his colleagues (1980) found that viewers who watch a lot of television were more likely to hold negative views of the elderly. The association was even stronger with younger persons who watch a lot of television. They also report that heavy viewing from grade 6 to grade 9 was more likely to estimate that people became "old" when they were age 51; light viewers estimated "old" at age 57. These effects might be limited because so many children do have so many real-life experiences with older family members and neighbors and because images of older adults may becoming more positive (e.g., Roy & Harwood, 1997).

Stereotypes of Racial–Ethnic Groups

Content analyses reveal that television's portrayal of racial–ethnic groups is limited. Perhaps the greatest amount of research has focused on the presentation of African Americans on television. It wasn't until the 1980s that African Americans began to be portrayed on television in about the same proportion as they are part of the U.S. population (Gerbner, Gross, Morgan, & Signorielli, 1982). Before then, African Americans were underrepresented and allowed to fill only a small range of roles. The early years of television especially point out the limited depictions of African Americans. Early television shows included *Beulah*, about a white household with a black maid, *The Jack Benny Show*, which featured Rochester as Benny's humorous valet, and *Amos 'n Andy*, a show where the only regularly employed character, Amos, was rarely seen. By the 1980s, though, African Americans were presented in a greater range of nonstereotyped occupations.

Now, most concerns about the images of African Americans on television focus on the roles in which they are seen. Gerbner and Signorielli (1979) noted that African Americans were more likely to be characters in situation comedies than in dramas. This trend has not changed. Prime-time television is segregated; sitcoms either have White or Black casts.[2] In the 1994 television season, for example, less than 20% of the five network's sitcoms had racially mixed casts (Storm, 1996). The National Association for the Advancement of Colored People (NAACP) charged that none of the 26 new shows in the 1999 television season featured a minority in a leading or starring role ("NAACP blasts TV networks," 1999).[3] Because African Americans are so commonly seen in comic settings, some writers are concerned that there is a recurrence of the buffoon stereotype of the minstrel show era reminiscent of the *Amos 'n' Andy* and the J. J. character of *Good Times* (Hammer, 1992; MacDonald, 1983). African Americans are also rarely seen in romantic contexts. Although soap operas highlight romance and sex, only 11.6% of intimate serial scenes showed African American couples (Bramlett-Solomon & Farwell, 1997). Sports programming also reinforced some stereotypes of African Americans. A content analysis of sports commentary found that announcers were more likely to mention the cognitive abilities of white football players but were more likely to comment on the physical abilities of African American players. Commentators used animal nicknames only for African American players. And, when announcers made disparaging comments about the cognitive abilities or character of a player, in all cases they were directed toward African American football players (Rada, 1997).

In general, television is not very culturally diverse. Based on a content analysis of Saturday morning television in 1992, Greenberg and Brand (1993) concluded that only NBC had programs that featured any racial–ethnic characters in major roles. Of the 20 shows on network children's prime-time television, three featured regular racial–ethnic characters. But, all regularly appearing racial–ethnic characters were Af-

---

[2]Television audiences are also segregated. *Seinfeld*'s popularity among white audiences was not shared by African American viewers. One reason might be the cavalier treatment of racial–ethnic characters. An African American security guard gets fired when he falls asleep in the chair George insisted on providing for the guard. Kramer burned John Paul, an African American marathon runner. Jerry first destroys the business of Babu, a Pakistani, and then causes him to be deported. Kramer burns a Puerto Rican Flag. In the 1994 season, *Seinfeld* was the most popular television program among White viewers. Among African American viewers, however, *Seinfeld* was ranked 118 out of 148 shows. The most popular program among African Americans was *Living Single* (Storm, 1994).

[3]Since that accusation, the major networks added some minority characters to the programs and pledged to increase diversity in their programming, program creation and writing, in their internship and training programs.

rican American. In 10.5 hours of programming, there was only one Hispanic character, no Asian Americans, and no Native Americans. Moreover, all featured minority characters were male. Greenberg and Brand (1993) did find, however, more racial diversity in the commercials than in the programs. But, except for a very few exceptions, almost all the nonwhite faces were African American. Once again, there were few Asians, Hispanics, or Native Americans. By contrast, the researchers found that Public Broadcasting System's (PBS) children's programs "yield a rich and broad array of cultural variability" (Greenberg & Brand, 1993, p. 141). All racial groups were integral to these children's programs and plots and characterizations were rarely stereotypic.

Beyond African Americans, other racial–ethnic groups are absent from television. Hispanic characters are relegated to the Spanish-language media and cable channels (Subervi-Vélez & Colsant, 1993). Native Americans, since the cancellation of *Northern Exposure* and the waning of the western drama, are rare occurrences on television (Geiogamah & Pavel, 1993). The short-lived *All-American Girl* in 1994 marked the first series to highlight an Asian family. Since its cancellation, there have been very few Asian characters on television.

Graves (1996) summarized recent research that reinforces the lack of racial–ethnic diversity on television: Just over 1% of characters are Asian and barely 1% were Hispanic. Asians and Hispanics are even less common in commercials. Native Americans are rarely seen. When they are on television, Hispanics are rarely featured characters, but they are twice as likely as African Americans to be presented negatively and be cast as delinquents and criminals. Compared to European Americans, Hispanics are three times as likely to be criminals; Asians and African Americans were two times as likely to be criminals.

One group is almost consistently presented negatively on television: Arabs or Middle Easterners. Shaheen (1984) reported that there are only a few images of Arabs on television: as terrorists, as wealthy, amoral and frivolous oil sheiks, or as villains (usually in children's programs). Except for belly dancers or harem dwellers, Arab women are nonexistent.

There are two kinds of potential effects of stereotyped media images of racial–ethnic groups: the creation of stereotypes and prejudice among nongroup members and negative effects on the children of racial–ethnic groups. Children are aware of stereotyped depictions of racial–ethnic groups. A survey of 1,200 children, age 10 to age 17, found that children associate White characters on television with "having lots of money," "being well-educated," "being leaders," "doing well in school," and "being intelligent." Minority characters are described as "breaking the law," "having a hard time financially," "being lazy," and "acting goofy" (Children Now, 1998). There is some limited evidence that children adopt these stereotypes as their own, especially if they are dependent on television for information about racial–ethnic groups (e.g., Greenberg, 1972). D. M. Zuckerman, Singer, and Singer (1980) found that White children with negative stereotyped attitudes of African Americans watched more violent television shows. This may be due, perhaps, to the images presented of African Americans as lawbreakers in those programs. Lawrence (1991) observed that White children interpreted the actions of African American characters more negatively than the same actions of White characters in drawings of ambiguous social scenarios. Evidence of the positive effects of counterstereotypes is stronger. Atkin, Greenberg, and McDermott (1983) found that White children who watched television programs with African American characters were more likely to believe that African Americans filled a greater variety of different roles in real world. But, despite speculation that television's images of African Americans would convey ideas that society does not place much value in African Americans (e.g., Powell, 1982), research has not found television viewing associated with negative effects on African American children. Stroman (1986), for example, found that television viewing was positively associated with self-esteem in African American children, especially for girls. She suggested that African American children's positive feelings toward African American characters in television shows might explain television's positive impact on self-esteem.

The ability of television to affect stereotypes is most strongly shown through the effects of counterstereotypes. Liebert and Sprafkin (1988) reported that cartoons that present positive attributes of African American characters (e.g., Bill Cosby and the Harlem Globetrotters) were associated with positive attitudes in White child viewers. When preschool children watched a positive presentation of interracial play on *Sesame Street*, they were more likely to play with children of different racial–ethnic groups (Gorn, Goldberg, & Kanungo, 1976).

Effects of Media Stereotypes

Stereotypes are sets of "generalized beliefs about a group that are widely held within a particular culture" (Hummert et al., 1995, p. 106). That is, stereotypes are sets beliefs held and recognized by large groups of people. Although we may not accept them as universal truths or behave as a result of them, we all recognize certain stereotypes. For example, if I said that I was going to visit my brother's child, who was attending college on a basketball scholarship, drove a pick-up truck, and liked to go hunting, you would probably conclude that it was my nephew, who came from a rural town. Stereotypes are not idiosyncratic; they are socially shared. In fact, there are only a limited number of stereotypes about any group in a culture. Hummert et al., (1995) summarized the various stereotypes that exist in the United States about the elderly: three positive (golden ager, perfect grandparent, John Wayne conservative) and four negative stereotypes (severely impaired, despondent, recluse, and shrew and/or curmudgeon). Some stereotypes may cut across cultures. Gender-role stereotypes in the United States and Australia, for example, are quite similar (Browne, 1998). Self-presentation behaviors, such as shyness and dominance, are fairly consistently gender-stereotyped in most cultures (Browne, 1998).

Stereotypes are not inherently good or bad, even though the term itself carries negative connotations. The stereotype of Asian high-school students scoring high on the math section of the Scholastic Aptitude Test (SAT) is certainly not negative. The stereotype of a traditional female is not negative: Being maternal, loving, and good with children are all positive traits. But, stereotypes can be negative, because they are limiting. When people violate stereotypical expectations, they are likely to be evaluated negatively (Mandler, 1982). The Asian high school student who does not excel in math or the woman who decides to give up custody of her child may all suffer from violating a stereotype. Hansen (1989), for example, found that women who conformed to stereotypes were rated more positively than women who violated stereotypes.

Stereotypes are also harmful because they objectify, depersonalize, and deny individuality (Enteman, 1996). The pervasiveness of stereotypes in the mass media drives concerns for effects because these are the dominant, if not only, images in the media of certain groups; there may be few positive images to counter negative images. These negative images may serve to justify inequitable conditions in society (e.g., Gray, 1989). Negative stereotypes offer potentially adverse effects, because they can be the basis for behavioral scripts (Van Evra, 1998). Racial-ethnic stereotypes may lead to fear and limit social interaction among different groups. Stereotypes about the elderly, for example, might affect how people interact with the elderly and lead to inappropriate or miscommunication between generations (Hummert, Nussbaum, & Wiemann, 1992).

Cognitive–Transactional Model

Another way to define stereotypes is as person schemas categorized along some dimension, such as gender, age, or ethnicity. As schemas, stereotypes help people deal with the overwhelming amount of information that they encounter in their daily lives. Stereotypes help people deal with uncertainty in their environment. For example, if we are stranded late at night in a neighborhood we have never visited, how do we know if we should go to one of the dwellings to ask for help? Even though we have no direct experience with the neighborhood, we might be more likely to go to the house with the children's bicycle on the porch and the dried flower wreath on the door, instead of the house with a Harley Davidson motor cycle parked in the driveway. Children and flowers seem to offer less threat. And, why do college students want to know the major of people that they meet? Does knowing what someone is studying tell more about the person? Do different majors have different stereotypes?

Stereotypes, though, are gross generalizations about some group. An early study by Allport and Postman (1945) supported the notion that stereotypes are schemas. The researchers showed their study participants a city subway scene in which a white man was holding an open straight razor. Later, when asked about the picture, white participants were more likely to remember that it had been an African American man holding the razor. Selective recall of the picture conformed to participants' stereotypes.

The cognitive–transactional model offers several explanations for (a) how media content is linked to the acquisition of stereotypes about social groups, (b) how media content affects the development of self-concept, or schemas about ourselves and the groups to which we belong, and (c) how media-primed stereotypes affect responses to members of those groups.

Acquisition of Stereotypes. Media content can affect the acquisition of new stereotyped schemas. Stereotypes have a basis in the real world. Stereotypes about groups develop from generalizations drawn from experiences with members of that group. The more similar our experiences with group members are, the more likely we are to develop stereotypes about the group, based on those experiences (Schneider et al., 1979). Salient examples, or exemplars, can also become the basis for stereotypes (Smith, 1990). For example, there are two ways that a college student could acquire a stereotypic view that college professors are eccentric: first, by noting that many professors seem to be idiosyncratic and "kooks" or by having experience with one particular professor who was especially outlandish. Based on the various models of learning (see chap. 5), stereotyped schemas are learned from salient experiences. Stereotyped schemas develop as new information is attached to preexisting information.

Television could be the basis for stereotyped schemas in children. Children have few opportunities to have direct experiences with people outside their own family. And, family members tend to be very much alike. So, children's sole experience with groups different from their family is most likely vicarious, through television. Because children are dependent on televison for information, that information is more likely to have an effect (Ball-Rokeach & DeFleur, 1976). Children may develop schemas about groups in society that they have no direct experience with, based on the images they see on television (see B. C. Armstrong, Neuendorf, & Brentar, 1992). This dependence on television may account for the relative lack of impact of television content on stereotypes of the elderly (Roy & Harwood, 1997). Children may have a good deal of experience with older, respected family members. So, it is not surprising that television's stereotyped images could be learned by children who have few direct experiences with the depicted groups.

Are stereotypes developed from television viewing during childhood representative of the schemas that children will carry with them for their entire lives? That is, are these effects from television viewing long-term? Schemas can be modified through experience (Fiske & Taylor, 1991). As children gain experiences, they may attach new knowledge to preexisting schemas, making them more complex. Stereotypes may become more specific, with greater knowledge. In adults, stereotypes tend not to be applied to groups as a whole. Adults recognize the variability among members of a group. Stereotypes, instead, become applied to subgroups that share the characteristics of exemplars of stereotypes (Hamilton & Mackie, 1990). For example, Hummert, and her colleagues (1995) found that negative stereotypes were most consistently applied to photos of elderly (75+), than to photos of people 65 to 74 years old. So, as people learn throughout their lives, stereotyped schemas developed in early childhood can develop and change. Interaction with a greater range of diverse groups of people may lead to changes in stereotypes (e.g., the contact hypothesis, Fiske & Taylor, 1991; Stephan & Brigham, 1985).

Encounters with counterstereotypes can also alter stereotyped schemas. Because people tend to view counterstereotypes as exceptions, Fiske and Taylor (1991) suggested three strategies that can be adopted for presenting effective counterstereotypic information via the mass media to change or eliminate stereotypes. First, counter-stereotypes should be depicted across a range of characters, so that the counterstereotypes are more generalizable to the group, as a whole. Second, the counterstereotyped characters should be otherwise typical of the group, so that they are not seen as exceptions or subcategories. Third, counterstereotypes should be presented over time; repetition may enhance schema change. There have been some studies of attempts to change stereotypes via the mass media (e.g., J. Johnston & Ettema, 1982, 1986), but, it is difficult to effect much change with media content (Hearold, 1986). This may be due to the impact of selective exposure (e.g., Vidmar & Rokeach, 1974) or the limited real-life experiences of child samples (Johnston & Ettema, 1982).

Development of Self-Schemas

Just as people hold schemas about others in society, they also hold self-schemas. *Self-schemas* are mental representations of one's "own personality attributes, social roles, past experience, future goals, and the like" (Fiske & Taylor, 1991, pp. 181-182). Self-schemas are self-concepts. They usually include attributes that are relevant and important to a person; self-schemas do not include irrelevant material. For example, if weight and physical appearance are important to an adolescent girl, then, they will be part of her self-schema. And, if physical strength is not important to her, the ability to lift weights will not be part of her self-schema. Self-schematic attributes can be positive (e.g., intelligence) or negative (e.g., shyness).

People are more attentive to self-schematic information that they encounter (Fiske & Taylor, 1991). So, self-relevant constructs should be important in selective attention to and perception of media content. There is not much research, though, on how the mass media affect self-concept. Even though television tends to show African Americans in stereotyped roles, Stroman (1986) found that television exposure was linked to positive self-concepts in African American children. R. L. Allen (1993) undertook an examination of the African American belief system (a cognitive schema). Preliminary studies with a national, adult sample revealed that exposure to television programs that depict the lives of African Americans was linked to positive aspects of self-concept for African Americans. Black-oriented television exposure was positively related to endorsing positive stereotypic beliefs (such as hard-working, honest, strong), Black autonomy (i.e., studying African languages, giving children African names), and feeling close to African American professionals and elected officials. Selective exposure and perception may insulate viewers from effects of television content on self-concept.

There is some limited evidence that suggests that media content may respond to self-schemas that adolescent girls hold about their body images. Myers and Biocca (1992) found that college females' personal body image responded to "body-image" television programming and commercials (e.g., *Star Search*, music videos). That is, body image seems to be "elastic" enough to change after viewing television.[4] Other researchers have found that media exposure may activate self-schemas and dissatisfaction with the appearance of one's body (e.g., Stice et al., 1994). Harrison and Cantor (1997), for example, observed that watching programs that featured heavier women (e.g., (*Designing Women* and *Roseanne*) was linked to college women's body dissatisfaction. It may be that the heavy female characters reminded women that thinner women are more desirable.

Responses Based on Media-Activated Stereotypes.   The cognitive–transactional model also points out that media content can be an effective prime. That is, media content can activate stereotypes and affect how people respond to various groups in society or evaluate themselves against media standards (Power, Murphy, & Coover, 1996). The priming of stereotypes is a result of automatic mental processing. Stereotypes are based on "snap judgments" that take little cognitive effort (Schneider et al., 1979). Stereotypes are based on the most salient characteristics of a person; physical appearance, for example, is a strong cue to a stereo-

---

[4]Contrary to expectation, however, watching this "body images" programming, however, led to decreases in perceived body size, not increases (Myers & Biocca, 1992).

type (Schneider et al., 1979). So, it is not surprising that television images could prime stereotypes.

There is evidence that some types of media content can activate stereotyped self-schemas. Tan (1979) found that adolescent girls who watched television ads were more likely to believe that being beautiful was important to popularity with men than girls who did not see the ads. Geis, Brown, Walsted, and Porter (1984) noted that college women who saw women in sex-typed commercials were more likely to emphasize homemaking in essays about what their lives would be like in 10 years. Presumably, media content can activate stereotypes that affect how viewers evaluate themselves. Davidson, Yasuna, and Tower (1979) found that little girls responded less stereotypically to questions after watching a television program with nontraditional roles for women.

Priming stereotypes can also influence how people respond to others. Both pornographic films (McKenzie-Mohr & Zanna, 1990) and music videos (C. H. Hansen & R. D. Hansen, 1988) have been found to activate stereotyped gender-role schemas and influence how men respond to women. Two experiments conducted by Power et al., (1996) support the ability of media content to prime stereotypes. College-student participants read fabricated news articles about a fictitious person, "Chris Miller," who was described in the first study as a Black male in either stereotypic or counterstereotypic terms. After reading the article, participants who had read the stereotypic article were more likely to assess personal blame on both Rodney King and Magic Johnson (see Iyengar, 1991) than those who had read the counterstereotypic article. In the second study, "Chris Miller" was described as a female in either stereotypic or counter-stereotypic terms. After reading, participants who had read the stereotyped article were less likely to find Anita Hill and Patricia Bowen were credible witnesses.[5] The authors concluded that "stereotypical or counter-stereotypic portrayals subsequently cued specific interpretations of media events" (Power et al., 1996, p. 53).

Cumulative Model

Another theory that connects media content and the acquisition of stereotypes is cultivation. *Cultivation* is a theory of media effects that is ex-

---

[5]Rodney King is an African American man whose beating by Los Angeles police officers had been captured on videotape. Magic Johnson is basketball star who developed HIV. Anita Hill is a law professor who accused Supreme Court Justice Clarence Thomas of sexual harassment. Patricia Bowen had accused William Kennedy Smith of rape at the Kennedy family's Palm Beach estate.

plained by the cumulative model. Content analyses consistently reveal that prime-time television content of the major broadcast networks is remarkably similar (Gerbner et al., 1994). That is, while there certainly are differences between specific television programs, overall, television presents a fairly consistent set of images: Men are overrepresented, women and minorities (except for African Americans) are underrepresented, and violence is pervasive and common. Moreover, groups tend to be presented stereotypically. Because the images are consistent and similar across television channels, greater immersion in the television world leads to believing that the real world resembles the television world. Although cultivation was initially proposed to describe and predict effects of violent media content, it is being used more often to describe how children's socialization is affected by television viewing. So, the cultivation hypothesis predicts that heavier television viewing is linked to holding more stereotyped views of social groups (Gerbner et al., 1994). There is support for cultivation. Viewers who watch a lot of television are more sexist (Morgan, 1982; Signorielli, 1993) and racist (Gerbner et al., 1982).

Cultivation is an appropriate theory to explain the effects of television content on children. Certainly repeated exposure to inaccurate images of social groups can contribute to what children learn about society. A question to be raised, however, is how long these cultivation effects last. There is some limited cultivation research that suggests that cultivation may persist as long as heavy viewing persists. Morgan (1982) found that over the course of 2 years, television viewing for middle-school students remained essentially unchanged. Moreover, for girls, first-year television viewing was related to sexism scores in the second year. But, television viewing declines as children get older (Nielsen Media Research, 1998). If children reduce their television viewing as they enter their teen years, do cultivation effects persist? There are two theoretical, yet untested, answers to that question. First, if television viewing does decline, we might expect cultivated, stereotyped beliefs to be modified, especially if children encounter real-life, unstereotyped and counterstereotyped information and examples. But, if television viewing remains heavy, adolescents are unlikely to encounter much information contrary to stereotypes that they might already hold, because television remains a dominant source of information. As Fiske and Taylor (1991) described, some stereotypes are "practically discomfirmable"(p. 153) if counter-stereotyped information is unlikely to be encountered.

Conditional Model

After reviewing the various theories that explain the effects of television content on children, Van Evra (1998) formulated a model that describes the effects as conditional on various aspects of the child (see Fig. 6.1).

Van Evra (1998) argued that there are several important individual differences in how social relationship and social category variables are important in understanding if and how television will affect a child:

- Viewing motives, or the reasons that the child watches television (entertainment or information);
- perceived reality, or how real and true-to-life the child believes the television content is;
- the amount of time that the child spends watching television (heavy or light viewing);
- the number of alternative information sources available to the child about the subjects in television programs (e.g., parental discussion, access to other media);
- age, program preferences, cognitive development, and television literacy.

According to this model, television should have its strongest impact on a child's body of knowledge when the child watches television as a source of information, when the child believes that television content is realistic, when the child watches television a lot, and has few other alternative sources of information. Alternately, television will have its least impact when the child views purely for entertainment and does not believe that television shows are particularly realistic. Television's effects are particularly minimized when the child does not watch much television and has many other sources of information about the world.

Although all aspects of this model have not been tested, there is theoretical support for several of its linkages. For example, it is clear that children watch television for different reasons (e.g., Greenberg, 1974). African American children watch television to learn about the world and seek role models from television performers (Greenberg, 1986). Children also vary in their beliefs about how real television is (e.g., Potter, 1988), and perceived realism does affect acceptance of some of television's messages (Hawkins & Pingree, 1980; Perse, 1986). Knowledge gap research (e.g., Tichenor, Donohue, & Olien, 1970, see also chap. 4, this volume) points out how education and income influence

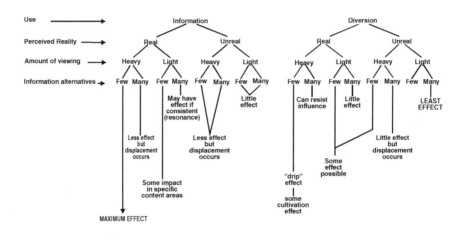

FIG. 6.1.   Van Evra's conditional model of socialization effects. From: Van Evra, J. (1998). *Television and child development* (2nd ed.). Mahwah, NJ: Lawrence Erlbaum Associates, p. 148. Reprinted with permission.

access to different mass media. Children from families with less income, for example, may find their media use limited to broadcast television because of the costs involved with cable, premium cable, and renting and buying children's educational videos. In all, then, socialization effects can be explained by the conditional model.

LEARNING UNHEALTHY BEHAVIORS

Adolescents are also the subject of concern about socialization effects of the mass media. Adolescence is a period of great change during which there is a tension between childhood and adulthood. During this time, adolescents begin to establish independence from their families, become more oriented toward relationships with friends and integration with peer groups, begin to form their sexual identity, and establish romantic and sexual relationships; also, they begin to move into more adult roles and accept more adult responsibilities (Strasburger, 1995).

These new roles are accompanied by a great deal of uncertainty. Because television is attractive and easily available, adolescents may turn to the mass media for information and advice (Alexander, 1985; Johnstone, 1974). Parents and scholars are concerned that the mass media might encourage adolescents to try adult behaviors (like drinking and sex) before they are mature enough to handle the consequences; or, the mass media might provide models for unhealthy behaviors associated with adulthood (e.g., smoking).

Much concern about socialization effects still focuses on television as a source of negative effects (Strasburger, 1995), especially the most commonly watched programs by adolescents: music videos and sitcoms (Children Now, 1998). But television viewing declines during the ages of 12 to 18 (Nielsen Media Research, 1998). The use of other media, especially movies, popular music, and magazines, increases during the teen years; so adolescents are exposed to a greater range of messages about adult behaviors.

Nutrition and Eating Disorders

In order to maintain good health, people need to know some of the principles of good nutrition. News stories, public service announcements, and food packaging rules ensure that more nutritional information is available to the public, yet television programming and commercials, for the most part, negate those positive messages. Food is a common element of programming and commercials; references to food occur about 10 times per hour in prime time (Story & Faulkner, 1990). But, many of these references involve snacking, rather than sit-down meals (Gerbner, Gross, Morgan, & Signorielli, 1981). And most of these references are to nonnutritious, snack foods (L. Kaufman, 1980; Story & Faulkner, 1990). Children's programming especially is surrounded by commercials for sweetened breakfast cereals, processed food product snacks (like pop tarts and fruit roll-ups), and high-fat fast foods. As children grow older, they might watch sports programming, which is flooded with soda, pizza, fast food, and snack food commercials. There are few opportunities to learn healthy eating practices by watching television (Signorielli & Lears, 1992).

Television programming does seem to have an impact on nutritional knowledge and behavior. Children who watch a lot of television, for example, know little about healthy eating practices (Signorielli & Lears, 1992). Most troubling, though, is the evidence that television viewing is associated with unhealthy eating. Commercials for snack foods are associated with children's choices of sugared snacks and cereals (Goldberg, Gorn, & Gibson, 1978). And, it is estimated that the average child sees about 5,000 commercials for these types of food over the course of 1 year (Signorielli & Lears, 1992). If childhood is the time in which one's eating habits are shaped, television is certainly not a good influence.

Overall, the most common unhealthy effect associated with television viewing is obesity (Dietz, 1990; Dietz & Gortmaker, 1985). The more television people watch, the more likely they are to be grossly overweight. There are several obvious explanations for this connection (Strasburger, 1995). Television viewing is a sedentary activity that burns few calories.[6] Moreover, the more time someone spends watching television, the less time they have to spend exercising. So, heavy television viewers become less physically fit and burn fewer calories (Tucker, 1986). Snacking often accompanies television viewing (Dietz, 1990). Most of those snacks are high fat (Wong et al., 1992).

As girls enter adolescence, new concerns about media effects center on eating disorders. Although the most common effect of television viewing is obesity, adolescents begin to watch less television (Nielsen Media Research, 1998) and begin to read more magazines and watch more videos and movies. Adolescence also marks puberty for most girls. Because estrogen helps bind fat, during puberty girls begin to acquire more fat, especially in the breasts and hips. But, adolescence also marks more interest in appearance and desire to be attractive. The widespread incidence of anorexia (eating too little food) and bulimia (induced vomiting after overeating) has focused researchers on the media messages about body weight in the mass media.

There is no doubt that thinness is valued in our culture. Moreover, the ideal female body type is growing thinner each year. Percy and Lautman (1994), for example, found that women portrayed in *McCalls* magazine advertisements became dramatically slimmer from 1905 through 1978. D. M. Garner, Garfinkel, Schwartz, and Thompson (1980) observed that both Miss America contestants and *Playboy* centerfolds became slimmer between 1960 and 1979. Magazines, movies, and

---

[6]One researcher found an ingenious way to encourage young and overweight "couch potatoes" to exercise. Neergaard (1999) connected exercise bicycles to television sets so that the sets would work only when the bicycle was being pedaled. After 10 weeks, compared to a control group, the overweight children ages 8 to 12 lost 2 to 3% of their body fat.

television associate female thinness with beauty, strength, independence, achievement, success, and self-control (Garfinkel & Garner, 1982; Wooley & Wooley, 1986).

Adolescent girls may be especially sensitive to media images of thinness because they experience a good deal of anxiety about their weight and physical appearance (e.g., Offer, Ostrov, & Howard, 1984). Magazines targeting teenage girls capitalize on these concerns; how to improve physical appearance is the main topic in most of these magazines (Evans, Rutberg, Sather, & Turner, 1991). The media now carry a wealth of messages that reinforce thinness. There have been an increase in women's fitness magazines in recent years that emphasize ways to improve physical appearance. Diet books frequently reach the best-seller lists. Health clubs and diet centers advertise regularly on television. Advertisements of diet products have dramatically increased (Stice & Shaw, 1994).

There is some evidence that the mass media contribute to females' eating disorders. Stice and Shaw (1994) located a significant association between reading magazines and college females' eating disorder symptoms. Another study (Stice, Schupak-Neuberg, Shaw, & Stein, 1994) found that media exposure was directly and indirectly linked to symptoms of eating disorders and indirectly linked through its impact on body dissatisfaction, internalization of ideal-body stereotypes, and gender-role endorsement. Harrison and Cantor (1997) found that in a college female sample, different media had different effects on various aspects of eating disorders. Reading fitness magazines was linked to Eating Attitudes Test (EAT) scores (a scale that assesses a range of attitudes and behaviors associated with eating disorders, Garner & Garfinkel, 1979), body dissatisfaction, and anorexic and bulimic eating behaviors.

Botta (1999) suggested that television's effects on eating disorders may be conditional on adolescent girls' mental activity while they are watching television. Although Botta did not find a connection between eating disorders and overall television exposure or watching dramatic programs that highlight thin women, Botta did find that television may indirectly affect eating disorders. Endorsing a thin ideal body type, being dissatisfied with one's own body, a personal drive for thinness, and bulimic action tendencies were all predicted by seeing media images of thin women as realistic and by comparing personal body type to the thin models on television.

Alcohol

Television presents drinking alcoholic beverages as a common, attractive, adult activity. Not only are alcoholic beverages the most common type of drink on television (Mathios, Avery, Bisogni, & Shanahan, 1998), but they are the most frequently advertised beverage in televised sports (Madden & Grube, 1992). Drinking is a common element of prime-time television (Signorielli, 1987) and music videos (DuRant et al., 1997; Jones, 1997). Some scholars estimate that children see over a million acts of drinking on television by the time they are age 18 (Postman, Nystrom, Strate, & Weingartner, 1987). Drinkers are typically wealthy, attractive, successful, and adventurous, and alcohol is associated with romance, adventure, comradery, and humor (Grube, 1993; Hundley, 1995). Moreover, drinking is an activity without any consequences, good or bad; harmful effects of drinking, even intoxication, are rarely mentioned (Grube, 1993; Hundley, 1995; Signorielli, 1987). Although drinking is legal only for those age 21 or older, television implies that it is common for young people to drink. Survey research has found that adolescents perceive that about 25% of the people in television beer advertisements were under the age of 21 (Slater et al., 1996).

The pervasiveness and glamor of these images of alcohol lead to concerns about underage drinking and abuse. These concerns about the effects of alcohol situations shown on television are not unfounded. Children enjoy alcohol ads and notice them more as they become adolescents (Aitken, Leathar, & Scott, 1988). Even children in grades 5 and 6 notice beer ads and are able to recognize "spokes-animals" and pair them with brands (Grube & Wallack, 1994). The researchers further found that awareness of beer ads was linked to more favorable attitudes about drinking in these children and intentions to drink when they became adults. Grube and Wallack (1994) concluded that ads might predispose children to drinking. Experiments have supported connections between drinking in programs and children's acceptance of alcohol. When children watched an episode of M*A*S*H with drinking scenes, they were more likely to say that they would offer adult guests "whiskey" rather than water than those children who saw the same episode without drinking depicted (Rychtarik Fairbank, Allen, Foy, & Drabman, 1983).

Studies have found connections between exposure to alcohol advertisements and adolescent drinking. Attraction to clever beer ads may have delayed effect. A longitudinal study found a relationship between males remembering ads at age 15 and drinking beer at age 18 (Connolly, Casswell, Zhang, & Silva, 1994). Atkin, Hocking, and Block (1984) observed that attention to beer and liquor ads predicted both beer and liquor consumption for grade 7 through grade 12. They also noted that adolescents are likely to drink heavily advertised brands. Based on heavy alcohol advertising in sports, Bloom, Hogan, and Blazing (1997) found a similar relationship between watching football and college basketball, and alcohol use for 13 to 18 year olds. Wyllie, Zhang, & Casswell (1998) conducted a study that ruled out the effects of selective exposure and memory for beer ads on drinking. In their phone survey of randomly sampled persons, ages 18 to 29, structural equation modeling found that liking beer advertisements had a direct and indirect influence on the amount of alcohol consumption (through its impact on positive beliefs about alcohol). The model did not support the effects of selective exposure hypothesis: that alcohol consumption predicted liking beer advertisements.

Tobacco

Since 1971, when tobacco ads were banned from the broadcast media, there have been some shifts in media presentations of smoking. Smoking on television has declined (Signorielli, 1990a) whereas smoking ads have increased in the print media (Centers for Disease Control, 1990). The tobacco companies, though, still seem to have a substantial impact on entertainment and editorial content because of their advertising for cigarettes and other products. Television characters rarely refuse to smoke or make derogatory comments about tobacco (Signorielli, 1990a) and the print media rarely mention the health risks of smoking, even if they do not carry ads for tobacco products (Kessler, 1989; Warner, Goldenhar, & McLaughlin, 1992). Smoking in films is more common than in real life; movie smoking rates have not declined over the years (Hazan, Lipton, & Glantz, 1994). Smoking is common even in G-rated films targeted toward younger children; Goldstein, Sobel, and Newman (1999) found that more than one-half of the films featured smoking in their sample of children's animated films. Tobacco companies aggressively use product placement to make sure that their products are used by highly visible and admired film stars (Action for Smoking and Health, 1996).[7] So, the dominant image of smoking is the one created by the tobacco companies. Smoking is presented as the action of glamorous, sexually attractive, independent, healthy, thin, macho, and active people (Altman, Slater, Albright, & Maccoby, 1987).

Young people have many opportunities to see tobacco ads and smoking in the media. These images may contribute to tobacco use by leading adolescents to form a positive attitude toward smoking. Cigarette companies place ads for youth-oriented brands in magazines that have high adolescent readership (King, Siegel, Celebucki, & Connolly, 1998). And, over one-quarter of MTV videos included tobacco use (DuRant et al., 1997).

Several studies point that concerns about the effects of tobacco advertising on adolescents is not unfounded. Pierce, Choi, Gilpin, Farkas, and Berry (1998) assessed the persuasive impact of tobacco advertising campaigns on adolescent smoking. The researchers argued that for the campaigns to lead to smoking, first, adolescents must be exposed to the ads, attend to and understand the messages, and finally, develop a cognitive or affective response to the message. Their longitudinal study of over 1,750 adolescents gives evidence that tobacco campaigns are linked to adolescent smoking. Over one-half of the sample named a favorite tobacco advertisement, and many owned or wanted to acquire promotional items (e.g., tee shirts). These two responses to tobacco advertising were significantly linked, over time, to smoking.

Pollay and his colleagues (1996) reported that young people, more than adults, are especially susceptible to tobacco advertising. Their research focused, not on the connection between advertising and smoking initiation, but on the brand choices of existing smokers. They found that adolescent smokers' brand choices were concentrated in the most heavily advertised brands and that the relationship between brand choice and advertising was stronger among adolescents than adults. These results mesh with those of Pierce and his colleagues (1991). Their random phone survey of over 24,000 adult and 5,000 adolescent smokers found that adolescent smokers were more likely than adult smokers to smoke the most heavily advertised brands (Marlboro and Camel).

---

[7]The most profitable movie of all time, *Titanic*, uses smoking as a way to show Rose's spirit of independence from her controlling fiancé. The notion of smoking as a sign of independence for woman became the basis of the Virginia Slim's advertising campaign: "You've come a long way, baby."

Both research teams concluded that there was a connection between tobacco advertising and adolescent smoking.

Kaufman (1994) believed that "young women may be uniquely vulnerable to enticements to smoke" (p. 629) because they are especially interested in fashion, physical appearance, thinness, and social desirability. Tobacco ads link smoking with all of these. It is not surprising, then, that after years of decline in smoking initiation, there was an increase in smoking in underage adolescent girls in 1967 (Pierce, Lee, & Gilpin, 1994), the year that marked the start of the tobacco advertising campaigns targeting women. There was a similar corresponding increase in sales of Camel cigarettes to adolescent smokers. Three years after the start of the Joe Camel advertising campaign, Camel's share increased from .5% to 32% of the adolescent market (DiFranza et al., 1991).

Pollay and his colleagues (1996) believed that exposure and attention to tobacco advertising begins in childhood. Exposure to and awareness of tobacco ads certainly begins before adolescence. Fischer and his associates (1991) asked children between age 3 and age 6 to match product logos with brand names. Children were able to match children's logos and brands readily; over 90% matched the logo and brand for the Disney channel, for example. McDonald's and Burger King were other recognizable logos (around 80% recognition rate). Tobacco logos were less recognizable; still, over 50% of the children were able to match Joe Camel and Camel cigarettes; around 33% of them recognized Marlboro logos.

Sexual Values and Behaviors

Adolescence is a time of growing interest in learning about and experimenting with sex. Unfortunately, most adolescents are underinformed about sex. J. D. Brown, Childers, and Waszak (1990) summarized the reasons that media may be a potent source of effects on adolescents' sexual knowledge and behavior: (a) they have little first-hand experience (either in action or observation); (b) their best sources—parents and educators—are reluctant to provide information and adolescents may be embarrassed to approach these sources; and (c) fear of appearing ignorant may lead them to rely on impersonal sources, such as the mass media. Unfortunately, media messages about sex are often inaccurate and incomplete and adolescents' interpretations of media sex may be incorrect and immature. Depictions of and discussions about sex are easily found in almost all media, from television soap operas, movies, magazines and books, and radio talk shows. The content of the mass media may become a source of effects on sexual knowledge and behavior in adolescents.

Sex is a common aspect of media content. Greenberg and his colleagues (1993b) observed that the 1986 prime-time programs preferred by adolescents presented just under three sexual acts an hour, of which 37% were visually presented. Adolescents' favorite soap operas during that same period depicted 3.67 sexual acts, of which 30% were visually portrayed. In both types of programs, the most common sexual act was intercourse between unmarried people. In all, intercourse accounted for 39% of prime-time sexual activity and 62% of all soap opera sexual activity. These findings reinforce the results of other content analyses. Sapolsky and Tabarlet (1991), for example, found that sexual activity in prime-time television had increased somewhat between 1979, when a sexual act was coded every 5 minutes, and 1989, when a sexual act was coded every 4 minutes. Signorielli (1987) noted that there was some sexual reference in 90% of all prime-time television programs. An analysis of 1997–1998 broadcast and cable programs found that sex is still a strong element of programming; overall, 56% of the programs featured some sexual content, with 36% of them containing at least one scene with a substantial focus on sex (Kunkel et al., 1999).

Other media content can be equally defined as sexual. Music videos, for example, focus a good deal on sexual activities that appeal to the young male target audience (Baxter, De Riemer, Landini, Leslie, & Singletary, 1985). Sexual activity has been coded in from 60% to 75% of sampled videos (Baxter et al., 1985; Sherman & Dominick, 1986). R-rated movies popular with adolescents are perhaps the most sexual of all; Greenberg and his associates (1993a) coded an average of 17.5 sexual acts each hour in these films, seven times the number found in the typical prime-time hour.

Not only is sexual content easily observed in the media, but its lessons are often inaccurate. Sexual activity is more common among unmarried couples (e.g., Greenberg, Siemicki, et al., 1993; Greenberg, Stankey, et al., 1993; Sapolsky & Tarberlet, 1991). The negative consequences of sexual activity are rarely presented or discussed. Lowry and Towles (1989b), for example, found no instances of pregnancy or disease prevention in their analysis of 1987 soap operas.[8] Subsequent content analyses of soap operas and prime-time programs observed similar deficiencies (e.g., Kunkel et al., 1999; Lowry & Schidler, 1993; Lowry & Towles, 1989a). And, sexual activity is often coupled with violence and drug and alcohol use (Signorielli, 1987). Sexual behavior in soap operas is often accompanied by deception (Larson, 1991). Homosexuality is invisible; gays and lesbians are rarely shown in normal roles. Any instances of same-sex sexual behavior are treated as taboo.

Concerns about the effects of sexual media content focus on its impact on the development of healthy sexual behaviors; that is, knowing when to have sex and having sex responsibly (e.g., protecting against disease and unplanned pregnancy). Greenberg (1994) suggested that exposure to sexual media may lead to several effects for adolescents: (a) greater concern with sexual matters, (b) perceptions that sex is common among young people, (c) greater acceptance of extra- and premarital sex, and (d) beliefs that sex has few negative consequences.

There is modest evidence that exposure to sexual media content is linked to attitudes about sex and sexual behaviors. Viewers of soap operas, for example, estimate a higher number of pregnancies outside of marriage (Carveth & Alexander, 1985; Perse, 1986) and believe that soap-opera relationships reflect real-life relationships (Corder-Bolz, 1981). Bryant and Rockwell (1994) found that exposure to televised scenes of sex outside marriage affected the moral values of adolescents ages 13 and 14; experimental participants were more likely to judge that sexual indiscretions were "wrong." Baran (1976) observed that watching sex on television was associated with less satisfaction with one's own sexual experiences. Other researchers have observed that exposure to more sexual television programs, such as MTV and soap operas, was linked to positive attitudes toward sexual permissiveness (Greeson & Williams, 1986; Strouse & Buerkel-Rothfuss, 1987).

Correlational studies have found connections between exposure to sexual media content and sexual activity. Adolescents who watch soap operas and "sexy" television programs have a greater number of sexual partners (Strouse & Buerkel-Rothfuss, 1987), and are more likely to

---

[8]This can be especially troubling, considering the relative promiscuity of some of the characters as well as their entangled sex histories. For example, a common soap opera theme is unknown paternity. A female character will have unprotected sex with two different partners so close in time that she cannot be sure which one is the father of her (usually unplanned) child.

engage in "precocious" sexual intercourse (J. D. Brown & Newcomer, 1991; Peterson, Moore, & Furstenberg, 1991).

Social Learning Theory

The most commonly invoked theory to explain television's effects on learning behaviors is *social learning theory* (also known as observational learning). Social learning theory is an approach that sees mass communication as a potentially powerful agent in directing human behavior. In the simplest of terms, social learning explains that people can model the actions that they observe in the media. Social learning theory is a cognitive approach that emphasizes the importance of mental activity as a precursor to action. In fact, external factors have an impact on an individual's behavior only through that individual's cognitive activity.

Bandura (1986, 1994) pointed out that the range of human knowledge would be severely limited if it were restricted only to what we can learn from our own actions. Human learning is certainly not due solely to operant conditioning, or performing a variety of acts, and learning only those that are reinforced (much as a pigeon learns to peck at a bar in a cage in order to release food pellets). Humans have the ability to conceptualize; so, humans can learn by modeling the behaviors of others that they observe.

Learning is a key element of social learning (see chap. 5). The theory posits long-term effects as a result of learning observed behaviors. Social learning is not a simple process, based on the simple observation of behavior followed by imitation. Social learning is a complex motivation process marked by four subprocesses: attention, retention, production, and motivation (see Fig. 6.2; Bandura, 1986, 1994).

The first step in social learning is attention to a behavior presented in the mass media; one cannot learn something that he or she has not paid attention to. Although it is clear that certain media content attributes increase the likelihood of attention (e.g., salience, prevalence), Bandura (1994) pointed out that attention is selective and voluntary, based on one's goals and interests. Media actions that have functional value are more likely to be attended to because they are seen as relevant and useful.

The next subprocess in social learning is retention. This is the mental learning of the observed behavior—integrating it into prior knowledge. Similar to the active learning models presented in chapter 5, retention involves cognitive rehearsal, reconstruction, comparing the

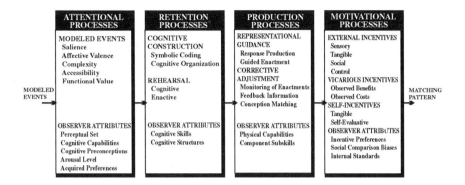

FIG. 6.2. Bandura's social learning theory. From: Bandura, A. (1994). Social cognitive theory of mass communication. In J. Bryant & D. Zillmann (Eds.), Media effects: Advances in theory and research (pp. 61–90). Hillsdale, NJ: Lawrence Erlbaum Associates, p. 67. Reprinted by permission.

action to already existing behavioral schemas, and "filing" the behavior into long-term memory.

Learning a behavior does not lead automatically to replicating it. The third subprocess of social learning involves the production of the learned behavior. First, the individual must have the physical abilities and skills to replicate the action. A child might watch a commercial for a particular bouncing toy (such as pogo ball) over and over, all the while paying a good deal of attention. But, if that child does not have the balance or physical skills to manipulate the toy, he or she will not be able to enact the behavior, even though the behavior may have been socially learned. Moreover, one must have the self-efficacy, or belief that they can enact the behavior, before attempting the action. Bandura (1986, 1994) also pointed out that social learning is more than simply duplicating an action. When the learned behavior is enacted, it often needs to be modified to suit the circumstances, and these modifications typically involve perfecting the learned skills.

Social learning recognizes that even socially learned behaviors that one can replicate may not be enacted unless one is motivated. The fourth subprocess involves various motivational incentives, or rewards (or punishments) associated with the action. If a behavior is rewarded, it is more likely to be produced; if it is punished, it becomes less likely to be produced. The rewards can be direct, self-produced, or vicarious (Bandura, 1994). Direct rewards (or punishments) involve the direct results of the action. Putting one's hand near a flame causes pain, for example; one is less likely to try that a second time. Self–produced rewards are those that emerge from self-satisfaction and sense of self-worth. After donating blood, for example, most people feel good about themselves. Vicarious rewards (or punishments) are socially observed. A character on a television program may challenge the school bully to a fight and gain the respect of his classmates. After watching that program, that outcome might motivate a school boy to challenge the bully at his own school—even though he knows that there might be some physical pain from the fight. Vicarious reinforcement is heightened by identification with the actor and perceived realism the of the media context.

Social learning theory provides a good explanation for the socialization effects of television. Some media images may be especially salient for adolescents. Thin female bodies and sexual actions, especially, can easily attract selective attention. Drinking and smoking, although not necessarily salient, may attract the attention of adolescents who are interested in learning about more adult behaviors (i.e., such actions may have functional value). The repetition of these same sorts of images and behaviors increase the likelihood that they will be learned. But, more important, television provides many more positive than negative reinforcements for harmful behaviors relating to eating, drinking alcohol, smoking, and sex. Although females are often thin, we rarely see the diet and exercise needed to maintain that slim ideal. In fact, on television, many of these slim models frequently snack on high calorie foods (e.g., Kaufman, 1980). Alcohol use is a common occurrence in the media and is associated with celebration and good times. But, television rarely shows any of the harmful effects of drinking; even drunkenness and hangovers are often depicted as comic (Signorielli, 1987). Sexual activities are almost always associated with positive reinforcement—young attractive participants who experience pleasure and romance. Negative consequences of sex are essentially invisible (e.g., Lowry & Towles, 1998a, 1989b). Media content, then, provides a wealth of opportunities to socially learn inappropriate or unhealthy behaviors. The rewards associated with these behaviors may reduce inhibitions and increase adolescents' motivation to model these behaviors.

Social learning theory is fairly broad in scope. Media content can be the basis for (a) learning novel or new behaviors (change effects), (b) the facilitation or inhibition of already learned behaviors, or (c) the prompting of learned behaviors (both reinforcement effects). But social learning theory is not an omnibus theory to explain all behavioral effects of mass communication. First, social learning theory cannot explain the effects of media content that only infers an action. Direct representation of the behavior is a key component. The behavior must be able to be observed in order to be socially learned: "all modeled information must be symbolically represented if it is to be retained as a guide for future action" (Bandura, 1986, p. 48). Even abstract modeling, or extracting the rules underlying behaviors to apply to innovative situations, involves observation (Bandura, 1986, 1994). Abstract modeling involves observing a range of actions, paying attention to rule-relevant aspects of the action, and extracting the underlying rule common to the actions. Bandura (1994) pointed out that abstract modeling is enhanced when "models verbalize their thoughts aloud as they engage in problem-solving activities (p. 70). So, social learning theory cannot explain the acquisition of behaviors that are not modeled in the mass media, such as bulimia, the use of many birth control devices, or sexual acts (which are not explicitly represented except in pornography).

Second, mere exposure is not sufficient for social learning. Observational learning is an active and motivated learning process that involves far more than simply observing a behavior and imitating it: "This is not to say that mere exposure to modeled activities is, in itself, sufficient to produce observational learning. Not all stimulation that impinges on individuals is necessarily observed by them, and even if it is noticed, what is registered may not be retained for any length of time" (Bandura, 1986, pp. 76–77). Social learning is a learning process that involves cognitive action and skills. Because social learning posits long-term effects, the modeled behavior must have some kind of cognitive representation. Some behaviors can be observed many times and not learned. Moreover, even an imitated behavior may not be socially learned. Mimicry is not social learning. Mimicry involves direct imitation of, or matching, a behavior to be imitated. Mimicry is usually a short-term effect, occurring immediately after the behavior. Without cognitive activity and mental representation of the rules underlying the action, the behavior is unlikely to be replicated in the longterm. Socialization effects of the mass media are not based on short-term mimicry.

The focus on social learning as the result of cognitive activity also limits social learning to observers who have the necessary cognitive skills to learn. According to Bandura (1986), "observational learning involved acquiring multiple subskills in selective observation, symbolic coding and rehearsal, coordinating sensory-motor and conceptual-motor systems, and judging probable outcomes for adopting another's behavior" (p. 81). Although even infants can mimic adult actions, they do not possess the cognitive abilities to retain, learn, and apply the behaviors in the longterm. So, very young children are not likely to socially learn behavior from television. Young children do not have the cognitive abilities to selectively attend to television or remember very much of what they have observed (Alwit et al., 1980; Collins, 1982). Children under age 4 may have difficulty socially learning from television, especially if the behaviors are complex (Anderson & Collins, 1988). Bandura et al. (1963) observed evidence of social learning with their sample of nursery school children, but these children averaged over age 4 (53 months). Observed behaviors in children younger than that are probably based on mimicry, not social learning.

Third, media content is only one source of social learning. Children may watch a good deal of television, but they also typically have a good many opportunities to observe parents, siblings, peers, and teachers. These presumably positive models should exert more influence on children's behavior because of salience, relevance, utility, and motivational factors. Austin, Roberts, and Nass (1990, see also Austin & Meili, 1994) pointed out that when television portrayals contradict what they observe in real life, children tend to reject television models as unrealistic, reducing the likelihood of social learning. Parental coviewing can also have an impact of social learning from television. Parents can make comments that reinforce the salience, relevance, and utility of prosocial behaviors (e.g., "Look what a good girl she is to help her brother") or diminish the reality, relevance, or reward of antisocial behaviors ("Do you think he felt bad when he realized he hurt the puppy?").

Social Learning as a Conditional Model of Effects

Social learning theory has some aspects of the cognitive–transactional model; the nature of the media content is important to understanding media effects. Bandura (1986, 1994) pointed out that the action must be observable, salient, and simple enough for the audience to comprehend. It is clear, however, that these media content attributes do not intrude on automatic attention. Social learning is primarily understood as an observer-motivated process. So, it falls clearly in the conditional model of media effects. Audience variables are central to understanding social learning.

Bandura' (1986, 1994) listed several of these variables; most reflect individual differences: (a) selective exposure based on preferences, arousal level, and perceptual abilities; (b) abilities to learn based on cognitive skills; (c) abilities to replicate the act based on physical capabilities and self-efficacy; and (d) motivation based on perceptions of rewards and preferences for incentives. Social category variables may also have relevance to social learning because social categories affect selective attention to and perception of media content. Age, as a social category, may reflect cognitive abilities and experiences. Social relationships may be important in understanding social learning effects. Social connections with others may serve as alternate, more salient models of behavior. Comments during media exposure may highlight certain behaviors, distract children from other behaviors, or lead children to discount certain behaviors as irrelevant. Social relationships may have their most important impact, however, on motivational processes. The social connections that we have with others can certainly serve as important normative influences that affect our willingness to act and our perceptions about the rewards and punishments associated with our actions (e.g., Fishbein & Ajzen, 1975). Adolescents, for example, may be more likely to drink alcohol if they expect that their peers will reward them for doing so (Atkin et al., 1984).

Summary

Although most of the research on socialization has focused on television as a source of negative effects, there are reasons to worry about the messages in other media that are targeted at children. Traditional fairy and folk tales often build on outdated images of women. In most of these stories, women's beauty and "femininity" are values, and women need to marry a "Prince Charming" to live happily ever after. Even children's videos contain stereotyped images of women and minority groups. And, much programming on children's and family cable channels is older off-network reruns. Those programs often are "wholesome" because they have little sex and violence, however, they often contain stereotyped images of the less aware and earlier days.

Scholars of media effects need to be aware of the media content available to children at various ages. We need to be concerned about media content that children will easily see—not necessarily the extreme content that some popular writers focus on that is located in magazines, books, and films that do not typically attract a child audience. It is also important to remember that children use different media at different times in their lives. Television use, for example, declines as children become older (Nielsen Media Research, 1998). Adolescents watch less television than other groups, so we need to be careful about affording television strong influence during adolescent years.

It is also important to remember that all socialization effects of the mass media are not negative. Socialization is a positive, functional aspect of the mass media (Wright, 1986). Television teaches many prosocial messages (e.g., J. Johnston & Ettema, 1986). The mass media can have important, prosocial effects on political socialization, or learning how to take interest in, learn about, and participate in government and politics (e.g., Chaffee & Yang, 1990).

Various models of media effects suggest different remedies to negative socialization effects. To reduce the more automatic effects of the cumulative and cognitive–transactional models, there have been suggestions that television programs and other media directed toward children and adolescents be improved. If children have well-produced content made available for them, they may be less likely to watch adult-oriented programs with inappropriate themes. Media producers should also consider the lessons that programs teach; negative as well as positive consequences of behaviors should be depicted.

Models of media effects that focus on active learning as the basis of socialization focus attention on the importance of media literacy. Media literacy is the set of skills needed to distinguish reality from fantasy in *media content* (Silverblatt, 1995; Singer, Zuckerman, & Singer, 1980). These skills serve as barriers to negative effects and involve knowledge about (a) the different types of programs and genres (e.g., the difference between news, commercials, comedy, and drama); (b) how programs are constructed (e.g., scripts, special effects, transitions, and editing); (c) the purpose and intent of commercials; (d) the operation of mass media as a business and the need for profit (e.g., importance of ratings); and (e) the focus of media content on entertainment. These skills should lead to a more critical and aware use of the mass media.

7

Effects of Violent Media Content

The Columbine High School shootings in Littleton, Colorado, in April, 1999, capped a year marked by youth violence. Once again, faced with public concerns, politicians moved to identify and eliminate the causes of aggression in the young. Fingers pointed at easy availability of guns and graphic depictions of violence in movies, television, and video games. The 106th Congress voted in June, 1999, to take no action to increase restrictions on gun sales, but continued plans to restrict access to violent media content.[1] Based on the mandate of the 1996 Telecommunications Bill, by January 1, 2000, all television sets with screens 13 inches or larger will be sold equipped with a V-chip, which will allow parents to block programs based on the TV Parental Guidelines ratings system.[2] At President Clinton's urging, the National Association of Theater Owners pledged to require youths unaccompanied by

---

[1]Interestingly, Congress has turned down legislation mandating child-proof locks on guns, but has endorsed the V-chip, which locks children out from objectionable television programming.

[2]The TV Parental Guidelines rating system is designed to give information about the program content so that parents can control their children's television viewing. The ratings are: TV-Y (acceptable for all children), TV-Y7 (designed for children age 7 or older), TV-Y7-FV (includes some intense fantasy violence), TV-G (acceptable for general audience, with little violence, strong language, or sexual dialogue or situations), TV-PG (may contain content unsuitable for younger children), TV-14 (contains content not suitable for children under the age of 14), and TV-M (designed for adults and not suitable for children under the age of 17). TV-PG, TV-14, and TV-MA programs may also carry additional ratings to describe specific content: V (intense violence), S (intense sexual situations), L (strong or coarse language), and D (sexually suggestive dialogue). For more information about and criticisms of the TV Parental Guidelines, see Federman (1998) and Heins (1998).

adults to produce a photo ID before being admitted to R-rated films. And, critics are wondering if the current voluntary rating system for video games is enough to keep violent games out of the hands of the young. The effects of media violence have once again become the topic of popular discussion and public policy.

Widespread concern about media violence is not new. DeFleur and Dennis (1994) reminded us that a "legacy of fear" has surrounded the adoption of almost every new mass medium. In the late 1880s, several states passed laws prohibiting the distribution of books, magazines, and newspapers that described in words or pictures accounts of crime or bloodshed (Saunders, 1996). Even comic books did not escape public scrutiny. In 1954, a Senate judiciary subcommittee led by Estes Kefauver investigated the impact of comic books on juvenile delinquency. And, over the past 40 years, Congress has held over 40 hearings about the impact of media violence (Cooper, 1996; Saunders, 1996).

There are good reasons to be concerned about the effects of media violence. Violence is common in media content. The Cultural Indicators group has analyzed prime-time and weekend daytime television dramatic programming since 1967. Over the years, the findings are remarkably consistent (Signorielli, 1990b). Between 1967 and 1985, about three-quarters of all prime-time dramatic programs contain violence; violent acts occur about 5 times an hour. Around 90% of all Saturday morning children's programs included violent acts for an average of about 20 acts per hour. The National Television Violence Study (Center for Communication and Social Policy, 1998) found a "strong consistency" in patterns of violence in their 3-year study from 1994 to 1997. In all, from 58% to 61% of all television programs contained violence. Programs broadcast on public television were the least violent; only about 1 in 5 showed violent acts. About one-half of the broadcast television programs (51%) included violence. Premium cable, however, was the most violent over the time of the study; just over 4 out of every 5 programs (83%) were violent. Clearly, television programming is filled with violence.

Few analyses have quantified the violence in popular film; however, anyone who has watched action films has noticed how common graphic violence is in this genre. The National Television Violence Study suggests how violent movies are. Of all the program genres, movies (which often are broadcasts of feature films) were the most violent; 89% of movies contained media violence. Hamilton's (1998) summaries of data from the National Coalition on Television Violence illustrated that movies can be quite violent. Although some prime-time television genres, such as action–adventure (27.6 violent acts per hour), western (22.6), science fiction (22.8), and mystery (25.5), as a whole, have more violent acts per hour than movies rated PG (20.1 violent acts per hour) or PG-13 (19.8), R-rated movies are quite a bit more violent than television fare; about 33.1 acts per hour.

Not surprising, home video, because it draws from theatrical films, is also a violent medium. The University of California, Los Angeles (UCLA) Television Violence Monitoring Project (UCLA Center for Communication Policy, 1998) considered the most-rented home videos over a 3-year period. They found that between 1995 and 1997, just over one-half of the videos had so much violence that they "would raise concerns" if they were shown unedited on broadcast television.

Public convictions that violent media content contributes to violence in society are supported by anecdotal reports of criminals' media use, naive beliefs in the connections between crime rates and media violence, media reports of "copycat" crimes, and the publicized reports of some highly visible research. News reports often mention connections between crimes and media content. "Gangsta rap" has been blamed for police shootings because the music playing in the accused's car included rap artists. Violent scenes in movies are linked to "imitation crimes" (Surette, 1998). The media reported that the Columbine High School shooters played violent video games, like *Doom*.

Perceptions are common that our violent media culture has bred a generation who are desensitized to crime and mayhem. These perceptions, though, are inaccurate. First of all, even though violence in the media has been rather constant over the years, violent crime is declining (Bureau of Justice Statistics, 1998). Overall, the FBI's violent crime index has been declining for the past 7 years; 1998 crime reports are 7% fewer than the previous year. California figures point out that youth crime has declined dramatically since the mid-1970s (Males, 1999). Nationally, firearm deaths in young people have declined since 1991 (Bureau of Justice Statistics, 1999a) and fewer high school students fight and carry guns and other weapons (Brener, Simon, Krug, & Lowry, 1999). In fact, there is an inverse relationship between the Nielsen ratings of violent television programs and criminal violence rates across 281 geographic areas (Messner, 1986).

It is clear that the most popular television programs and movies are not the most violent.[3] Most people don't find media violence appealing. But media violence does appeal to certain demographic groups—those most valued by advertisers. The most desirable target audiences are people age 18 to 49, especially women age 18 to 34. Although these age groups spend less money than older adults, advertisers believe that they are more susceptible to advertising influence because they have not established product and brand preferences. Moreover, they watch less television overall, so advertisers are more interested in funding programs they are likely to watch. Young people are the largest market for media violence. According to Hamilton (p. 55), "nearly 75% of the heavy viewers of violence programming [e.g., fictional crime, real-life police programs, and action-adventure films] are concentrated in three of the demographic groups, males 18-34, females 18-34 (21% of heavy viewers), and males 35-49 (19%)" (p. 55).

Certain scholarly reports capture political and public attention to support the connection between media violence and aggression in society. One analysis that has received perhaps the most publicity connects television and homicide rates. Centerwall's (1989a, 1989b) reports compared Western countries' homicide rates between 1945 and 1975 to that of South Africa during that same time period. Centerwall, a medical doctor, took an epidemiological approach to the effects of media violence. He explored how the introduction of television into Western societies was associated with an increase in the homicide rate. He used South Africa as a "control" population; because of concerns that English-language imported television programming would undermine the Afrikaans language of the White minority, television broadcasting in South Africa was prohibited until 1975. After controlling for several alternate explanations, such as economic growth, gun ownership, alcoholism, urbanization, and age distribution of the population, Centerwall found that the homicide rates among Whites in many Western nations skyrocketed 15 years after television ownership increased, but remained fairly stable in South Africa. Centerwall con-

---

[3]The television programs with the highest ratings for the 1998–1999 television season were *ER*, *Friends*, *Frasier*, *Monday Night Football*, *Jesse*, *Veronica's Closet*, *60 Minutes*, *Touched by an Angel*, *Sunday Movie on CBS*, and Wednesday evening's edition of 20/20—none of which are action or violence oriented. Of the 50 most profitable films of all time, only 8 are R-rated. The top-10 (as of June, 1999) are *Titanic*, *Star Wars*, *E. T.*, *Jurassic Park*, *Forrest Gump*, *Star Wars: The Phantom Menace*, *The Lion King*, *Return of the Jedi*, *Independence Day*, and *The Empire Strikes Back* (Movieweb, 1999).

cluded that television alone was the cause for the increase in homicide; he believes that about one-half of the violent crime in the United States can be attributed to television violence. He explains that television violence desensitizes children viewers and makes them more violent. Centerwall also believes that homicide is committed only by the most violent in society. Television, then, increases the number of children who are violent enough to kill. As these children become older (accounting for the 15-year lag in homicides), they commit homicides.

Centerwall has been a witness before Congressional hearing at least twice (Cooper, 1996) and his analyses have been widely cited. Communication scholars have been relatively uncritical, however, of his findings. Some comments about his work are warranted. Although Centerwall was limited in locating an industrialized society without television, South Africa might not have been an accurate comparitor to Western nations. Under apartheid, South Africa was a highly repressive and controlled society. Pally (1994) suggested that because South African Whites were such an overwhelming minority, a "siege" mentality might have reduced aggression among that group. Figlio (n.d.) points out that South Africa's self-isolation and climate of repression limits the credibility of White crime rates.[4] Centerwall's data ignore some of the realities of homicide rates. For example, his use of standardized homicide rates obscures the fact that South Africa had a much higher homicide rate than the United States before television was widely adopted. Moreover, his analyses use data beginning in the mid-1940s, a time of great societal cohesion in Western nations, due to the end of World War II. In fact, homicide rates in the 1940s had dropped dramatically from the 1930s (when homicide rates were among the highest historically).[5] Nor can Centerwall's method explain the current trend of decreasing homicide rates. Because his analytical technique was a relatively simple bivariate graphical analysis, Centerwall's findings could well be the re-

[4]During those years, South Africa was not a member of the World Health Organization, which monitors and records death rates (including homicide) among member nations.

[5]Homicide rates during the depression were rather high: 8.8 per 100,000 people in 1930, 9.2 (1931), 9.0 (1931), 9.7 (1933), 9.5 (1934). By 1945 (the first year of Centerwall's study), rates were much lower: 5.7 per 100,000 people. After remaining rather low (e.g., 4.7 in 1960), homicide rates climbed dramatically in the 1970s: 10.1 per 100,000 people (1974), 9.9 (1975), 9.0 (1976), 9.1 (1977), 9.2 (1978), 10.0 (1979), and 10.7 (1980; the highest recorded U.S. homicide rate). In 1998, the homicide rate dropped to the lowest rate since 1967: 6 homicides per 100,000 people (U.S. Department of Justice, 1999).

sult of a spurious correlation, or a "relationship" between two variables that is really due to the impact of a third variable.[6]

Although politicians and the public rely on anecdotal evidence and widespread beliefs that the preponderance of media violence must be linked to societal aggression, scholars are more convinced by evidence provided by the results of field and laboratory experiments and metaanalyses that consistently demonstrate a connection between exposure to violent media content and aggressive behavior. There is a general and widespread conclusion among most media scholars that there is a connection between media violence and aggressive behavior. Although no reputable media scholar holds that media violence is the largest reason for violence in society, most accept that media violence is a small, but significant contributor to aggressive behavior. This consensus is based on bodies of research and conclusions from large-scale research analyses, including the 1972 surgeon general's report (Surgeon General's Scientific Advisory Committee, 1972), the 1982 report from the National Institutes of Mental Health (NIMH; 1982), Centers for Disease Control (1991), National Academy of Science (1993), and the American Psychological Association (1993). As summarized in the 1982 NIMH report: "After 10 more years of research, the consensus among most of the research community is that violence on television does lead to aggressive behavior by children and teenagers who watch the programs" (p. 6).

This conclusion is drawn over 25 years of research using a variety of methods and measures. Especially compelling are the results of *metaanalyses*, a statistical aggregation of research results across a large number of studies that assesses direction and size of effects. Metaanalyses of media violence studies conducted from 1956 through 1990 have consistently found a significant effect of media violence on violent behavior and attitudes (Andison, 1977; Hearold, 1986; Paik & Comstock, 1994; Wood et al., 1991). Also notable are the results of longitudinal studies that conclude that television viewing in early years leads to aggressive behavior in later years. The late introduction of tele-

---

[6]A classic example of a spurious correlation is the strong positive relationship between the number of bars and the number of churches in a town. Although one might be tempted to conclude that drinking leads to repentance and prayer, the relationship is spurious, accounted for in the population of a town. As the number of people in a town increases, so does the number of bars, churches, schools, stores, and so on. Another classic spurious relationship is the one between the size of the big toe and math ability.

vision to a Canadian town, for example, gave researchers the chance to observe how children respond to viewing. Among other findings, direct observation of children in playground activities revealed that children became significantly more physically and verbally aggressive 2 years after the introduction of television (Joy et al., 1986). Panel studies, which examined television viewing and aggression in the same children over time, have also concluded that television leads to aggressive behavior (e.g., Huesmann & Eron, 1986; Lefkowitz, Eron, Walder, & Huesmann, 1977).[7]

There are some scholars who deny the causal conclusion between media violence and aggressive behavior (e.g., Freedman, 1984; Wurtzel & Lometti, 1987), but most interest in media violence has moved from determining if violent media content has an effect to how its effects occur. The variety of contingent conditions that intervene in the effects of violent media content (e.g., Paik & Comstock, 1994; Van Evra, 1998; T. M. Williams, 1986) pointed out that the dominant model of media effects of media violence is the conditional model. Several theories have evolved to explain the conditions under which viewing violent media content may lead to aggressive behavior.

THEORIES OF BEHAVIORAL EFFECTS OF VIOLENT MEDIA CONTENT

Cognitive Theories

There is a group of theories that base their explanation for violent media content's process of effects on a cognitive process. That is, people's aggressive behavior grows out of mental activity generated as a result of, or in response to violent media content. These theories rely on three types of mental activity as the basis for aggressive behavior: learning, attitude formation, and priming.

Learning

Social Learning.   The dominant cognitive approach to connecting violent media content and aggressive behavior is based on learning. That is, through exposure to media content, viewers learn how and when to act aggressively. These learning approaches are based on the same

---

[7]These panel studies have been widely scrutinized and criticized (e.g., Becker, 1972; Howitt, 1972; Kaplan, 1972; Kay, 1972; Milavsky, Kessler, Stipp, & Rubins, 1982; Sohn, 1982).

learning processes discussed in chapter 5. Learning is a conditional process that involves mental engagement and effort; it is not the result of passive exposure to media content. Learning also is a relatively long-term effect, so learning approaches assume that effects of learning media violence are fairly enduring.

The most prominent cognitive theory to explain how watching violent media content translates into aggressive behavior is social learning theory (also known as observational learning; see chap. 6). Bandura (1986, 1994) explained that people learn, not only through direct experience, but also by observing others. Media content provides many opportunities for observational learning; unfortunately, many of these involve antisocial actions. Because violence is so common in the visual media, television, movies, and video provide many models for aggressive actions. There are two keys to social learning: People will be more likely to learn behaviors that are relevant and adaptive.

Relevant behaviors are those that have some connection to one's life. So, social learning is enhanced when viewers perceive the content to be more realistic (e.g., Potter, 1988). In general, violence in film and video is more likely to be learned than animated violence (e.g., Hapkiewicz & Stone, 1974); violence in news has stronger social learning effects than violence in drama (e.g., Atkin, 1983). Social learning is also enhanced when the violent action is depicted as justified. Good reasons for violent actions heighten the perceived utility of violent behavior, making it more likely to be used in the future. In experimental settings, justified violence has been found to have significantly larger effects on aggression than unjustified violence (e.g., Berkowitz & Powers, 1978). Relevance is also increased when the violent actor is similar to the viewer. There is evidence that identification with a violent actor may increase social learning of aggression. Children, for example, are more likely to imitate characters of the same age and gender (e.g., Hicks, 1965; Bandura et al., 1963; Jose & Brewer, 1984).

Another key to social learning is that people learn behaviors that are *adaptive*, or those that will help them in their own lives. So, people will model violent behavior if it is rewarded; they will not model violent behavior that is punished (Bandura et al., 1963; Lando & Donnerstein, 1978). Social sanctions can be powerful inhibitors of violent behavior. But, there are indications that simple lack of punishment (even in the absence of explicit rewards) is enough to trigger social learning (e.g., Walters & Parke, 1964). Bandura (1994) explained that much media violence makes aggressive behavior appear more adaptive by depicting violence as morally justified, relatively inconsequential, and by depersonalizing the victim and thus reducing the blame on the actor.

Although recent extensions of social learning have suggested that people can learn abstract processes underlying actions by simply observing the action (Bandura, 1994), social learning theory has its greatest applicability and support in explaining enactments that resemble the media depiction. That is, social learning theory explains why a child might imitate wrestling moves after watching those same moves on televised wrestling. But, it is less successful in explaining why a child punches another after watching a wrestling match in which there is no punching. It is also important to remember that social learning is learning; a process that involves attention, comprehension, and elaboration (Bandura, 1994). Still, visual media offer many images that enhance the likelihood that viewers will socially learn violent acts. Content analyses consistently demonstrate that violence is the behavior of attractive, successful, and rewarded characters (e.g., Potter & Ware, 1987). Moreover, violence is arousing and likely to attract and hold attention, which increases the likelihood that it will be learned (e.g., A. Lang, 1990).

Information-Processing Model

It is clear that not all aggressive behavior associated with media exposure resembles the action in the media. Based on his work on youth violence, Huesmann (1986) articulated another learning model to explain the effects of media violence on aggressive behavior. Huesmann modified social learning theory to move its explanations beyond the impact of media content attributes (e.g., nature of the actor, victim, and reinforcement) and more to the context of the individual learner. The *information-processing model* is an adaptation of schema theory and network learning models (chap. 2 and chap. 4) to learning violence. According to this model, learning violent behaviors is the result of learning violent media scripts. These scripts are schemas about courses of action that are stored in memory. When retrieved, they become guides for behavior.

Like the social learning process, this information-processing model requires that media content be salient, and that viewers must pay attention, encode the action, and commit it to LTM. Unlike social learning theory, this approach does not hold that the scripts will be identical to the observed action. Through encoding and elaboration, scripts may become idiosyncratic or combined with other already learned scripts. So, the behaviors may deviate from the models. This approach might provide a better explanation for learning violence in the absence of explicit rewards (Huesmann, 1982). The behavior needs only to be noticeable and useful. Reinforcement also plays a different role in this model. Mental rehearsal reinforces violent scripts, more than actual rewards shown in the media. Evidence for mental rehearsal of violent scripts is found in the connection between violent fantasies and viewing aggressive media content (Huesmann & Eron, 1986).

Huesmann (1986) was clear, however, in pointing out that this information-processing model is a conditional one, based, to a large extent, on children's social development. Huesmann holds that a child's social environment affects violent television viewing as well as the acquisition of violent scripts. For example, children who are violent tend not to be popular. So, they have fewer social activities and might spend more time watching television. Children rejected by their parents might spend less time with them at home, and watch more televison. And, these children might act aggressively, out of frustration. So, the acquisition of violent scripts is the interaction of television viewing within the social context.

Priming by Aggressive Media Cues

Another cognitive approach to connecting violent media content with aggressive behavior is one that stresses short-term effects. Based on schema theory and the cognitive transactional model, violent media content can be a potent prime to activate aggressive mental scripts, which might then lead to aggressive behavior. Scholars who study priming effects of media content (e.g., Jo & Berkowitz, 1994) do not deny the potential long-term effects of social learning or information processing models. Instead, they recognize that there is another process, a temporary one, by which aggressive cues in media content can stimulate, for a short time, aggressive scripts. *Priming* is the automatic activation of a preexisting schema by a salient cue in the environment. Once a schema is activated, it is, in a sense, "top of mind," and likely to affect how people think, feel, and act. So, aggressive media cues may stimulate, or prime, aggressive thoughts that can affect how people respond to the social setting.

There is a good deal of research evidence that violent media content can prime, or activate, aggressive scripts. Films with hostile interactions lead to more hostile responses in research participants (e.g., Carver et al., 1983). Even violent comic books, comic routines, and video games are associated with temporary aggressive thoughts and feelings (Berkowitz, 1970; Mehrabian & Wixen, 1986). Priming by violent media cues may also be an explanation for some of the short-term violence that accompanies some violent movies and sporting matches.

Further support for the aggressive cue model is provided by research that finds that the use of specific salient objects can cue aggression (Josephson, 1987). In one study, elementary school boys were shown excerpts from either a violent or nonviolent television program. The violent program began with the villains using walkie-talkies. After watching television and being frustrated by not being able to watch promised cartoons, the boys were given a chance to play floor hockey. Before playing, each boy was "interviewed" by a play-by-play commentator using either a tape recorder or a walkie-talkie. Aggression was measured by counting aggressive actions during the game. Consistent with priming, boys who watched the aggressive television program were more aggressive than boys who did not. Interestingly, among those boys who saw the aggressive program, those who were interviewed with the walkie-talkie were the most aggressive. Josephson (1987) explained that the violent television program served to activate aggressive scripts for those boys with higher levels of characteristic aggressiveness. The additional cue of the walkie-talkie, though, was an especially potent prime.[8]

Together with Huesmann's information-processing model, the aggressive cue approach provides a more complete explanation of long-term and short-term effects of media violence based on schematic learning. Exposure to violent media content may be one way that people acquire aggressive scripts. These scripts can become the basis for violent behaviors. People might consciously activate aggressive scripts in controlled mental processing as a way to solve solutions in the real world. Or, salient media cues might prime aggressive scripts that affect how people respond for a short period of time.

---

[8]Because guns are used so often in violent drama and news, they may serve as especially potent aggressive cues in the real world.

Attitude Change

Another cognitive approach to hypothesizing a relationship between violent media content and aggressive behavior focuses on the attitudes that people have toward violence. Exposure to violence in the mass media leads people to be more accepting of violence as a societal norm and as a solution to problems. In a sense, through exposure to media violence, people become disinhibited to violence (as opposed to habituation, which is discussed later in this chapter).

Media content fosters acceptance of violence because much media violence is justified, rewarded, and committed by attractive characters (Potter & Ware, 1987). Moreover, media content rarely shows the consequences of violence, leading some viewers to believe that violence is not so harmful. Research has shown that even short-term exposure to violent media content is associated with greater acceptance of violence (Dominick & Greenberg, 1972; Thomas & Drabman, 1975). Gerbner and his associates (Gerbner, Gross, Jackson-Beeck, Jeffries-Fox, & Signorielli, 1978) found that viewers who watch a lot of television were more likely to agree that it was acceptable to hit someone in anger. Other research has found that heavy television viewing is linked to beliefs that violence is more common (e.g., Gerbner et al., 1994).

The basis of all research on attitudes is that attitudes are important because they predict behavior (Ajzen & Fishbein, 1980). So, holding positive attitudes about violence should lead to aggressive behavior. It is this connection to aggressive behavior that marks the attitude change approach as a conditional effect of media violence. Research typically finds only a modest connection between attitudes and actions; people don't always act in accordance with their attitudes. One of the earliest studies to demonstrate this lack of correspondence was in the 1930s. In his investigation of racial prejudice, LaPiere (1934) traveled around the United States with a Chinese couple. After visiting 251 hotels and restaurants, they were denied service only once. But, responses to a questionnaire sent to those same establishments about 6 months later recorded that over 90% of respondents would refuse service to Chinese people. Clearly, attitudes and behaviors are not isomorphic. This may illustrate that just because someone holds positive attitudes about violence does not necessarily mean that they will act on those attitudes.

Ajzen and Fishbein's (1980) and Fishbein and Ajzen's (1975) theory of reasoned action (TRA) provides a conditional explanation for how attitudes about violence lead to aggressive behavior. Their formula to describe the connection between attitudes and behavior is:

$$B \sim BI = w_1 A_{act} + w_2 SN_{act}$$

B = a specific behavior
BI = intention to behave
A_{act} = attitude about a specific act
SN_{act} = the attitudes that relevant others hold about the act
w = the situational weights applied in specific contexts

The *theory of reasoned action* (TRA) is a cognitive approach that assumes that people have reasons for acting and that attitudes predict behavior, within a social context. Note that Ajzen and Fishbein (1980) held that it is impractical to predict behavior directly. Intentions are not stable; as time passes, intentions can change and situations can intervene that make a specific action less likely. Generally, the shorter the time period between intention formation and opportunity to act, the greater the correspondence between intention and behavior. So, the TRA focuses on predicting intentions to behave (BI).

There are two influences on behavioral intention: attitudes about the specific act and perceptions of subjective norms. The attitude toward the act is a very specific attitude—about a very specific act. In the case of attitudes about violence, an attitude that violence in general is a solution to societal problems is not specific enough to predict specific behavior. If, however, a child holds the attitude that hitting a bully in the playground is a good solution to being bullied, that specific attitude might lead to intentions to punch the bully the next time he or she accosts the child. *Subjective norms* are perceptions or evaluations of the attitudes held by significant others about the specific act. In other words, subjective norms are beliefs that important others think the behavior is a good or bad idea. So, a child who believes that friends and parents would agree that he or she should punch the bully will probably have greater intention to do so.

In any specific context, however, both attitude and subjective norm are weighted. That is, each is assigned a specific importance, based on the situation. A child might believe that punching bullies in the playground is a good idea but not actually punch the bully because a teacher (who disapproves of punching) is watching. The influence of the subjective norm (the teacher) overrides the positive attitude toward punching. The next recess, however, if that teacher is not in sight, the child might be likely to punch the bully.

Media violence can have an impact on both attitudes toward behaviors and subjective norms. The positive presentation of violence in the mass media, as justified, rewarded, and committed by attractive characters might lead to positive attitudes toward specific violent acts. And, media content can also lead to beliefs that society approves of violence in certain settings. But, specific acts based on those attitudes and perceptions are conditional, based on the context in which the act occurs. Even the most violent and provoked person might be hesitant to act aggressively if there are police officers nearby.

PHYSIOLOGICAL THEORIES

Another set of theories that hypothesize that aggressive behavior can grow out of exposure to violent media content recognizes that humans react affectively as well as cognitively to their environment. Key to these approaches are physiological responses to violent media content.

Arousal

Arousal is an affective, nonspecific physiological response that is marked by alertness, faster breathing, and increased heart-rate (Lang, 1994). Arousal is a fairly common reaction to media exposure. People become caught up in the action of movies and television programs and become excited (in the case of action films), frightened (horror movies), sad ("tear jerkers"), sexually aroused (pornography), and involved (quiz programs). Certainly one important reason people use the mass media is for excitement and to help relieve boredom (e.g., Perse, 1996; Rubin, 1983; Zillmann & Bryant, 1985).

Violent media content has the potential to be quite arousing. Based on stimulus generalization, images that depict danger and threat to personal safety can engender arousal. Arousal is an adaptive response because it readies humans to action and increases survival if threats are imminent. Beyond content, the techniques used in violent media content can increase arousal. Fast pacing, numerous cuts and edits, and object movement toward the screen increase arousal (e.g., Lang,

1990; A. Lang, Geiger, Strickwerda, & Sumner, 1993). Indeed, researchers have observed evidence of physiological arousal during exposure to violent film clips (e.g., Bushman & Geen, 1990). So, violent media content can increase arousal. Duration of this arousal, though, is fairly short term, lasting anywhere from a few minutes to no more than 1 hour or so (Tannenbaum & Zillmann, 1975). The effects based on arousal, then, are short term.

There are three related mechanisms that explain how the arousal induced by violent media content might be linked to aggressive behavior for a short time. First, arousal simply increases the likelihood of action. Zillmann (1982) conceptualized arousal as "a unitary force that energizes or intensifies behavior that receives direction by independent means" (p. 53). When aroused, "the individual will do as he would ordinarily—but with increased energy and intensity due to the available residual arousal" (Tannenbaum & Zillmann, 1975, p. 161). Arousal, then, leads to more intense behavior. After exposure to arousing violent media content, people may act intensely. This approach does not argue that aroused action will be aggressive—only that it will be more intense. Actions may be prosocial as well as antisocial. But, if provoked, the antisocial action will be stronger.

The second mechanism that explains the connection between arousal and violent behavior is based on individual differences. Optimal level of arousal is an individual difference variable (Donohew, Finn, & Christ, 1988). That is, people differ on the level of arousal that makes them feel content. When people are below their optimal level of arousal, they feel uncomfortable and bored. When they have exceeded their optimal level of arousal, they also feel uncomfortable; they feel stressed. For some people, with characteristically lower optimal levels of arousal, the arousing aspects of media violence might lead to overstimulation and stress. Overstimulation leads to physical activity to relieve the stress.[9] Once again, this approach does not hold that the physical activity will be necessarily aggressive. Certainly, people pace and fidget when stressed.

The third mechanism is based on the transfer of arousal. Excitation transfer might increase the likelihood of aggressive action for a short time after exposure to violent media content. Arousal, as a physiologi-

---

[9]Most of us have observed children who have been watching action-filled cartoons. Often, they cannot sit still.

cal response, is nonspecific. People, however, label their arousal based on their appraisal of the context (Schachter, 1964). For example, an exciting sporting match is associated with a good deal of arousal. A viewer will label that arousal as either positive (happiness or joy) or negative (sadness, disappointment, or anger) based on the outcome of the game. An important implication of excitation transfer is that residual arousal can increase affective reactions to subsequent events. Arousal can be relabeled, based on a changing context. So, arousal produced by an exciting sports contest can first be labeled as disappointment, but then be relabeled as anger, if one is cut off by another car when leaving the stadium parking lot. Excitation transfer provides a theoretical reason to expect aggression to follow arousal as a result of exposure to violent media content. Violent media content produces arousal in a viewer. Three actions might occur as a result of that arousal: (a) the viewer is likely to act more intensely than when unaroused; (b) the viewer may become overstimulated; (c) in the context of media violence, that arousal might be labeled as fear, anger, or hostility. So, for a short time after exposure to violent media content (while the arousal still persists), behavior will be more likely to be intense and grow out of feelings of hostility or anger.

Habituation Desensitization

Another physiological effect of television violence is *habituation*. Habituation is an adaptive response to the environment. Stimuli that we regularly encounter lose their ability to arouse us. So, with repeated exposure, stimuli that were initially arousing begin to lose their ability to arouse. With repeated exposure, initially strong arousal reactions to media violence diminish. There is a good deal of evidence that people can become habituated to media violence. Children who are viewers of a lot of television violence showed less physiological arousal when watching violence than do viewers of a light amount of television (Cline, Croft, & Courrier, 1973; Thomas, Horton, Lippincott, & Drabman, 1977).

This habituation may have several negative consequences. If people seek out arousing media content to help them achieve optimal levels of arousal, they will need to seek out increasingly more arousing content. Indeed, action film sequels typically become more violent to satisfy repeat viewers (Jhally, 1994). Exposure to increasingly more violent media fare provides fodder for other potential cognitive effects: social learning, aggressive script acquisition, and aggressive cue activation. Moreover, viewing increasingly aggressive media content may lead to callousness, or disregard for the suffering of others as a result of loss of empathy and sympathy. As Zillmann (1991) hypothesized, viewers might become less disturbed when witnessing violence in real life and, hence, "less inclined to intervene in, and attempt to stop, aggression among others" (p. 120). There is research evidence to support Zillmann's views. After longer term exposure to violent "slasher" films, research participants began to report fewer emotionally disturbing reactions to later films. When they were asked to review the report of a sexual assault trial, compared to men who had not viewed the films, participants perceived that the victim had suffered less and reported less sympathy for her (Linz et al., 1984). Repeated exposure to violence led to calloused perceptions and reactions.

Summary

Together, these theoretical approaches offer different, but complementary explanations for aggressive behavior as a consequence of exposure to violent media content. Cognitively, people may learn from the violent actions that they watch and model these actions in their daily lives. But, not all aggressive behavior connected to media exposure mimics media action. Viewers may also learn the principles of violence from the mass media and integrate violence into their own behavioral scripts and repertoire. Or, media content may lead to the acquisition of attitudes that might foster violent behavior. Physiologically, violent media content can be arousing. Arousal can stimulate more intense action, that might be more likely to grow out of anger or hostility labeled as a result of the context of exposure to violent media content.

It is important to note that all of these explanations grow out of the conditional model. None holds that exposure to violence leads irrevocably to violent behavior. Whether violent media content becomes the basis for cognitive or physiological processes leading to aggressive behavior depends on many social category, social relationship, and individual difference variables.

THEORIES OF COGNITIVE AND AFFECTIVE EFFECTS OF VIOLENT MEDIA CONTENT

Although much of the research on violent media content has focused on its effects on aggressive behavior, there is a body of research that focuses on cognitive and affective effects. These approaches hold that the thoughts and feelings evoked by media violence are important, undesirable effects.

Fear in Children

Fear is "an *immediate emotional response* that is typically of relatively short duration, but that may endure, on occasion, for several hours or days, or even longer" (Cantor, 1994, p. 214). Fear is not necessarily a negative effect of media violence. Studies using nonchild samples show that fear is one of the appeals of certain media genres. Suspense, for example, is a highly sought-after aspect of television programs and movies. Generally, more suspenseful movies are more successful movies because suspense produces enjoyment (Zillmann, 1980). Even horror movies have their fans—those who like being scared (e.g., P. A. Lawrence & Palmgreen, 1996). For children, however, fear is not necessarily pleasurable. There is much concern that some children become quite frightened by some media content, and that fear will have some enduring, negative effects.

Over the years, there has been a good deal of research and anecdotal evidence that children do become frightened by some media content. In one of the Payne Fund studies, Blumer (1933) concluded that some children were so affected emotionally by the movies that they were "emotionally possessed." Fear was one of the common emotional reactions to the movies. Over the years, certain movies and television programs have been anecdotally linked to childhood fear. Some movies (e.g., *Indiana Jones and the Temple of Doom*, and *Gremlins*), rated PG, were so frightening that another category to the MPAA movie code was created: PG-13. Parents were cautioned to keep children from watching *The Day After*, a two-part miniseries about a nuclear attack on the United States, and *Jurassic Park*, a popular 1993 film about a rampage of cloned dinosaurs in a modern-day theme park, because of the fearful situations they depicted.

Children become frightened by dangers and injuries (a large part of television drama, reality programs, and news), monsters and "unnatural" creatures, distortions of natural forms (e.g., deformed people and extra-large creatures), and by witnessing fear and danger to others (Cantor, 1994). Concerns about childhood fears have increased as technical expertise and computer effects have increased distortions and the graphic portrayal of violence.

It is not always possible to predict when children will be frightened. Movies such as *Poltergeist* and the Stephen King miniseries *It* have left some children afraid of clowns, for example. Research has shown that children's cognitive immaturity can lead to fear reactions. Sparks and Cantor (1986), for example, noted that young children were quite frightened by the television program *The Incredible Hulk*, in which a scientist transforms into a super-strong green monster to correct injustices. The Hulk was a good character, but he frightened children because he looked scary. At young ages, appearances lead to fear, regardless of the motives or underlying character. As children grow older, they are more likely to be frightened by real, rather than fantasy media content (Cantor, 1994). With cognitive maturity, children realize that fiction is not real. But, frightening real-world characters and events can be great sources of fear. For older children, the realistic violence of reality programs and news may be more frightening than drama (e.g., J. Cantor, Mares, & Oliver, 1993).

Cultivation

Cultivation is perhaps the body of research with the greatest visibility outside our field. Cultivation is grounded in the evidence of a long-term program of content analysis[10] of dramatic prime-time television content that television presents a pattern of images that deviates from reality: Violence is far more common on television than in reality. Cultivation researchers acknowledge that this television violence may lead to some behavioral effects, but they believe that the most common and subtle effect of television violence is that it shapes viewers' beliefs about the real world. Viewers of a lot of television are more likely to believe that violence is common in the real world, to be fearful of crime and personal injury, to be distrustful of others, and to take precautions to protect themselves against crime (Gerbner et al., 1994). According to cultivation, then, the dominant effects of television violence are cognitive (beliefs about social reality) and affective (fear of crime).

Cultivation is a media effect that is explained by the cumulative model of media effects. Selective exposure to specific television programs is not relevant for two reasons. First, content analyses demonstrate that the pattern of images pervades all prime-time content, so it is pointless to try to avoid television's dominant message about vio-

---

[10]Content analyses of prime-time television have been conducted every year since 1967.

lence. Second, television is used nonselectively; people watch television by the clock, rather than choosing specific programs (Gerbner & Gross, 1976). Through repeated exposure to similar messages across the range of television channels, viewers of a lot of television begin to adopt television's world as their view of reality.

This perspective was initially grounded in the Marxist view that explained that television's patterns of violence served to reinforce society's existing power structure. Middle-class White males are more likely to be aggressors and women and minorities are more likely to be victims (e.g., Signorielli, 1990b). So, television teaches minorities and women their place in society, and threatens them with violence should they try to challenge society's power structure. According to Gerbner and Gross (1976), heavy television viewing should lead to "a heightened sense of risk and insecurity (different for groups of varying power) [that] is more likely to increase acquiescence to and dependence upon established authority, and to legitimize its use of force" (p. 194).

Cultivation research has attracted a good of criticism over the years. Scholars and industry representatives questioned the definition of violence that drives the content analyses: "the overt expression of physical force against self or other, compelling action against one's will on pain of being hurt or killed, or actually hurting or killing" (Gerbner & Gross, 1976, p. 184). Because this definition includes unintentional and accidental acts of violence as well as acts of nature, critics argued that the content analyses over-estimated the amount of television violence (e.g., Blank, 1977). Cultivation scholars responded that even accidental violence teaches lessons of power (Gerbner et al., 1977).

Still other scholars pointed out that controlling for sociodemographic variables reduces or eliminates cultivation effects (e.g., Hughes, 1980). Cultivation scholars modified their approach to introduce mainstreaming and resonance to account for the impact of sociodemographic characteristics of people (Gerbner et al., 1980). With mainstreaming, heavy television viewing overrides views outside the television "mainstream" that are due to sociodemographic characteristics. So, heavy television viewers of all sociodemographic groups tend to be more similar. With resonance, television's messages reinforce real-life experiences of people who watch a lot of television, so that certain sociodemographic groups tend to get a "double dose" from television viewing. These reformulations broaden cultivation's scope, but cultivation research has been criticized for using them only as post-hoc explanations (Hirsch, 1981).

Other critics have questioned whether cultivation effects reflect survey respondents' tendencies to overestimate both their television viewing and their chances of victimization (Wober & Gunter, 1986). In fact, studies note that respondents, as a whole, overestimate (e.g., Perse, 1986; Potter, 1986). There is also evidence that a response bias may account for some cultivation effects; effects are more commonly found with negatively rather than positively phrased questions (Rubin, Perse, & Taylor, 1988). And, as television viewing becomes more fragmented and selective, cultivation as a cumulative effect might be less common (Perse et al., 1994). Finally, some critics have offered conceptual criticisms (e.g., Zillmann, 1980; 1991). It seems strange that people would willingly watch media content that leaves them upset and unhappy. Selective exposure research has demonstrated that people watch television to maximize pleasant feelings and minimize negative affect (Zillmann & Bryant, 1985). And, habituation would argue that repeated exposure to violent media content would lead viewers who watch a lot of television to be less affected over time, not more fearful.

These critics have all questioned if the cultivation effect exists. Studies have identified cultivation effects, though, across a wide range of samples and social reality effects (Morgan & Shanahan, 1997). Given the small, but consistent significant effect of television viewing on social reality beliefs, many scholars have assumed that cultivation exists and have attempted to uncover the psychological process that underlies the acquisition of social reality beliefs from television. In general, evidence supports that cultivation may be a result of a psychological process similar to the automatic route of the cognitive-transaction model. That is, cultivated perceptions may be the result of less thoughtful, automatic, heuristic judgments. As Shrum (1997) explained, "the cultivation effect can be explained as an instance of the application of the availability heuristic (Tversky & Kahneman, 1973), which posits that people infer the prevalence of a construct (e.g, crime, violence, occupations) from the ease with which relevant examples can be recalled from memory" (p. 350). For people who watch a lot of television, the easiest examples to recall may be based on television viewing. In a sense, television viewing primes certain notions about the television world. When making judgments about the real world, these viewers have these television notions at top of mind. So, they become the basis of perceptions of social reality.

Support for automatic processing being the basis for cultivation effects is found in experimental studies that found that cultivation effects could be primed by a single exposure, instead of long-term exposure (Tamborini, Zillmann, & Bryant, 1984). Other studies have found that cultivation effects occur when viewers "forget" the source of their information (Mares, 1996). Shrum and his colleges (Shrum, Wyer, & O'Guinn, 1998) found that cultivation effects were stronger when participants were not primed to discount television information. Reminding people of television as a source of information significantly reduces cultivation effects (Morgan & Shanahan, 1997). So, a more mindless, ritualistic approach to television viewing is associated with adopting its pattern of images as the source of social reality beliefs.

Summary

The effects of violent media content on aggressive behavior are a major concern to scholars and policymakers, but there are also concerns about nonbehavioral effects. There are a number of reports that violent media content frightens children and may have enduring effects on their health and well-being. What frightens children changes as they grow older, as do their abilities to cope with their fear. Interestingly, concerns about children's fear responses should focus not only on fictional media content, but on realistic content. Reality programs and news are often quite violent and graphic. The realism associated with these portrayals may increase fear effects for children.

One of the most discussed bodies of research about television violence focuses on the cognitive and affective effects of heavy television viewing. Cultivation research has shown that people who spend more time in the television world are more likely to believe that the real world is like the television world. Viewers of a lot of television, then are more likely to believe that violence is common and that people are at risk. Originally formulated as a cumulative effect of television viewing, recent investigations on the psychological processes underlying the cultivation effect suggest that the effect is a result of more automatic processing of television content, in which easily assessable exemplars are the basis for evaluations about social reality.

THEORIES OF NULL EFFECTS

Although most scholars accept that media violence is a small, but significant contributor to aggressive behaviors, thoughts, and feelings, there are some approaches that argue that media content does not cause aggression. Justification holds that there is a connection between exposure to media violence and aggressive behavior, but the causal direction is from aggression to exposure. Catharsis is an approach that holds that not only is there no effect between viewing media violence and aggression, but the relationship is a negative one.

Justification

The *justification* approach argues that it is aggressive people who watch violent media content to justify their own actions and feelings. In other words, selective exposure accounts for the relationship between aggressive behavior and viewing violent media content. There is some evidence that aggressive tendencies are linked to viewing violence. Huesmann (1982) reported a modest, but significant, connection between aggression and watching violent television a year later. Fenigstein (1979) observed that experimental participants who were given a chance to act aggressively were more likely to select media content that featured violence. Later, Fenigstein and Heyduk (1985) noted that participants who were primed to think violent thoughts by creating imaginary stories including 10 words with aggressive connotations were also more likely to select violent films to watch. McIlwraith and Schallow (1983) found evidence that obsessional emotional daydreaming (i.e., guilt and hostile aggressive daydreams) was linked to reading violent drama and watching television, including violent drama.

There are several theoretical explanations for selective exposure to violent media content as justification. Festinger's (1954) *social comparison theory* holds that selective exposure is motivated to reduce dissonance, or negative feelings, about one's own actions. Seeing media violence might help aggressive people believe that their own thoughts, feelings, and actions are acceptable. Uses and gratifications might explain that aggressive people might seek out violent media content to get information about how to deal with their own violence or to learn new ways to commit violence. Zuckerman (1996) posited that the arousal potential of violent horror films may appeal to high sensation seekers. Zillmann (1998) offered several other explanations for the appeal of media violence. The appeal of violent content might be found in (a) notions of protective vigilance, or satisfying curiosity about how to deal with threatening situations (e.g., Boyanowski, 1977); (b) being able to show mastery in social settings by hiding fear (Zillmann et al.,

1986); (c) to provide a setting for unleashing socially unacceptable emotional responses (e.g., glee at the misfortune of villains); and (d) to maximize entertainment and amusement through excitation transfer, in which the arousal engendered by media violence is transformed into pleasure.

Although justification approaches and research that examines widespread exposure to media violence are relatively unresearched, it is clear that selective exposure offers some valid explanation for the connection between aggressive tendencies and exposure to media violence. Most scholars agree that the connection between aggression and media violence is likely a reciprocal one, in which personal predispositions and media violence are interlinked in patterns of violent lifestyles.

Catharsis

Catharsis is an unusual theory connecting media violence and aggressive behavior. Catharsis holds that watching media violence provides a healthy venue for viewers to "purge" their aggressive feelings. According to catharsis, the connection between watching media violence and aggressive behavior is a negative one; the more one watches violence, the less aggressive they will be. The notion of catharsis is drawn from dramatic theory as far back as Aristotle. In trying to explain the appeal of tragic drama (e.g., the Greek or Shakespearean tragedies) aestheticians argue that through identification with a great and tragic hero, the audience is able to purge themselves of harmful emotions, and feel relieved and more healthy afterward.

The idea that violent media content could be cathartic and healthy was advanced by Feshbach (1955, 1972) who believed that engaging in aggressive fantasies helped reduce aggressive drives. Media content, of course, could help stimulate violent fantasies. There was some limited support for catharsis in a single field study (Feshbach & Singer, 1971). Now, however, catharsis is generally discredited. The overwhelming evidence is that there is a positive, not a negative, relationship between exposure to media violence and aggressive behavior (Paik & Comstock, 1994). Moreover, catharsis is directly counter to priming and arousal theories. Media violence has an arousing, not a calming effect on audiences and tends to activate aggressive, not pleasant thoughts.

Some scholars are reluctant to reject catharsis out of hand, however. Comstock, Chaffee, Katzman, McCombs, and Roberts (1978) suggested that there are two types of catharsis. *Vicarious behavior catharsis*, which is based on purging negative emotions simply by participating vicariously in drama, finds few advocates among the scholarly community. It is not considered a valid apology for media violence. *Overt behavior catharsis*, however, is based on the positive impact of "acting out" emotional responses on purging negative affect. Comstock and his colleagues (1978) summarized the results of several studies that support the effects of overt behavior catharsis. Scheff and Scheele (1980) also presented evidence of overt behavior catharsis. Laughter helps reduce stress and arousal levels. Overt behavior catharsis might explain the appeal of a "good cry" while watching tear-jerkers, or how pornography might help reduce sexual tension.

Summary

Mass communication scholars overwhelmingly accept that media violence bears some responsibility for violent behavior. Media violence is certainly not the largest contributor to violence in society, but it may be one aspect that is more easily solved. Accumulated research evidence has allowed scholars to identify the aspects of violent media content that are most likely to be associated with aggressive behavior (Donnerstein, Slaby, & Eron, 1994):

- when violence is rewarded;
- when violence is justified;
- when aggressive cues are common in everyday life;
- when the aggressor is similar to the audience;
- when the audience can identify with the aggressor;
- when the violence is motivated by a desire to cause harm;
- when the violence has few negative consequences;
- when the violence is presented realistically;
- when there is little criticism of the violence;
- when the violence is physiologically arousing;
- when the audience is predisposed to aggression.

Despite this general agreement, the ideas of scholars who are critical of this research are worth noting (e.g., Freedman, 1984; Wurtzel & Lometti, 1987). Correlation is not the same as correlation. Finding connections between aggressive behavior and exposure to violent media content does not exclude alternate explanations (e.g., selective exposure) or the impact of other influences (e.g., overconsumption of alcohol). Experimental studies can offer evidence of causation, but research ethics do not allow scholars to use measures of realistic aggression. Punching a Bobo doll, administering shocks, or committing fouls in floor hockey are not the kind of violence that our society fears. Research designs may have demonstrated a connection between exposure to violent media content and more socially (or experimenter) acceptable "aggressive" acts, but have been unable to uncover links to real-life violent behavior.

Although most communication scholars are loath to recommend censorship (more communication is generally considered better than less), there have been a number of policy solutions proposed to the problem of media violence. Saunders (1996) suggested limiting the First Amendment protection of media violence by applying the same obscenity exception that is applied to sexual content to violent content. So, "sufficiently explicit and offensive depictions of violence" (p. 4) could be found to be legally obscene. This would allow various levels of government to regulate, or even ban such content. Hamilton (1998) proposed that media violence be treated as environmental pollution. Hamilton argues that media violence, like pollution, has negative externalities, or costs, that are borne by society, but not by the producers. This notion suggests solutions, such as programming taxes, to make producers bear some of the costs of their product and to discourage production of harmful content. Another solution might be based on zoning laws that limit the locations and times of operation of certain pollution-producing businesses to reduce their harm. This would involve channeling violent content to hours when children would be less likely to be in the audience. A first attempt to channel violent content was the 1975–1976 Family Viewing Time policy, in which the Federal Communications Commission (FCC) strongly encouraged television broadcasters to limit violence during the first hour of prime time. The policy, though, was overturned in federal court as a result of improper FCC action and seen as a violation of broadcasters' First Amendment rights. Channeling, however, has been more successful with indecent broadcast material.

A solution adopted by government and industry that can limit the impact of media violence is based on the film model. Television programs are now labeled to make parents more aware of age-appropriate programs and to give them information as to what sort of content (i.e., violence, sex, dialogue, or adult situations) makes the program less suitable for children. The 1996 Telecommunications bill mandates that by January 1, 2000, all television sets with screens 13-inches or larger include the V-chip, a device that allows parents to block programs with certain ratings.

Another way to limit children's viewing of violent media content is to provide children with other, less violent programming. The popularity of *Sesame Street* and other educational entertainment programs for children shows that violence is not necessary for popularity. Scholars believe that if there were more well done entertaining and educational children's programs, children would spend their time watching them, instead of less educational, or violent, or adult-oriented programming.

Research on the effects of violent media content offers guidelines to reduce the negative impact of media violence. Research demonstrates that parental mediation of violent television programming seems to limit aggressive effects (Nathanson, 1999). When parents limit their children's viewing of violent television, there is less exposure to violence. Parents' comments during television viewing also limit aggressive effects. Parents can teach children critical viewing skills, such as reminding them that content is not real, that aggressors are not justified, and that there are real, negative consequences of violent behavior. These can all encourage children to discount television drama as a model. By providing information not included by media producers, parents should be able to minimize the negative impact of media violence. Parents can also provide the normative influence that lets children see that violence is not a socially acceptable solution to problems. As Nathanson (1999) concluded, "parents can socialize children into an orientation toward violent TV that makes them more or less vulnerable to its negative effects" (p. 138). Exposure to violence does not have to lead to negative effects; there are ways to mitigate negative effects and enhance positive effects of media content.

It is important to remember that the prosocial effects of television are stronger and more common than its negative effects (Hearold, 1986; Paik, 1995). As Hearold (1986) concluded, "Although fewer studies exist on prosocial effects, the effect size is so much larger, holds up better under more stringent conditions, and is consistently higher for boys and girls, that the potential for prosocial effects overrides the smaller but persistent negative effects of antisocial programs" (p. 116).

8

Effects of Sexually Explicit
Media Content

Sex is a common theme in most media content. Some type of sexual reference is found in 90% of all television programs (Signorielli, 1987) and in 60-75% of all music videos (Baxter et al., 1985; Sherman & Dominick, 1986). Chapter 6 discussed how this sexual content can play a role in adolescent socialization effects. But, the most commonly available sexual content is often not very explicit. On television, sex is often a topic of conversation or implied in visual euphemisms (e.g., Baxter et al., 1985; Greenberg & D'Alessio, 1985). Other media, though, provide more sexually explicit presentations of sexual behavior. R-, X-, NC-17-rated and unrated movies, adult magazines and books, pub-lic-access cable channels, videotapes, and the WWW all deliver con-tent that depicts graphic sexual acts (e.g., D. Brown & Bryant, 1989). It is difficult to get accurate estimates of interest in or exposure to sexu-ally explicit materials, but there are indications that they are widely available and used by a large audience (Bryant & D. Brown, 1989).

Although sexually graphic material can certainly contribute to child and adolescent sexual socialization, most graphic material is not as readily available to those audiences as the less explicit content found on television. Parents, educators, and public policy analysts all try to find ways to channel this explicit content, to keep it from being easily accessed by younger children. Because of these restrictions on avail-ability, most of the research on the effects of sexually graphic media content focuses on older adolescents and sexually active adults.

Sexually explicit media content is often referred to as pornography, erotica, or obscenity. These terms are often used interchangeably, although they have slightly different meanings and connotations (Hawkins & Zimring, 1988). *Obscenity*, for example, is a legal term that defines sexual content that is not protected by the First Amendment.[1] *Erotica*, derived from the Greek word *eros* (love), refers to sexually explicit content, without the connotation of degradation. *Pornography* is derived from the Greek words meaning writings of or about prostitutes. This term tends to define sexual content that includes violence or actions that degrade and demean women (e.g., Longino, 1980). These different terms reflect the different assumptions and views about sexually explicit content that guide research on effects.

THREE RESEARCH PERSPECTIVES ON SEXUALLY EXPLICIT MEDIA CONTENT

Linz and Malamuth (1993) organized and analyzed much of the research on the effects of sexually explicit materials and concluded that there are three "normative theories" that guide research into the effects of sexually explicit materials. These normative theories grow out of the connotations of the different terms used to describe sexually explicit materials. They also are based on certain assumptions about the functions and effects of sexually explicit media content. And, each implies different societal responses to sexually explicit material. Like Seibert et al.'s (1956) four theories of the press, these three perspectives are based on assumptions about humans and definitions of truth and morality. These assumptions guide research and color the types of studies that are conducted and how the results are interpreted.

Moralist Perspective

This perspective is similar to the authoritarian media theory (Siebert et al., 1963). According to both moralist and authoritarian approaches, there is an absolute truth that is revealed by a higher authority (e.g., God) to a chosen few in society. These chosen few are usually recog-

---

[1]The Supreme Court ruled in *Miller v. California* (1973) that obscenity was determined by applying these three rules: (1) The average person, applying contemporary community standards, finds the material, taken as a whole, appeals to prurient interests; (2) The work depicts, in a patently offensive way, sexual conduct defined by the applicable state law; (3) The work lacks any serious literary, artistic, political, or scientific value.

nized by society as having authority and power (e.g., ruling class, religious leaders). Those with access to knowledge of truth and morals have the obligation to protect others in society who do not possess that knowledge. So, authoritarian systems are marked by censorship of content that authorities deem to be harmful to society.

Linz and Malamuth (1993) pointed out that within this perspective, sexually explicit material is believed to cause societal disruption by creating an unhealthy or excessive interest in sex. An overemphasis on sex could corrupt morals and lead people to act in ways that undermine marriage and family. Sexual media content might also distract people from other important societal roles. Sexual content might have the overall impact of lessening society's moral climate as people pursue sexual self-gratification. This moralist approach sees no benefit to sexually explicit material. Sexual behavior is private and making it public can only encourage distasteful or immoral acts. This approach appears to have been the basis for current obscenity and broadcast indecency laws. Both laws make reference to sexual content that is "patently offensive." Obscenity law also defines outlawed material as content that "appeal[s] to the prurient interest."[2]

Some research in our field has considered effects of pornography from this perspective. There is little doubt that sexually explicit media content has the ability to sexually arouse (e.g., Malamuth & Check, 1980). Over time, however, the arousal response can diminish. People can become habituated to sexual materials so that these materials no longer have the potential to arouse. Zillmann and Bryant (1984, 1986b) observed that research participants (male and female college students as well as nonstudent adults) became habituated after exposure to sexually explicit films of heterosexual, oral, and anal intercourse. After massive exposure to these films (from just under 5 hours to about 6 hours), research participants lost some of their ability to be aroused by sexual content. Heart rates were not as pronounced as the control groups' heart rates when exposed to suggestive content. There is additional evidence that commonly available sexual materials can lead to habituation. Research partici-

[2]*Prurient* has a few definitions. It can mean "appeals to sexual desire" or "unwholesome" or "unhealthy."

pants were given opportunities to watch a film privately from a group of films that included family-oriented (G-rated) films, common pornography (heterosexual and oral sex), and less common pornography (i.e., bondage, sadomasochism, and bestiality). Those who had been massively exposed to common heterosexual pornography were more likely to watch films depicting less common sexual acts. Zillmann and Bryant (1986b) concluded that

> our findings support the view that continued exposure to generally available, nonviolent pornography that exclusively features heterosexual behavior among consenting adults arouses an interest in and creates a taste for pornography that portrays less commonly practiced sexual activities, including those involving the infliction of pain. (p. 574)

Zillmann and Bryant's (1982, 1986b) research noted other effects of exposure to sexually explicit materials. Over time, research participants report to be less repulsed by sexually explicit content and tend to report more enjoyment of it. In addition, after massive exposure to common heterosexual pornography, research participants are more likely to believe that certain sexual acts are more common in society than groups who have not been massively exposed to common heterosexual pornography. The experimental group, for example, estimated that almost two-thirds of adults engage in oral sexual practices, compared to just over one-third of a control group that viewed no pornography. In addition, the experimental group estimated that 28.5% of adults engaged in anal intercourse (compared to 12.1% estimated by the no-exposure control group), 30.2% engaged in group sex (compared to 10.9%), 14.2% engaged in sadomasochism (compared to 7.4%), and 12.0% engaged in bestiality (compared to 6.6%).

Massive exposure to sexually explicit materials also appears to affect family values (Zillmann & Bryant, 1988). Compared to the control group, the exposure group reported more tolerance for pre- and extramarital sexual activity, less endorsement of marriage as an institution, were reported to want fewer children, and were more likely to believe that there were health risks in sexual repression. Together these results suggest a view that sexually explicit media content fosters exposure to deviance and may undermine societal values. This moralist perspective bears some similarities to the cumulative effects model. Repeated exposure to sexual materials leads to effects that are negative and relatively long term.

Feminist Perspective

This perspective is referred to as a *feminist perspective* not because it is endorsed by all feminists, but because its focus is on the negative effects of sexually explicit materials on women. According to this view, sexual content is pornography, or material produced for men that demeans and devalues women. Pornography contributes to the sexualization of women, discrimination against women, and a societal climate that is more accepting of violence against women.

This perspective is based on a social responsibility media philosophy (Siebert et al., 1963). Social responsibility is based on the recognition that societal structure affects the availability and interpretation of media content. For example, in the United States, the First Amendment guarantees the right of free speech. Based on libertarian philosophy, U.S. democratic principles hold that all ideas have the right to be expressed. In reality, however, those ideas with political and economic value are most likely to have a platform. Social responsibility media theory argues that media should make room to express ideas and present content for underserved groups in society (e.g., children, nondominant political parties, the poor). Moreover, the goal of mass media should be to improve society, not merely to give people what they want. So, the feminist perspective on sexual content holds that pornography is irresponsible media content that harms women.

The feminist perspective is based on evidence that pornography is replete with antifemale images and themes. Weaver (1991d) pointed out that there are three major categories of sexually explicit media content. The first, that with standard nonviolent themes, is probably the most common. Even though this category does not contain aggression against women, it is clearly produced with a male audience in mind. As such, it focuses on explicit sexual acts and ignores nonsexual relationships among people. Because the focus is on sexual gratification, foreplay and affection are rarely shown. Women are usually portrayed as sexually available, eager, and promiscuous. In all, this violent content promotes the view that women's greatest value may be as sexual objects, who satisfy the sexual needs of men, with few needs of their own.

The second type of sexually explicit media content, that with violent or coercive themes, causes considerable concern because of the linkage of sex and violence. Slasher films, or films that depict graphic violence, commonly include violence against women (Molitor & Sapolsky, 1993; Weaver, 1991a). In fact, about one-third of all sexual acts in slasher films are accompanied by violence and over 20% of all female victims of violence are killed in sexual circumstances (Molitor & Sapolsky, 1993). This type of media content especially might be linked to cognitive, affective, and behavioral negative effects against women.

A third type of sexually explicit material is that which focuses on idealized sexual themes. This is the content that feminists would not consider pornography because it does not demean women. Some writers have suggested that it is sexual content written for women that would present sexual activity in a romantic and affectionate way. There is, however, little evidence that very much of this sort of material is produced (Weaver, 1991d).

Much of the research conducted on the effects of pornography support the conclusions of the feminist perspective. Exposure to pornography appears to be associated with harmful consequences. In experimental settings, pornography primes unrealistic expectations about women and sex. After exposure, male research participants report that their partners are less sexually attractive (Weaver et al., 1984) and that they are less sexually satisfied with their partners' physical attraction, affection, and sexual performance (Zillmann & Bryant, 1988). Using survey methodology, Perse (1994) observed that exposure to sexually explicit materials, as well as using those materials for sexual enhancement (mood enhancement, information, and foreplay) were linked to greater acceptance of sex-role stereotypes and sexual conservatism, or views that men, not women, should be sexually active. Perse (1994) suggested that the use of sexual material by males to sexually prime their partners "might cause, reinforce, or grow out of views that dehumanize women and see them as objects needing to be 'turned on'" (p. 507).

Even more troubling to feminists is evidence that exposure to pornography is linked to acceptance of violence against women. Several studies have found that, compared to control groups, experimental groups who have been exposed to sexually explicit material are more likely to accept violence against women (Malamuth & Check, 1981), express less compassion for female rape victims (Zillmann & Bryant,

1982), and recommend lighter prison sentences for convicted rapists (Zillmann & Bryant, 1982). Metaanalyses have found that, in experimental settings, there is an average correlation of $r = .146$ ($N = 2,248$) between exposure to sexual materials and acceptance of rape myths[3] (Allen, Emmers, Gebhardt, & Giery, 1995) and an average correlation of $r = .132$ ($N = 2,040$) between exposure to pornography and behavioral aggression (Allen, D'Alessio, & Brezgel, 1995). Exposure to sexually violent material has also been linked to increased aggression (administering shocks) against women in laboratory settings (Donnerstein & Berkowitz, 1981).

In all, the feminist perspective sees this research suggesting that pornography's most potentially harmful effects are on the attitudes and beliefs of those who use it. Because pornography fosters beliefs and attitudes that reinforce male dominance over women, pornography may promote discrimination and abuse against women. Any potential beneficial effects of sexually explicit media content, therefore, cannot override these negative effects.

Liberal Perspective

In direct contrast to moralist and feminist approaches, a liberal approach focuses on the benefits and functions that pornography serves. Most of the research locating negative effects has been conducted in laboratory settings. Those who hold the liberal perspective reject, for the most part, the findings of experimental laboratory research because of concerns about ecological validity and experimenter demand. (Critiques of this research will be discussed later in this chapter.) Instead, they rely on research that shows little connection between the availability of sexually explicit material and crime rates.

This perspective grows out of liberal media theory philosophy (Siebert et al., 1963) and is based on a functionalist approach to mass communication (e.g., C. R. Wright, 1986). A *liberal media theory philosophy* holds that knowledge and truth are available to everyone. So, in order to discover the truth and benefit society, everyone should have

---

[3]*Rape myths* are stereotyped, inaccurate, outdated, and calloused beliefs about rape and attitudes about women that reflect lack of sympathy for rape victims. Rape myths are usually measured with a scale developed by Burt (1980). Sample items are: "Any healthy woman can successfully resist a rapist if she really wants to", "When women go around braless or wearing short skirts and tight tops, they are just asking for trouble", and "If a girl engages in necking or petting and she lets things get out of hand, it is her own fault if her partner forces sex on her."

the right to free speech and all ideas should be heard and evaluated. Even inaccurate ideas offer benefits because they stimulate discussion that can lead to enlightenment. *Functionalist approaches* hold that things exist because they serve some benefit for society. If something is not useful, it will not be used. Liberal approaches to sexually explicit media content, then, argue that the value of pornography should be judged by the individual who uses it and the functions that it serves for individuals and society.

Outside of the laboratory, there is only limited research to suggest that exposure to sexually explicit media content is harmful. Across a wide range of different countries, analyses reveal that rape has not increased any more than other violent crimes when circulation of sexually explicit materials increases (Kutchinsky, 1991). In the United States, correlations between rape rates and circulation of sex magazines become nonsignificant when attitudes toward violence are introduced as a control variable (Baron & Straus, 1984). The 1971 Commission on Obscenity and Pornography concluded that sexually explicit materials could have a cathartic effect and displace antisocial sexual acts.[4] In fact, some studies found that sex offenders and people who engaged in "abnormal" sexual behaviors were less exposed to sexually explicit materials (Cook & Fosen, 1971; Johnson, Kupperstein, & Peters, 1971; Walker, 1971).

The liberal perspective focuses on the therapeutic aspects of sexually explicit media content. Sexual materials have been used successfully in therapy with adolescents, medical students, physically disabled adults, and sexually dysfunctional people (Yaffe, 1982). Others argue that sexual materials can prevent sexual problems because they provide information about sex, relieve sexual anxieties and inhibitions, and facilitate communication about sex among partners (e.g., W. C. Wilson, 1978). Surveys support liberal conclusions. People find sexually explicit media content entertaining and educational. Patrons of adult movies report that the films encourage safe sexual fantasies and sexually primed them for their partners (Nawy, 1973; Winick, 1971). Women report to read sexually explicit books for entertainment, escape, to pass time, to satisfy their curiosity about sex, to learn more about sex, and to relax (Coles & Shamp, 1984; Lawrence & Herold, 1988). A uses and gratifications study (Perse, 1994)

---

[4]See the discussion of Comstock et al.'s (1978) notion of overt behavior catharsis in chap. 7.

found that the most salient reason for using sexually explicit materials was for diversionary reasons, such as entertainment and relaxation. Respondents also reported to use sexual materials for sexual enhancement, or to get ideas for sex and to facilitate sex with one's partner, or for solitary sexual release.

The liberal perspective recognizes that sexual materials can be dysfunctional as well as functional. Harm, though, is not due to the nature of the media content, but to the interpretations of the content by individuals. Like the conditional model of media effects, the liberal perspective holds that, for the most part, sexual materials have only beneficial or reinforcement effects. It is aspects of individuals that lead to harmful effects.

THEORIES TO EXPLAIN THE EFFECTS OF SEXUALLY EXPLICIT MEDIA CONTENT

There are few theories proposed to explain specifically the effects of sexually explicit media content. Scholars rely on various other theories to explain how the audience can adopt beliefs, attitudes, or behaviors depicted in sexual materials. The most comprehensive set of theories are those used to explain the effects of media violence (see chap. 7).

Social Learning

There is little research that explicitly tests social learning as the theoretical explanation behind the effects of sexually explicit material (Allen, Emmers, et al., 1995). This is understandable, given the focus of social learning on the learning and imitation of specific behaviors depicted in media content (Bandura, 1994). It would be unethical and impractical to assess social learning of private sexual behaviors or sexual violence. But, there are good reasons to suggest that sexually explicit media content might be the basis for social learning (Check & Malamuth, 1981). Sexually explicit behaviors in media content are usually quite salient. That is, they capture the attention of the audience. Much of the audience is quite attentive to sexually explicit action because sexually explicit materials usually present behaviors that are both relevant and adaptive. Sexually explicit media content often has some connection to the audience members' lives. Some individuals expect to be able to learn about sex and get ideas for their own sexual relationship (Duncan, 1990; Perse, 1994). Sexually explicit behavior is usually associated with especially potent rewards: sexual pleasure and satisfaction. Moreover, sexually explicit materials typically present sexual behavior as justified. That is, victims of sexual violence don't appear to suffer; female victims often appear to begin to enjoy the sex and become willing participants (Palys, 1986; Slade, 1984). In all, the salience of the presentation, the utility and rewards of sexual behavior, and the justification of the action suggest that sexually explicit media content may be the basis for social learning of sexual acts as well as sexual violence.

Information Processing

Huesmann's (1986) information-processing model of the effects of violence media content may also provide some explanation for the effects of sexually explicit materials. The *information-processing model* holds that the connection between media content and subsequent behaviors arises from a learning process. Unlike social learning theory, which explains how specific observed behaviors are learned, this model focuses on the learning of scripts, or patterns of behaviors. According to the information-processing approach, the learned behaviors are not necessarily the same as those observed. Through mental encoding and elaboration, scripts adapted from sexually explicit media content may be combined with preexisting scripts. So, patterns of behavior might resemble the scripts used in sexually explicit materials, and integrate violence against partners, callous disregard for feelings of others, or actions that objectify and demean women. Although there has been no research to test specifically audiences' learning of scripts based on sexually explicit media content, this process can explain some behavioral effects of exposure.

Priming

A good deal of the research on the effects of sexually explicit media content is conducted in laboratory settings, with dependent variables measured shortly after exposure. Much of this evidence of short-term effects of exposure to sexually explicit materials can be explained by priming (Zillmann & Weaver, 1989). Sexually explicit media content is a potent prime. It is salient, and content that features this sort of content uses production techniques, such as close-ups and enhanced sounds to make these images and actions even more prominent. Those who have written about the biological connections between attention to media content and arousal (e.g., Malamuth, 1996) would certainly recognize the biological basis for attention to sexual media. In laboratory settings, especially, where selective exposure is often overridden due to experimental procedures, sexual media content may activate schemas in research participants, schemas "that are likely to encourage men to focus on women's sexuality and foster high expectations for women's sexual attractiveness, sexual interest, and sexual permissiveness" (Jansma, Linz, Mulac, & Imrich, 1997, p. 4).

There is research to support priming effects of sexually explicit media content. Pornography appears to prime sexually oriented schemas that lead male participants to see their own partners as less sexually attractive (Weaver et al., 1984; Zillmann & Bryant, 1988). For sex-typed males, those males who are guided by "a readiness to encode all cross-sex interaction in sexual terms and all members of the opposite sex in terms of sexual attractiveness" (Bem, 1981, p. 31), priming effects may be particularly strong. McKenzie-Mohr and Zanna (1990) observed that sex-typed males (compared to non sex-typed males) interacted with female confederates in a way that marked sexual interest. They moved physically closer to the confederate and were judged to pay more attention to her physical appearance and disregard her intellectual abilities. Jansma and her colleagues (1997) observed naturalistic male–female interactions after exposure to sexually explicit films. They found that, compared to non-sex-typed males, sex-typed males who watched a degrading, sexually explicit film rated a woman's intellectual abilities lower. As Jansma and her colleagues (1997) noted, one-shot laboratory studies reveal modest priming effects. Exposure to pornography over time, however, would lead to frequent priming of sexist schemas. Long-term exposure to pornography might increase the chance that those schemas will be used to guide how men interact with and evaluate women in daily life.

Attitude Change

Research supports the conclusion that exposure to sexually explicit media content is linked to calloused attitudes toward women. In both laboratories and natural settings, the more sexually explicit material that men watch, the more likely they are to endorse rape myths and be accepting of sexual violence against women (Allen, D'Alessio, et al., 1995; Allen, Emmers, et al., 1995; Malamuth & Check, 1985; Perse, 1994). Exposure to sexual materials has also been linked to less sympathy toward rape victims (Linz et al., 1984; Zillmann & Bryant, 1982) and less support for the women's movement (Zillmann & Bryant, 1982). Sexually explicit media content fosters these attitudes because of the themes and images that cut across pornography. Sexually aggressive behavior is typically enacted by attractive characters and although women initially resist forced sexual advances, they quickly become wanton and willing participants (Palys, 1986; Slade, 1984). Because pornography ignores relationship development, romance, and foreplay, women are typically objectified, valued only for their sexual attraction and skills. With repeated exposure, these themes translate into calloused attitudes toward women and beliefs that rape is not particularly harmful (Zillmann & Bryant, 1982).

Arousal

Physiological and sexual arousal are fairly common reactions to sexually explicit media content (M. Brown, Amoroso, & Ware, 1976; Donnerstein & Barrett; 1978; Harris, 1994b). Arousal might facilitate the effects of sexual materials. The arousal produced by sexual material might lead to more intense responses (Tannenbaum & Zillmann, 1975). There is evidence that exposure to sexual materials leads to heightened aggression in angered men. Early studies on the impact of violent pornography found that already angered research participants were more likely to administer harmful electric shocks after watching film clicks with sexual content (Donnerstein & Berkowitz, 1981; Zillmann, 1971). Excitation-transfer theory (e.g., Zillmann, 1980) offers additional support for a connection between heightened arousal as a result of exposure to sexually explicit media content and more intense action. *Arousal* is a nonspecific physiological response. Humans define the arousal based on their appraisal of the environmental context (Schachter, 1964). If they are already angry, the arousal is interpreted as increased anger. Clearly, excitation transfer would predict that increased anger is not the only response to sexual arousal. If one is feeling happy or romantic, those feelings could also be heightened.

Habituation–Desensitization

Just as viewers of violent media content can become less aroused with repeated exposure, so too viewers of sexually explicit media content will find that it loses its potential to arouse. Zillmann and Bryant's research (1984, 1986b) noted that research participants became habituated to more common forms of pornography with repeated exposure. Not only was there evidence of reduced physiological arousal (heart rate), but research participants seemed to be more likely to seek out more deviant types of pornography than participants who had not been massively exposed to pornography. Beyond evidence to support moralists' desires to suppress pornography, these research findings have some additional implications. The pornography that might be sought out by habituated audiences is likely to depict more arousing types of content, such as less common sexual practices or sexual violence and coercion. This combination of sexual activity and violence might have other, cognitive effects, based on social learning, attitude change, or priming.

Cultivation

Cultivation is a theoretical approach that hypothesizes that exposure to television leads viewers who watch a lot of television to adopt a view of social reality that is consistent with television's content. Cultivation might not be the most appropriate theory to apply to the effects of pornography. First, cultivation focuses on television as the medium that is most widely accessible and used in our society. Because most viewing takes place during the evening, television is likely to be watched nonselectively, more by the clock than because of specific programs (Gerbner & Gross, 1976). Moreover, content analyses show that certain patterns of themes and images cut across almost all of television's programming. Pornography is not used like television. It is not as widely available as television and because of that restricted availability, exposure to pornography might not be so nonselective. Among heavy users of pornography, however, cultivation of a sort might occur. Patterns of certain types of images, however, do cut across most types of pornography: various sorts of sexual behavior.

There are two general types of perceptions that can be cultivated. First-order effects, or beliefs about the factual world of the media, and second-order effects, or attitudes that grow out of those facts (Gerbner, Gross, Morgan, & Signorielli, 1986). Zillmann and Bryant (1982) observed evidence of cultivation of first-order cultivation effects. Compared to research participants who were not exposed to sexually explicit movie clips, college students who had been massively exposed to pornography over a period of 6 weeks were more likely to estimate that the sexual acts common in pornography (e.g., oral, anal, and group sex) were common across society. And, although scholars have not explicitly used cultivation to explain the acquisition of rape myths, it is conceivable that prolonged exposure to pornography, because of its common theme of sexual coercion, could lead to the cultivation of rape myths in people who view a lot of pornography (Allen, Emmers, et al., 1995).

Justification

Justification is an approach that holds that the causal direction between negative effects of media content and exposure to that content is based on selective exposure; that is, it is sexually violent or calloused people who prefer sexually explicit media content because it justifies their preexisting beliefs, attitudes, and behavioral tendencies. There may be evidence to support this approach. First, not everyone uses or seeks out sexually explicit media content (Bryant & Brown, 1989). Even accounting for social desirability, different types of media content have different size audiences. Sexually explicit R-rated films are viewed by a large number of people, men's magazines that feature sexually explicit photographs and letters are read by somewhat fewer people, and sexually explicit movies and videos are watched regularly by about a quarter of adults (Bryant & Brown, 1989).

Different types of people have different reactions to sexually explicit media content. Malamuth and Check (1983) observed that men who have a self-admitted high "likelihood of rape" became more sexually aroused when they listened to aggressive, coercive, and nonconsenting sexual acts than when they listened to consenting sex. Check and Guloien (1989) observed differential negative effects of sexually violent and dehumanizing pornography based on psychoticism. Research participants viewed, over a period of 6 days, either three videos containing sexually violent scenes, or three videos with sex in which the woman was objectified and dehumanized, or three videos containing romantic, sexual acts. For those participants low in psychoticism, compared to a no-exposure control group, exposure did not have any effect on their self-admitted likelihood of committing rape or forcing sex acts. But, compared to the control group, those participants high in psychoticism who were exposed to violent and dehumanizing pornography were significantly more likely to say they would rape or force a woman to engage in sex against her will. Based on his research on men who have been convicted of sexually violent crimes, Marshall (1989) believed that sexual criminals have a different use for and reliance on pornography than nonviolent men. There is some evidence that sadistic rapists become more aroused by violent pornography and rapists generate rape fantasies even when they view consenting sexual acts (Marshall, 1989). For certain especially violent men, pornography may serve, in part, as justification for their acts.

Catharsis

It is obvious that vicarious behavior catharsis is not a valid explanation for effects of pornography. All evidence contradicts the proposition that sexual feelings can be purged or satisfied simply by viewing or reading sexually explicit materials. Overt behavior catharsis, however, might be an outcome of use. *Overt behavior catharsis* is based on the positive impact of "acting out" emotional responses on purging negative affect (Comstock et al., 1978). Sexually explicit media content is used, at times, to generate sexual fantasies, for masturbation, and to reduce sexual tension (Duncan, 1990; Perse, 1994).

Models of Effects

The effects of sexually explicit content draw explanations from all four models of media effects. The almost uniform arousal effects of sexual material points out that sexual content, itself, can evoke automatic, short-term physiological effects. Gender differences might explain how different types of content appeals to males and females, but the predictability of these effects can be explained by innate links between the mind and body (Malamuth, 1996). The cognitive–transaction model is supported by research that demonstrates that salient features of sexually explicit material prime gender-stereotyped schemas that affect, for a short time, real-life appraisals (J. B. Weaver et al., 1984; Jansma et al., 1997). Content analyses of pornography conclude that there is a good deal of consistency in the kinds of actions that are presented. J. B. Weaver's (1991d) analysis of these studies concludes that 90% of visual pornography involves heterosexual intercourse. The settings and action are stylized and vary little. Moreover, because most of the material is targeted to a male audience, pornography tends to focus on sexual gratification at the expense of expressions of affection and depictions of relationship development. The cumulative model would explain that these consonant and consistent themes and images, over time, might lead to cognitive or attitudinal effects in heavy consumers.

The conditional model explains that effects of sexual materials is indirect, conditional on aspects of the audience. First, although sexually explicit materials are certainly widely available, not everyone chooses to watch or read them (Bryant & Brown, 1989). The social undesirability associated with sexually explicit materials also implies that those who are interested in pornography need to take somewhat active steps to acquire it. So, selective exposure is relevant to effects of use. Some research has suggested that preexisting attitudes about rape (Malamuth & Check, 1983) and personality traits (Check & Guloien, 1989) affected arousal and attitudinal responses to pornography. Perse (1994) found that holding rape myths was, in part, conditional on reasons for using sexual materials. Those respondents who used erotica for sexual release were less likely to hold rape myths; those who used erotica as a substitution for a partner were more likely to hold rape myths. And, using erotica for diversionary, entertainment reasons or for sexual enhancement (information and foreplay) had an indirect impact on rape myths, through respondents' links to greater exposure to sexual materials and through their impact on holding hostile beliefs about women.

Malamuth and Briere (1986) proposed a model of indirect effects of pornography. According to their model, sexually explicit materials can lead indirectly to antisocial effects in the presence of other conditions. They suggest that media content, in connection with individual experiences, such as home environment, social network, and personality characteristics, can be linked to hostility toward women and the acquisition of attitudes that might favor the connections between sexuality and violence. In the presence of opportunity, acute arousal, or forces that lessen disinhibition (e.g., alcohol), sexual aggression might result. Marshall's (1989) analysis of research on adult rapists illuminates the indirect influence of pornography on aggression. Research on men who have been convicted of rape and child molestation paint a grim portrait of their early family lives. Rapists are raised typically in violent and abusive homes with alcoholic and neglectful parents. As a result, these boys have low self-esteem and lack the social skills that would allow them to develop normal romantic relationships. Because of their lack of social skills and as a result of the abuse they have suffered, these boys often turn to inappropriate sexual acts. Marshall hypothesizes that pornography has the potential to have a stronger impact on these malsocialized young men. Without adult models of normal male–female relationships, the skewed and inaccurate relationships depicted in pornography might have more potent cognitive and affective effects, leading to beliefs about sexual acts and attitudes about women that mimic those in pornography. Violent pornography, especially, might be more likely to be modeled, because the violence in it mirrors abusive home life. Violent effects of pornography, then, are highly conditional on a host of individual, social, and cultural factors.

Are Negative Effects Due to the Sex or the Violence?

Research on the effects of sexually explicit materials has been motivated by concerns about negative societal effects. Many of these studies grow out of the feminist social responsibility perspective and focus on how sexually explicit materials are linked directly to aggression against women or indirectly by fostering tolerance for violence or calloused attitudes toward women as sexual partners and as crime victims. Research consistently supports experimental connections between sexually violent and explicit materials and attitudes that reflect acceptance of violence and proclivity to engage in violence toward women (Allen, D'Alessio, et al., 1995; Linz et al., 1984; Paik & Comstock, 1994). Most pornography, however, is not violent (Weaver, 1991d). Most pornography features nonviolent focus on sexual acts, typically heterosexual intercourse, lesbianism, oral–genital contact, and ejaculation (Hebditch & Anning, 1988). Most of this content, however, focuses solely on sexual activity from a male viewpoint and ignores the romantic aspects of sexual activity. Sex partners are not presented as relationship partners; women tend to be objectified and valued solely for their abilities to satisfy males' sexual desire. Most pornography, then, is not violent, but it demeans and devalues women. Are there negative effects of this nonviolent but demeaning material?

Social scientists disagree about concluding that nonviolent pornography fosters acceptance of violence against women. Zillmann and Bryant's (1982, 1984) research supported conclusions that nonviolent but degrading pornography is linked to calloused beliefs about and attitudes toward women. Experimental groups who viewed clips of pornographic movies over a period of time, compared to control groups who saw clips of nonsexual movies, recommended shorter sentences for convicted rapists and indicated less support for the women's liberation movement. Zillmann (1989) noted that these findings were corroborated by two unpublished studies (Linz, 1985; J. B. Weaver, 1987). The research observed that, compared to control groups who watched nonsexual films, experimental participants who watched nonviolent sexual films reported less sympathy and compassion for rape victims and victims of sexual abuse. Check and Guloien (1989) also found that, compared to control groups who did not watch any sexually oriented films, those who were exposed to both violent and nonviolent but dehumanizing pornography reported greater willingness to force women into sexual acts (a proclivity to rape). Allen, D'Alessio, and their colleague's (1995) metaanalysis of the effects of pornography concludes that nonaggressive pornography is significantly related to aggressive outcomes in laboratory settings, though not as strongly as is aggressive pornography.

Other communication scholars, though, are not convinced that pornography that is not explicitly violent is harmful: "While it seems that certain types of pornography can influence aggression and other asocial attitudes and behaviors toward women, this is not the case for other forms of pornography, especially nonaggressive pornography" (Donnerstein, 1984, p. 78). These scholars base their conclusion on several arguments. First, media content does not need to be sexual to lead to attitudes that reflect an acceptance of violence against women. In a field experiment, Malamuth and Check (1981) found that R-rated movies that included scenes of implied coercive sex were linked to acceptance of violence against women and endorsement of rape myths. Donnerstein et al. (1987) caution that to focus concern about violence against women on pornography is misguided, because it ignores the effects of readily available, R-rated content that includes nonsexual violence against women.

These scholars also conclude that any negative attitudinal effects of nonaggressive pornography are unlikely in the real world; laboratory effects have been based on long-term, massive exposure in the presence of few constraints against aggression (Donnerstein, 1984). Studies have found that angered research participants who watched nonviolent pornography, compared to participants who were not angered and watched a neutral film, were more aggressive (they administered shocks against targets, male or female) after the film (Donnerstein & Barrett, 1978). But, there was little support for an aggressive focus on women. Exposure to nonviolent pornography led to greater aggression against male targets than against female targets. Even though measures of physiological arousal indicated that subjects who had an opportunity to aggress against female targets were more aroused, they administered significantly fewer shocks against female targets than participants who had opportunities to aggress against male targets. Still other studies find little support for aggressive outcomes of nonviolent sexual content (see Donnerstein, 1984, for a summary).[5]

This issue of whether the negative effects of sexually explicit material are associated with nonaggressive pornography is still unresolved. Scholars have criticized studies that have found effects for a number of reasons, such as not controlling for experimenter demand, not including appropriate control groups (e.g., J. B. Weaver, 1991c), or not varying pornographic content to assess what specific content aspects of nonviolent pornography are linked to calloused attitudes toward women (Donnerstein et al., 1987). There are several theories of effects, however, that would support a connection between exposure to nonviolent sexual content and adversarial beliefs and attitudes about women.

Information processing (Huesmann, 1986) holds that, as a result of cognitive activity, media content can be learned and become the basis of schemas and scripts. According to this approach, these stereotypes and adversarial beliefs common in nonviolent pornography could become the basis for schemas and sexual scripts. There is some indication that males especially use sexually explicit materials for information (e.g., Duncan,1990; Perse, 1994). Moreover, the stereotyped content in these materials has also been linked to gender-role stereotypes (Perse, 1994), to adversarial beliefs about women (e.g., Perse, 1994), and to acceptance of rape myths (Malamuth & Check, 1985).

Arousal approaches have been especially supported in research (Allen, D'Alessio, et al., 1995). Overall, excitation transfer is a viable explanation for some of the relationship between exposure to sexually

---

[5]J. B. Weaver (1991c) argues that many of these studies that fail to replicate use flawed methods. Specifically, studies often cue participants by asking them to think about how sexually explicit content demeans and degrades women. Scholars (e.g., Mares, 1996; Shrum, 1997) illustrated that when people are aware of the source of information that might be inaccurate (e.g, cultivation effects from inaccurate television content), they are likely to discount it.

explicit media content (violent and nonviolent) and aggression. When research participants have been angered (i.e., placed in an unpleasant state of arousal) and then shown sexually stimulating content, they tend to act more aggressively than participants who have not been angered. Excitation transfer would explain that the increased arousal depicted in the sexual material increases the arousal, which might be labeled unpleasant, because of the state of anger. So, according to excitation transfer, nonviolent sexual content could result in aggression under certain circumstances, that is, when the participant is already unpleasantly aroused (e.g., angered) and when the sexual material does not cause the arousal to be relabeled as a pleasant feeling (e.g., Zillmann, Bryant, Comisky, & Medoff, 1981). Exposure to nudity alone does not appear to be associated with aggression (Allen, D'Alessio, et al., 1995). According to excitation transfer, nudity might not increase arousal or nudity alone might be associated with pleasant feelings that cause arousal to be relabeled as a positive affect.

Criticisms of Research on the Effects of Sexually Explicit Media Content

There has been a good deal of scrutiny and criticism of the research on the effects of sexually explicit materials. In fact, some of the writings have been marked by somewhat accusatory and unpleasant tones. Disagreements grow out of conflicting concerns. Scholars are socially responsible and hope that their research work will improve society. At the same time, advocating restrictions on speech and media content is not a comfortable position for communication scholars. For the most part, the results of pornography research have been used by those who advocate more restrictions on nonobscene sexual materials (e.g., Attorney General's Commission on Pornography, 1986). Major areas of criticism of the research on the effects of sexually explicit media content focus on the reliance on experimental methods, restricted explanations offered for the findings, and the focus on sexual content as the major cause for negative effects.

Laboratory experiments offer the most conclusive evidence that sexually explicit materials are linked to negative effects. Although the laboratory offers many benefits to researchers, such as control of extraneous influences and evidence of time order, the artificial nature of the laboratory makes it difficult to generalize the results to the real world. Laboratory experiments that vary levels of sexually explicit material eliminate the influence of selective exposure. Compliant participants might view content that they might never select on their own. The generalizability of most pornography experiments has been limited by the restricted samples. Most studies have relied on college student samples, who might not represent the range of all those who use sexual materials. Moreover, research participants who are offended by being part of a study of pornography might choose not to participate, leaving a sample composed of those who are interested in and even approving of sexual materials.[6]

Another criticism of laboratory research on the effects of pornography holds that the experimental procedures themselves might lead participants to infer that the researchers approve of sexually explicit materials or believe that they are innocuous because they are so casually shown in the experiment (Zillmann & Bryant, 1982). Encouraging participants to act violently toward others in the lab setting (e.g., shock) might also lead participants to believe that the researcher condones violence or that aggression in the lab causes no real harm. In other words, the artificial laboratory setting removes social sanctions against aggression that are present in the real world (see also the discussion of the theory of reasoned action in chap. 7).

The experimental procedures themselves might be flawed and yield invalid results. For example, several studies anger or frustrate the participants before exposure to sexual materials in order to disinhibit them enough to aggress. Although some who use pornography in the real world might be disinhibited because of alcohol or drug use, it has not been established that anger is a common precursor to pornography use. This might be an uncommon and artificial aspect of laboratory research that does not translate to the real-world use of pornography. The laboratory also offers a very restricted range of responses to the experimental conditions. In many of these studies, the participants are presented with only one way (e.g., shocking someone) to help release their anger and frustration. Other, more socially acceptable ways to release frustration (e.g., exercise) are not permitted.

Brannigan and Goldenberg (1987) pointed out that the experiments that involve participants exhibiting aggression by shocking anonymous

---

[6]This may not be a problem with college samples, however. Zillmann and Bryant (1987) reported that they had no subject attrition in their 6-week study of the effects of massive exposure to pornography (Zillmann & Bryant, 1982).

and unseen targets use procedures very similar to those used by Milgram (1974) in his study of obedience to authority. If the target's reaction to the pain was part of the design, Brannigan and Goldenberg (1987) suggested that the amount of aggression in those studies would certainly have been reduced, just as it was in Milgram's experiments.

Researchers might also create conditions that heighten social desirability. Linz and Donnerstein (1988) pointed out that some studies motivated volunteer participants by telling them that their recommendations about sexual materials would be reported directly to the Canadian government. So, these participants might have been influenced by a kind of third-person effect (e.g., Davison, 1983) and made stronger recommendations against sexual materials because they believed that others would be negatively affected by these materials.

Other critics have suggested that researchers are too quick to interpret their results to support beliefs that exposure to sexual materials leads to negative effects. Christensen (1986) argued for alternate explanations for Zillmann and Bryant's (1982) findings. Instead of inferring that research participants become calloused toward women and sex after massive exposure to sexually explicit films, Christensen suggests that instead they might have become more comfortable with sex. Although it is clear that items in Mosher's (1971) sexual callousness scale are phrased in "callous" terms themselves (Zillmann & Bryant, 1986a), other items could be interpreted as reflecting an adventurous orientation toward sexual experimentation, which might also be affected if one becomes more comfortable with sex (less taboo) as a result of massive exposure to pornography. This, Christensen (1986) argues, might be the real outcome of massive exposure to sexual media content.

Brannigan (1987) provided a related alternate explanation for these effects of pornography. Participants massively exposed to sexually explicit films estimated that the uncommon sexual acts were significantly more common (Zillmann & Bryant, 1982). Brannigan (1987) pointed out that, although it is impossible to know exactly how many people engage in different sorts of sexual practices (i.e., oral and anal intercourse, group sex, sadomasochism, and bestiality) that prior surveys suggest that these higher estimates might actually be more accurate than the lower estimates of groups not massively exposed to pornography. Sexual films might give people a more accurate view of sex or lead them to feel more comfortable with sexual acts and see them as less deviant.

Perhaps the major criticism of this body of research grows out of the policy recommendations that it drives. Social science, as a whole, is still not convinced that the negative effects of sexually explicit materials are due to the sexuality, instead of the aggressive and degrading content and themes. Some communication scholars have argued that instead of advocating greater restrictions on sexual material, research should focus on education to understand how to mitigate the negative effects of sexually explicit media content.

Mitigating the Negative Effects of Sexually Violent and Degrading Media Content

Obscene materials are not protected by the First Amendment. But, many feminists and moralists advocate censorship of sexually explicit media content that is not obscene. There are several problems with censorship as a way to eliminate the negative effects of this material (Fisher & Barak, 1989). First, censorship itself teaches negative values—intolerance for controversial and distasteful ideas. Moreover, censorship would tend to make the public discussion of sexual matters even more taboo, and might increase sexual guilt and ignorance. Prior experiences with prohibition of alcohol and drug restrictions point out that the censorship is not likely to be effective. Sexually explicit materials might be pushed underground, but will still be available, but perhaps from less reputable outlets. It is clear that censoring pornography would not eliminate all sexist, demeaning, and degrading media content. These themes are common in nonsexual media content. Censorship might be used by groups to eliminate healthy educational materials. Already, books that deal with sex education (e.g., *Our Bodies Ourselves*; Boston Women's Health Book Collective, 1973) has been removed from several libraries, because the book discusses sexual health. These concerns about censorship, coupled with the lingering questions about the true nature of the effects of sexually explicit material lead scholars to advocate using other strategies to combat the potential negative effects of sexually explicit media content.

It is clear that it is possible to reduce and even eliminate the negative effects of short- and relatively long-term exposure to sexually violent and demeaning materials. Ethics demand that researchers do not harm their participants. So, studies on the effects of sexually explicit materials always include substantial debriefing: disclosing the purpose of the study, alerting the participants that they might be affected in various ways, and discussing how the messages in the content are inaccurate. Debriefing also involves long-term follow-up to reinforce positive messages (e.g., Linz et al., 1984). Debriefing is effective (e.g., Donnerstein & Berkowitz, 1981; Check & Malamuth, 1984; Malamuth & Check, 1984) and its effects appear to be fairly enduring (as long as 7 to 8 months), despite long-term and massive exposure to sexually violent materials.

Malamuth and Check (1984) observed that debriefing (including education about the inaccuracies about rape and the fallaciousness of rape myths) led their research participants who had watched a sexually violent film to be less accepting of rape than a comparable group who had watched a sexually explicit film that did not include rape and were also not debriefed. Prebriefing research participants also appears to reduce negative effects (Intons-Peterson, Roskos-Ewoldsen, Thomas, Shirley, & Blut, 1989). Before watching a slasher film segment, the researchers gave the experimental group information that debunked rape myths. Then the group watched a reenactment of a rape trial. Compared to a group that was not prebriefed, this group held fewer rape myths and saw more harm in the rape.[7] Debriefing appears to cure the effects of exposure to sexually violent materials; prebriefing seems to work as a sort of inoculation protecting people against negative effects.

Outside the laboratory, scholars recommend sex education and media literacy training to reduce the likelihood of negative effects of sexually demeaning and violent media content. Metaanalyses (Allen, D'Alessio, Emmers, & Gebhardt, 1996; Flores & Hartlaub, 1998) found that various educational interventions, such as human sexuality courses, rape education workshops and video interventions, as well as educational briefings and debriefings reduce acceptance of rape myths. Within our own field, we believe that educated people are more likely to reject effects. Media literacy training will help reduce the negative effects of media content.

---

[7]Donnerstein at al. (1987) reported an interesting unintended effect of prebriefing found by one of their students (Bross, 1985): The experimental group that was prebriefed experienced a higher drop-out rate over the 2-week project (45%) compared to the group that was not prebriefed (32%). Those who dropped out reported to see more violence in the films, found the film more degrading to men and women, and were aware of potential harm to themselves. These findings offer some support to critics who argue that some of the effects in laboratory experiments might be because participants believe that the materials are not particularly harmful.

Media literacy is mentally active selection and use of mass communication (Potter, 1998; Silverblatt, 1995). It involves an understanding of how producers use forms, genres, and production techniques to create certain effects. The media literate audience members also understand the financial constraints on media production, the inaccuracies in representations, as well as the potential effects that can emerge from media use. Research on mitigating the effects of television violence (e.g., Huesmann, Eron, Klein, Brice, & Fischer, 1983) observed that certain educational strategies, such as teaching children that television violence is unrealistic, inappropriate, and unacceptable, are linked to lower levels of aggression over a period of time.

The encouraging results of violence interventions and debriefing and prebriefing in pornography recommend that material about pornography and rape myths be part of sex education and media literacy training (Donnerstein et al., 1987). Moreover, these results give scholars, educators, and parents guides to creating educational materials to mitigate the effects of sexually violent or degrading media content:

1. Reduce the likelihood that the messages of sexually violent or degrading material will be viewed realistically. Point out the inaccuracies of the material, especially the linkage of sex and violence. Dispel rape myths. Lower perceived realism is associated with fewer effects.
2. Reduce the credibility of the material by educating adolescents about the financial aims and intended audiences for sexual materials. Less credible messages have fewer effects.
3. Educate about the realities of rape and about the inaccuracies in the depictions of rape in sexually explicit media so that there will be less identification with the aggressors to reduce the likelihood of social learning.
4. Create awareness of the typical reactions to the material, so that the audience will know the source of their own reactions. Knowing the source of feelings and thoughts reduces the likelihood that these feelings and thoughts will be generalized beyond the exposure context.

Despite the evidence that it is possible to mitigate the effects of sexually violent and degrading material, not all interventions have been successful at reducing negative effects. Mullin et al. (1996) hypothesized that creating awareness of date rape would make participants less sympathetic to the accused rapist in a trial. They were specifically interested in the sorts of material that might be part of pre-trial publicity. Their hypothesis was not supported. They found that males who read magazine-like articles about predatory date rape were not more sympathetic toward the victim in a mock rape trial. Instead, they were more likely to generate prodefendant thoughts and question the credibility of the rape victim.

A large-scale field test of the effects of a made-for-television movie about acquaintance rape (Wilson, Linz, Donnerstein, & Stipp, 1992) found increases in awareness of acquaintance rape as a social problem. And, after watching the movie, older female viewers were less likely to attribute blame to the victim. But, similar to the findings of Mullin and his colleagues (1996), older males who watched the movie were more likely to blame the victim. These "boomerang effects" certainly need to be explored to make educational efforts more effective.

Linz, Fuson, and Donnerstein (1990) compared the effectiveness of educational materials versus role-playing strategies to reduce the negative effects of slasher films on college men. They found that educational interventions had a modest impact on rape myths, self-reports of sexually coercive behaviors, and perceptions that rape victims were less responsible for their victimization. The strongest intervention was in a role-playing condition in which the experimental group was told that they would be participating in making a video to educate adolescents "who have been fooled by mass media depictions into thinking that women desire sexual violence" (Linz et al., 1990, p. 654). They composed essays about the topic, read the essays while being videotaped, and then watched their tape as it was played back. This classic role-playing technique is based on cognitive consistency approaches (e.g., Festinger, 1957), which hold that the discomfort that people feel when they are advocating a stand contrary to their own views leads to acceptance of the advocated position. Self-perception approaches (e.g., Bem, 1965) further explained that people infer their own attitudes by making attributions about their own actions. Observing oneself advocating a position leads to acceptance of that position. Role-playing techniques offer additional strategies to reducing negative effects of pornography.

Summary

The widespread concern about the negative effects of sexually explicit materials grows out of evidence that these materials are becoming even more widely available with the increase in media channels, especially the VCR and WWW. It is also clear that most sexually explicit material is degrading and demeaning to women; some even includes depictions of sexual violence and rape. All four models of media effects provide some explanation for the effects of sexually explicit materials. Consistent with the direct effects model, sexual content has an almost universal ability to attract attention and stimulate some sort of arousal reaction. The cumulative model explains that over time, exposure to sexually explicit materials may affect attitudes toward sexual behaviors and women as sexual partners. Over time, exposure affects the arousal response to these materials; people can become desensitized to them. Aspects of pornography are quite noticeable and salient, capable of priming schemas that affect subsequent thoughts and behaviors, consistent with the cognitive-transactional model. Most evidence, though, supports the conditional model. Sexually explicit materials' effects are conditional on certain characteristics of the individual: gender, personality, family background, prior attitudes, and context of exposure.

Evidence that exposure to these materials leads to sexual callousness, or acceptance of sexual violence, and lack of sympathy for victims of sexual violence had led some feminists and moralists to call for limits on the availability of these materials. Public policy has been attentive to these concerns and responded by enacting various legal remedies to the "problem" of pornography. Censorship, however, is not a solution easily adopted by communication scholars. First, there is evidence that sexually explicit materials can be functional. They can provide information, educate, help reduce guilt and taboos, and provide sexual stimulation and outlets for sexual fantasy and release. There are also concerns about relying on the evidence from laboratory experiments to infer a causal connection between exposure to sexual violence and degrading media content and sexual callousness and aggression. There are suspicions that the methods may not be ecologically valid and subjects might be responding to some experimenter demand.

Communication scholars and students have shown that censorship does not have to be the only solution to mitigating the negative effects of sexually explicit materials. Our field's work on media literacy offers several suggestions that involve education, skills training, and techniques to increase audience awareness. Media literacy and audience education might be a way to reduce the likelihood of negative effects and increase the possibility for positive uses of sexually explicit media content.

Afterword: Social Impacts of New Mass Media Technology

One of the exciting aspects of studying mass communication is the dynamic nature of our field. Media technology regularly changes and improves. Over the past 100 years, we have seen the introduction of radio and television, which altered traditional orientations toward print media. The widespread use of communications satellites has allowed the almost-instantaneous delivery of media content and changed mass communication from a national to a global enterprise. The expansion and adoption of cable moved television toward multichannel offerings. Now, home satellite dishes and the WWW are delivering huge numbers of channels into the home. The VCR and the remote control device delivered control over when and what to watch into the hands of the audience. On the horizon, high definition digital television and video and the WWW promise to change the appearance and delivery of home media.

The eager adoption of each new mass communication technology has stimulated two major areas of research. The first has been research on *displacement effects*. These kinds of studies explore if the adoption and use of new technologies displace or replace media-related activities and other activities. So, early research on children's use of television focused on whether television replaced reading, which was assumed to be a more educational and beneficial pastime for children (e.g., Schramm et al., 1961). Some of the early research on the effects of cable television focused on whether watching cable networks displaced viewing local broadcast channels (e.g., Webster, 1983). Although some of this concern was driven by economic interests, scholars also recognized that a move toward viewing cable networks might displace attention to and awareness of local news (e.g., Hill & Dwyer, 1981). One recurring theme has reemerged with widespread use of the Internet and the WWW—that media use will reduce social interaction and lead to individual isolation from society (Kraut et al., 1998; see also Gerbner & Gross, 1976, for an application of this view to television viewing).

A second major area of research has centered on the content delivered by new media technologies. For the most part, this research has focused on content associated with negative effects, such as violence and sex. Concerns about "sexual agitation" effects were associated with the movies as early as the 1920s (Jowett, Jarvie, & Fuller, 1996) and continue as the WWW has become a primary distributor of pornography. Fears about the effects of violent media content continue with the increasing technical sophistication of special effects and video and/or computer games (e.g., Griffiths, 1997).

New issues might arise in the study of media effects, but for now, media scholars can approach the changing media environment with a wealth of questions and concerns that build on traditionally important areas of study such as:

- Are video and/or computer games related to aggressive behavior?
- What are the effects of WWW pornography?
- Do changes in the delivery of news affect agenda-setting effects?
- How is computer and/or WWW use related to academic achievement?
- What are the effects of trials that are broadcast?
- What are the effects of changes to the home television receiver (higher definition, larger screen)?
- What effects does the WWW have on political interest and activity?
- Will the WWW increase or decrease knowledge gaps?
- Will the proliferation of news outlets (on cable and the WWW) increase public affairs knowledge?

Our field is poised to research these ideas and others. Mass communication already has an abundance of theories to explain media effects. Scholars only need to apply these theories appropriately to new media contexts to understand how new media technologies alter traditional processes of effects. We have already begun to see this research emerging. Scholars have considered such traditional questions in the context of new media such as: (a) how cable television subscription and VCRs affect cultivation effects (e.g., Morgan & Shanahan, 1991; Perse et al., 1994); (b) if electronic text delivery of news alters agenda-setting effects (Heeter, Brown, Soffin, Stanley, & Salwen, 1989); (c) exploring the impact of video game use on attitudes toward aggression (Dominick, 1984); (d) comparing learning from Web pages and other media (Sundar, Narayan, Obregon, & Uppal, 1998); and (e) examining the impact of the WWW on politics (Kaid & Bystrom, 1999).

Throughout this book, I have applied a framework to understanding the process of media effects based on four models. Each of these models offers an incomplete, but focused analysis of media effects. These four models can be a useful framework for venturing into new areas of study. Because each of the models focuses on different aspects of the cause of media effects, different models can be useful as initial ways to examine the effects of new mass communication technologies.

DIRECT EFFECTS

The *direct effects model* focuses on media content as the major cause for understanding media effects. This model is relevant in situations where media content affects most people similarly and automatically. So media content attributes that are relevant to this model are those associated with involuntary responses (e.g., orienting response and arousal). The direct effects model is relevant to understanding media effects of new technologies that are associated with involuntary attention. We already know that certain aspects of media content cause orienting responses (OR) and arousal (e.g., Detenber, & Reeves, 1996; Lang, 1990). Larger screens, especially those that display higher definition images, might trigger orienting responses, more involuntary attention to the screen, and stimulate more arousal. This heightened attention and arousal might then be linked indirectly to effects that grow out of attention to media content, such as learning effects. It might be more difficult, for example, to ignore programming on large, high definition screens, so children might learn more rapidly from educational programs. On the other hand, the arousal so easily produced by high-definition, large images might become the basis of arousal processes leading to greater effects of violent and/or sexually explicit content.

Some scholars expect that new media technology will be marked by interactive use, rather than one-way reception (e.g., Williams, Rice, & Rogers, 1988). Interactivity means that the audience will have greater control over pacing, structure, and content of media content. Interactivity is already a component of video and/or computer games, and the integration of the WWW and video media promises to add interactivity to the delivery of other entertainment. Interactivity might have impacts on media effects. Interactivity might increase arousal, which might enhance the likelihood of arousal-based media effects. On the other hand, interactivity might lead to more overt behavior catharsis, or acting out emotional responses in order to unleash them.

The direct effects model also builds on the importance of the realism of the content. With traditional television and video, images are low definition and relatively small. Higher definition images, coupled with larger presentations, better quality sound, and improved special effects might enhance the reality of certain depictions. Future research could explore whether these improvements are associated with not only greater orienting and physiological responses, but also heightened impressions of realism. The key to implementing the direct effects model, then, is to explore the involuntary human responses to new images and presentations, and then test the impact of those responses on other media effects.

CONDITIONAL EFFECTS

The *conditional model* of media effects looks to the audience as the prime explanation for media effects. According to this model, audience attributes, such as social categories, social relationships, and individual differences act as conditions that either mitigate or enhance media effects. A central concept in this model is selectivity. People selectively expose themselves to specific media content, selectively attend to specific aspects of media messages, selectively perceive what they pay attention to, and selectively recall certain information afterward. So, the key to exploring the effects of new media technologies within the framework of the conditional model is to focus on how the access to, use of, and reactions to new technologies are affected by aspects of the audience.

The application of the conditional model to the new media environment is rather straightforward. It requires, however, an analysis of the audience attributes that could act as conditions that mitigate or enhance selectivity. For example, there are certain social categories that are linked to access to and use of newer technologies. Education and income are still linked to access to and use of computers and the WWW, although as the technology becomes less expensive and easier to use, those variables will become less important. But, because knowledge gaps are conditional on media access, communication skills, and social utility based on SES, effects that are based on learning and using material available via the Internet might still be conditional on income and education. Similarly, the growing use of the WWW for political discussion and campaigns may have limited media effects on political nonelites, because these nonelites may have less expertise and interest in accessing technology for political information.

Uses and gratifications research has shown that the reasons that people use mass communication affects media effects. Although we know a good deal about the motives driving more traditional media, it is clear that use of new technologies might grow out of different motives. Rubin and Bantz (1987), for example, found that some VCR use was motivated by new reasons that utilized the capabilities of the VCR. So, researchers should explore new reasons for the audience to select content delivered by the new media.

Many of the new technological developments increase the ease with which people can be selective. The remote control device, for example, made it easier to change channels to seek out programming and avoid other content (e.g., Perse, 1998). Cable television, coupled with the remote control led to increased channel repertoires, or increases in the number of channels that people regularly watch (Ferguson & Perse, 1993). Increased selectivity might change some media effects. People can find it much easier to avoid certain types of content that they are not interested it, such as political campaign ads (e.g., Walker & Bellamy, 1991), so they might be less likely to be affected by that content. On the other hand, there are now more options to select types of content that might have been difficult to get before. One recurring concern about the WWW is that adolescents have easier access to sexually explicit materials. In earlier years, adolescents might have been barred from adult bookstores, movie theaters, and video rentals, but the WWW erases those barriers. Similarly, people who prefer to

watch violent media content have many more options available including video, premium, and pay cable. Easier access might increase
conditions leading to some media effects.

CUMULATIVE EFFECTS

The *cumulative effects model* emphasizes the consistency and consonance of media content within and across channels. That is, certain
patterns of images are so constant and regular that selective exposure
is irrelevant. In the era before cable television, when there were only
three major networks and few independents with wide viewership,
content analyses demonstrated that violence and stereotyping were
consistent across prime-time programming (e.g., Signorielli, 1990b). At
the same time, news outlets used by most people were easily identified—newspapers, news magazines, and broadcast network newscasts. Once again, content analyses showed a remarkable consistency
in the topics of the main stories. Selective exposure was not relevant;
people who watched or read the news were exposed to the same major news stories.

The cumulative effects model considers that media effects can be
explained by understanding the nature of media content; and, content
defines effects. And, the more that audience members are exposed to
media content, the more likely they are to be affected. So, in the case of
cultivation, the more time someone spends watching television (i.e.,
living in the "television world"), the more likely he or she is to fashion a
view of the world that mirrors the content of television. In the case of
agenda setting, the more someone uses the news, the more likely they
are to adopt the news' ranking of important stories, issues, events, and
media (i.e., adopt the media agenda).

The cumulative model is an appropriate framework to use to explore
effects that focus on consistency of media content across channels. For
example, will cultivation effects be maintained while the audience
share of the three major networks declines? Will the increasing use of
"nontraditional" news outlets diminish agenda-setting effects? To answer such questions, scholars need to examine whether the conditions
undergirding the cumulative model are maintained in a media environment different from that of the 1970s (the decade in which these theories were introduced). Content analyses need to examine whether the
content of the most watched cable and broadcast channels is conso-

nant; whether new and traditional news outlets have similar agendas. Then, audience analysts need to explore audience behavior. Does the audience still watch television "by the clock," during prime time? Do newer channels and technologies (e.g., VCRs) pull some of the audience away from prime-time viewing? There is good reason to expect that television use will become polarized, that is become more like radio, print media, and film use, where certain content is preferred to the exclusion of other content (e.g., Webster & Phalen, 1997). Is selective exposure still irrelevant? Does selection of specific channels, programs, and news outlets allow some viewers to be exposed to patterns of images that differ from the patterns viewed by people who select different channels, networks, and news outlets? Is it possible that channel and/or content diversity, coupled with greater abilities to exercise selective exposure, reduce the cumulative effects of the mass media?

COGNITIVE-TRANSACTIONAL EFFECTS

The *cognitive-transactional model* focuses on the role of active and passive mental activity on media effects. When audiences are active and goal oriented, they direct attention and mental activity to seek out media content to satisfy their goals. So, schemas that are used are under the control of the individual. When audiences are passive, or relaxing, salient aspects of media content have greater potential to prime, or activate schemas that will then influence how people interpret media content and respond to other stimuli in their environment. This transactional model emphasizes the importance of both individual audience factors and aspects of media content in understanding media effects.

This model offers three routes to exploring the effects of new media technologies. First, it might be important to understand the schemas that people have about various communication channels (e.g., Perse & Courtright, 1993). If people believe that certain technologies are too difficult to use, for example, they might be reluctant to use them (e.g., Salomon, 1983). So, preconceptions might hold certain groups back from benefiting from using certain technologies. Or, some people might avoid using certain technologies because they believe that they offer too-ready access to offensive or harmful media content.

A second application of the cognitive-transactional model to the study of the effects of new technologies is to consider the nature of the mental activity while using newer technologies. Researchers should explore whether new technology use is more or less likely to be ritualistic and automatic, compared to use of traditional media. There is some early evidence, for example, that Web surfing might not be as relaxing a pastime as television use (Ferguson & Perse, 2000). Users need to pay attention to click to hyperlinks and often wait frustratingly long times for pages and graphics to load. Time spent on an average Web session is not very long (about ½ hour a day; Ferguson & Perse, 2000), suggesting that people are instrumentally getting what they want and then logging off. Mathematical analysis of Web surfing activity suggests that the number of pages within a site that people visit is related to the amount of value they receive from the page compared to the cost of waiting for the page to load (Huberman, Pirolli, Pitkow, & Lukose, 1998)—an instrumental cost–benefit analysis. And, the most visited sites on the Web appear to offer more instrumental gratification. These sites are search engines (e.g., Yahoo!), software distribution sites (e.g., Netscape, Microsoft, CNET), news (e.g., CNN, MSN), and entertainment (e.g., Disney). If controlled mental activity dominates the use of some newer technologies, then the effects associated with that use might be more likely to be shaped by preexisting schemas and individual goals. Researchers need to explore the use of new technologies over time, however. While the WWW might demand more controlled mental effort in its current form, future developments might change that. Improvements to browsers, increase in bandwidth, and delivery via television (rather than computer) might make Web surfing as easy as changing channels, giving rise to more automatic use of the WWW.

A third area of research suggested by the cognitive transactional model focuses on the aspects of new technologies that might be associated with ability to prime—salience. Certainly the increases in definition and size associated with some the developments in special effects and video delivery suggest that media content may become even more intrusive and salient with far greater potential to prime and activate audience schemas. Research might explore whether larger images, stereo sound, and computer-enhanced special effects have stronger priming effects than the traditional media.

SUMMARY

Wimmer and Dominick (2000) explained how research on any mass medium follows a logical and predictable progression: (a) research on the medium itself, how it operates, and the content that it delivers; (b) research on the uses and users of the medium, who makes up the audience, and what are their reasons for using the medium; (c) research on the effects of the medium; and finally (d) research on how to improve the medium. The study of the social effects of new media technology involve all of these kinds of research. The study of direct effects should center on aspects of the medium and the content that are related to involuntary responses by the audience. The study of conditional effects mandates an understanding of the audience of new technologies: their make-up, the social nature, and aspects of individuals that affect selective exposure, attention, perception, and recall. The cumulative effects model suggests that researchers examine the nature of the content of new media, to see if similar topics and images are still consonant across channels to see if selective exposure is relevant. The cognitive-transactional model suggests a focus on both the content and the audience of the new media. As the media environment changes with reallocation of time spent on different media, as well as the refinements of technology, researchers can examine the different effects of controlled and automatic use of newer media. As mass communication students and scholars, we should always keep in mind that the goal of our study is improvement—to find ways to mitigate the negative effects and enhance the positive effects of mass communication.

References

Abramson, P. R., & Hayashi, H. (1984). Pornography in Japan: Cross-cultural and theoretical considerations. In N. M. Malamuth & E. Donnerstein (Eds.), *Pornography and sexual aggression* (pp. 173–183). Orlando, FL: Academic Press.

Action on Smoking and Health. (1996). ASH seeks federal investigation of smoking in movies; action featured in "Eye of American" on CBS-TV news. [Online press report]. Available: http://ash.org/legal/eye.htm

Aitken, P. P., Leathar, D. S., & Scott, A. C. (1988). Ten- to sixteen-year-olds' perceptions of advertisements for alcoholic drinks. *Alcohol and Alcoholism 23*, 491–500.

Ajzen, I., & Fishbein, M. (1980). *Understanding attitudes and predicting social behavior*. Englewood Cliffs, NJ: Prentice-Hall.

Alexander, A. (1985). Adolescents' soap opera viewing and relational perceptions. *Journal of Broadcasting & Electronic Media, 29*, 295–308.

Alexander, A., Ryan, M. S., & Munoz, P. (1984). Creating a learning context: Investigations on the interaction of siblings during television viewing. *Critical Studies in Mass Communication, 1*, 345–364.

Allen, M., D'Alessio, D., & Brezgel, K. (1995). A meta-analysis summarizing the effects of pornography II: Aggression after exposure. *Human Communication Research, 22*, 258–283.

Allen, M., D'Alessio, D., Emmers, T. M., & Gebhardt, L. (1996). The role of educational briefings in mitigating effects of experimental exposure to violent sexually explicit material: A meta-analysis. *Journal of Sex Research, 33*, 135–141.

Allen, M., Emmers, T., Gebhardt, L., & Giery, M. A. (1995). Exposure to pornography and acceptance of rape myths. *Journal of Communication, 45*(1), 5–26.

Allen, R. L. (1993). Conceptual models of an African-American belief system. In G. L. Berry & J. K. Asamen (Eds.), *Children & television: Images in a changing sociocultural world* (pp. 155–176). Newbury Park, CA: Sage.

Allport, G. W., & Postman, L. J. (1945). The basic psychology of rumor. *Transactions of the New York Academy of Sciences, Series II, 8*, 61–81.

Altman, D. G., Slater, M. D., Albright, C. L., & Maccoby, N. (1987). How an unhealthy product is sold: Cigarette advertising in magazines, 1960–1985. *Journal of Communication, 37*(4), 95–105.

Alwitt, L. F., Anderson, D. R., Lorch, E. P., & Levin, S. R. (1980). Preschool children's visual attention to attributes of television. *Human Communication Research 7*, 52–67.

American Psychological Association. (1993). *Violence and youth: Psychology's response*. Washington, DC: Author.

Anderson, D. R., Alwitt, L. F., Lorch, E. P., & Levin, S. R. (1979). Watching children watch television. In G. Hale & M. Lewis (Eds.), *Attention and cognitive development* (pp. 331–361). New York: Plenum Press.

Anderson, D. R., & Burns, J. (1991). Paying attention to television. In J. Bryant & D. Zillmann (Eds.), *Responding the to the screen: Reception and reaction processes* (pp. 3–25). Hillsdale, NJ: Lawrence Erlbaum Associates.

Anderson, D. R., & Collins, P. A. (1988). *The impact on children's education: Television's influence on cognitive development* (Working paper No. 2). Washington, DC: U.S. Department of Educational Research and Improvement, U.S. Department of Education.

Anderson, D. R., & Levin, S. R. (1976). Young children's attention to Sesame Street. *Child Development, 47*, 806–811.

Anderson, J. A., & Meyer, T. P. (1988). *Mediated communication: A social action perspective*. Newbury Park, CA: Sage.

Anderson, J. R. (1995). *Cognitive psychology and its implications* (4th ed.). New York: W. H. Freeman.

Andison, F. S. (1977). TV violence and viewer aggression: A cumulation of study results 1956–1976. *Public Opinion Quarterly, 41*, 314–331.

Andreasen, M. (1985). Listener recall for call-in versus structured interview radio formats. *Journal of Broadcasting & Electronic Media, 29*, 421–430.

Ansolabehere, S., & Iyengar, S. (1996). The craft of political advertising: A progress report. In D. C. Mutz, P. M. Sniderman, & R. A. Brody (Eds.), *Political persuasion and attitude change* (pp. 101–122). Ann Arbor: University of Michigan.

Armstrong, G. B. (1993). Cognitive interference from background television: Structure effects on verbal and spatial processing. *Communication Studies, 44*, 56–70.

Armstrong, G. B., Boiarsky, G. A. & Mores, M. (1991). Background television and reading performance. *Communication Monographs, 58*, 235–253.

Armstrong, G. B., & Greenberg, B. S. (1990). Background television as an inhibitor of cognitive processing. *Human Communication Research, 16*, 355–386.

Armstrong, B. C. , Neuendorf, K. A., & Brentar, J. E. (1992). TV entertainment, news, and racial perceptions of college students. *Journal of Communication, 42*(3), 153–176.

Asch, S. E. (1956). Studies of independence and conformity: I. A minority of one against a unanimous majority. *Psychological Monographs, 70*(9), 1–70.

Atkin, C. K. (1983). Effects of realistic TV violence vs. fictional violence on aggression. *Journalism Quarterly, 60*, 615–621.

Atkin, C., K., Greenberg, B. S., & McDermott, S. (1983). Television and race role socialization. *Journalism Quarterly, 60*, 407–414.

Atkin, C. K., Hocking, J., & Block, M. (1984). Teenage drinking: Does advertising make a difference? *Journal of Communication, 34*(20), 157–167.

Attorney General's Commission on Pornography. (1986). *Final report*. Washington, DC: U.S. Department of Justice.

Austin, E. W., & Meili, H. K. (1994). Effects of interpretations of televised alcohol portrayals on children's alcohol beliefs. *Journal of Broadcasting & Electronic Media, 38*, 417–435.

Austin, E. W., Roberts, D. F., & Nass, C. I. (1990). Influences of family communication on children's television-interpretation processes. *Communication Research, 17*, 545–564.

Axsom, D., Yates, S., & Chaiken, S. (1987). Audience response as a heuristic cue in persuasion. *Journal of Personality and Social Psychology, 53*, 30–40.

Baker, S. M., & Petty, R. E. (1994). Majority and minority influences: Source-position imbalance as a determinant of message scrutiny. *Journal of Personality and Social Psychology, 67*, 5–19.

Ball, S., & Bogatz, G. A. (1970). *The first year of "Sesame Street ": An evaluation.* Princeton, NJ: Educational Testing Services.

Ball, S., Palmer, P., & Milward, E. (1986). Televison and its educational impact: A reconsideration. In J. Bryant & D. Zillmann (Eds.), *Perspectives on media effects* (pp. 129–142). Hillsdale, NJ: Lawrence Erlbaum Associates.

Ball-Rokeach, S. J., & DeFleur, M. L. (1976). A dependency model of mass-media effects. *Communication Research, 3*, 3–21.

Bandura, A. (1986). *Social foundations of thought and actions: A social cognitive theory.* Englewood Cliffs, NJ: Prentice-Hall.

Bandura, A. (1994). Social cognitive theory of mass communication. In J. Bryant & D. Zillmann (Eds.), *Media effects: Advances in theory and research* (pp. 61–90). Hillsdale, NJ: Lawrence Erlbaum Associates.

Bandura, A., Ross, D., & Ross, S. A. (1963). Imitation of film-mediated aggressive models. *Journal of Abnormal and Social Psychology, 66*, 3–11.

Baran, S. J. (1976). How TV and film portrayals affect sexual satisfaction in college students. *Journalism Quarterly, 53*, 468–473.

Baran, S. J., & Blasko, V. J. (1984). Social perceptions and the by-products of advertising. *Journal of Communication, 34*(3), 12–20.

Baran, S. J., & Davis, D. K. (1995). *Mass communication theory: Foundations, ferment, and future.* Belmont, CA: Wadsworth.

Bargh, J. A. (1988). Automatic information processing: Implications for communication and affect. In L. Donohew, H. E. Sypher, & E. T. Higgins (Eds.), *Communication, social cognition, and affect* (pp. 9–32). Hillsdale, NJ: Lawrence Erlbaum Associates.

Baron, L., & Straus, M. A. (1984). Sexual stratification, pornography, and rape in the United States. In N. M. Malamuth & E. Donnerstein (Eds.), *Pornography and sexual aggression* (pp. 186–209). Orlando, FL: Academic Press.

Bartlett, F. A. (1932). *A study in experimental and social pscyhology.* New York: Cambridge University Press.

Bassiouni, M. C. (1982). Media coverage of terrorism: The law and the public. *Journal of Communication, 32*(2), 128–143.

Baxter, R. L., De Riemer, C., Landini, A., Leslie, L., & Singletary, M. W. (1985). A content analysis of music videos. *Journal of Broadcasting & Electronic Media, 29*, 245–257.

Bechtel, R. B., Achelpohl, C., & Akers, R. (1972). Correlates between observed behavior and questionnaire response on television viewing. In E. A. Rubenstein, G. A. Comstock, & J. P. Murray (Eds.), *Television and social behavior: Vol. 4. Television in day-to-day life, patterns of use* (DHEW publication HSM 72-9059, pp. 274–344). Washington, DC: Government Printing Office.

Becker, G. (1972). Causal analysis in R-R studies: Television violence and aggression. *American Psychologist, 27*, 967–968.

Bem, D. J. (1965). An experimental analysis of self-persuasion. *Journal of Experimental Social Psychology, 1*, 199–218.

Bem, S. L. (1981). Gender schema theory: A cognitive account of sex typing. *Psychological Review, 88*, 354–364.

Bemmaor, A. C. (1984). Testing alternative econometric models on the existence of advertising threshold effect. *Journal of Marketing Research, 21*, 298–308.

Berelson, B. (1948). Communication and public opinion. In W. Schramm (Eds.), *Communications in modern society* (pp. 167–185). Chicago: University of Illinios Press.

Berelson, B. (1959). The state of communication research. *Public Opinion Quarterly, 23*, 1–17.

Berkowitz, L. (1970). Aggressive humor as a stimulus to aggressive responses. *Journal of Personality and Social Psychology, 16*, 710–717.

Berkowitz, L., & Alioto, J. T. (1973). The meaning of an observed event as a determinant of its aggressive consequences. *Journal of Personality and Social Psychology, 28*, 206–217.

Berkowitz, L., & Powers, P. C. (1978). Effects of timing and justification of witnessed aggression on the observers' punitiveness. *Journal of Research in Personality, 13*, 71–80.

Berkowitz, L., & Rogers, K. H. (1986). A priming effect analysis of media influences. In J. Bryant & D. Zillmann (Eds.), *Perspectives on media effects* (pp. 57–81). Hillsdale, NJ: Lawrence Erlbaum Associates.

Berlyne, D. E. (1960). *Conflict, arousal, and curiosity*. New York: McGraw-Hill.

Berlyne, D. E. (1970). Attention as a problem in behavior theory. In D. I. Mostofsky (Ed.), *Attention: Contemporary theory and analysis* (pp. 25–49). New York: Appleton Century Crofts.

Bernard, R. M., & Coldevin, G. O. (1985). Effects of recap strategies on television news recall and retention. *Journal of Broadcasting & Electronic Media, 29*, 407–419.

Berry, C. (1983). Learning from television news: A critique of the research. *Journal of Broadcasting, 27*, 359–370.

Beuf, A. (1974). Doctor, lawyer, household drudge. *Journal of Communication, 24*(2), 142–154.

Biocca, F. (Ed.). (1991). *Television and political advertising: Vol 1. Psychological processes*. Hillsdale, NJ: Lawrence Erlbaum Associates.

Bishop, G. F., Oldendick, R. W., Tuchfaber, A. J., & Bennett, S. E. (1980). Pseudo-opinions on public affairs. *Public Opinion Quarterly, 44*, 198–209.

Bishop, J. M., & Krause, D. R. (1984). Depictions of aging and old age on Saturday morning television. *Gerontologist, 24*, 91–94.

Blank, D. M. (1977). The Gerbner violence profile. *Journal of Broadcasting, 21*, 273–279.

Bloom, P. M., Hogan, J. E., & Blazing, J. (1997). Sports promotion and teen smoking: An exploratory study. *American Journal of Health Behavior, 21*(2), 100–109.

Blumer, H. (1946). Collective behavior. In A. M. Lee (Ed.), *New outlines of the principles of sociology* (pp. 167–222). New York: Barnes and Noble.

Blumler, H. (1933). *Movies and conduct*. New York: Macmillan.

Bogart, L. (1989). *Press and public: Who reads what, when, where, and why in American newspapers* (2nd ed.). Hillsdale, NJ: Lawrence Erlbaum Associates.

Bogart, L. (1995). *Commercial culture: The media system and the public interest*. New York: Oxford.

Boston Women's Health Book Collective. (1973). *Our bodies ourselves*. New York: Simon & Schuster.

Botta, R. A. (1999). Television images and adolescent girls' body image disturbance. *Journal of Communication, 49*(2), 22–41.

Bowen, G. L. (1989). Presidential action in public opinion about U.S. Nicaraguan policy: Limits to the "rally 'round the flag" syndrome. *PS: Political Science and Politics, 22*, 793–800.

Bowen, L. (1994). Time of voting decision and use of political advertising: The Slade Gorton-Brock Adams senatorial campaign. *Journalism Quarterly, 71*, 665–675.

Boyanowski, E. O. (1977). Film preference under conditions of threat: Whetting the appetite for violence, information, or excitement? *Communication Research, 4*, 133–145.

Bramlett-Solomon, S., & Farwell, T. (1997). Sex on soaps: An analysis of black, white and interracial couple intimacy. In S. Biagi & M. Kern-Foxworth (Eds.), *Facing difference: Race, gender, and mass media* (pp. 3–10). Thousand Oaks, CA: Pine Forge Press.

Brannigan, A. (1987). Pornography and behavior: Alternate explanations. *Journal of Communication, 37*(3), 185–189.

Brannigan, A., & Goldenberg, S. (1987). The study of aggressive pornography: The vissitudes of relevance. *Critical Studies in Mass Communication, 4*, 262–283.

Brannigan, A., & Kapardis, A. (1986). The controversy over pornography and sex crimes: The criminological evidence and beyond. *Australian & New Zealand Journal of Criminology, 19*, 259–284.

Brener, N. D., Simon, T. R., Krug, E. G., & Lowry, R. (1999). Recent trends in violence-related behaviors among high school students in the United States. *JAMA, 282*, 440–446.

Brigham, J. C., & Giesbrecht, L. W. (1976). "All in the Family": Racial attitudes. *Journal of Communication, 26*(4), 69–74.

Brock, R. C., & Balloun, J. L. (1967). Behavioral receptivity to dissonant information. *Journal of Personality and Social Psychology, 6*, 413–428.

Brosius, H., Donsbach, W., & Birk, M. (1996). How do text-picture relations affect the informational effectiveness of television newscasts? *Journal of Broadcasting & Electronic Media, 40*, 180–195.

Brosius, H., & Kepplinger, H. M. (1990). The agenda-setting function of television news. *Communication Research, 17*, 183–211.

Bross, M. (1985). *Mitigating the effects of mass media sexual violence*. Unpublished master's thesis, University of Wisconsin-Madison.

Brown, D., & Bryant, J. (1989). The manifest content of pornography. In D. Zillmann & J. Bryant (Eds.), *Pornography: Research advances & policy considerations* (pp. 3–24). Hillsdale, NJ: Lawrence Erlbaum Associates.

Brown, J. (1958). Some tests of the decay theory of immediate memory. *Quarterly Journal of Experimental Psychology, 10*, 12–21.

Brown, J. D., Childres, K. W., & Waszak, C. S. (1990). Television and adolescent sexuality. *Journal of Adolescent Health Care, 11*, 62–70.

Brown, J. D., & Newcomer, S. F. (1991). Television viewing and adolescents' sexual behavior. *Journal of Homosexuality, 21*, 77–91.

Brown, M., Amoroso, D. M., & Ware, E. E. (1976). Behavioral effects of viewing pornography. *Journal of Social Psychology, 98*, 235–245.

Browne, B. A. (1998). Gender stereotypes in advertising on children's television in the 1900s: A cross-national analysis. *Journal of Advertising, 27*, 83–96.

Bryant, J., & Brown, D. (1989). Uses of pornography. In D. Zillmann & J. Bryant (Eds.), *Pornography: Research advances & policy considerations* (pp. 25–55). Hillsdale, NJ: Lawrence Erlbaum Associates.

Bryant, J., & Rockwell, S. C. (1994). Effects of massive exposure to sexually oriented prime-time television programming on adolescents' moral judgment. In

D. Zillmann, J. Bryant, & A. C. Huston (Eds.), *Media, children, and the family* (pp. 183–195). Hillsdale, NJ: Lawrence Erlbaum. Associates

Bryant, J., & Zillmann, D. (1984). Using television to alleviate boredom and stress: Selective exposure as a function of induced excitational states. *Journal of Broadcasting, 28*, 1–20.

Bryant, J., & Zillmann, D. (Eds.). (1994). *Media effects: Advances in theory and research.* Hillsdale, NJ: Lawrence Erlbaum Associates.

Bryant, J., Zillmann, D., & Brown, D. F. (1983). Entertainment features in children's educational television: Effects on attention and information acquisition. In J. Bryant & D. R. Anderson (Eds.), *Children's understanding of television: Research on attention and comprehension* (pp. 221–240). New York: Academic Press.

Budd, R. W., MacLean, M. S., Jr., Barnes, A. M. (1966). Regularities in the diffusion of two major news events. *Journalism Quarterly, 43*, 221–230.

Bureau of Justice Statistics. (1998). Serious violent crime levels continued to decline in 1997. [Online report]. Available: http://www.ojp.usdoj.gov/bjs/glace/cv2.htm

Bureau of Justice Statistics. (1999). Firearm death by intent, 1991–96. [Online report]. Available: http://www.ojp.usdoj.gov/bjs/glace/frmdth.txt

Burt, M. R. (1980). Cultural myths and supports for rape. *Journal of Personality and Social Psychology, 38*, 217–230.

Bushman, B. J., & Geen, R. G. (1990). Role of cognitive-emotional mediators and individual difference in the effects of media violence on aggression. *Journal of Personality and Social Psychology, 58*, 156–163.

Cacioppo, J. T., & Petty, R. E. (1979). Effects of message repetition and position on cognitive response, recall, and persuasion. *Journal of Personal and Social Psychology, 37*, 97–109.

Cacioppo, J. T., & Petty, R. E. (1982). The need for cognition. *Journal of Personality and Social Psychology, 42*, 116–131.

Cacioppo, J. T., Petty, R. E., Kao, C., & Rodriguez, R. (1986). Central and peripheral routs to persuasion: An individual difference perspective. *Journal of Personality and Social Psychology, 51*, 1032–1043.

Campbell, A., Converse, P. E., Miller, W. E., & Stokes, D. E. (1966). *The American voter.* New York: Wiley.

Cantor, J. (1994). Fright reactions to mass media. In J. Bryant & D. Zillmann (Eds.), *Media effects: Advances in theory and research* (pp. 213–245). Hillsdale, NJ: Lawrence Erlbaum Associates.

Cantor, J., Mares, M. L., & Oliver, M. B. (1993). Parents' and children's emotional reactions to televised coverage of the Gulf War. In B. Greenberg & W. Gantz (Eds.), *Desert storm and the mass media* (pp. 325–340). Cresskill, NJ: Hampton Press.

Cantor, M. G., & Orwant, J. (1980). Differential effects of television violence on girls and boys. In T. McCormack (Ed.), *Studies in communications: A research annual* (Vol. 1, pp. 63–83). Greenwich, CT: JAI Press.

Cantril, H., Gaudet, H., & Herzog, H. (1940). *The invasion from Mars: A study in the psychology of panic.* Princeton, NJ: Princeton University Press.

Capuzzo, M. (1990, December 7). Unsportsmanlike conduct. *Philadelphia Inquirer*, pp. C1, C5.

Carrocci, N. M. (1985). Diffusion of information about cyanide-laced Tylenol. *Journalism Quarterly, 62*, 630–633.

Carver, C. S., Ganellen, R. J., Froming, W. J., & Chambers, W. (1983). Modeling: An analysis in terms of category accessibility. *Journal of Experimental Social Psychology, 19*, 403–421.

Carveth, R., & Alexander, A. (1985). Soap opera viewing motivations and the cultivation process. *Journal of Broadcasting & Electronic Media, 29*, 259–273.

Ceci, S. J., & Kain, E. L. (1982). Jumping on the bandwagon with the underdog: The impact of attitude polls on polling behavior. *Public Opinion Quarterly, 46*, 228–242.

Center for Communication and Social Policy. (Ed.). (1998). *National television violence study 3*. Thousand Oaks, CA: Sage.

Centers for Disease Control. (1990). Cigarette advertising—United States, 1970–1980. *Morbidity & Mortality Weekly Report, 39*, 261–265.

Centers for Disease Control. (1991). *Position papers from the Third National Injury Conference: Setting the national agenda for injury control in the 1990s*. Washington, DC: Department of Health and Human Services.

Centerwall, B. S. (1989a). Exposure to television as a cause of violence. In G. Comstock (Ed.), *Public communication and behavior* (Vol. 2, pp. 1–58). Orlando, FL: Academic Press.

Centerwall, B. S. (1989b). Exposure to television as a risk factor for violence. *American Journal of Epidemiology, 129*, 643–652.

Chaffee, S. H. (1977). Mass media effects: New research perspectives. In D. Lerner & L. M. Nelson (Eds.), *Communication research—A half-century appraisal* (pp. 210–241). Honolulu: University of Hawaii Press.

Chaffee, S. H. (1992). [Review of *Is anyone responsible? How television frames political issues*]. *Journal of Broadcasting & Electronic Media, 36*, 239–241.

Chaffee, S. H., & Hochheimer, J. L. (1982). The beginnings of political communication research in the United States: Origins of the "limited effects" model. In E. M. Rogers & F. Balle (Eds.), *The media revolution in America and western Europe* (pp. 263–283). Norwood, NJ: Ablex.

Chaffee, S. H., McLeod, J. M., & Atkin, C. K. (1971). Parental influences on adolescent media use. *American Behavioral Scientist, 14*, 323–340.

Chaffee, S. H., McLeod, J. M., & Wackman, D. B. (1973). Family communication patterns and adolescent political participation. In J. Dennis (Ed.), *Socialization to politics: A reader* (pp. 349–364). New York: Wiley.

Chaffee, S. H., & Schleuder, J. (1986). Measurement and effects of attention to media news. *Human Communication Research, 13*, 76–107.

Chaffee, S. H., & Yang, W. M. (1990). Communication and political socialization. In O. Ichilov (Ed.), *Political socialization, citizenship education, and democracy* (pp. 137–157). New York: Teachers College Press.

Chaiken, S. (1979). Communicator physical attractiveness and persuasion. *Journal of Personality and Social Psychology, 37*, 1387–1397.

Chaiken, S., & Eagly, A. H. (1983). Communication modality as a determinant of message persuasiveness and message comprehensibility. *Journal of Personality and Social Psychology, 34*, 605–614.

Chang, H. (1998). The effect of news teasers in processing TV news. *Journal of Broadcasting & Electronic Media, 42*, 327–339.

Check, J. V. P., & Guloien, T. H. (1989). Reported proclivity for coercive sex following repeated exposure to sexually violent pornography, nonviolent pornography, and erotica. In D. Zillmann & J. Bryant (Eds.), *Pornography: Research advances & policy considerations* (pp. 159–184). Hillsdale, NJ: Lawrence Erlbaum Associates.

Check, J. V. P., & Malamuth, N. M. (1981). Pornography and social aggression: A social learning theory analysis. In M. L. McLaughlin (Ed.), *Communication Yearbook 9*, (pp. 181–213). Beverly Hills, CA: Sage.

Check, J. V. P., & Malamuth, N. (1984). Can there be positive effects of participation in pornography experiments? *Journal of Sex Research, 20,* 14–31.

Chew, F., & Palmer, S. (1994). Interest, the knowledge gap, and television programming. *Journal of Broadcasting & Electronic Media, 38,* 271–287.

Children Now. (1998, May 6). New study finds children see inequities in media's race and class portrayals. [Online press release]. Available: http://www.childrennow.org/media/race.html

Christensen, F. (1986).Sexual callousness: Re-examined. *Journal of Communication, 36*(1), 174–184.

Cline, V. B., Croft, R. G., & Courrier, S. (1973). Desensitization of children to television violence. *Journal of Personality and Social Psychology, 27,* 360–365.

Cohen, B. (1963). *The press and foreign policy.* Princeton, NJ: Princeton University Press.

Cohen, J. (1988). *Statistical power analysis for the behavioral sciences* (2nd ed.). Hillsdale, NJ: Lawrence Erlbaum Associates.

Cohen, J., & Davis, R. G. (1991). Third-person effects and the differential impact in negative political advertising. *Journalism Quarterly, 68,* 680–688.

Coles, C. D., & Shamp, M. J. (1984). Some sexual, personality, and demographic characteristics of women readers of erotic romances. *Archives of Sexual Behavior, 13(3),* 187–209.

Collins, W. A. (1982). Cognitive processing in television viewing. In D. Pearl, L. Bouthilet, & J. Lazar (Eds.), *Television and behavior: Ten years of scientific progress and implications for the eighties* (DHHS Publication No. ADM 82-1196, Vol. 2, pp. 9–23). Washington, DC: U.S. Government Printing Office.

Commission on Obscenity and Pornography. (1970). *The report of the Commission on Obscenity and Pornography.* Washington, DC: U.S. Government Printing Office.

Comstock, G. (1989). *The evolution of American television.* Newbury Park, CA: Sage.

Comstock, G., Chaffee, S., Katzman, N., McCombs, M., & Roberts, D. (1978). *Television and human behavior.* New York: Columbia University Press.

Condry, J. (1989). *The psychology of television.* Hillsdale, NJ: Lawrence Erlbaum Associates.

Connolly, G. M., Casswell, S., Zhang, J. F., & Silva, P. A. (1994). Alcohol in the mass media and drinking by adolescents: A longitudinal study. *Addiction, 89,* 1255–1263.

Converse, P. E. (1975). Public opinion and voting behavior. In F. Greenstein & N. Polsby (Eds.), *Handbook of political science, Vol. 4* (pp. 75–169). Reading, MA: Addison-Wesley.

Cook, R. F., & Fosen, R. H. (1971). Pornography and the sex offender: Patterns of exposure and immediate arousal effects of pornographic stimuli. *Technical report of the Commission on Obscenity and Pornography* (Vol. 7, pp. 149–162). Washington, DC: U. S. Government Printing Office.

Cook, T. D., Appleton, H., Conner, R. F., Shaffer, A., Tamkin, G., & Weber, S. J. (1975). *Sesame Street revisited: A case study in evaluation research.* New York: Russell Sage.

Cooper, C. A. (1996). *Violence on television: Congressional inquiry, public criticism and industry response. A policy analysis.* Lanham, MD: University Press.

Corder-Bolz, C. (1981). Television and adolescents' sexual behaviors. *Sex Education Coalition News, 3,* 40.

Corteen, R. S., & Williams, T. M. (1986). Television and reading skills. In T. M. Williams (Ed.), *The impact of television: A natural experiment in three communities* (pp. 39–86). Orlando, FL: Academic Press.

Coser, L. A. (1956). *The functions of social conflict*. New York: Free Press.

Cotton, J. L. (1985). Cognitive dissonance in selective exposure. In D. Zillmann & J. Bryant (Eds.), *Selective exposure to communication* (pp. 11–33). Hillsdale, NJ: Lawrence Erlbaum Associates.

Craik, F. I. M., & Lockhart, R. S. (1972). Levels of processing: A framework for memory research. *Journal of Verbal Learning and Verbal Behavior, 11*, 671–684.

Curran, J., Gurevitch, M., & Woollacott, J. (1982). The study of the media: Theoretical approaches. In M. Gurevitch, T. Bennett, J. Curran, & J. Woollacott (Eds.), *Culture, society and the media* (pp. 11–29). New York: Methuen.

David, P., & Johnson, M. A. (1998). The role of self in third-person effects about body image. *Journal of Communication, 48*(4), 37–58.

Davidson, E. S., Yasuna, A., Tower, A. (1979). The effects of television cartoons on sex-role stereotyping in young girls. *Child Development, 50*, 597–600.

Davis, D. K., & Robinson, J. P. (1986). News story attributes and comprehension. In J. P. Robinson & M. R. Levy (Eds.), *The main source: Learning from television news* (pp. 179–210). Beverly Hills: Sage.

Davis, R., & Owen, D. (1998). *New media in American politics*. New York: Oxford.

Davison, W. P. (1983). The third-person effect in communication. *Public Opinion Quarterly, 47*, 1–15.

Dayan, D., & Katz, E. (1992). *Media events: Live broadcasting of history*. Cambridge, MA: Harvard University Press.

Dearing, J. W., & Rogers, E. M. (1996). *Communication concepts 6: Agenda-setting*. Thousand Oaks, CA: Sage.

Dee, J. L. (1987). Media accountability for real-life violence: A case of negligence or free speech? *Journal of Communication, 37*(2), 106–138.

Deemers, D. P., Craff, D., Choi, Y. & Pessin, B. M. (1989). Issue obtrusiveness and the agenda-setting effects of national network news. *Communication Research, 16*, 793–812.

DeFleur, M. L. (1987). The growth and decline of research on the diffusion of the news, 1945–1985. *Communication Research, 14*, 109–130.

DeFleur, M. L., & Ball-Rokeach, S. (1989). *Theories of mass communication* (5th ed.). New York: Longman.

DeFleur, M. L., & Dennis, E. E. (1994). *Understanding mass communication: A liberal arts perspective* (5th ed.). Dallas: Houghton Mifflin.

Dennis, E. E., Stebenne, D., Pavlik, J., Thalhimer, M., LaMay, C., Smillie, D., FitzSimon, M., Gazsi, S., & Rachlin, S. (1991). *The media at war: The press and the Persian Gulf conflict*. New York: Gannett Foundation.

Detenber, B. H., & Reeves, B. (1996). A bio-informational theory of emotion: Motion and image size effects on viewers. *Journal of Communication, 46*(3), 66–84.

Diamond, E., & Bates, S. (1992). *The spot: The rise of political advertising on television* (3rd ed.). Cambridge, MA: MIT Press.

Dietz, W. H. (1990). You are what you eat—What you eat is what you are. *Journal of Adolescent Health Care, 11*, 76–81.

Dietz, W. H., & Gortmaker, S. L. (1985). Do we fatten our children at the TV set? Television viewing and obesity in children and adolescents. *Pediatrics, 75*, 807–812.

DiFranza, J. R., Richards, J. W., Paulman, P. M., Wolf-Gillespie, N., Fletcher, C., Jaffe, R. D., & Murray, D. (1991). RJR Nabisco's cartoon camel promotes Camel cigarettes to children. *JAMA, 266*, 3149–3153.

Dobkin, B. A. (1992). *Tales of terror: Television news and the construction of the terrorist threat*. New York: Praeger.

Dominick, J. R. (1984). Videogames, television violence, and aggression in teenagers. *Journal of Communication, 34*(2), 136–147.

Dominick, J. R., & Greenberg, B. S. (1972). Attitudes towards violence: The interaction of television, exposure, family attitudes, and social class. In G. A. Comstock & E. A. Rubinstein (Eds.), *Television and social behavior: Vol. 3. Television and adolescent aggressiveness* (pp. 314–335). Washington, DC: U.S. Government Printing Office.

Donnerstein, E. (1984). Pornography: Its effects on violence again women. In N. Malamuth & E. Donnerstein (Eds.), *Pornography and sexual aggression* (pp. 53–81). New York: Academic Press.

Donnerstein, E., & Barrett, G. (1978). The effects of erotic stimuli on male aggression towards females. *Journal of Personality and Social Psychology, 36*, 180–188.

Donnerstein, E., & Berkowitz, L. (1981). Victim reactions in aggressive-erotic films as a factor in violence against women. *Journal of Personality and Social Psychology, 41*, 710–724.

Donnerstein, E., Linz, D., & Penrod, S. (1987). *The question of pornography: Research findings and policy implications*. New York: Free Press.

Donnerstein, E., Slaby, R. G., & Eron, L. D. (1994). The mass media and youth aggression. In L. D. Eron, J. H. Gentry, & P. Schlegel (Eds.), *Reason to hope: A psychosocial perspective on violence & youth* (pp. 219–250). Washington, DC: American Psychological Association.

Donnerstein, E., Wilson, B., & Linz, D. (1992). On the regulation of broadcast indecency to protect children. *Journal of Broadcasting & Electronic Media, 36*, 111–117.

Donohew, L., Finn, S., & Christ, W. G. (1988). "The nature of news" revisited: The roles of affect, schemas, and cognition. In L. Donohew, H. E. Sypher, & E. T. Higgins (Eds.), *Communication, social cognition, and affect* (pp. 195–218). Hillsdale, NJ: Lawrence Erlbaum Associates.

Donohue, G. A., Tichenor, P. J., & Olien, C. N. (1975). Mass media and the knowledge gap: A hypothesis reconsidered. *Communication Research, 2*, 3–23.

Doob, A. N., & Macdonald, G. E. (1979). Television viewing and fear of victimization: Is the relationship causal? *Journal of Personality and Social Psychology, 37*, 170–179.

Dorr, A. (1986). *Television and children: A special medium for a special audience*. Beverly Hills, CA: Sage.

Duncan, D. (1990). Pornography as a source of sex information for university students. *Psychological Reports, 66*, 442.

DuRant, R. H., Rome. E. S., Rich, M., Allred, E., Emans, S. J., & Woods, E. R. (1997). Tobacco and alcohol use behaviors portrayed in music videos: A content analysis. *American Journal of Public Health, 87*, 1131–1135.

Durkheim. E. (1964). *The division of labor in society* (G. Simpson, Trans.). New York: Free Press. (Original work published 1893)

Durkin, K. (1985). Television and sex-role acquisition. 2: Effects. *British Journal of Social Psychology, 24*, 191–210.

Dynes, R. (1970). *Organized behavior in disaster*. Lexington, MA: Heath Lexington.

Edwards, E. D. (1991). The ecstasy of horrible expectations: Morbid curiosity, sensation seeking, and interest in horror movies. In B. A. Austin (Ed.), *Current re-*

search in film: Audiences, economics, and law (Vol. 5, pp. 19–38). Norwood, NJ: Ablex.

Edwardson, M., Grooms, D., & Proudlove, S. (1981). Television news information gain from interesting video vs. talking heads. *Journal of Broadcasting, 25*, 15–24.

Edwardson, M., Kent, K., & McConnell, M. (1985). Television news information gain: Videotex versus a talking head. *Journal of Broadcasting & Electronic Media, 29*, 367–378.

Elliott, P. (1974). Uses and gratifications research: A critique and sociological alternative. In J. G. Blumler & E. Katz (Eds.), *The uses of mass communication: Current perspectives on gratifications research* (pp. 249–268). Beverly Hills, CA: Sage.

Enteman, W. F. (1996). Stereotyping, prejudice, and discrimination. In P. W. Lester (Ed.), *Images that injure: Pictural stereotypes in the media* (pp. 10–14). Westport, CN: Praeger.

Entman, R. M. (1993). Framing: Toward clarification of a fractured paradigm. *Journal of Communication, 43*(4), 51–58.

Ettema, J. S., & Kline, F. G. (1977). Deficits, difference, and ceilings: Contingent conditions for understanding knowledge gap. *Communication Research, 4*, 179–202.

Evans, E. D., Rutberg, J., Sather, C., & Turner, C. (1991). Content analysis of contemporary teen magazines for adolescent females. *Youth and Society, 23*, 99–120.

Eveland, W. P., Jr. (1997). Interactions and nonlinearity in mass communication: Connecting theory and methodology. *Journalism and Mass Communication Quarterly, 74*, 400–416.

Eveland, W. P., McLeod, D. M., & Signorielli, N. (1995). Actual and perceived U.S. public opinion: The spiral of silence during the Persian Gulf War. *International Journal of Public Opinion Research, 7*, 91–109.

Eysenck, M. W. (1993). *Principles of cognitive psychology*. Hillsdale, NJ: Lawrence Erlbaum Associates.

Eysenck, M. W., & Keane, M. T. (1992). *Cognitive psychology: A student's handbook*. Hillsdale, NJ: Lawrence Erlbaum Associates.

Federal Election Commission. (1998). About elections and voting. [Online report]. Available: http://www.fec.gov/pages/electpg.htm

Federman, J. (1998). Media ratings systems: A comparative review. In M. E. Price (Ed.), *The V-chip debate: Content filtering from television to the Internet* (pp. 99–132). Mahwah, NJ: Lawrence Erlbaum Asociates.

Fenigstein, A. (1979). Does aggression cause a preference for viewing media violence? *Journal of Personality and Social Psychology, 37*, 2307–2317.

Fenigstein, A., & Heyduk, R. G. (1985). Thought and action as determinants of media exposure. In D. Zillmann & J. Bryant (Eds.), *Selective exposure to communication* (pp. 113–139). Hillsdale, NJ: Lawrence Erlbaum Associates.

Ferguson, D. A., & Perse, E. M. (1993). Media and audience influences on channel repertoire. *Journal of Broadcasting & Electronic Media, 37*, 31–47.

Ferguson, D. A.. & Perse, E. M. (2000). The World Wide Web as a functional alternative to television. *Journal of Broadcasting & Electronic Media*, 155–174.

Feshbach, S. (1955). The drive-reducing function of fantasy behavior. *Journal of Abnormal and Social Psychology, 50*, 3–11.

Feshbach, S. (1972). Reality and fantasy in filmed violence. In J. P. Murray, E. A. Rubinstein, & G. A. Comstock (Eds.), *Television and social behavior. Vol. 2: Tele-*

vision and social learning (pp. 318–345). Rockville, MD: National Institute of Mental Health.

Feshbach, S., & Singer, R. D. (1971). *Television and aggression: An experimental field study.* San Francisco: Jossey-Bass.

Festinger, L. (1954). A theory of social comparison. *Human Relations, 7,* 117–140.

Festinger, L. (1957). *A theory of cognitive dissonance.* Stanford, CA: Stanford University.

Fetler, M. (1984). Television viewing and school achievement. *Journal of Communication, 34*(2), 104–118.

Figlio, R. M. (n.d.). *Review and critique: Report to the American Broadcasting Company regarding: Centerwall, Brandon S., "Exposure to televison as risk factor for violence."* Unpublished report, University of California-Riverside, Department of Sociology.

Findahl, O., & Höijer, G. (1985). Some characteristics of news memory and comprehension. *Journal of Broadcasting & Electronic Media, 29,* 379–396.

Fischer, P. M., Schwartz, M. P., Richards, J. W., Goldstein, A. O., & Rojas, T. H. (1991). Brand logo recognition by children aged 3 to 6 years: Mickey Mouse and Old Joe the Camel. *JAMA, 266,* 3145–3148.

Fishbein, M., & Ajzen, I. (1975). *Belief, attitude, intention and behavior: An introduction to theory and research.* Reading, MA: Addison-Wesley.

Fisher, W. A., & Barak, A. (1989). Sex education as a corrective: Immunizing against possible effects of pornography. In D. Zillmann (Ed.), *Pornography: Research advances & policy considerations* (pp. 289–320). Hillsdale, NJ: Lawrence Erlbaum Associates.

Fiske, S. T., & Kinder, D. R. (1991). Involvement, expertise, and schema sue: Evidence from political cognition. In N. Cantor & J. F. Kihlstrom (Eds.), *Personality, cognition, and social interaction* (pp. 171–190). Hillsdale, NJ: Lawrence Erlbaum Associates.

Fiske, S. T., & Taylor, S. E. (1991). *Social cognition* (2nd ed.). New York: McGraw-Hill.

Flavell, J. H. (1963). *The developmental psychology of Jean Piaget.* New York: Van Nostrand.

Flores, S. A., & Hartlaub, M . G. (1998). Reducing rape-myth acceptance in male college students: A meta-analysis of intervention studies. *Journal of College Student Development, 39,* 438–448.

Frankovic, K. A. (1998). Public opinion and polling. In D. Graber, D. McQuail, & P. Norris (Eds.), *The politics of news: The news of politics* (pp. 150–170). Washington, DC: Congressional Quarterly Press.

Freedman, J. L. (1984). Effect of television violence on aggressiveness. *Psychological Bulletin, 96,* 227–246.

Fuchs, D. A. (1966). Election-day radio-television and western voting. *Public Opinion Quarterly, 30,* 226–236.

Funkhouser, G. R. (1973a). The issues of the sixties: An exploratory study in the dynamics of public opinion. *Public Opinion Quarterly, 37,* 62–75.

Funkhouser, G. R. (1973b). Trends in media coverage of the issues of the sixties. *Journalism Quarterly, 50,* 533–538.

Gallup Organization. (1991, January). Buildup to war. *Monthly Report,* pp. 2–13.

Gantz, W. (1978). How uses and gratifications affect recall of television news. *Journalism Quarterly, 55,* 664–672, 681.

Gantz, W. (1983). The diffusion of news about the attempted Reagan assassination. *Journal of Communication, 33*(1), 56–66.

Gantz, W., Krendl, K. A., & Robertson, S. R. (1986). Diffusion of a proximate news event. *Journalism Quarterly, 63*, 282–287.

Gantz, W., & Tokinoya, H. (1987). Diffusion of news about the assassination of Olof Palme: A trans-continental, two-city comparison of the process. *European Journal of Communication, 2*, 197–210.

Garfinkel, P. E., & Garner, D. M. (1982). *Anorexia nervosa: A multidimensional perspective*. New York: Brunner-Mazel.

Garner, P. E., & Garfinkel, P. E. (1979). The Eating Attitudes Test: An index of symptoms of anorexia nervosa. *Psychological Medicine, 9*, 273–279.

Garner, D. M., Garfinkel, P. E., Schwartz, D., & Thompson, M. (1980). Cultural expectations of thinness in women. *Psychological Reports, 47*, 483–491.

Garramone, G. M. (1983). Issue versus image orientation and effects of political advertising. *Communication Research, 18*, 59–76.

Garramone, G., Atkin, C. K., Pinkleton, B. E., & Cole, R. T. (1990). Effects of negative political advertising on the political process. *Journal of Broadcasting & Electronic Media, 34*, 299–311.

Gartner, M. (1976). Endogenous bandwagon and underdog effects. *Public Choice, 25*, 83–89.

Gaunt, J. (1991, January 23). War briefly shoots down video rentals. *The Philadelphia Inquirer*, p. 7C.

Gaziano, C. (1985). The knowledge gap: An analytical review of media effects. In M. Gurevitch & M. Levy (Eds.), *Mass communication review yearbook* (Vol. 5, pp. 462–501). Beverly Hills: Sage.

Gaziano, C. (1988). How credible is the credibility crisis? *Journalism Quarterly, 65*, 267–278, 375.

Gaziano, C., & McGrath, K. (1986). Measuring the concept of credibility. *Journalism Quarterly, 63*, 451–462.

Geiogamah, H., & Pavel, D. M. (1993). Developing television for American Indian and Alaska Native children in the late 20th century. In G. L. Berry & J. K. Asamen (Eds.), Children & television: Images in a changing sociocultural world (pp. 191–204). Newbury Park, CA; Sage.

Geis, F. L., Brown, V., Walstedt, J., & Porter, N. (1984). TV commercials as achievement scripts for women. *Sex Roles, 10*, 513–525.

Genova, B. K. L., & Greenberg, B. S. (1979). Interests in news and the knowledge gap. *Public Opinion Quarterly, 43*, 79–91.

Gerbner, G. (1990). Epilogue: Advancing on the path of righteousness (maybe). In N. Signorielli & M. Morgan (Eds.), *Cultivation analysis: New directions in media effects research* (pp. 249–262). Newbury Park, CA: Sage.

Gerbner, G., & Gross, L. (1976). Living with television: The violence profile. *Journal of Communication*, 26(2), 173–199.

Gerbner, G., Gross, L., Eleey, M., Jackson-Beeck, M., Jeffries-Fox, S., & Signorielli, N. (1977). The Gerbner violence profile—An analysis of the CBS report. *Journal of Broadcasting, 21*, 280–286.

Gerbner, G., Gross, L., Jackson-Beeck, M., Jeffries-Fox, S., & Signorielli, N. (1978). Cultural Indicators: Violence profile no. 9. *Journal of Communication, 28*(3), 176–207.

Gerbner, G., Gross, L., Morgan, M., & Signorielli, N. (1980). The "mainstreaming" of American: Violence profile no. 11. *Journal of Communication, 30*(3), 10–29.

Gerbner, G., Gross, L., Morgan, M., & Signorielli, N. (1981). Health and medicine on television. *New England Journal of Medicine, 305*, 901–904.

Gerbner, G., Gross, L., Morgan, M., & Signorielli, N. (1982). Charting the mainstream: Television's contributions to political orientations. *Journal of Communication, 32*(2), 100–127.

Gerbner, G., Gross, L., Morgan, M., & Signorielli, N,. (1986). Living with television: The dynamics of the cultivation process. In J. Bryant & D. Zillmann (Eds.), *Perspectives on media effects* (pp. 17–40). Hillsdale, NJ: Lawrence Erlbaum Associates.

Gerbner, G., Gross, L., Morgan, M., & Signorielli, N. (1994). Growing up with television: The cultivation perspective. In J. Bryant & D. Zillmann (Eds.), *Media effects: Advances in theory and research* (pp. 17–41). Hillsdale, NJ: Lawrence Erlbaum Associates.

Gerbner, G., Gross, L., Signorielli, N., & Morgan, M. (1980). Aging with television: Images on television drama and conceptions of social reality. *Journal of Communication, 30*(1), 37–47.

Gerbner, G., & Signorielli, N. (1979). *Women and minorities in television drama 1969–1978*. Philadelphia: Annenberg School for Communication, University of Pennsylvania.

Ghanem, S. (1997). Filling in the tapestry: The second level of agenda setting. In M. McCombs, D. L. Shaw, & D. Weaver (Eds.), *Communication and democracy: Exploring the intellectual frontiers in agenda-setting theory* (pp. 3–14). Mahwah, NJ: Lawrence Erlbaum Associates.

Gitlin, T. (1978). Media sociology: The dominant paradigm. *Theory and Society, 6*, 205–253.

Gitlin, T. (1980). *The whole world is watching: Mass media and the making and unmaking of the new left*. Berkeley: University of California Press.

Glynn, C. J., Hayes, A. F., & Shanahan, J. (1997). Perceived support for one's opinions and willingness to speak out: A meta-analysis of survey studies on the "spiral of silence." *Public Opinion Quarterly, 61*, 452–463.

Glynn, C. J., & McLeod, J. M. (1985). Implications of the spiral of silence theory of communication and public opinion research. In K. R. Sanders, L. L. Kaid, & D. Nimmo (Eds.), *Political communication yearbook 1984* (pp. 43–65). Carbondale, IL: Southern Illinois University Press.

Goldberg, M. E., Gorn, G. J., & Gibson, W. (1978). TV messages for snack and breakfast foods: Do they influence children's preferences? *Journal of Consumer Research, 5*, 73–81.

Goldman, K., & Reilly, P. M. (1992, September 10). Untold story: Media's slow grasp of hurricane's impact helped delay response. *Wall Street Journal*, pp. A1, A9.

Goldstein, A. O., Sobel, R. A., & Newman, G. R. (1999). Tobacco and alcohol use in G-rated children's animated films. *JAMA, 281*, 1131–1136.

Goltz, J. D. (1984). Are the news media responsible for the disaster myth? A content analysis of emergency response imagery. *International Journal of Mass Emergencies and Disasters, 2*, 345–368.

González, H. (1988). Mass media and the spiral of silence: The Philippines from Marcos to Aquino. *Journal of Communication, 38*(4), 33–48.

Gorn, G. J., Goldberg, M. E., & Kanungo, R. N. (1976). The role of educational television in changing the intergroup attitudes of children. *Child Development, 47*, 277–280.

Graber, D. A. (1982). The impact of media research on public opinion studies. In D. C. Whitney, E. Wartella, & S. Windahl (Eds.), *Mass communication review yearbook* (Vol. 3, pp. 555–563). Beverly Hills: Sage.

Graber, D. A. (1988). *Processing the news: How people tame the information tide* (2nd ed.). New York: Longman.

Graber, D. A. (1989). *Mass media and American politics* (3rd ed.). Washington, DC: Congressional Quarterly Press.

Graber, D. A. (1990). Seeing is remembering: How visuals contribute to learning from television news. *Journal of Communication, 40*(3), 134–155.

Graber, D. A. (1993). *Mass media and American politics* (4th ed.). Washington, DC: Congressional Quarterly Press.

Graves, S. B. (1993). Television, the portrayal of African Americans, and the development of children's attitudes. In G. L. Berry & J. K. Asamen (Eds.), *Children & television: Images in a changing sociocultural world* (pp. 179–190). Newbury Park, CA: Sage.

Graves, S. B. (1996). Diversity on television. In T. M. MacBeth (Ed.), *Tuning in to young viewers: Social science perspectives on television* (pp. 61–86). Thousand Oaks, CA: Sage.

Gray, H. (1989). Television, black Americans, and the American dream. *Critical Studies in Mass Communication, 6*, 376–386.

Greenberg, B. S. (1965). Diffusion of news about the Kennedy assassination. In B. S. Greenberg & E. B. Parker (Eds.), *The Kennedy assassination and the American public: Social communication in crisis* (pp. 89–98). Stanford, CA: Stanford University Press.

Greenberg, B. S. (1972). Children's reactions to TV blacks. *Journalism Quarterly, 49*, 5–14.

Greenberg, B. S. (1974). Gratifications of television viewing and their correlates for British children. In J. G. Blumler & E. Katz (Eds.), *The uses of mass communications: Current perspectives on gratifications research* (pp. 71–92). Beverly Hills: Sage.

Greenberg, B. S. (1986). Minorities and the mass media. In J. Bryant & D. Zillmann (Eds.), *Perspectives on media effects* (pp. 165–188). Hillsdale, NJ: Lawrence Erlbaum Associates.

Greenberg, B. S. (1988). Some uncommon television images and the drench hypothesis. In S. Oskamp (Ed.), *Applied social psychology annual. Vol. 8: Television as a social issue* (pp. 88–102). Newbury Park, CA: Sage.

Greenberg, B. S. (1994). Content trends in media sex. In D. Zillmann, J. Bryant, & A. C. Huston (Eds.), *Media, children, and the family: Social scientific, psychodynamic, and clinical perspectives* (pp. 165–182). Hillsdale, NJ: Lawrence Erlbaum Associates.

Greenberg, B. S., & Brand, J. E. (1993). Cultural diversity on Saturday morning television. In G. L. Berry & J. K. Asamen (Eds.), Children & television: Images in a changing sociocultural world (pp. 132–142). Newbury Park, CA; Sage.

Greenberg, B. S., Cohen, E., & Li, H. (1993). How the U.S. found out about the war. In B. S. Greenberg & W. Gantz (Eds.), *Desert Storm and the mass media* (pp. 145–152). Cresskill, NJ: Hampton.

Greenberg, B. S., & D'Alessio, D. (1985). Quantity and quality of sex in the soaps. *Journal of Broadcasting & Electronic Media, 29*, 309–321.

Greenberg, B. S., Siemicki, M., Dorfman, S., Heeter, C., Stanley, C., Soderman, & Linsangan, R. (1993). Sex content in R-rated films viewed by adolescents. In B.

S. Greenberg, J. D. Brown, & N. L. Buerkel-Rothfuss (Eds.), *Media, sex, and the adolescent* (pp. 45–58). Cresskill, NJ: Hampton Press.

Greenberg, B. S., Stanley, C., Siemicki, M., Heeter, C., Soderman, A., & Linsangan, R. (1993). Sex content on soaps and prime-time television series most viewed by adolescents. In B. S. Greenberg, J. D. Brown, & N. L. Buerkel-Rothfuss (Eds.), *Media, sex, and the adolescent* (pp. 29–44). Cresskill, NJ: Hampton Press.

Greenwald, A. G., & Leavitt, C. (1984). Audience involvement in advertising: Four levels. *Journal of Consumer Research, 11*, 581–592.

Greeson, L. E., & Williams, R. A. (1986). Social implications of music videos for youth: An analysis of the content and effects of MTV. *Youth & Society, 18*, 177–189.

Griffith, R. (1986). *Battle in the Civil War: Generalship and tactics in America 1861–65*. Camberley, England: Fieldbooks.

Griffiths, M. (1997). Video games and aggression. *The Psychologist, 9*, 397–401.

Grube, J. W. (1993). Alcohol portrayals and alcohol advertising on television. *Alcohol Health & Research World, 17*, 61–11.

Grube, J. W., & Wallack, L. (1994). Television beer advertising and drinking knowledge, beliefs, and intentions among school children. *American Journal of Public Health, 84*, 254–259.

Gunter, G. (1985). New sources and news awareness: A British survey. *Journal of Broadcasting & Electronic Media, 29*, 397–406.

Gunter, B. (1987). *Poor reception: Misunderstanding and forgetting broadcast news*. Hillsdale, NJ: Lawrence Erlbaum Associates.

Gunther, A. C. (1995). Overrating the X-rating: The third-person perception and support censorship of pornography. *Journal of Communication, 45*(1), 27–38.

Gunther, A. G., & Thorson, E. (1992). Perceived persuasive effects of product commercials and public service announcements: third-person effects in new domains. *Communication Research, 19*, 574–596.

Gurevitch, M., & Blumler, J. G. (1990). Political communication systems and democratic values. In J. Lichtenberg (Ed.), *Democracy and the mass media: A collection of essays* (pp. 269–289). Cambridge: Cambridge University Press.

Hamilton, D. L., & Mackie, D. M. (1990). Specificity and generality in the nature and use of stereotypes. In T. K. Srull & R. S. Wyer, Jr. (Eds.), *Advances in social cognition: Vol. III. Content and process specificity in the effects of prior experiences* (pp. 99–110). Hillsdale, NJ: Lawrence Erlbaum Associates.

Hamilton, J. T. (1998). *Channeling violence: The economic market for violent television programming*. Princeton, NJ: Princeton University Press.

Hammer, J. (1992, October 26). Must blacks be buffoons? *Newsweek*, 70–71.

Hansen, C. H. (1989). Priming sex-role stereotypic event schemas with rock music videos: Effects on impression favorability, trait inferences, and recall of a subsequent male–female interaction. *Basic and Applied Social Psychology, 10*, 371–391.

Hansen, C. H., & Hansen, R. D. (1988). How rock music videos can change what is seen when boy meets girl: Priming stereotypic appraisal of social interaction. *Sex Roles, 19*, 287–316.

Hapkiewicz, W. G., & Stone, R. D. (1974). The effect of realistic versus imaginary aggressive models on children's interpersonal play. *Child Study Journal, 4*(2), 47–58.

Harris, A. J., & Feinberg, J. F. (1977). Television and aging: Is what you see what you get? *Gerontologist, 17*, 464–468.

Harris, R. J. (1994a). *A cognitive psychology of mass communication* (2nd ed.). Hillsdale, NJ: Lawrence Erlbaum Associates.

Harris, R. J. (1994b). The impact of sexually explicit media. In J. Bryant & D. Zillmann (Eds.), *Media effects: Advances in theory and research* (pp. 247–272). Hillsdale, NJ: Lawrence Erlbaum Associates.

Harrison, K., & Cantor, J. (1997). The relationship between media consumption and eating disorders. *Journal of Communication, 47*(1), 40–67.

Hastie, R. (1981). Schematic principles in human memory. In E. T. Higgins, C. P. Herman, & M. P. Zanna (Eds.), *Social cognition: The Ontario Symposium* (Vol. 1, pp. 39–88). Hillsdale, NJ: Lawrence Erlbaum Associates.

Hastorf, A. H., & Cantril, H. (1954). They saw a game: A case study. *Journal of Abnormal and Social Psychology, 49*, 129–134.

Hawkins, G., & Zimring, F. E. (1988). *Pornography in a free society*. Cambridge, England: Cambridge University Press.

Hawkins, R. P., & Pingree, S. (1980). Some processes in the cultivation effect. *Communication Research, 7*, 193–226.

Hawkins, R. P., & Pingree, S. (1982). Television's influence on social reality. In D. Pearl, L. Bouthilet, & J. Lazar (Eds.), *Television and behavior: Ten years of scientific progress and implications for the eighties* (DHHS Publication No. ADM 82-1196, Vol. 2, pp. 224–247). Washington, DC: U.S. Government Printing Office.

Hazan, A. R., Lipton, H. L., & Glantz, S. A. (1994). Popular films do not reflect current tobacco use. *American Journal of Public Health, 84*, 998–1000.

Hearold, S. (1986). A synthesis of 1043 effects of television on social behavior. In G. Comstock (Ed.), *Public communication and behavior* (Vol. 1, pp. 65–133). Orlando, FL: Academic Press.

Hebditch, D., & Anning, N. (1988). *Porn gold: Inside the pornography business*. London: Faber & Faber.

Heeter, C., Brown, N., Soffin, S., Stanley, C., & Salwen, M. (1989). Agenda-setting by electronic text news. *Journalism Quarterly, 66*, 101–106.

Heins, M. (1998). Three questions about television ratings. In M. E. Price (Ed.), *The V-chip debate: Content filtering from television to the Internet* (pp. 47–58). Mahwah, NJ: Lawrence Erlbaum Associates.

Helregel, B. K., & Weaver, J. B. (1989). Mood-management during pregnancy through selective exposure to television. *Journal of Broadcasting & Electronic Media, 33*, 15–33.

Henshel, R. L., & Johnston, W. (1987). The emergence of bandwagon effects: A theory. *Sociological Quarterly, 28*, 493–511.

Herman, E. S., & Chomsky, N. (1988). *Manufacturing consent: The political economy of the mass media*. New York: Pantheon Books.

Herrett-Skjellum, J., & Allen, M. (1996). Television programming and sex stereotyping: A meta-analysis. In B. R. Burleson (Ed.), *Communication yearbook* (Vol. 19, pp. 157–185). Thousand Oaks, CA: Sage.

Hickman, H. (1991). Public polls and election participants. In P. J. Lavrakas & J. K. Holley (Eds.), *Polling and presidential election coverage* (pp. 100–133). Newbury Park, CA: Sage.

Hicks, D. J. (1965). Imitation and retention of film-mediated aggressive peer and adult models. *Journal of Personality and Social Psychology, 2*, 97–100.

Hill, D. B. (1985). Viewer characteristics and agenda setting by television news. *Public Opinion Quarterly, 49*, 340–350.

Hill, D. B., & Dyer, J. A. (1981). Extent of diversion of newscasts from distant stations by cable viewers. *Journalism Quarterly, 58*, 552–555.

Hill, R. J., & Bonjean, C. M. (1964). News diffusion: A test of the regularity hypothesis. *Journalism Quarterly, 41*, 336–342.

Hirsch, P. (1981). On not learning from one's own mistakes: A reanalysis of Gerbner et al.'s findings on cultivation analysis: Part II. *Communication Research, 8*, 3–17.

Hirschburg, P. L., Dillman, D. A., & Ball-Rokeach, S. J. (1986). Media system dependency theory: Responses to the eruption of Mount St. Helens. In S. J. Ball-Rokeach & M. G. Cantor (Eds.), *Media, audience, and social structure* (pp.117–126). Newbury Park, CA: Sage.

Hirschman, E. C. (1987). Consumer preferences in literature, motion pictures, and television programs. *Empirical Studies of the Arts, 5*, 31–46.

Hogben, M. (1998). Factors moderating the effect of televised violence on viewer behavior. *Communication Research, 25*, 220–247.

Hollander, B. A. (1994). Patterns in the exposure and influence of the old news and the new news. *Mass Communication Review, 21*, 144–155.

Hollenbeck, A. R., & Slaby, R. G. (1979). Infant visual and vocal responses to television. *Child Development, 50*, 41–45.

Holloway, S., Tucker, L., & Hornstein, H. A. (1977). The effects of social and nonsocial information on interpersonal behavior of males: The news makes news. *Journal of Personality and Social Psychology, 35*, 514–522.

Hornik, R. (1978). Television access and the slowing of cognitive growth. *American Educational Research Journal, 15*, 1–15.

Hornstein, H. A., LaKind, E., Frankel, G., & Manne, S. (1975). Effects of knowledge about remote social events on prosocial behavior, social conceptual, and mood. *Journal of Personality and Social Psychology, 32*, 1038–1046.

Hovland, C. I., Janis, I. L., & Kelley, J. J. (1953). *Communication and persuasion*. New Haven, CT: Yale University.

Hovland, C. I., Luchins, A. S., Mandell, W., Campbell, E. H., Brock, T. C., McGuire, W. J., Feierabend, R. L., & Anderson, N. H. (1957). *The order of presentation in persuasion*. New Haven, CT: Yale University Press.

Hovland, C. I., Lumsdaine, A. A., & Sheffield, F. D. (1949). *Experiments on mass communication*. Princeton, NJ: Princeton University Press.

Hovland, C. I., & Mandell, W. (1952). An experimental comparison of conclusion-drawing by the communicator and by the audience. *Journal of Abnormal and Social Psychology, 47*, 581–588.

Howitt, D. (1972). Television and aggression: A counterargument. *American Psychologist, 27*, 969–970.

Hsu, M. L., & Price, V. (1993). Political expertise and affect. *Communication Research, 20*, 671–695.

Huberman, B. A., Pirolli, P. L. T., Pitkow, J. E., & Lukose, R. M. (1998, April 3). Strong regularities in World Wide Web surfing. *Science, 280*, 95–97.

Huesmann, L. R. (1982). Television and violence and aggressive behavior. In D. Pearl, L. Bouthilet, & J. Lazar (Eds.), *Television and behavior: Ten years of scientific progress and implications for the eighties* (DHHS Publication No. ADM 82-1196, Vol. 2, pp. 126–137). Washington, DC: Government Printing Office.

Huesmann, L. R. (1986). Psychological processes promoting the relation between exposure to media violence and aggressive behavior by the viewer. *Journal of Social Issues, 42*(3), 125–140.

Huesmann, L. R., Eron, L. D. (1986). The development of aggression in American children as a consequence of television violence viewing. In L. R. Huesmann & L. D. Eron (Eds.), *Television and the aggressive child: A cross-national comparison* (pp. 45–80). Hillsdale, NJ: Lawrence Erlbaum Associates.

Huesmann, L. R., Eron, L. D., Klein, R., Brice, P., & Fischer, P. (1983). Mitigating the imitation of aggressive behavior by changing children's attitudes about media violence. *Journal of Personality and Social Psychology, 44*, 899–910.

Hughes, M. (1980). The fruits of cultivation analysis: A reexamination of some effects of television watching. *Public Opinion Quarterly, 44*, 287–302.

Hummert, M. L., Nussbaum, J. F., & Wiemann, J. M. (1992). Communication and the elderly. *Communication Research, 19*, 413–422.

Hummert, M. L., Shaner, J. L., & Garstka, T. A. (1995). Cognitive processes affecting communication with older adults: The case for stereotypes, attitudes, and beliefs about communication. In J. F. Nussbaum & J. Coupland (Eds.), *Handbook of communication and aging research* (pp. 105–131). Mahwah, NJ: Lawrence Erlbaum Associates.

Hundley, H. L. (1995). The naturalization of beer in *Cheers. Journal of Broadcasting & Electronic Media, 39*, 350–359.

Huston, A. C., Wright, J. C. (1983). Children's processing of television: The informative functions of formal features. In J. Bryant and D. R. Anderson (Eds.), *Children's understanding of television: Research on attention and comprehension* (pp. 35–68). New York: Academic Press.

Huston, A. C., Wright, J. C., Wartella, E., Rice, M. L., Watkins, B. A., Campbell, T., & Potts, R. (1981). Communicating more than content: Formal features of children's television programs. *Journal of Communication, 31*(3), 32–48.

Hyde, T. S., & Jenkins, J. J. (1973). Recall for words as a function of semantic, graphic, and syntactic orienting tasks. *Journal of Verbal Learning and Verbal Behavior, 12*, 471–480.

Immerwahr, J., & Doble, J. (1982). Public attitudes toward freedom of the press. *Public Opinion Quarterly, 46*, 177–194.

Itons-Peterson, M. J., & Roskos-Ewoldsen, B., Thomas, L., Shirley, M., & Blut, D. (1989). Will educational materials reduce negative effects of exposure to sexual violence? *Journal of Social and Clinical Psychology, 50*, 455–457.

Iwao, S., Pool, I. de Sola, & Hagiwara, S. (1981). Japanese and U.S. media: Some cross-cultural insights into TV violence. *Journal of Communication, 31*(2), 28–36.

Iyengar, S. (1991). *Is anyone responsible: How television frames political issues.* Chicago: University of Chicago Press.

Iyengar, S., & Kinder, D. R. (1987). *News that matters: Television and American public opinion.* Chicago: University of Chicago Press.

Iyengar, S., Peters, M. D., & Kinder, D. R. (1982). Experimental demonstrations of the "not-so-minimal" consequences of television news programs. *American Political Science Review, 76*, 848–858.

Iyengar, S., & Simon, A. (1993). News coverage of the gulf crisis and public opinion. *Communication Research, 20*, 365–383.

Jackson, J. E. (1983). Election night reporting and voter turnout. *American Journal of Political Science, 27*, 615–635.

Jaglom, L. M., & Gardner, H. (1981). The preschool television viewer as anthropologist. In H. Kelly & H. Gardner (Eds.), *Viewing children through television* (pp. 9–30). San Francisco: Jossey-Bass.

Jamieson, K. H., & Birdsell, D. W. (1988). *Presidential debates: The challenge of creating an informed electorate*. New York: Oxford.

Jansma, L. L., Linz, D. G., Mulac, A., & Imrich, D. J. (1997). Men's interactions with women after viewing sexually explicit films: Does degradation make a difference? *Communication Monographs, 64*, 1–24.

Jhally, S. (Producer and Director). (1994). *The killing screens* [Film]. Northhampton, MA: Media Education Foundation.

Jhally, S., Lewis, J., & Morgan, M. (1991). The Gulf War: A study of the media, public opinion and public knowledge. *Propaganda Review, 8*, 14–15, 50–52.

Jo, E., & Berkowitz, L. (1994). A priming effect analysis of media influences: An update. In J. Bryant & D. Zillmann (Eds.), *Media effects: Advances in theory and research* (pp. 43–60). Hillsdale, NJ: Lawrence Erlbaum Associates.

Johnson, B. T., & Eagly, A. H. (1990). Involvement and persuasion: Types, traditions, and the evidence. *Psychological Bulletin, 107*, 375–384.

Johnson, W. T., Kupperstein, L. R., & Peters, J. J. (1971). Sex offenders' experience with erotica. *Technical report of the Commission on Obscenity and Pornography* (Vol. 7, pp. 163–171). Washington, DC: U.S. Government Printing Office.

Johnston, J., & Ettema, J. S. (1982). *Positive images: Breaking stereotypes with children's television*. Beverly Hills, CA: Sage.

Johnston, J., & Ettema, J. S. (1986). Using television to best advantage: Research for prosocial television. In J. Bryant & D. Zillmann (Eds.), *Perspectives on media effects* (pp.143–164). Hillsdale, NJ: Lawrence Erlbaum Associates.

Johnstone, J. W. C. (1974). Social integration and mass media use among adolescents: A case study. In J. G. Blumler & E. Katz (Eds.), *The uses of mass communication: Current perspectives on gratifications research* (pp. 35–47). Beverly Hills, CA: Sage.

Jones, K. (1997). Are rap videos more violent? Style differences and the prevalence of sex and violence in the age of MTV. *Howard Journal of Communication, 8*, 343–356.

Jose, P. E., & Brewer, W. G. (1984). Development of story liking: Character identification, suspense, and outcome resolution. *Developmental Psychology, 20*, 911–924.

Josephson, W. L. (1987). Television violence and children's aggression: Testing the priming, social script, and disinhibition predictions. *Journal of Personality and Social Psychology, 53*, 882–890.

Jowett, G. S., Jarvie, I. C., & Fuller, K. H. (1996). *Children and the movies: Media influence and the Payne Fund controversy*. New York: Cambridge University Press.

Joy, L. A., & Kimball, M. M., & Zabrack, M. L. (1986). Television and children's aggressive behavior. In T. M. Williams (Ed.), *The impact of television: A natural experiment in three communities* (pp. 303–360). Orlando, FL: Academic Press.

Kahneman, D. (1973). *Attention and effort*. Englewood Cliffs, NJ: Prentice-Hall.

Kaid, L., & Bystrom, D. G. (Eds.). (1999). *The electronic election: Perspectives on the 1996 campaign communication*. Mahwah, NJ: Lawrence Erlbaum Associates.

Kaid, L. L., Harville, B., Ballotti, J., & Wawrzyniak, M. (1993). Telling the Gulf War story: Coverage in five papers. In B. S. Greenberg & W. Gantz (Eds.), *Desert Storm and the mass media* (pp. 61–73). Cresskill, NJ: Hampton Press.

Kaplan, R. M. (1972). On television as a cause of aggression. *American Psychologist, 27*, 968–969.

Katz, D. (1960). The functional approach to the study of attitudes. *Public Opinion Quarterly, 24*, 163–204.

Katz, E. (1968). On reopening the question of selectivity in exposure to mass communications. In R. P. Abelson, E. Aronson, W. J. McGuire, T. M. Newcomb, M. J. Rosenberg, & P. H. Tannenbaum (Eds.), *Theories of cognitive consistency: A sourcebook* (pp. 788–796). Chicago: Rand McNally.

Katz, E. (1980). Media events: The sense of occasion. *Studies in Visual Anthropology, 6*, 84–89.

Katz, E., Adoni, H., & Parness, P. (1977). Remembering the news: What the picture adds to recall. *Journalism Quarterly, 54*, 231–239.

Katz, E., & Lazarsfeld, P. F. (1955). *Personal influence: The part played by people in the flow of mass communications.* New York: Free Press.

Katzman, N. (1974). The impact of communication technology: Promises and prospects. *Journal of Communication, 24*(4), 47–58.

Kaufman, L. (1980). Prime time nutrition. *Journal of Communication, 30*(3), 37–46.

Kaufman, N. J. (1994). Smoking and young women: The physician's role in stopping an equal opportunity killer. *JAMA, 271*, 629–630.

Kay, H. (1972). Weaknesses in the television-causes-aggression analysis by Eron et al. (1972). *American Psychologist, 27*, 970–973.

Kaye, E. (1989, September). Peter Jennings. *Esquire*, 158–176.

Kellerman, K. (1985). Memory processes in media effects. *Human Communication Research, 12*, 83–131.

Kellner, D. (1993). The crisis in the Gulf and the lack of critical media discourse. In B. S. Greenberg & W. Gantz (Eds.), *Desert Storm and the mass media* (pp. 37–47). Cresskill, NJ: Hampton Press.

Kennamer, J. D. (1990). Self-serving biases in perceiving the opinions of others: Implications for the spiral of silence. *Communication Research, 17*, 393–404.

Kepplinger, H. M. (1997). Political correctness and academic principles: A reply to Simpson. *Journal of Communication, 47*(4), 102–117.

Kerlinger, F. N. (1973). *Foundations of behavioral research* (2nd ed.). New York: Holt, Rinehart & Winston.

Kern, M. (1989). *30-second politics: Political advertising in the eighties.* New York: Praeger.

Kessler, M. (1989). Women's magazines' coverage of smoking related health hazards. *Journalism Quarterly, 66*, 316–322, 445.

Kim, J., & Rubin, A. M. (1997). The variable influence of audience activity on media effects. *Communication Research, 24*, 107–135.

Kinder, D. R., & Sanders, L. M. (1990). Mimicking political debate with survey questions: The case of white opinion on affirmative action for blacks. *Social Cognition, 8*, 73–103.

Kinder, D. R., & Sears, D. O. (1985). Public opinion and political action. In G. Lindzey & E. Aronson (Eds.), *Handbook of social psychology: Vol. 2. Special fields and applications* (pp. 659–741). New York: Random House.

King, C., Siegel, M., Celebucki, C., & Connolly, G. N. (1998). Adolescent exposure to cigarette advertising in magazines: An evaluation of brand-specific advertising in relation to youth readership. *JAMA, 279*, 516–520.

Kipper, P. (1986). Television camera movement as a source of perceptual information. *Journal of Broadcasting & Electronic Media, 30*, 295–307.

Klapper, J. T. (1960). *The effects of mass communication.* New York: Free Press.

Klatzky, R. L. (1980). *Human memory: Structures and processes* (2nd ed.). New York: W. H. Freeman.

Kozma, R. B. (1991). Learning with media. *Review of Educational Research, 61*,179–211.

Kraft, R. N. (1987). The influence of camera angle on comprehension and retention of pictorial events. *Memory & Cognition, 15*, 291–307.

Kraus, S. (1962). *The great debates: Background, perspective, effects.* Bloomington: Indiana University Press.

Kraus, S. (1996). Winners of the first 1960 televised presidential debate between Kennedy and Nixon. *Journal of Communication, 46*(4), 78–96.

Kraut, R., Patterson, M., Lundmark, V., Kiesler, S., & Mukopadhyay, R., & Scherlis, W. (1998). Internet paradox: A social technology that reduces social involvement and psychological well-being? *American Psychologist, 53*, 1017–1031.

Krugman, H. E. (1965). The impact of television advertising: Learning without involvement. *Public Opinion Quarterly, 29*, 349–356.

Kubey, R., & Csikszentmihalyi, M. (1990). *Television and the quality of life: How viewing shapes everyday experience.* Hillsdale, NJ: Lawrence Erlbaum Associates.

Kubey, R. W., & Peluso, T. (1990). Emotional response as a cause of interpersonal news diffusion: The case of the space shuttle tragedy. *Journal of Broadcasting & Electronic Media, 34*, 69–76.

Kueneman, R. M., & Wright, J. E. (1975). New policies of broadcast stations for civil disturbances and disasters. *Journalism Quarterly, 52*, 670–677.

Kunkel, D., Cope, K. M., Farinola, W. J. M., Biely, E., Rollin, E., & Donnerstein, E. (1999). *Sex on TV: Content and context.* Menlo Park, CA: The Henry Kaiser Family Foundation.

Kutchinsky, B. (1991). Pornography and rape: theory and practice? Evidence from crime data in four countries where pornography is easily available. *International Journal of Law and Psychiatry, 14*, 147–164.

Lamb, B., & Associates. (1988). *C-SPAN: American's town hall.* Washington, DC: Acropolis Books.

Lando, H. A., & Donnerstein, E. I. (1978). The effects of a model's success or failure on subsequent aggressive behavior. *Journal of Research in Personality, 12*, 225–234.

Lang, A. (1990). Involuntary attention and physiological arousal evoked by structural features and emotional content in TV commercials. *Communication Research, 17*, 275–299.

Lang, A. (1994). What can the heart tell us about thinking? In A. Lang (Ed.), *Measuring psychological responses to media* (pp. 99–111). Hillsdale, NJ: Lawrence Erlbaum Associates.

Lang, A. (1995). Defining audio/video redundancy from a limited capacity information processing perspective. *Communication Research, 22*, 86–115.

Lang, A., Geiger, S., Strickwerda, M., & Sumner, J. (1993). The effects of related and unrelated cuts on television viewers' attention, processing capacity, and memory. *Communication Research, 20*, 4–29.

Lang, A., Newhagen, J., & Reeves, B. (1996). Negative video as structure: Emotion, attention, capacity, and memory. *Journal of Broadcasting & Electronic Media, 40*, 460–477.

Lang, K., & Lang, G. E. (1968). *Voting and nonvoting: Implications of broadcasting returns before polls are closed.* Waltham, MA: Blaisdell.

Lang, K., & Lang, G. E. (1984). The impact of polls on public opinion. *Annals of the American Academy of Political and Social Science, 472*, 129–142.

LaPiere, R. T. (1934). Attitudes vs. actions. *Social Forces, 13*, 230–237.

Larson, J. F. (1980). A review of the state of the art in mass media disaster reporting. In *Disasters and the mass media: Proceedings of the Committee on Disasters and the Mass Media Workshop* (pp. 75–136). Washington, DC: National Academy of Sciences.

Larson, S. G. (1991). Television's mixed messages: Sexual content on *All My Children. Communication Quarterly, 39*, 156–163.

Lasorsa, D. L. (1989). Real and perceived effects of 'Amerika.' *Journalism Quarterly, 66*, 373–378, 529.

Lasswell, H. (1927). *Propaganda technique in the world war*. New York: Knopf.

Lasswell, H. D. (1948). The structure and function of communication in society. In L. Bryson (Ed.), *The communication of ideas* (pp. 37–51). New York: Harper.

Lau, R. R. (1986). Political schemata, candidate evaluations, and voting behavior. In R. R. Lau & D. O. Sears (Eds.), *Political cognition: The 19th Annual Carnegie Symposium on Cognition* (pp. 95–126). Hillsdale, NJ: Lawrence Erlbaum Associates.

Lau, R. R., & Sears, D. O. (1986). Social cognition and political cognition: The past, the present, and the future. In R. R. Lau & D. O. Sears (Eds.), *Political cognition: The 19th Annual Carnegie Symposium on Cognition* (pp. 347–366). Hillsdale, NJ: Lawrence Erlbaum Associates.

Lavarkas, P. J., Holley, J. K., & Miller, P. V. (1991). Public reactions to polling news during the 1988 presidential election campaign. In P. J. Lavrakas & J. K. Holley (Eds.), *Polling and presidential election coverage* (pp. 151–183). Newbury Park, CA: Sage.

Lawrence, K., & Herold, E. S. (1988). Women's attitudes toward and experience with sexually explicit materials. *Journal of Sex Research, 24*, 161–169.

Lawrence, P. A., & Palmgreen, P. C. (1996). A uses and gratifications analysis of horror film preference. In J. B. Weaver, III, & R. Tamborini (Eds.), *Horror films: Current research on audience preferences and reactions* (pp. 161–178). Mahwah, NJ: Lawrence Erlbaum Associates.

Lawrence, V. W. (1991). Effect of socially ambiguous information on white and black children's behavioral and trait perceptions. *Merrill-Palmer Quarterly, 37*, 619–630.

Lazarsfeld, P. F., Berelson, B., & Gaudet, H. (1968). *The people's choice: How the voter makes up his mind in a presidential election* (3rd ed.). New York: Columbia University Press.

Lazarsfeld, P. F., & Merton, R. K. (1948). Mass communication, popular taste and organized social action. In L. Bryson (Ed.), *The communication of ideas* (pp. 95–118). New York: Harper.

Ledingham, J. A., & Walters, L. M. (1989). The sound and the fury: Mass media and hurricanes. In L. M. Walters, L. Wilkins, & T. Walters (Eds.), *Bad tidings: Communication and catastrophe* (pp. 35–45). Hillsdale, NJ: Lawrence Erlbaum Associates.

Lee, A., & Lee, E. B. (1939). *The fine art of persuasion: A study of Father Coughlin's speeches*. New York: Harcourt, Brace.

Lefkowitz, M. L., Eron, L., Walder, L., & Huesmann, L. R. (1977). *Growing up to be violent: A longitudinal study of the development of aggression*. New York: Pergamon Press.

Lemish, D. (1987). Viewers in diapers: The early development of television viewing. In T. R. Lindlof (Ed.), *Natural audiences: Qualitative research of media uses and effects* (pp. 33–57). Norwood, NJ: Ablex.

Levin, S. R., & Anderson, D. R. (1976). The development of attention. *Journal of Communication, 26*(2), 126–135.

Levy, M. R. & Windahl, S. (1984). Audience activity and gratifications: A conceptual clarification and exploration. *Communication Research, 11*, 51–78.

Liebert, R. M., & Sprafkin, J. (1988). *The early window: Effects of television on children and youth.* New York: Pergamon.

Linn, T. (1996). Media methods that lead to stereotypes. In P. M. Lester (Ed.), *Images that injure: Pictural stereotypes in the media* (pp. 15–18). Westport, CT: Praeger.

Linz, D. (1985). Sexual violence in the media: Effects on male viewers and implications for society. (Doctoral dissertation, University of Wisconsin-Madison). *Dissertation Abstracts International, 46*, 4604B.

Linz, D., & Donnerstein, E. (1988). The methods and merits of pornography research. *Journal of Communication, 38*(2), 180–184.

Linz, D., Donnerstein, E., & Penrod, S. (1984). The effects of multiple exposures to filmed violence against women. *Journal of Communication, 34*(3), 130–147.

Linz, D., Fuson, I. A., & Donnerstein, E. (1990). Mitigating the negative effects of sexually violent mass communications through preexposure briefings. *Communication Research, 17*, 641–674.

Linz, D., & Malamuth, N. (1993). *Pornography.* Newbury Park: CA: Sage.

Lippmann, W. (1922). *Public opinion.* New York: Macmillan.

Litle, P., & Zuckerman, M. (1986). Sensation seeking and music preference. *Personality and Individual Differences, 4*, 575–577.

Longino, H. E. (1980). Pornography, oppression, and freedom: A closer look. In L. Lederer (Ed.), *Take back the night: Women on pornography* (pp. 40–54). New York: William Morrow.

Lorch, E. P., Anderson, D. R., & Levin, S. R. (1979). The relationship of visual attention to children's comprehension of television. *Child Development, 50*, 722–727.

Lowry, D. T., & Shidler, J. A. (1993). Prime time TV portrayals of sex, "safe sex" and AIDS: A longitudinal analysis. *Journalism Quarterly, 70*, 628–637.

Lowry, D. T., & Towles, D. W. (1989a). Prime time TV portrayals of sex, contraception, and venereal diseases. *Journalism Quarterly, 66*, 347–352.

Lowry, D. T., & Towles, D. W., (1989b). Soap opera portrayals of sex, contraception, and sexually transmitted diseases. *Journal of Communication, 39*(2), 76–83.

Lyle, J., & Hoffman, H. R. (1972). Children's use of television and other media. In E. A. Rubinstein, G. A. Comstock, & J. P. Murray (Eds.), *Television and social behavior: Vol. 4. Television in day-to-day life: Patterns of use* (DHEW publication HSM 72-9059, pp. 129–256). Washington, DC: U.S. Government Printing Office.

Maccoby, E. (1954). Why do children watch television? *Public Opinion Quarterly, 18*, 239–244.

MacDonald, J. F. (1983). *Blacks and white TV: Afro-Americans in television since 1948.* Chicago: Nelson-Hall.

MacKuen, M. B., & Coombs, S. L. (1981). *More than news: Media power in public affairs.* Beverly Hills: Sage.

Madden, P. A., & Grube, J. W. (1994). The frequency and nature of alcohol and tobacco advertising in televised sports, 1990 through 1992. *American Journal of Public Health, 84*, 297–299.

Malamuth, N. M. (1996). Sexually explicit media, gender differences, and evolutionary theory. *Journal of Communication, 46*(3), 8–31.

Malamuth, N. M., & Briere, J. (1986). Sexual violence in the media: Indirect effects on aggression against women. *Journal of Social Forces, 42*, 75–92.

Malamuth, N. M., & Check, J. V. P. (1980). Penile tumescence and perceptual responses to rape as a function of the victim's perceived reactions. *Journal of Applied Social Psychology, 10*, 528–547.

Malamuth, N. M., & Check, J. V. P. (1981). The effects of mass media exposure on acceptance of violence against women: A field experiment. *Journal of Research in Personality, 15*, 436–446.

Malamuth, N. M., & Check, J. V. P. (1983). Sexual arousal to rape depictions: Individual differences. *Journal of Abnormal Psychology, 92*, 55–67.

Malamuth, N. M., & Check, J. V. P. (1984). Debriefing effectiveness following exposure to pornographic rape depictions. *Journal of Sex Research, 20*, 14–31.

Malamuth, N. M., & Check, J. V. P. (1985). The effects of aggressive pornography on beliefs in rape myths: Individual differences. *Journal of Research in Personality, 19*, 299–320.

Malamuth, N. M., Haber, S., & Feshbach, S. (1980). Testing hypotheses regarding rape: Exposure to sexual violence, sex differences, and the "normality" of rapists. *Journal of Research in Personality, 14*, 121–137.

Males, M. (1999, January/February). Drive-by journalism. *Extra!*, pp. 11–12.

Mandler, G. (1982). The structure of value: Accounting for taste. In M. S. Clarke & S. T. Fiske (Eds.), *Affect and cognition: The seventeenth annual Carnegie Symposium on cognition* (pp. 3–36). Hillsdale, NJ: Lawrence Erlbaum Associates.

Mares, M. (1996). The role of source confusions in television's cultivation of social reality judgments. *Human Communication Research, 23*, 278–297.

Marsh, C. (1984). Do polls affect what people think? In C. F. Turner & E. Martin (Eds.), *Surveying subjective phenomena* (Vol. 2, pp. 565–591). New York: Russell Sage Foundation.

Marshall, W. L. (1989). Pornography and sex offenders. In D. Zillmann & J. Bryant (Eds.), *Pornography: Research advances & policy considerations* (pp. 185–214). Hillsdale, NJ: Lawrence Erlbaum Associates.

Martin, H. H. (1984). President Reagan's return to radio. *Journalism Quarterly, 61*, 817–821.

Mathios, A., Avery, R., Bisogni, C., & Shanahan, J. (1998). Alcohol portrayal on prime-time television: Manifest and latent messages. *Journal of Studies on Alcohol, 59*, 302–310.

May, M. D., Sundar, S. S., & Williams, R. B. (1997, May). *The effects of hyperlinks and site maps on the memorability of enjoyability of Web content*. Paper presented at the International Communication Association annual convention, Montreal.

Mayer, M. E., Gudykunst, W. B., Perrill, N. K., & Merrill, B. D. (1990). A comparison of competing models of the news diffusion process. *Western Journal of Speech Communication, 54*, 113–123.

McArthur, L. Z., & Post, D. L. (1977). Figural emphasis and person perception. *Journal of Experimental Social Psychology, 13*, 520–535.

McArthur, L. Z., & Solomon, L. K. (1978). Perceptions of an aggressive encounter as a function of the victim's salience and perceiver's arousal. *Journal of Personality and Social Psychology, 36*, 1278–1290.

McCain, T. A., Chilberg, J., & Wakshlag, J. (1977). The effect of camera angle on source credibility and attraction. *Journal of Broadcasting, 21*, 35–46.

McClure, R. D., & Patterson, T. E. (1974). Television news and political advertising: The impact of exposure on voter beliefs. *Communication Research, 1*, 3–31.

McCombs, M. (1994). News influence on our pictures of the world. In J. Bryant & D. Zillmann (Eds.), *Media effects: Advances in theory and research* (pp. 1–16). Hillsdale, NJ: Lawrence Erlbaum Associates.

McCombs, M., Einsiedel, E., & Weaver, D. (1991). *Contemporary public opinion.* Hillsdale, NJ: Lawrence Erlbaum Associates.

McCombs, M. E., & Shaw, D. L. (1972). The agenda-setting function of mass media. *Public Opinion Quarterly, 36,* 176–187.

McCombs, M. E., & Weaver, D. H. (1985). Toward a merger of gratifications and agenda-setting research. In K. E. Rosengren, L. A. Wenner, & P. Palmgreen (Eds.), *Media gratifications research: Current perspectives* (pp. 95–108). Beverly Hills, CA: Sage.

McCubbins, M. D. (1992). Party decline and presidential campaigns in the television age. In M. D. McCubbins (Ed.), *Under the watchful eye: Managing presidential campaigns in the television era* (pp. 9–57). Washington, DC: Congressional Quarterly.

McGhee, P. E., & Frueh, T. (1980). Television viewing and the learning of sex-role stereotypes. *Sex Roles, 6,* 179–188.

McGuire, A. J. (1985). Attitudes and attitude change. In G. Lindzey & E. Aronson (Eds.), *The handbook of social psychology: Vol 2. Special fields and applications* (3rd ed., pp. 233–346). New York: Random House.

McGuire, W. J. (1986). The myth of massive media impact: Savagings and salvagings. In G. Comstock (Ed.), *Public communication and behavior* (Vol. 1, pp. 173–257). Orlando, FL: Academic Press.

McIlwraith, R. D., & Schallow, J. R. (1983). Adult fantasy life and patterns of media use. *Journal of Communication, 33*(1), 78–91.

McKenzie, R. (1993). Comparing breaking TV newscasts of the 1989 San Francisco earthquake: How socially responsible was the coverage? *World Communication, 22,* 13–20.

McKenzie-Mohr, D., & Zanna, M. P. (1990). Treating women as sexual objects: Look to the (gender schematic) male who has viewed pornography. *Personal and Social Psychology Bulletin, 16,* 296–308.

McLaughlin, B. (1965). "Intention" and "incidental" learning in human subjects: The role of instructions to learn and motivation. *Psychological Bulletin, 63,* 359–376.

McLeod, D. M. (1995). Communicating deviance: The effects of television news coverage of social protest. *Journal of Broadcasting & Electronic Media, 39,* 4–19.

McLeod, D. M., & Detenber, B. H. (1999). Framing effects of television news coverage of social protest. *Journal of Communication, 49*(3), 3–23.

McLeod, D. M., Eveland, W. P., Jr., & Nathanson, A. I. (1997). Support for censorship of violent and misogynic rap lyrics: An analysis of the third-person effect. *Communication Research, 24,* 153–174.

McLeod, D. M., Eveland, W. P., Jr., & Signorielli, N. (1994). Conflict and public opinion: Rallying effects of the Persian Gulf War. *Journalism Quarterly, 72,* 20–31.

McLeod, D. M., & Hertog, J. K. (1992). The manufacture of pubic opinion by reporters: Informal cues for public perceptions of protest groups. *Discourse and Society, 3,* 259–275.

McLeod, D. M., & Perse, E. M. (1994). Direct and indirect effects of socioeconomic status on public affairs knowledge. *Journalism Quarterly, 71,* 433–442.

McLeod, D. M., Perse, E., Signorielli, N., & Courtright, J. A. (1993). Public perceptions and evaluations of the functions of the media in the Persian Gulf War. In B.

S. Greenberg & W. Gantz (Eds.), *Desert Storm and the mass media* (pp. 197–212). Cresskill, NJ: Hampton Press.

McLeod, D. M., Perse, E. M., Signorielli, N., & Courtright, J. A. (1999). Public hostility toward freedom of expression during international conflicts: A case study of public opinion during the Persian Gulf War. *Free Speech Yearbook, 36*, 104–117.

McLeod, J. M., Becker, L. B., & Byrnes, J. E. (1974). Another look at the agenda-setting function of the press. *Communication Research, 1*, 131–166.

McLeod, J. M., Kosicki, G. M., & Pan, A. (1991). On understanding and misunderstanding media effects. In J. Curran & M. Gurevitch (Eds.), *Mass media and society* (pp. 235–266). London: Edward Arnold.

McLeod, J. M., & McDonald, D. G. (1985). Beyond simple exposure: Media orientation and their impact on political processes. *Communication Research, 12*, 3–33.

McLeod, J. M., & Reeves, B. (1980). On the nature of mass media effects. In S. Withey & R. Abels (Eds.), *Television and social behavior: Beyond violence and children* (pp. 17–54). Hillsdale, NJ: Lawrence Erlbaum Associates.

McQuail, D. (1994). *Mass communication theory* (3rd ed.). London: Sage.

McQuail, D., & Windahl, S. (1993). *Communication models: For the study of mass communication* (2nd ed.). New York: Longman.

Meadowcroft, J. M., & Reeves, B. (1989). Influence of story schema development on children's attention to television. *Communication Research, 16*, 352–374.

Meadowcroft, J. M., & Zillmann, D. (1987). Women's comedy preferences during the menstrual cycle. *Communication Research, 14*, 204–218.

Mehrabian, A., & Wixen, W. J. (1986). Preference for individual video games as a function of their emotional effects on players. *Journal of Applied Social Psychology, 16*, 3–15.

Mendelsohn, H. (1964). Broadcast and personal sources of information in emergent public crises: The presidential assassination. *Broadcasting, 8*, 147–156.

Mendelsohn, H. (1966). Western voting and broadcasts of results on presidential election day. *Public Opinion Quarterly, 30*, 212–225.

Merton, R. K. (1946). *Mass persuasion: The social psychology of a war bond drive*. New York: Harper.

Merton, R. K. (1949). Patterns of influence: A study of interpersonal influence and communication behavior in a local community. In P. F. Lazarsfeld & F. N. Stanton (Eds.), *Communications research 1948–49* (pp. 180–219). New York: Harper.

Merton, R. K. (1968). *Social theory and social structure*. New York: Free Press.

Messaris, P. (1986). Parents, children, and television. In G. Gumpert & R. Cathcart (Eds.), *Inter/media: Interpersonal communication in a media world* (3rd ed., pp. 519–536). New York: Oxford.

Messaris, P., & Kerr, D. (1983). Mothers' comments about TV: Relation to famiy communication patterns. *Communication Research, 10*, 175–194.

Messner, S. E. (1986). Television violence and violent crime: An aggregate analysis. *Social Problems, 33*, 218–235.

Meyrowitz, J. (1982). Television and interpersonal behavior: Codes of reception and response. In G. Gumpert & R. Cathcart (Eds.), *Inter/media: Interpersonal communication in a media world* (2nd ed., pp. 221–241). New York: Oxford.

Milavsky, J. R., Kessler, R., Stipp, H., & Rubens, W. S. (1982). Television and aggression: Results of a panel study. In D. Pearl, L. Bouthilet, & J. Lazar (Eds.), *Television and behavior: Ten years of scientific progress and implications for the eighties* (DHHS Publication No. ADM 82-1196, Vol. 2, pp. 138–157). Washington, DC: U.S. Government Printing Office.

Milgram, S. (1974). *Obedience to authority: An experimental view.* New York: Harper & Row.

Miller v. California, 413 U.S. 15 (1973).

Mindak, W. H., & Hursh, D. (1965). Television functions on the assassination weekend. In B. S. Greenberg & E. B. Parker (Eds.), *The Kennedy assassination and the American public: Social communication in crisis* (pp. 130–141). Stanford, CA: Stanford University Press.

Molitor, F., & Sapolsky, B. S. (1993). Sex, violence, and victimization in slasher films. *Journal of Broadcasting & Electronic Media, 37*, 233–242.

Morgan, M. (1982). Television and adolescents' sex role stereotypes: A longitudinal study. *Journal of Personality and Social Psychology, 43*, 947–955.

Morgan, M. (1986). Television and the erosion of regional diversity. *Journal of Broadcasting & Electronic Media, 30*, 123–139.

Morgan, M. (1987). Television, sex-role attitudes, and sex-role behavior. *Journal of Early Adolescence, 7*, 269–282.

Morgan, M., & Gross, L. (1982). Television and educational achievement and aspiration. In D. Pearl, L. Bouthilet, & J. Lazar (Eds.), *Television and behavior: Ten years of scientific progress and implications for the Eighties* (DHHS Publication No. ADM 82-1196, pp. 78–90). Washington, DC: U.S. Government Printing Office.

Morgan, M., & Shanahan, J. (1991). Do VCRs change the TV picture? VCRs and the cultivation process. *American Behavioral Scientist, 35*, 122–135.

Morgan, M., & Shanahan, J. (1997). Two decades of cultivation research: An appraisal and meta-analysis. In B. R. Burleson (Ed.), *Communication yearbook 20*, (pp. 1–45). Thousand Oaks, CA: Sage.

Morwitz, V. G., & Pluzinski, C. (1996). Do polls reflect opinions or do opinions reflect polls? The impact of political polling on voters' expectations, preferences, and behavior. *Journal of Consumer Research, 23*, 53–67.

Mosher, D. L. (1971). Sex callousness toward women. In *Technical report of the Commission on Obscenity and Pornography* (Vol. 7, pp. 313–325). Washington, DC: U.S. Government Printing Office.

Movieweb. (1999). Top 50 all time highest grossing movies. [Online report]. Available: http://www.movieweb.com/movie/alltime.html

Mueller, J. E. (1970). Presidential popularity from Truman to Johnson. *American Political Science Review, 64*, 18–34.

Mullin, C., Imrich, D. J., & Linz, D. (1996). The impact of acquaintance rape stories and cast-specific pre-trial publicity on juror decision making. *Communication Research, 23*, 100–135.

Mutz, D. C., Roberts, D. F., & van Vuuren, D. P. (1993). Reconsidering the displacement hypothesis: Television influence on children's time use. *Communication Research, 20*, 51–75.

Myers, P. N., Jr., & Biocca, F. A. (1992). The elastic body image: The effect of television advertising and programming on body image distortions in young women. *Journal of Communication, 42*(3), 108–133.

NAACP Blasts TV Network Fall Season Whitewash. (1999, July 12). [Online press release]. Available:http://www.naacp.org/president/releases/naacp_tv_networks.htm

Nacos, B. L. (1990). *The press, presidents, and crises.* New York: Columbia University Press.

Nathanson, A. I. (1999). Identifying and explaining the relationship between parental mediation and children's aggression. *Communication Research, 26,* 124–143.

National Academy of Science. (1993). *Understanding and preventing violence.* Washington, DC: National Academy Press.

National Association of Broadcasters. (1995). Radio activities [On-line]. Available: http://www.nab.org/www/userguid/radio.htm

National Institute for Mental Health. (1982). *Television and behavior: Ten years of scientific progress and implications for the eighties. Vol. 1: Summary report* (DHHS Pub. No. ADM 82-1195). Washington, DC: U.S. Government Printing Office.

Nawy, H. (1973). In the pursuit of happiness? Consumers of erotica in San Francisco. *Journal of Social Issues, 29*(3), 147–161.

Neergaard, L. (1999, April 19). A novel way to keep children in shape. *Philadelphia Inquirer,* p. A2.

Nestvold, K. J. (1964). Oregon radio–TV response to the Kennedy assassination. *Journal of Broadcasting, 8,* 141–146.

Neuendorf, K. A., & Fennell, R. (1988). A social facilitation view of the generation of humor and mirth reactions: Effects of a laugh track. *Communication Studies, 39,* 37–48.

Neuman, R. (1976). Patterns of recall among television news viewers. *Public Opinion Quarterly, 40,* 115–123.

Neuman, S. B. (1991). *Literacy in the television age: The myth of the TV effect* (2nd ed.). Norwood, NJ: Ablex.

Neuman, W. R., Just, M. R., & Crigler, A. N. (1992). *Common knowledge: News and the construction of political meaning.* Chicago: University of Chicago Press.

Newhagen, J. E. (1994). The relationship between censorship and the emotional and critical tone of television news coverage of the Persian Gulf War. *Journalism Quarterly, 71,* 32–42.

Newhagen, J. E., & Reeves, B. (1991). Emotion and memory responses for negative political advertising: A study of television commercials used in the 1988 presidential election. In F. Biocca (Ed.), *Television and political advertising: Vol. 1. Psychological processes* (pp. 197–220). Hillsdale, NJ: Lawrence Erlbaum Associates.

Newhagen, J. E., & Reeves, B. (1992). The evening's bad news: Effects of compelling negative television news images on memory. *Journal of Communication, 42*(2), 25–41.

News flash! Women M.I.A. in print and broadcast. (1993, July). *Working Woman,* 9.

Nielsen Media Research. (1998). *1988 report on television.* New York: Author.

Noelle-Neumann, E. (1973). Return to the concept of powerful mass media. *Studies in Broadcasting, 9,* 68–105.

Noelle-Neumann, E. (1984). *The spiral of silence: Public opinion—Our social skin.* Chicago: University of Chicago Press.

Noelle-Neumann, E. (1991). The theory of public opinion: The concept of the spiral of silence. In J. A. Anderson (Ed.), *Communication yearbook* (Vol. 14, pp. 256–287). Newbury Park, CA: Sage

Noelle-Neumann, E. (1993). *The spiral of silence: Public opinion—Our social skin* (2nd ed.). Chicago: University of Chicago Press.

Offer, D., Ostrov, E., & Howard, K. I. (1984). *Patterns of adolescent self-image.* San Francisco: Jossey-Bass.

O'Keefe, M. T., & Kissel, B. C. (1971). Visual impact: An added dimension in the study of news diffusion. *Journalism Quarterly, 48*, 298–303.

Paik, H. (1995). Prosocial television programs and altruistic behavior: A meta-analysis. *Mass Communication Review, 22*, 147–165.

Paik, H., & Comstock, G. (1994). The effects of television violence in antisocial behavior. *Communication Research, 21*, 516–546.

Pally, M. (1994). *Sex & sensibility: Reflections on forbidden mirrors and the will to censor*. Hopewell, NJ: Ecco Press.

Palmgreen, P., Wenner, L. A., & Rayburn, J. D., III. (1980). Relations between gratifications sought and obtained: A study of television news. *Communication Research, 7*, 161–192.

Palmgreen, P., Wenner, L. A., & Rayburn, J. D., III. (1981). Gratifications discrepancies and news program choice. *Communication Research, 8*, 451–478.

Palys, T. S. (1986). Testing the common wisdom: The social content of video pornography. *Canadian Psychology, 27*, 22–35.

Patton, J., Stinard, T., & Routh, D. (1983). Where do children study? *Journal of Educational Research, 76*, 280–286.

Pauly, H. (1996, August 4). As athletes collect the gold, retailers count losses. *Philadelphia Inquirer*, p. D-1.

Peled, T., & Katz, E. (1974). Media functions in wartime: The Israel home front in October 1973. In J. G. Blumler & E. Katz (Eds.), *The uses of mass communication: Current perspectives on gratifications research* (pp. 49–69). Beverly Hills, CA: Sage.

Percy, L., & Lautman, M. R. (1994). Advertising, weight loss, and eating disorders. In E. M. Clark, T. C. Brock, & D. W. Steward (Eds.), Attention, attitude, and affect in response to advertising (pp. 301–311). Hillsdale, NJ: Lawrence Erlbaum Associates.

Perloff, R. M. (1993). Ego-involvement and the third person effect of televised news coverage. *Communication Research, 16*, 236–262.

Perloff, R., Wartella, E., & Becker, L. (1982). Increasing learning from TV news. *Journalism Quarterly, 59*, 83–86.

Perse, E. M. (1986). Soap opera viewing patterns of college students and cultivation. *Journal of Broadcasting & Electronic Media, 30*, 175–193.

Perse, E. M. (1990a). Audience selectivity and involvement in the newer media environment. *Communication Research, 17*, 675–697.

Perse, E. M. (1990b). Cultivation and involvement with local television news. In N. Signorielli & M. Morgan (Eds.), *Cultivation analysis: New directions in media effects research* (pp. 51–69). Newbury Park, CA: Sage.

Perse, E. M. (1990c). Involvement with local television news: Cognitive and emotional dimensions. *Human Communication Research, 16*, 556–581.

Perse, E. M. (1990d). Media involvement and local news effects. *Journal of Broadcasting & Electronic Media, 34*, 17–36.

Perse, E. M. (1990e). Predicting attention to local television news: Need for cognition and motives for viewing. *Communication Reports, 5*, 40–49.

Perse, E. M. (1994). Uses of erotica and acceptance of rape myths. *Communication Research, 21*, 488–515.

Perse, E. M. (1996). Sensation seeking and the use of television for arousal. *Communication Reports, 9*, 37–48.

Perse, E. M. (1998). Implications of cognitive and affective involvement for channel changing. *Journal of Communication, 48*(3), 49–68.

Perse, E. M., & Courtright, J. A. (1993). Normative images of communication media: Mass and interpersonal channels in the new media environment. *Human Communication Research, 19*, 485–503.

Perse, E. M., Ferguson, D. A., & McLeod, D. M. (1994). Cultivation in the newer media environment. *Communication Research, 21*, 79–104.

Peterson, J. L., Moore, K. A., & Furstenberg, F. F. (1991). Television viewing and early initiation of sexual intercourse: Is there a link? *Journal of Homosexuality, 21*, 93–119.

Petty, R. E., & Cacioppo, J. T. (1980). Effects of issue involvement on attitudes in an advertising context. In G. Gorn & M. Goldberg (Eds.), *Proceedings of the Division 23 program* (pp. 75–79). Montreal: American Psychological Association.

Petty, R. E., & Cacioppo, J. T. (1984). The effects of involvement on responses to argument quantity and quality: Central and peripheral routes to persuasion. *Journal of Personality and Social Psychology, 46*, 69–81.

Petty, R. E., & Cacioppo, J. T. (1986). *Communication and persuasion: Central and peripheral routes to attitude change*. New York: Springer-Verlag.

Petty, R. E., Cacioppo, J. T., & Goldman, R. (1981). Personal involvement as a determinant of argument-based persuasion. *Journal of Personality and Social Psychology, 41*, 847–855.

Petty, R. E., Cacioppo, J. T., & Heesacker, M. (1981). The use of rhetorical questions in persuasion: A cognitive response analysis. *Journal of Personality and Social Psychology, 40*, 432–440.

Petty, R. E., Ostrom, T. M., & Brock, T. C. (1981). *Cognitive responses in persuasion*. Hillsdale, NJ: Lawrence Erlbaum Associates.

Petty, R. E., & Priester, J. R. (1994). Mass media attitudes change: Implications of the Elaboration Likelihood Model of Persuasion. In J. Bryant & D. Zillmann (Eds.), *Media effects: Advances in theory and research* (pp. 91–122). Hillsdale, NJ: Lawrence Erlbaum Associates.

Petty, R. E., Wegener, D. T., Fabrigar, L. R., Priester, J. R., & J. T. Cacioppo. (1993). Conceptual and methdological issues in the Elaboration Likelihood Model of persuasion: A reply to the Michigan State critics. *Communication Theory, 3*, 336–362.

Pew Reseracher Center For The People & The Press. (1996, May). Fall off greater for young adults and computer users [On-line]. Available: http://www.people-press.org/ mediamor.htm

Pfau, M., & Parrott, R. (1993). *Persuasive communication campaigns*. Boston: Allyn & Bacon.

Picard, R. G. (1993). *Media portrayals of terrorism: Functions and meaning of news coverage*. Ames: Iowa State University Press.

Pierce, J. P., Choi, W. S., Gilpin, E. A., Farkas, A. J., & Berry, C. C. (1998). Tobacco industry promotion of cigarettes and adolescent smoking. *JAMA, 279*, 511–515.

Pierce, J. P., Gilpin, E., Burns, D. M., Whalen, E., Rosbrook, B., Shopland, D., & Johnson, M. (1991). Does tobacco advertising target young people to start smoking? *JAMA, 266*, 3154–3158.

Pierce, J. P., Lee, L., & Gilpin, E. A. (1994). Smoking initiation by adolescent girls, 1944 through 1988. *JAMA, 217*, 608–611.

Pollay, R. W., Siddarth, S., Siegel, M., Haddix, A., Merritt, R. K., Giovino, G. A., & Eriksen, M. P. (1996). The last straw? Cigarette advertising and realized market shares among youths and adults, 1979–1993. *Journal of Marketing, 60*, 1–16.

Postman, N. (1985). *Amusing ourselves to death: Public discourse in the age of show business*. New York: Penguin.

Postman, N., Nystrom, C., Strate, L., & Weingartner, C. (1987). *Myths, men, & beer: An analysis of beer commercials on broadcast television, 1987*. Falls church, VA: AAA Foundation for Traffic Safety.

Potter, W. J. (1986). Perceived reality and the cultivation hypothesis. *Journal of Broadcasting & Electronic Media, 30*, 159–174.

Potter, W. J. (1987). Does television viewing hinder academic achievement among adolescents? *Human Communication Research, 14*, 27–46.

Potter, W. J. (1988). Perceived reality in television effects research. *Journal of Broadcasting & Electronic Media, 32*, 23–41.

Potter, W. J. (1998). *Media literacy*. Thousand Oaks, CA: Sage.

Potter, W. J., & Ware, W. (1987). An analysis of the contexts of antisocial acts on prime-time television. *Communication Research, 14*, 664–686.

Powell, G. J. (1982). The impact of television on the self-concept development of minority group children. In G. L. Berry & C. Mitchell-Kerman (Eds.), *Television and the socialization of the minority child* (pp. 105–131). New York: Academic Press.

Power, J. G., Murphy, S. T., & Coover, G. (1996). Priming prejudice: How stereotypes and counter-stereotypes influence attribution of responsibility and credibility among ingroups and outgroups. *Human Communication Research, 23*, 36–58.

Price, V. (1992). *Communication concepts 4: Public opinion*. Newbury Park, CA: Sage.

Price, V., & Allen, S. (1990). Opinion spirals, silent and otherwise: Applying small group research to public opinion phenomena. *Communication Research, 17*, 369–392.

Price, V., & Czilli, E. J. (1996). Modeling patterns of news recognition and recall. *Journal of Communication, 46*(2), 55–78.

Price, V., & Tewksbury, D. (1997). News values and public opinion: A theoretical account of media priming and framing. In G. Barnett & F. J. Boster (Eds.), *Progress in communication sciences* (Vol. 13, pp. 173–212). Greenwich, CT: Ablex.

Price, V., Tewksbury, D., & Huang, L. (1998). Third-person effects on publication of a holocaust-denial advertisement. *Journal of Communication, 48*(2), 3–26.

Price, V., Tewksbury, D., & Powers, E. (1997). Switching trains of thought: The impact of news frames on readers' cognitive responses. *Communication Research, 24*, 481–506.

Price, V., & Zaller, J. (1993). Who gets the news? Alternative measures of news reception and its implications for research. *Public Opinion Quarterly, 57*, 133–164.

Quarantelli, E. L. (1981). The command post view in local mass communication systems. *International Journal of Communication Research, 7*, 57–73.

Rada, J. A. (1997). Color blind-sided: Racial bias in network television's coverage of professional football games. In S. Biagi & M. Kern-Foxworth (Eds.), *Facing difference: Race, gender, and mass media* (pp. 23–29). Thousand Oaks, CA: Pine Forge Press.

Rayburn, J. D., II, Palmgreen, P., & Acker, T. (1984). Media gratifications and choosing a morning news program. *Journalism Quarterly, 61*, 149–156.

Record-Breaking TV audience. (1991, January 28). *Newsweek*, 6.

Reep, D. C., & Dambrot, F. H. (1987). Television professional women: Working with men in the 1980s. *Journalism Quarterly, 64*, 376–381.

Reese, S. (1984). Visual verbal redundancy effects on television news learning. *Journal of Broadcasting, 28*, 79–87.

Reeves, B., Newhagen, E., Mailbach, E., Basil, M., & Kurz, K. (1991). Negative and positive television messages: Effects of message type and message context on attention and memory. *American Behavioral Scientist, 34*, 679–694.

Reeves, B., Thorson, E., & Schleuder, J. (1986). Attention to television: Psychological theories and chronometric measures. In J. Bryant & D. Zillmann (Eds.), *Perspectives on media effects* (pp. 251–279). Hillsdale, NJ: Lawrence Erlbaum Associates.

Rhee, J. W., & Cappella, J. N. (1997). The role of political sophistication in learning from news: Measuring schema development. *Communication Research, 24*, 197–233.

Riffe, D., & Stovall, J. G. (1989). Diffusion of news of shuttle disaster: What role for emotional response? *Journalism Quarterly, 66*, 551–556.

Ritchie, D., Price, V., & Roberts, D. F. (1987). Television, reading, and reading achievement: A reappraisal. *Communication Research, 14*, 292–315.

Roberts, D. F., & Maccoby, N. (1985). Effects of mass communication. In G. Lindzey & E. Aronson (Eds.), *The handbook of social psychology: Vol 2. Special fields and applications* (3rd ed., pp. 539–598). New York: Random House.

Robinson, J. D., & Skill, T. (1995). The invisible generation: Portrayals of the elderly on prime-time television. *Communication Reports, 8*, 111–119.

Robinson, J. P. (1981). Television and leisure time: A new scenario. *Journal of Communication, 31*(1), 120–130.

Robinson, J. P., & Levy M. R. (Eds.). (1986). *The main source: Learning from television news*. Beverly Hills, CA: Sage.

Robinson, J. P., & Levy, M. R. (1996). New media use and the informed public: A 1990s update. *Journal of Communication, 46*(2), 129–135.

Rogers, E. M. (1994). *A history of communication study: A biographical approach*. New York: Free Press.

Rogers, E. M. (1995). *Diffusion of innovations* (4th ed.). New York: Free Press.

Rogers, E. M., & Dearing, J. W. (1988). Agenda-setting research: Where has it been, where is it going? In J. A. Anderson (Ed.), *Communication yearbook* (Vol. 11, pp. 555–594). Newbury Park, CA: Sage.

Rojas, H., Shah, D. V., & Faber, R. J. (1996). For the good of others: Censorship and the third-person effect. *International Journal of Public Opinion Research, 8*, 163–186.

Roper Starch Worldwide. (1995). *America's watching: Public attitudes toward television*. New York: Author.

Rosengren, K. E. (1987). Conclusion: The comparative study of news diffusion. *European Journal of Communication, 2*, 227–255.

Rosengren, K. E., McQuail, D., & Blumler, J. G. (1987). News diffusion [Special issue]. *European Journal of Communication, 2*(2).

Rosenthal, R. (1979). The "file drawer problem" and tolerance for null results. *Psychological Bulletin, 86*, 638–641.

Rosenthal, R. (1984). *Meta-analytic procedures for social* research. Newbury Park, CA: Sage.

Rosenthal, R., & Rubin, D. B. (1982). A simple, general purpose display of magnitude of experimental effect. *Journal of Educational Psychology, 74*, 708–712.

Rothenbuhler, E. W. (1988). The living room celebration of the Olympic games. *Journal of Communication, 38*(4), 61–81.

Rothschild, M. L., & Ray, M. L. (1974). Involvement and political advertising effects: An exploratory experiment. *Communication Research, 1*, 264–283.

Rowland, W. D., Jr. (1983). *The politics of TV violence: Policy uses of communication research*. Beverly Hills, CA: Sage.

Roy, A., & Harwood, J. (1997). Underrepresented, positively portrayed: Older adults in television commercials. *Journal of Applied Communication Research, 25*, 39–56.

Rubin, A. M. (1981a). An examination of television viewing motivations. *Communication Research, 8*, 141–165.

Rubin, A. M. (1981b). A multivariate analysis of "60 Minutes" viewing motivations. *Journalism Quarterly, 58*, 529–534.

Rubin, A. M. (1983). Television uses and gratifications: The interactions of viewing patterns and motivations. *Journal of Broadcasting, 27*, 37–51.

Rubin, A. M. (1984). Ritualized and instrumental television viewing. *Journal of Communication, 34*(3), 66–77.

Rubin, A. M. (1986). Age and family control influences on children's television viewing. *The Southern Speech Communication Journal, 52*, 35–51.

Rubin, A. M. (1994). Media uses and effects: A uses-and-gratifications perspective. In J. Bryant & D. Zillmann (Eds.), *Perspectives on media effects: Advances in theory and research* (pp. 417–436). Hillsdale, NJ: Lawrence Erlbaum Associates.

Rubin, A. M., & Bantz, C. R. (1987). Utility of videocassette recorders. *American Behavioral Scientist, 30*, 471–485.

Rubin, A. M., & Perse, E. M. (1987). Audience activity and television news gratifications. *Communication Research, 14*, 58–84.

Rubin, A. M., Perse, E. M., & Powell, R. A. (1985). Loneliness, parasocial interaction, and local television news viewing. *Human Communication Research, 12*, 155–180.

Rubin, A. M., Perse, E. M., & Taylor, D. S. (1988). A methodological examination of cultivation. *Communication Research, 15*, 107–134.

Rucinski, D. (1992). Personalized bias in the news: The potency of the particular? *Communication Research, 19*, 91–108.

Rucinski, D., & Salmon, C. T. (1990). The "other" as the vulnerable voter: A study of the third person effect in the 1988 U.S. presidential campaign. *International Journal of Public Opinion Research, 2*, 345–368.

Rychtarik, R. G., Fairbank, J. A., Allen, C. M., Foy, D. W., & Drabman, R. S. (1983). Alcohol use in television programming: Effects on children's behavior. *Addictive Behaviors, 8*, 19–22.

Sabato, L. J. (1993). *Feeding frenzy: How attack journalism has transformed American politics*. New York: Free Press.

Salmon, C. T., & Kline, F. G. (1985). The spiral of silence ten years later. In K. R. Sanders, L. L. Kaid, & D. Nimmo (Eds.), *Political communication yearbook 1984* (pp. 3–30). Carbondale, IL: Southern Illinois University Press.

Salmon, C. T., & Neuwirth, K. (1990). Perceptions of opinion "climates" and willingness to discuss the issue of abortion. *Journalism Quarterly, 67*, 567–577.

Salomon, G. (1983). The differential investment of mental effort in learning from different sources. *Educational Psychologist, 18*, 42–50.

Salomon, G., & Leigh, T. (1984). Predispositions about learning from print and television. *Journal of Communication, 34*(2), 119–135.

Salwen, M. B., & Driscoll, P. D. (1997). Consequences of third-person perception in support of press restrictions in the O.J. Simpson trial. *Journal of Communication, 47*(2), 60–78.

Sapolsky, B. S., & Tabarlet, J. O. (1991). Sex in primetime television: 1979 versus 1989. *Journal of Broadcasting & Electronic Media, 35*, 505–516.

Saunders, K. W. (1996). *Violence as obscenity: Limiting the media's First Amendment protection*. Durham, University of North Carolina Press.

Schachter, S. (1964). The interaction of cognitive and physiological determinants of emotional state. In L. Berkowitz (Ed.), *Advances in experimental social psychology* (Vol. 1, pp. 49–80). New York: Academic Press.

Scheff, T. J., & Scheele, S. C. (1980). Humor and catharsis: The effect of comedy on audiences. In P. H. Tannenbaum (Ed.), *The entertainment functions of television* (pp. 165–182). Hillsdale, NJ: Lawrence Erlbaum Associates.

Scheufele, D. A. (1999). Framing as a theory of media effects. *Journal of Communication, 49*(1), 103–122.

Schleuder, J. D., White, A. V., & Cameron, G. T. (1993). Priming effects of television news bumpers and teasers on attention and memory. *Journal of Broadcasting & Electronic Media, 37*, 437–452.

Schneider, D. J., Hastorf, A. H., & Ellsworth, P. C. (1979). *Person perception* (2nd ed.). Reading, MA: Addison-Wesley.

Schneider, W., & Pressley, M. (1997). *Memory development between two and twenty* (2nd ed.). Mahwah, NJ: Lawrence Erlbaum Associates.

Schramm, W. (1965). Communication in crisis. In B. S. Greenberg & E. B. Parker (Eds.), *The Kennedy assassination and the American public: Social communication in crisis* (pp. 1–25). Stanford, CA: Stanford University Press.

Schramm, W., Lyle, J., & Parker, E. (1961). *Television in the lives of our children*. Stanford, CA: Stanford University Press.

Schuman, H., & Presser, S. (1980). *Questions and answers in attitude surveys: Experiments on question form, wording, and context*. Orlando, FL: Academic Press.

Schwartz, D. A. (1973–1974). How fast does news travel? *Public Opinion Quarterly, 37*, 625–627.

Shaheen, J. G. (1984). *The TV Arab*. Bowling Green, OH: Bowling Green State University Popular Press.

Shannon, C. E., & Weaver, W. (1949). *The mathematical theory of communication*. Urbana: University of Illinois Press.

Sharkey, J. (1991). *Under fire: U.S. military restrictions on the media from Grenada to the Persian Gulf*. Washington, DC: Center for Public Integrity.

Sheatsley, P. B., & Feldman, J. J. (1965). A national survey on public reactions and behavior. In B. S. Greenberg & E. B. Parker (Eds.), *The Kennedy assassination and the American public: Social communication in crisis* (pp. 149–177). Stanford, CA: Stanford University Press.

Sherif, C. W., Sherif, M., & Nebergall, R. E. (1965). *Attitude and attitude change: The social judgment-involvement approach*. Philadelphia: Saunders.

Sherman, B. L., & Dominick, J. R. (1986). Violence and sex in music videos: TV and rock 'n' roll. *Journal of Communication, 36*(1), 79–93.

Shoemaker, P. J. (1989). Predicting media uses. In F. Williams (Ed.), *Measuring the information society* (pp. 229–242). Newbury Park, CA: Sage.

Shoemaker, P. J. (1996). Hardwired for news: Using biological and cultural evolution to explain the surveillance function. *Journal of Communication, 46*(3), 32–47.

Shrum, L. J. (1997). The role of source confusion in cultivation effects may depend on processing strategy: A comment on Mares (1996). *Human Communication Research, 24*, 349–358.

Shrum, L. J., Wyer, R. S., Jr., & O'Guinn, T. C. (1998). The effects of television consumption on social perceptions: The use of priming procedure to investigate psychological processes. *Journal of Consumer Research, 24*, 447–458.

Siebert, F. S., Peterson, T., & Schramm, W. (1963). *Four theories of the press*. Urbana: University of Illinois Press.

Signorielli, N. (1987). Drinking, sex, and violence on television: The cultural indicators perspective. *Journal of Drug Education, 17*, 245–260.

Signorielli, N. (1990a). Television and health: Images and impact. In C. Atkin & L. Wallack (Eds.), *Mass communication and public health: Complexities and conflicts* (pp. 96–113). Newbury Park, CA: Sage.

Signorielli, N. (1990b). Television's mean and dangerous world: A continuation of the Cultural Indicators Perspective. In N. Signorielli & M. Morgan (Eds.), *Cultivation analysis: New directions in media effects research* (pp. 285–106). Newbury Park, CA: Sage.

Signorielli, N. (1993). Television, the portrayal of women, and children's attitudes. In G. L. Berry & J. K. Asamen (Eds.), *Children & television: Images in a changing sociocultural world* (pp. 229–242). Newbury Park, CA: Sage.

Signorielli, N., & Lears, M. (1992). Television and children's conceptions of nutrition: Unhealthy messages. *Health Communication, 4*, 245–257.

Silverblatt, A. (1995). *Media literacy: Keys to interpreting media messages*. Westport, CT: Praeger.

Simon, A. F. (1997). Television news and international earthquake relief. *Journal of Communication, 47*(3), 82–93.

Simon, H. A. (1974). How big is a chunk? *Science, 183*, 482–488.

Simpson, C. (1994). *Science of coercion: Communication research & psychological warfare 1945–1960*. New York: Oxford.

Simpson, C. (1996). Elisabeth Noelle-Neumann's "spiral of silence" and historical context of communication theory. *Journal of Communication, 46*(3), 149–173.

Simpson, C. (1997). Response to Kepplinger. *Journal of Communication, 47*(4), 139–141.

Singer, D. G., Zuckerman, D. M., & Singer, J. (1980). Helping elementary school children learn about TV. *Journal of Communication, 30*(3), 84–93.

Singer, J. (1980). The power and limitations of television: A cognitive-affective analysis. In P. H. Tannenbaum (Ed.), *The entertainment functions of television* (pp. 31–65). Hillsdale, NJ: Lawrence Erlbaum Associates.

Singhal, A., & Rogers, E. M. (1989). Prosocial television for development in India. In R. E. Rice & C. K. Atkin (Eds.), *Public communication campaigns* (2nd. ed., pp. 331–350). Newbury Park, CA: Sage.

Slade, J. W. (1984). Violence in the hard-core pornographic film: A historical survey. *Journal of Communication, 34*(3), 148–63.

Slater, M. D., Rouner, D., Beauvais, F., Murphy, K., Domenech-Rodriguez, M., & Van Leuven, J. (1996). Adolescent perceptions of underage drinkers in TV beer ads. *Journal of Alcohol and Drug Education, 42*, 43–56.

Smith, E. R. (1990). Reply to commentaries. In T. K. Srull & R. S. Wyer, Jr. (Eds.), *Advances in social cognition: Vol. III. Content and process specificity in the effects of prior experiences* (pp. 181–202). Hillsdale, NJ: Lawrence Erlbaum Associates.

Sohn, D. (1982). On Eron on television violence and aggression. *American Psychologist, 37*, 1292–1293.

Sood, R., Stockdale, G., & Rogers, E. M. (1987). How the news media operate in natural disasters. *Journal of Communication, 37*(3), 27–41.

Sparks, G. G., & Cantor, J. (1986). Development differences in fright responses to a television program depicting a character transformation. *Journal of Broadcasting & Electronic Media, 30*, 309–322.

Squire, L. R., & Slater, P. C. (1975). Forgetting in very long-term memory as assessed by an improved questionnaire technique. *Journal of Experimental Psychology: Human Learning and Memory, 1*, 50–54.

Stauffer, J., Frost, R., & Rybolt, W. (1983). The attention factor in recalling network television news. *Journal of Communication, 33*(1), 29–37.

Stein, A. H., & Friedrich, L. K. (1975). Impact of television on children and youth. In E. M. Hetherington (Ed.), Review of child development research (Vol. 5, pp. 183–256). Chicago, University of Chicago Press.

Stempel, G. H., III, & Hargrove, T. (1996). Mass media audiences in a changing media environment. *Journalism and Mass Communication Quarterly, 73*, 549–558.

Stempel, G. H., & Windhauser, J. W. (1989). Coverage by the prestige press of the 1988 presidential campaign. *Journalism Quarterly, 66*, 894–896, 919.

Stephen, W. G., & Brigham, J. C. (Eds.). (1985). Intergroup contact [Special issue]. *Journal of Social Issues, 41*(3).

Stice, E. M., Schupak-Neuberg, E., Shaw, H. E., & Stein, R. I. (1994). Relation of media exposure to eating disorder symptomatology: An examination of mediating mechanisms. *Journal of Abnormal Psychology, 103*, 836–840.

Stice, E. M., & Shaw, H. E. (1994). Adverse effects of the media portrayed thin-ideal women and linkages to bulimic symptomatology. *Journal of Social and Clinical Psychology, 13*, 288–308.

Stiff, J. B. (1986). Cognitive processing of persuasive message cues: A meta-analytic review of the effects of supporting information on attitudes. *Communication Monographs, 53*, 75–89.

Stiff, J. B., & Boster, (1987). Cognitive processing: Additional thoughts and a reply to Petty, Kasmer, Haughtvedt, and Cacioppo. *Communication Monographs, 54*, 250–256.

Stokes, L. C., & Pankowski, M. L. (1988). Incidental learning of aging adults via television. *Adult Education Quarterly, 38*, 88–100.

Storm, J. (1996, April 14). Segregated situation on television comedies. *Philadelphia Inquirer*, pp. A1, A18.

Story, M., & Faulkner, P. (1990). The prime time diet: A content analysis of eating behavior and food messages in television program content and commercials. *American Journal fo Public Health, 80*, 738–740.

Strasburger, V. C. (1995). *Adolescents and the media: Media and psychological impact*. Thousand Oaks, CA: Sage.

Stroman, C. A. (1986). Television viewing and self-concept among black children. *Journal of Broadcasting & Electronic Media, 30*, 87–93.

Strouse, J. S., & Buerkel-Rothfuss, N. L. (1987). Media exposure and the sexual attitudes and behaviors of college students. *Journal of Sex Education and Therapy, 13*, 43–51.

Subervi-Vélez, F. A., & Colsant, S. (1993). The television worlds of Latino children. In G. L. Berry & J. K. Asamen (Eds.), Children & television: Images in a changing sociocultural world (pp. 213–228). Newbury Park, CA; Sage.

Sudman, S. (1986). Do exit polls influence voting behavior? *Public Opinion Quarterly, 50*, 331–339.

Sundar, S., Nurayan, S., Obregon, R., & Uppal, C. (1998). Does web advertising work: Memory for print vs. online media. *Journalism & Mass Communication Quarterly, 75*, 822–835.

Surette, R. (1998). *Media, crime, and criminal justice: Images and realities* (2nd ed.). Belmont, CA: West/Wadsworth.

Surgeon General's Scientific Advisory Committee on Television and Social Behavior. (1972). *Television and growing up: The impact of televised violence*. Washington, DC: U. S. Government Printing Office.

Tamborini, R., Zillmann, D., & Bryant, J. (1984). Fear and victimization: Exposure to television and perceptions of crime and fear. In R. N. Bostom (Ed.), *Communication Yearbook 8* (pp. 492–513). Beverly Hills, CA: Sage.

Tan, A. S. (1979). TV beauty ads and role expectations of adolescent female viewers. *Journalism Quarterly, 56*, 283–288.

Tan, Z. C. W. (1988). Media publicity and insurgent terrorism: A twenty-year balance sheet. *Gazette, 42*, 2–32.

Tannenbaum, P. H. (1986). Policy options for early election projections. In J. Bryant & D. Zillmann (Eds.), *Perspectives on media effects* (pp. 189–302). Hillsdale, NJ: Lawrence Erlbaum Associates.

Tannenbaum, P. H., & Zillmann, D. (1975). Emotional arousal in the facilitation of aggression through communication. In L. Berkowitz (Ed.), *Advances in experimental social psychology* (Vol. 8, pp. 149–192). New York: Academic Press.

Tavris, C. (1988). Beyond cartoon killings: Comments on two overlooked effects of television. In S. Oskamp (Ed.), *Applied social psychology annual. Vol. 8: Television as a social issue* (pp. 189–197). Newbury Park, CA: Sage.

Taylor, S. E. (1975). On inferring one's attitudes from one's behavior: Some delimiting conditions. *Journal of Personality and Social Psychology, 31*, 126–131.

Taylor, S. E., & Crocker, J. (1981). Schematic bases of social information processing. In E. T. Higgins, C. P. Herman, & M. P. Zanna (Eds.), *Social cognition: The Ontario Symposium* (Vol. 1, pp. 89–134). Hillsdale, NJ: Lawrence Erlbaum Associates.

Television Information Office. (1985). *A broadcasting primer with notes on the new technologies*. New York: Author.

Thomas, M. H., & Drabman, R. S. (1975). Toleration of real life aggression as a function of exposure to televised violence and age of subject. *Merrill-Palmer Quarterly, 21*, 227–232.

Thomas, M. H., Horton, R. W., Lippencott, E. C., & Drabman, R. S. (1977). Desensitization to portrayals of real-life aggression as a function of exposure to television violence. *Journal of Personality and Social Psychology, 35*, 450–458.

Thompson, T. L., & Zerbinos, E. (1995). Gender roles in animated cartoons: Has the picture changed in 20 years? *Sex Roles, 32*, 651–673.

Thorson, E., & Lang, A. (1992). The effects of television videographics and lecture familiarity on adult cardiac orienting responses and memory. *Communication Research, 19*, 346–369.

Tichenor, P. J., Donohue, G. A., & Olien, C. N. (1970). Mass media flow and the differential growth in knowledge. *Public Opinion Quarterly, 34*, 159–170.

Toch, H., & Klofas, J. (1984). Pluralistic ignorance, revisited. In G. M. Stephenson & J. H. David (Eds.), *Progress in applied social psychology* (Vol. 2, pp. 129–159). New York: Wiley.

Tönnies, F. (1957). *Community and society* (C. P. Loomis, Trans.). East Lansing: Michigan State University Press.

Traugott, M. W. (1992). The impact of media polls on the public. In T. E. Mann & G. R. Orren (Eds.), *Media polls in American politics* (pp. 125–149). Washington, DC: Brookings Institution.

Treisman, A. (1979). The psychological reality of level of processing. In L. S. Cermak & F. I. M. Craik (Eds.), *Levels of processing in human memory* (pp. 301–330). Hillsdale, NJ: Lawrence Erlbaum Associates.

Tuchman, G. (1978). *Making news: A study in the construction of reality*. New York: Free Press.

Tuchman, S., & Coffin, T. E. (1971). The influence of election night television broadcasts in a close election. *Public Opinion Quarterly, 35*, 315–326.

Tucker, L. A. (1986). The relationship of television viewing to physical fitness and obesity. *Adolescence, 21*, 797–806.

Turner, C. W., & Berkowitz, L. (1972). Identification with film aggressor (covert role taking) and reactions to film violence. *Journal of Personality and Social Psychology, 21*, 256–264.

Tversky, A., & Kahneman, D. (1973). Availability: A heuristic for judging frequency and probability. *Cognitive psychology, 5*, 207–232.

UCLA Center for Communication Policy. (1998). 1997 TV violence report. Part IV: Findings in other television media. [Online report]. Available: http://ccp.ucla.edu/Webreport96/other.htm

U.S. Bureau of the Census. (1990). 1990 US census data. [Online document]. Available: http://venus.census.gov/cdrom/lookup/91002709

U.S. Department of Justice, Federal Bureau of Investigation. (1999, October 17). Crime in the United States, 1998. [Online report]. Available: http://www.fbi.gov/pressrm/pressrel/ucr98.htm

Valkenberg, P. M., Semetko, H. A., & de Vresse, C. H. (1999). The effects of news frames on readers' thoughts and recall. *Communication Research, 26*, 550–569.

Van Evra, J. (1998). *Television and child development* (2nd ed.). Mahwah, NJ: Lawrence Erlbaum Associates.

Vancil, D. L., & Pendell, S. D. (1987). The myth of viewer listener disagreement in the first Kennedy-Nixon debate. *Central State Speech Journal, 38*, 16–27.

Vidmar, N., & Rokeach, M. (1974). Archie Bunker's bigotry: A study in selective perception and exposure. *Journal of Communication, 24*(1), 36–47.

Viswanath, K., & Finnegan, J. R., Jr. (1996). The knowledge gap hypothesis: Twenty-five years later. *Communication yearbook* (Vol. 19, pp. 187–227). Thousand Oaks, CA: Sage.

Viswanath, K., Kahn, E., Finnegan, J. R., Jr., Hertog, J., & Potter, J. D. (1993). Motivation and the knowledge gap: Effects of a campaign to reduce diet-related cancer risk. *Communication Research, 20*, 546–563.

Walker, C. E. (1971). Erotic stimuli and the aggressive sexual offender. *Technical report of the Commission on Obscenity and Pornography* (Vol. 7, pp. 91–147). Washington, DC: U. S. Government Printing Office.

Walker, J. R., & Bellamy, R. V., Jr. (1991). The gratifications of grazing: An exploratory study of remote control use. *Journalism Quarterly, 68*, 422–431.

Walters, R. H., & Parke, R. D. (1964). Influence of response consequences to a social model on resistance to deviation. *Journal of Experimental Child Psychology, 1*, 269–280.

Wanta, W. (1997). *The public and the national agenda: How people learn about important issues*. Mahwah, NJ: Lawrence Erlbaum Associates.

Warner, K. E., Goldenhar, L. M., & McLaughlin, C. G. (1992). Cigarette advertising and magazine coverage of the hazards of smoking. *New England Journal of Medicine, 326*, 305–309.

Warner, S. (1993, September 9). Show business is big business. *Philadelphia Inquirer*, pp. E-1, E-9.

Wartella, E. (1980). Children's impressions of television mothers. In M. Grewe-Partsch & G. J. Robinson (Eds.), *Women, communication, and careers* (pp. 76–84). New York: K. G. Saur.

Wartella, E., Heintz, K. E., Aidman, A. J., & Mazzarella, S. R. (1990). Television and beyond: Children's video media in one community. *Communication Research, 17*, 45–64.

Wartella, E., & Reeves, B. (1985). Historical trends in research on children and the media: 1900–1960. *Journal of Communication, 35*(2), 118–133.

Watt, J. H., Jr. (1979). Television form, content attributes, and viewer behavior. In M. J .Voight & G. J. Hanneman (Eds.), *Progress in communication sciences* (Vol. 1, pp. 51–89). Norwood, NJ: Ablex.

Watt, J. H., & Krull, R. (1977). An examination of three models of television viewing and aggression. *Human Communication Research, 3*, 99–112.

Watt, J. H., Mazza, M., & Snyder, L. (1993). Agenda-setting effects of television news coverage and the effects decay curve. *Communication Research, 20*, 408–435.

Waxman, J. J. (1973). Local broadcast gatekeeping during natural disaster. *Journalism Quarterly, 50*, 751–758.

Weaver, D. H., Graber, D. A., McCombs, M. E., & Eyal, C. H. (1981). *Media agenda-setting in a presidential election: Issues, images and interest*. New York: Praeger.

Weaver, J., & Wakshlag, J. (1986). Perceived vulnerability to crime, criminal victimization experience, and television viewing. *Journal of Broadcasting & Electronic Media, 30*, 141–158.

Weaver, J. B., III. (1987). Effects of portrayals of female sexuality and violence against women on perceptions of women (Doctoral dissertation, University of Indiana). *Dissertation Abstracts International, 48*, 2482-A.

Weaver, J. B., III (1991a). Are "slasher" horror films sexually violent? A content analysis. *Journal of Broadcasting & Electronic Media, 35*, 385–392

Weaver, J. B., III. (1991b). Exploring the links between personality and media preferences. *Personality and Individual Differences, 12*, 1293–1299.

Weaver, J. B., III. (1991c). The impact of exposure to horror film violence on perceptions of women: Is it the violence or an artifact? In B. A. Austin (Ed.), *Current research in film: Audiences, economics, and law* (Vol. 5, pp. 1–18). Norwood, NJ: Ablex.

Weaver, J. B., III. (1991d). Responding to erotica: Perceptual processes and dispositional implications. In J. Bryant & D. Zillmann (Eds.), *Responding to the screen: Reception and reaction processes* (pp. 329–354). Hillsdale, NJ: Lawrence Erlbaum Associates.

Weaver, J. B., III, Brosius, H., & Mundorf, N. (1993). Personality and movie prefer-ences: A comparison of American and German audiences. *Personality and In-dividual Differences, 14*, 307–315.

Weaver, J. B., III, Masland, J. L., & Zillmann, D. (1984). Effect of erotica on young men's aesthetic perception of their female partners. *Perceptual and Motor Skills, 58*, 929–930.

Weaver, J., & Wakshlag, J. (1986). Perceived vulnerability to crime, criminal victim-ization experience, and television viewing. *Journal of Broadcasting & Elec-tronic Media, 30*, 141-158.

Weaver-Lariscy, R. A., Sweeney, B., & Steinfatt, T. (1984). Communication during assassination attempts: Diffusion of information in attacks on President Reagan and the pope. *Southern Speech Communication Journal, 49*, 258–276.

Webster, J. G. (1983). The impact of cable and pay cable television on local station audiences. *Journal of Broadcasting, 27*, 119–126.

Webster, J. G., & Phalen, P. F. (1997). *The mass audience: Rediscovering the domi-nant model*. Mahwah, NJ: Lawrence Erlbaum Associates.

Webster, J. G., & Wakshlag, J. (1985). Measuring exposure to television. In D. Zillmann & J. Bryant (Eds.), *Selective exposure to communication* (pp. 35–62). Hillsdale, NJ: Lawrence Erlbaum Associates.

Weibull, L., Lindahl, R., & Rosengren, K. E. (1987). News diffusion in Sweden: The role of the media. *European Journal of Communication, 2*, 143–170.

Weimann, G. (1983). The theater of terror: Effects of press coverage. *Journal of Communication, 33*(1), 38–45.

Weimann, G. (1987). Media events: The case of international terrorism. *Journal of Broadcasting & Electronic Media, 31*, 21–39.

Weimann, G., & Winn, C. (1994). *The theater of terror: Mass media and interna-tional terrorism*. New York: Longman.

Weinstein, N. D. (1980). Unrealistic optimism about future life events. *Journal of Personality and Social Psychology, 39*, 806–820.

Welch A. J., & Watt, J. H., Jr. (1982). Visual complexity and young children's learn-ing from television. *Human Communication Research, 8*, 133–145.

Wenger, D. E. (1980). A few empirical observations concerning the relationship between the mass media and disaster knowledge: A research report. In *Disas-ters and the mass media: Proceedings of the Committee on Disasters and the Mass Media Workshop* (pp. 241–266). Washington, DC: National Academy of Sciences.

Williams, F., Rice, R. E., & Rogers, E. M. (1988). *Research methods and the new me-dia*. New York: Free Press.

Williams, P. A., Haertel, E. H., Haertel, G. D., & Walberg, H. J. (1982). The impact of leisure-time television on school learning: A research synthesis. *Amercian Edu-cational Research Journal, 19*, 19–50.

Williams, T. M. (1986). Summary, conclusions, and implications. In T. M. Williams (Ed.), *The impact of television: A natural experiment in three communities* (pp. 395–430). Orlando, FL: Academic Press.

Williams, W. (1985). Agenda setting research. In J. R. Dominick & J. E. Fletcher (Eds.), *Broadcasting research methods* (pp. 189–201). Boston: Allyn & Bacon.

Wilson, B. J., Linz, D., Donnerstein, E., & Stipp, H. (1992). The impact of social issue television programming on attitudes toward rape. *Human Communication Re-search, 19*, 179–208.

Wilson, W. C. (1978). Can pornography contribute to the prevention of sexual problems? In C. B. Qualls, J. P. Wincze, & D. H. Barlow (Eds.), *The prevention of sexual disorders: Issues and approaches* (pp. 159–179). New York: Plenum.

Wimmer, R. D., & Dominick, J. R. (2000). *Mass media research: An introduction* (6th ed.). Belmont, CA: Wadsworth.

Winick, C. (1971). A study of consumers of explicitly sexual materials: Some function served by adult movies. *Technical report of the Commission on Obscenity and Pornography* (Vol. 4, pp. 245–262). Washington, DC: U. S. Government Printing Office.

Wober, J. M. (1978). Televised violence and paranoid perception: The view from Great Britain. *Public Opinion Quarterly, 42*, 315–321.

Wober, J. M., & Gunter, B. (1986). Television audience research at Britain's Independent Broadcasting Authority, 1974–1984. *Journal of Broadcasting & Electronic Media, 30*, 15–31.

Wong, N. D., Hei, T. K., Qaqundah, P. Y., Davidson, D. M., Bassin, S. L., & Gold, K. V. (1992). Television viewing and pediatric hypercholesterolemia. *Pediatrics, 90*, 75–79.

Wood, W., Wong, F. Y., & Chachere, J. G. (1991). Effects of media violence on viewers' aggression in unconstrained social interaction. *Psychological Bulletin, 109*, 371–383.

Woodward, G. C. (1993). The rules of the game: The military and the press in the Persian Gulf War. In R. E. Denton, Jr. (Ed.), *The media and the Persian Gulf War* (pp. 1–26). Westport, CT: Praeger.

Wooley, O. W., & Wooley, S. (1986, October). Thinness mania. *American Health*, 68–74.

Wright, C. R. (1986). *Mass communication: A sociological perspective* (3rd ed.). New York: Random House.

Wright, P. L. (1974). Analyzing media effects on advertising responses. *Public Opinion Quarterly, 38*, 192–205.

Wright, P. L. (1981). Cognitive responses to mass media advocacy. In R. E. Petty, T. M. Ostrom, & T. C. Brock (Eds.), *Cognitive responses to persuasion* (pp. 263–282). Hillsdale, NJ: Lawrence Erlbaum Associates.

Wurtzel, A., & Lometti, G. (1987). Researching television violence. In A. A. Berger (Ed.)., *Television in society* (pp. 117–132). New Brunswick, NJ: Transaction.

Wyer, R. S., Jr., & Srull, T. K. (1986). Human cognition in its social context. *Psychological Review, 93*, 322–359.

Wyllie, A., Zhang, J. F., & Casswell, S. (1998). Positive responses to televised beer advertisements associated with drinking and problems reported by 18–29-year olds. *Addiction, 93*, 749–760.

Yaffe, M. (1982). Therapeutic uses of sexually explicit material. In M. Yaffe & E. C. Nelson (Eds.), *The influence of pornography on behavior* (pp. 119–150). London, Academic Press.

Young, J. T. (1923). *The new American government and its work*. New York: Macmillan.

Zak, A. (1998). Presidential elections 1948–96. Elections U.S.A. [Online report]. Available: http://www.geocitied/CapitolHill/6228/elections2.htm

Zaller, J. (1996). The myth of mass media impact revived. In D. C. Mutz, P. M., Sniderman, & R. A. Brody (Eds.), *Political persuasion and attitude change* (pp. 17–78). Ann Arbor: University of Michigan Press.

Zettl, H. (1973). *Sight sound motion: Applied media aesthetics.* Belmont, CA: Wadsworth.

Zillmann, D. (1971). Excitation-transfer in communication-mediated aggressive behavior. *Journal of Experimental Social Psychology, 7,* 419–434.

Zillmann, D. (1980). Anatomy of suspense. In P. H. Tannenbaum (Ed.), *The entertainment functions of television* (pp. 133–163). Hillsdale, NJ: Lawrence Erlbaum Associates.

Zillmann, D. (1982). Television viewing and arousal. In D. Pearl, L. Bouthilet, & J. Lazar (Eds.), *Television and behavior: Ten years of scientific progress and implications for the Eighties* (DHHS Publication No. ADM 82-1196, pp. 53–67). Washington, DC: U.S. Government Printing Office.

Zillmann, D. (1989). Effects of prolonged consumption of pornography. In D. Zillmann & J. Bryant (Eds.), *Pornography: Research advances & policy considerations* (pp. 127–157). Hillsdale, NJ: Lawrence Erlbaum Associates.

Zillmann, D. (1991). Television viewing and arousal. In J. Bryant & D. Zillmann (Eds.), *Responding to the screen: Reception and reaction processes* (pp. 103–133). Hillsdale, NJ: Lawrence Erlbaum Associates.

Zillmann, D. (1998). The psychology of the appeal of portrayals of violence. In J H. Goldstein (Ed.), *Why we watch: The attractions of violent entertainment* (pp. 170–211). New York: Oxford.

Zillmann, D., & Bryant, J. (1974). Effect of residual excitation on the emotional response to provocation and delayed aggressive behavior. *Journal of Personality and Social Psychology, 30,* 782–791.

Zillmann, D., & Bryant, J. (1982). Pornography, sexual callousness, and the trivialization of rape. *Journal of Communication, 32*(4), 10–21.

Zillmann, D., & Bryant, J. (1984). Effects of massive exposure to pornography. In N. M. Malamuth & E. Donnerstein (Eds.), *Pornography and sexual aggression* (pp. 115–138). New York: Academic Press.

Zillmann, D., & Bryant, J. (1985). Affect, mood, and emotion as determinants of selective exposure. In D. Zillmann & J. Bryant (Eds.), *Selective exposure to communication* (pp. 157–190). Hillsdale, NJ: Lawrence Erlbaum Associates.

Zillmann, D., & Bryant, J. (1986a) A response. *Journal of Communication, 36*(1), 184–188.

Zillmann, D., & Bryant, J. (1986b). Shifting preferences in pornography consumption. *Communication Research, 13,* 560–578.

Zillmann, D., & Bryant, J. (1987). A reply. *Journal of Communication, 37*(3), 189–192.

Zillmann, D., & Bryant, J. (1988). Pornography's impact on sexual satisfaction. *Journal of Applied Social Psychology, 18,* 438–453.

Zillmann, D., Bryant, J., Comisky, P. W., & Medoff, N. J. (1981). Excitation and hedonic valence in the effect of erotica on motivated intermale aggression. *European Journal of social Psychology, 11,* 233–252.

Zillmann, D., Bryant, J., & Sapolsky, B. S. (1989). Enjoyment from sports spectatorship. In J. H. Goldstein (Ed.), *Sports, games, and play: Social and psychological viewpoints* (2nd ed., pp. 241–278). Hillsdale, NJ: Lawrence Erlbaum Associates.

Zillmann, D., Hezel, R. T., & Medoff, N. J. (1980). The effect of affective states on selective exposure to televised entertainment fare. *Journal of Applied Social Psychology, 10,* 323–339.

Zillmann, D., & Weaver, J. B. (1989). Pornography and men's sexual callousness toward women. In D. Zillmann & J. Bryant (Eds.), *Pornography: Research advances & policy considerations* (pp. 95–125). Hillsdale, NJ: Lawrence Erlbaum Associates.

Zillmann, D., Weaver, J., Mundorf, N., & Aust, C. (1986). Effects of an opposite-gender companion's affect to horror on distress, delight, and attraction. *Journal of Personality and Social Psychology, 51*, 586–594.

Zucker, H. G. (1978). The variable nature of news influence. In B. D. Ruben (Ed.), *Communication yearbook* (Vol. 2, pp. 225–240). New Brunswick, NJ: Transaction.

Zuckerman, D. M., Singer, D. G., & Singer, J. L. (1980). Children's television viewing, racial, and sex-role attitudes. *Journal of Applied Social Psychology, 10*, 281–294.

Zuckerman, M. (1979). Attribution of success and failure revisited: The motivational bias is alive and well in attribution theory. *Journal of Personality, 47*, 245–287.

Zuckerman, M. (1994). *Behavioral expressions of biosocial bases of sensation seeking*. Cambridge, England: Cambridge University Press.

Zuckerman, M. (1996). Sensation seeking and the taste for vicarious horror. In J. B. Weaver, III, & R. Tamborini (Eds.), *Horror films: Current research on audience preferences and reactions* (pp. 147–160). Mahwah, NJ: Lawrence Erlbaum Associates.

Zuckerman, M., & Litle, P. (1986). Personality and curiosity about morbid and sexual events. *Personality and Individual Differences, 7*, 49–56.

Author Index

Subject Index